Football Hooligans

Knowing the Score

Gary Armstrong

BERG

Oxford • New York

First published in 1998 by
Berg
Editorial offices:
150 Cowley Road, Oxford, OX4 1JJ, UK
70 Washington Square South, New York, NY 10012, USA

Paperback edition reprinted in 1998

Berg is the imprint of Oxford International Publishers Ltd.

Library of Congress Cataloging-in-Publication Data

A catalogue record for this book is available from the Library of Congress.

British Library Cataloguing-in-Publication Data

A catalogue record for this book is available from the British Library.

ISBN   1 85973 952 0 (Cloth)
       1 85973 957 1 (Paper)

Typeset by JS Typesetting, Wellingborough, Northants.
Printed in the United Kingdom by Biddles Ltd, Guildford and King's Lynn.

Contents

(Figures 1–10 can be found between pp. 138 and 139.)

Acknowledgements

The study of one's native city is always related to memories; and, hopefully mine of Sheffield and the time I spent there have not been wasted, for the memories and occasions have become an investment in the production of this book. This work is thus the end product of a recollection of collisions with a range of places, persons and personalities who knowingly or unwittingly assisted in my strivings.

Usually an academic work will chronicle the unfolding intellectual influences on the author. I found this to be only half the story. The journey from schoolboy to Ph.D., in this instance, runs parallel with another journey – and encompasses the transitions that occurred between the first football match I attended and the latter research process that saw the devoted fan crystalise into one considered to be of quotable value by the national news media. In a sense the two processes could be encapsulated under the headings 'Emotional' and 'Intellectual'. However, there is another category – 'Financial' – which I feel needs to be acknowledged. And unsure of which is the more significant, I will set out my indebtedness in a chronological order.

A very big thank you is due to the Reverend Tony Frain for taking me in 1969, and for the next six years, to Bramall Lane. I proved a more fanatical and enduring devotee to Sheffield United perhaps than to Catholicism. Next I am indebted to my school teacher, John Civico, who suggested to an innocent 15-year-old that University was a realistic ambition, and advised me well for years. Then came University – a strange experience, made more bearable by the one person responsible for the thesis that lies behind this book being started and, more importantly, being completed – my friend and mentor, Dr Rosemary Harris. A few others deserve special mention: David Cowell, sadly deceased, who assisted me with my first publication and employed me for my first lecture, was always the source of a drink and a lend of money, a truly generous man. Many thanks are due to Richard Giulianotti, for the hours of phone calls and his support across days of academic isolation. Gratitude is also due to Malcolm Young who, as a reader, managed to hone down my literary and combative excesses that this publication, at one time, contained. Thanks are also due to Dick Hobbs who, as a teaching colleague in the late 1980s, gave me refreshingly lucid advice on how to proceed; namely, 'fuck the ethics and get on with it'.

As for those who helped me financially throughout all this, it goes without saying that Mum and Dad are the most important. Without their financial sacrifice University life would have been much harder. Others, unaware of their contribution, assisted in my days as Ph.D. researcher and provided me with the expenses and conditions required to continue to study. So, thanks are due to John Salmons for three summers on building sites, to Paddy Limb for the delivery jobs, to George and Geoff for the hours given at the swimming pool, to Catch 22 Employment Agency for all the work they supplied, to the crew on O'Keefes (night shift) on the Broadgate Development, to Ian and Janet for the hundreds of hours of exam invigilation, to Ian Baxter for employing me as a Youth Worker, and Pauline Booker who gave loans without hesitation when times were hard. Then again, my thanks are also due to those people who helped put a roof over my head at little cost throughout much of this time: John Pryor, Mrs Eileen King, Charles Fletcher and Martyn Edwards. Gratitude is also due to the Economic and Social Research for their funding between the years 1986–88 and to the Guggenheim Foundation of New York for theirs in 1990.

In recent years a few academics and non-academics have helped kick-start the book in its various stages and have offered personal encouragement. Contributing in various ways and for various lengths of time I list them as one: Allan Abrahamson, Rohan Bastin, Sue Edwards, Penri Griffiths, Robin Theobald, and Clive Norris. The advice received from Eduardo Archetti was always invaluable, and his professionalism, alongside that of Paul Richards, as my PhD Examiners at the Department of Anthropology, University College London, will always be remembered. Another group of academics unwittingly helped produce this book. Lauded as hooligan 'experts', and prominently in the portals of academe, your cowardly attempts to prevent my work being published and personal attacks on me ensured that I would never give in – you know who you are.

I am indebted to a variety of women who know nothing about football or football hooliganism. Firstly, to Karen Kinnaird for typing my various efforts and seeing through the evolution of my thinking, and for not decrying too much my structural and grammatical errors. Then to Kathryn Earle, the commissioning editor of this work and, alongside her, Sara Everett for having the confidence and competence to publish it. I also owe an unpayable debt to Hani Darlington for suffering this work being strewn around her living-room and across my brain between 1991 and 1997.

Finally, I have a collective thank-you towards those who made this work possible; namely, the Blades. I am grateful for your allowing me into your lives, enduring my questions, and tolerating my presence in a variety of situations. For those of you who stood up for me in my absence, when suspicion abounded, I am particularly indebted. Whilst all the names in the text have been changed to protect both the guilty and the innocent, I feel a need to personally thank Joe, Pete, Steve, John, Jay, Daryll, Vinny, Dwane, Sammy, Andy, Pat, Glenn, Perfect, Dave, Kaz, Herman, Ronnie, Mick, Carl, and Ernie and the hundreds of other Blades who gave me the time of day. Wider thanks are due to all the other supporters of Sheffield United and Sheffield Wednesday, who have helped make my life so interesting for the past 27 years.

I hope it was all worth it.

Preface: Sheffield: May 1984

In their last match, Sheffield United lost 2–1. Promotion was now almost impossible. On the final whistle four hundred Blades chanted slogans from the picket lines of the Miners' dispute. Some threw coins at forty police gathered in front of the terrace fencing. Eventually twenty officers entered the terrace to assault those gathered there, effectively breaking up the event. Outside, a few Blades threw stones at the police ranks. Their response was a charge by six mounted police followed by officers with truncheons drawn, striking out at whoever they could. One Blade, Benny, ran at a mounted policeman, dragging him off his horse. Onlookers and Blades cheered. Blades remained in the city centre, some two hundred strong, in futile expectation of Owls returning from their own match. Police followed the Blades' pub-crawl. Hours later two unmanned police vehicles were damaged – an unattended and empty police dog van was overturned by a dozen striking miners who were also Blades, and a police transit van rolled into a wall when its handbrake was released by the same contingent.

Four days later the Supporters Clubs refused to run coaches to the game at Burnley. This was entirely reasonable, for it was not United who were playing Burnley, but Hull City. If the latter won by three goals they would gain promotion to Division Two; if they did not United would go up. Blades organised their own transport – four coaches – and two hundred went. The vehicles stopped at a pub; two Blades climbed the stairs to the living quarters looking for money to steal; two others stole bottles from the bar. A shaven-headed black youth announced that he was 'Johann Sebastian Bach' and played the composer's tunes on the pub's piano. The landlord phoned the police. Six officers arrived. One Blade, Dempsey, resolved this situation, saying 'the two were looking for the toilet', and, if he collected money to 'cover the cost of the bottles, could they leave?' A beer-tray laden with Blades' coins paid the debt, and the journey continued. Hull won, but only by two goals. United were thus promoted. Blades shook hands with Burnley fans, exchanged abuse with Hull fans and, that night, rejoiced in Sheffield nightclubs, singing their hatred of Sheffield Wednesday.

* * *

This research was not conducted in order to try to prevent Blades from being Blades. This research project was not established to 'cure' football hooliganism, and I believe it is naive to suggest that something as complex as the human ability to construct the phenomenon of real and symbolic 'enemies' is something that can be 'curable'. This inevitably raises issues around the ethical aspect of academic research. As Becker (1967) asked: 'Whose side are we on?, and as Bauman (1987) asks 'Do we legislate or interpret?' In this situation I was not on anyone's side, and I certainly did not consider it my job to work as an agent of State control. As Polsky (1969) points out, he has nothing against social workers, probation workers, policemen or anyone else trying to stop people from breaking the law: 'If a man wants to make that sort of thing his life work, I have no objection; that is his privilege. I suggest merely that he not do so in the name of sociology, criminology, or any other social science.' (140). On this issue I am at variance with others in Britain spoken of as academic experts on hooliganism, for they are often funded by various bodies of control, and act as what Baritz (1965) would call 'servants of power'.

For years I was a presence amongst the Blades, and throughout those years I do not consider my presence affected a single incident nor any views held. This was mainly because I never saw it as my job to be a missionary against types of behaviour or to act as a moral example to others. The answer to the question, 'why did I take this stance' is twofold. Firstly, there was nothing to be gained from any display of personal arrogance. Secondly, I found that the business of carrying out extended participant observation to be pervaded by pragmatism, and the milieu to be one in which personal values have to be submerged (cf. Bruyn 1966; Hobbs 1989: 7).

Being Sheffield-born and a United fan, this was never going to be some wondrous journey by a middle-class PhD student researching the horribly violent or exotic working class. Obviously I sought to be detached, but was able to bring a degree of reflexivity to the research, for all ethnographers find the task of the researcher must always be to 'fit in' and act as naturally as possible. This I had no problem in doing, for I had what Bourdieu (1984: 2) called the 'cultural competence' to participate with this specific gathering; and with my background had no need to 'go native' or achieve 'over-rapport'. At the same time it must be stressed that this research is not a narrative of a former or reformed hooligan participant. Whilst from a similar class background to many of those so classified, my aspirations took me away from the city to University. That I remained in contact with peers is the reason this book has been written.

Getting the feel of a society or social group in one's bones was achievable here because of the way via prolonged ethnography the subjects realise the researcher is different, recognise this distinction, and react accordingly.

This is something which those who never attempt prolonged research find difficult to comprehend. The task is to become accepted while making it clear there is a distinction between oneself and those studied. This has been better stated by Powdermaker (1967) who contends: 'The ethnographer must be intellectually poised between familiarity and strangeness, while socially, he or she is poised between "'stranger' and 'friend'". Following this advice, Freilich (1970: 100) called himself a 'marginal native'. I saw myself in the same role, taking comfort in the words of Agar (1980: 456), who writes: 'to be knowledgeable is to be capable of understanding on the basis of minimal cues', and be sensitive enough to look beyond words for what Geertz (1975) called the intentionality which distinguishes the wink from the twitch. Not all researchers are capable of this. As Baudrillard (1988: 54) suggested in significant metaphorical form: 'The point is not to write the sociology or psychology of the car, the point is to drive. That way you can learn more about this society than all academia could ever tell you.'

Sometimes the researcher must wonder whether we can account for the behaviour of small groups we know intimately. By 'account' I mean explain to others the reasons for behaviour that is apparently anomalous. One of the aims of the research here was to try to seek motives, but this was a massive problem, not least because the form and motivation for individuals varied over time. From a theoretical viewpoint, constructing a model of what motivates people is probably impossible, because meaning only has value in its interpretation. The way that you, as a researcher, interpret meaning depends upon your outlook, and this should never be forgotten. In my own case I was not a mirror of the Blades, and I cannot claim to represent them. I recognise I am what Parker (1974: 63) calls the 'third man', who both reconstructs the action and interprets these in writing-up my version of events.

There was a reality to be represented here, but there was no set mode for representing the reality that I saw. As Clifford and Marcus (1986) tell us, there is no such thing as a culture which is finite, and so someone else doing the same job could write about different aspects of the Blades. Individuals within the Blades might also see matters differently, either because they were more involved or saw events from another perspective. Every ethnography, then, is incomplete, and extra (or additional) work has always to be done. Meanwhile I can only aim through description to present myself as what Atkinson (1990: 27) would call a 'credible witness', all the while remembering, as Humphrey (1970: 170) has said of ethnography, that it 'is always a matter of greater or lesser misrepresentation'. My main aim was to seek an 'understanding' of the fans and their various behaviours, and my task was to explain, not justify.

Part I

Presenting the Hooligan

This study has limitations, for it is about only one group of fans in one city. Such a study, however, can address the theoretical debate on the role of the individual in 'structuring the structure' (Giddens 1984). Indeed, it is possible to build up a detailed moving picture of particular 'hooligans' in this 'local state' of Sheffield; then follow the pronouncement of policemen, politicians, and media reporters, and then examine the ways in which various individuals make decisions that influence the behaviour of others or alter the environment within which others have to move and make their decisions. Essentially, what football hooliganism involves is the participants taking upon themselves various roles and identities. Identity of any type is always psycho-social and, as Schlesinger (1991: 173) argues, is continually constructed and reconstructed. However, the very concept of identity is underplayed in most studies of hooligan causation, because crucial to Us is the construction and existence of Them or the Other. The problem, then, is how to interpret just how, in the hooligan debate, is the *'other'* constructed and maintained and given sufficient status to be worth confronting. This is meat and drink to the anthropologist, but is sometimes not addressed by the psychologist, the sociologist, or the statistician. As Feldman (1993: 79) noted anthropologists' examinations of violence can teach more than sociologists, for violence can transcend classifications and symbolic orders to produce another symbolic order. This, however, is dependent on agreement as to what is symbolically and culturally relevant to the participants. This creates other problems for, as Simmel (1971: 23) argued, we need to always be aware of the segmentary aspects of the person, and, as A. Cohen (1994: 11) cogently suggests, individuals have a 'basket of selves'. We, therefore, will see how, at times, the Blade animates a character (Goffman 1975: 547), whilst, at other times, he leaves the role because *'self, a combination of character and performance, is a changeable formula'* (ibid.: 573). The actor/role-player can, thus, hold incompatible beliefs and desires. No one can be the subject of fixed definition for constructions of self are dependent on reflexivity (cf. Giddens 1991: 52–3), sometimes responding to events then creating them, and sometimes acting in reverse order.

Chapter 1

'Blades', 'Pigs' and 'Their Boys'

'. . . My response to any comment about the intolerable behaviour of football supporters was to go red in the face, point at the interlocuter, and yell "shut your fucking mouth or I'll kill you, you gutless bastard", which, while it did bring discussions to an abrupt end, was hardly a winning intellectual gambit.'

(Harry Pearson (1994: 10) *The Far Corner*)

In an attempt to redress gaps in knowledge about what football hooligans do and who the football hooligan is, what follows is an anthropological study of one particular group of football fans, nicknamed 'the Blades'.[1] The sinister-sounding name of these supporters of Sheffield United FC derives from the founding of the club in 1889 in a city renowned for its steel industry. This origin is reflected in the club badge of crossed swords beneath a Yorkshire rose. Borrowing from this heritage, the Club is nicknamed 'The Blades' and all United supporters call themselves and each other 'Blades'. The 'Hooligan Element' are similarly known as Blades, and when reference is made to this term it will refer specifically to them. Other fans of the club will be referred to as United followers/supporters/Unitedites. Those who constitute Blades know they are 'Football Hooligans', but never refer to themselves by such a term except in jest and ridicule. Instead, by various practices, they define themselves as participants in *'It'*, whilst their opponents (their equivalents in age and appearance) are *'Them'*. Such rivals are more commonly known as *'Their Boys'* or *'Their Lads'* if originating from another city, or as *'Pigs'* if their allegiance is to the city rivals of Sheffield Wednesday, whose fans have themselves adopted the club nickname of 'The Owls'. Blades (and most Unitedites) prefer the derisory term 'Pigs' to Owls, and Owls in turn prefer 'Pigs' to 'Blades'; for some this hostility extends beyond words, and rivalry has become since the late 1960s a frequently violent affair.[2]

Team Mates: Football and Disorder

Blades are involved in a range of complex and varied social activities, the enactment of which periodically involves a complex negotiation of rivalries. One scenario would involve an individual Blade, in a company of up to 200 similar Blades, journeying to another city, where their equivalents would await their arrival. Upon recognition the two groups would be prepared to fight, despite having never met and being unlikely ever to see each other again. As a parallel to the match they had travelled to watch, Blades could decide if they (as a parallel team) had won, lost, or drawn their competitive engagement. Not that this mattered too much, for future weeks would bring other groups of lads and similar scenarios in a repetitive process.

The other, more frequent, scenario did not always need a football match, and was most often manifested in Sheffield city centre around pubs and clubs during the accepted 'hooligan' time of Friday and Saturday evenings. On these occasions the opposition was the Owls, and the issue far more complex than that pertaining to simple rivalry with groups from another city. Even so, both types of scenarios and competitions were reduced in the eyes of non-combatants to football hooliganism, and this meant a prefix or adjoinder of criticism of both the act and the participants. To millions these fans were the bottom of the social and moral barrel by virtue of their activities.

The idea of football hooliganism might seem to be a new phenomenon, yet it has its roots in the age-old masculine pursuit of revelry. The game, it seems, has always troubled the authorities, perhaps because it reflects the spirit and wayward energy of the mob – the early eighteenth-century *mobile vulgus*, or 'fickle crowd'. Legislation has long been used to control football-related disorders, and as far back as 1314 football was banned in London in an attempt to preserve public tranquillity, for it was feared the tumult and disorder surrounding these games might well give occasion to the forces of sedition and treason.

At a local level the game could always provoke rowdy behaviour both at the football grounds and in the streets. (In 1908 Sheffield Wednesday had their ground closed because of the rowdy behaviour of spectators.) Fishwick (1989) cites letters from 'Ratepayers' to the Sheffield press in the 1920s and 1930s complaining about noise, swearing, rowdiness, and betting consequent on the football that disturbed their Saturday afternoons. Because of this, the provision of football pitches for native young men was not a priority of the Socialist City Council, and, in the inter-war years, they even banned collections for junior football club funds. In 1928 Sheffield Magistrates discovered they had been sending youths to *prison* for playing football in the streets. Unknown to them, the exact nature of the crime had been changed in the prosecution evidence to a charge of Disorderly Behaviour (S. Jones 1988: 137).

Despite this, and rather contrarily, football was encouraged by industrialists in times of social worry. In 1912 pit-managers organised teams and competitions for striking miners, reportedly to keep the men from Trade Union activity (Fishwick 1986: 19, 27). Whether this worked is not known. Similarly, the city's one-time largest employer, steel magnate, Sir Robert Hadfield, promoted the game with the intention of combating industrial unrest and post-First World War fears of Bolshevism, as well as to increase fitness and productivity (Fishwick 1989: 13). Later, the game was seen as a way of absorbing the monotony of unemployment in the 1930s (Fishwick 1986: 44). Unemployed leagues were organised by the local FA, now with the support of the local press and city council, but hand-in-hand with property owners. Private pitches were made available, representing, in Fishwick's words, a paternalism of those with power and money towards those with neither (1989: 13–16). Nevertheless this did not stop a 6,000-strong riot in 1935, nor the barracking of police football teams by unemployed spectators.

Fandom: Spatial and Affective Dimension

The big question is: why does so much conflict take place around the game of football? The answer obviously lies in the symbiosis between the game and local male cultural mores. But why has this developed, and what are the peculiarities that may lie in this region? In Sheffield the game has an unparalleled significance as the birthplace of organised football. The world's oldest football club, founded in 1855, was, and still is, named Sheffield FC. In origin the team consisted mainly of the ex-pupils of the Sheffield Collegiate School where the sons of the city's middle-class were educated (Holt 1986: 84). The opposition they played were similarly from middle-class organisations (Mason 1980: 9–35). This elitist origin soon disseminated its knowledge as the same author noted: *'In spite of itself it is clear that the Sheffield Club helped to stimulate the formation of other local organisations of a much more socially heterogeneous nature than itself'* (24). By the 1860s Sheffield had fifteen teams, and advised on the rules of the game when the Football League was founded in 1863. Football has always been played in the Sheffield region: Young (1964) mentions a game in 1793, and industrialised society has simply changed the rules somewhat. Since its codification (in Sheffield) and popularisation nationally and internationally in the nineteenth century, the game of Association Football, and the football ground, has been, and remains, the male working-class leisure space *par excellence*, alongside the public house, and still provides *the* focal point of leisure, interest, passion and a focus for implicit masculinity for tens of thousands of men.

Even today it is the city's spectator and participant sport *par excellence*. No other winter sport in Sheffield can compete with football, be it for player or spectator. Options *are* available in Greyhound Racing, Rugby League and Motorcycle Speedway, but the first and last have seen better days, whilst professional Rugby League, after only a decade of existence in Sheffield, is still striving to attract more than a few thousand supporters. Meanwhile Modernity challenges traditional sports and sporting venues via Americanisation and the transglobal diffusion of sport. This has brought the indoor spectacles of ice hockey and basketball, the former in particular capable of attracting crowds of 8,000; but nothing, as yet, can compete with the crowds that watch football.[3]

The appeal of the game is its simplicity. The prerequisites for playing the game are simply four limbs and two lungs and, at the higher level, a brain that can produce moments of genius. The prerequisites for being a fan are easily learned, with gestures, actions, and words for the correct expression of joy set against indignation and ridicule. The South Yorkshire region is well known for producing footballers (see Bale 1982: 34), and in 1990 in South Yorkshire there were over 500 amateur clubs in Saturday Leagues, and nearly 1,200 teams played on Sundays. Many of the participants also watched the two professional clubs in Sheffield, and having played the game, of course, all men become self-proclaimed football experts. For the past century the one place *par excellence* to hear unreserved male commentary has been, and still is, the football ground. These icons to the community from which the club draws its followers are revered emblems of local identity.

Personal Geography: The Football Ground

The simplest way of experiencing a Sheffield United/Blade identity is by entering United's Bramall Lane ground. To borrow from Portelli (1993: 100), the ground gives shape to the image of unity, and 'spectacularises' the social relations of a city (cf. Bromberger *et al.* 1993a: 130–1). This space encapsulates (football) culture, which, as Shields (1991: 274) argues, is nothing until it is 'spatialised' and allowed its 'regimes of articulation'.

Football grounds enjoy the personality of place, and have always been subject to social segregation. Areas are self-selecting, and demarcations for decades were dependent on price differentials. Today, these separations are mostly informal, with people choosing the space to suit their personal preferences and pockets. The main concern for all fans is for visibility and numbers; though a few care more for a 'good', i.e. a well-behaved, fan image presented to a wider public. Not all agree on what is important in this respect, and the 'community' of football fans is not completely in accord on how to support 'their' team. For some, pride is misplaced or mistreated when it is combined with hostility, though generations of Blades have fought rivals whilst expressing pride in their team and their city. In effect, this should not be seen as being something completely deviant, simply because the game has always provided degrees of identity. The nature of support permits the committed to 'go with the flow' (Finn 1994: 109) in the liminal experience the game offers. The events on the pitch can provoke ecstasy; they can also depress and for some offer a reflexive awareness. Emotions can run riot, and sometimes so do the fans, in what is one of the last spectacles in British life offering the chance of intense emotion and social relationships.

Over the generations at United's Bramall Lane ground, those colonising the *Shoreham End* (better known to regulars as the 'Kop') were considered rough in manner, uncouth in their support, and predominantly male and working-class. Historically, this terracing was always home to the most vociferous of die-hard fans, and, from the mid-1960s it became the home of the younger, partisan and rowdier element, i.e. the hooligans. It was here that rival fans fought for fifteen years (1965–80), and from here came the chants that shocked older and more polite fans. A roof covered 95 per cent of those who stood here, and when seats were installed 100 per cent were protected from the elements. By 1994, even though seating had stifled participation, this remained the most vociferous and partisan area.

The next most populated and partisan area was the *John Street Terrace*, which until 1994 ran the length of the pitch. At the forefront this covered section housed those who wished to stand, but preferred either a sidelong view of the match and/or more polite company. Always 95 per cent male, traditionally the fans here were older (30–50) than those on the Kop, and seemed to contain many who attended alone. Split by an earlier 'Players Tunnel' into the East and West terrace, from 1980 until 1994 the place became the spot where many Blades gathered, for this was the closest section to visiting fans, towards whom chants and taunts were directed. In accordance with the requirements of the 1991 Taylor Report, this terracing was reduced to rubble in June 1994, with plans to replace it with an all-seater stand. Behind the terrace was the *John Street Stand*, originating in the nineteenth century, and at one time *the* place for social aspirants to be seen, with the Board of Directors sitting directly above the players' changing rooms and tunnel. Having lost its gentility in the 1960s with the building of both the Bramall Lane Stand and the subsequent South Stand, it became under-used and renowned from the 1970s as the home of the elderly *'thermos flask and blanket brigade'*. Symbolic of another era, made of wood and unspectacular in appearance, its days were numbered, and it, too, was demolished in 1994, to be replaced by a £6m. state-of-the-art all-seater stand complete with private 'executive' boxes.

Opposite the Kop was a small terracing known as the *Bramall Lane End*. This became the 'Visiting Supporters Only' terrace in the early 1980s, and, until 1994, remained exclusively for away fans. It was then converted for Unitedites' use whilst a new John Street stand was being built. Above it was the *Bramall Lane Stand*, built in 1966. In its mid-1970s heyday it was regarded as *the* area for the *nouveaux riches*, and by the mid-1980s few United fans were to be found there (they preferred the South Stand). In 1986, this Stand was designated for visitors only. Finally there is the *South Stand* opened in 1975. Its 8,000 seats permitted status demarcations, with the centre for the Directors and, after 1982, the 250-strong 'Executive Club'. The East and West wings provided cheaper seating for those who had 'not quite "arrived"'! Ironically, after 1980 and until 1987, Blades occasionally occupied the West wing in their hundreds, producing a total breakdown of social demarcations. One could, perhaps flippantly, remark that there the contented and the demented now sat cheek by jowl, for by the 1980s the old, traditionally recognised, class demarcations had broken down in the Bramall Lane football ground.

The streets and pubs around the ground are, for thousands of fans, the most comfortable urban surroundings of the city after their home neighbourhoods. Visiting fans do not always see matters in such cosy terms. For some, such spaces provoke fear and/or excitement. Over the past three decades some visitors to Bramall Lane have faced the prospect of running a gauntlet of abuse and potential assault, and may have warily and stealthily approached the ground. Certain home fans, however, loved this atmosphere of intimidation and the various scenarios that unfolded around this. And in the 1960s it was attending such a site, combined with the adolescent pursuits of a desired form of masculinity based in the excitement of competing with similar rivals, that produced the first manifestations of football hooliganism. From this time on, match-going for many adolescents took on the aura of a credibility test. Via the turnstile and then the 200 steps to the back of the Kop the first thing hundreds did was to look across to the away end and comment on their visitors. Thus, older heads could reminisce contemptuously:

Fuck all compared to last year.
I remember when they used to pack Lane End out.

Alternatively one could be impressed:

They've brought a reyt mob.
There's thousands of the bastards.

While a poor following was dismissed via:

Two donkeys and a bubble car.
They never come here . . . they daren't.

Thus was modern Football Hooliganism born in its embryonic form. It was Sheffield United 'Boot Boys' from the Shoreham End 'Kop' versus the rest, and rival fans had to learn that Sheffield Unitedites were 'hard' and the ground intimidating to visit. Football thus became bound up with the reputation of a section of men in that city, and one which similar men from other cities wanted to contest. Whilst such scenarios were being played out across Britain, at times the hooligan issue was intra-city, and these events deserve detailed attention.

The Constant Other: The Owls

Antagonisms and oppositions around football identities in Sheffield take many forms, but have always centred round the conflicting loyalties of Blades and Owls. Since the mid-1960s, Blades, like most other Unitedites in my experience, have always wanted the Wednesday team to lose. A United victory and Wednesday defeat achieved what the victorious faction terms a *'Sheffield Double'*. United fans generally (and Blades certainly) enjoy a certain *Schadenfreude* at their rivals' misfortunes, be they at a club, player or fan level. Their misfortunes were relished, whether failed attempts at signing players, or the public pronouncements of a disgruntled current player; and, obviously, there was celebrating of any games that Wednesday lost. No Sheffield loyalty ever led Unitedites to celebrate the success of Wednesday for its city-wide benefits. At fan level, any publicity about Owls' fans being involved in any form of misfortune was sufficient to provoke a laugh at Blade gatherings.

Yet there is no obviously *good* social or historically apparent reason why the United–Wednesday hostility should be so strong. The bitterness

manifest from both sides seems quite remarkable. In a search for explanations, the history of the two Clubs provides some clues as to some of the
later rivalry (cf. Young 1964; Farnworth 1982; Clareborough 1989). The
Wednesday team were founded in 1867 out of a Cricket Club consisting of
traders with a day off on a Wednesday. The football team was established
to keep members together through the winter. United were formed in 1889
out of the Sheffield United Cricket Club when a member of the ground
staff at Bramall Lane saw an FA Cup semi-final played there. The revenue
it had grossed added to the appeal the game held, and no doubt he
translated this into profit and suggested to the Directors that another
football club could be founded. The owners of Bramall Lane formed a
football team (Sheffield United) and advertised for players. Strangely, it
was in Scotland that the Club drew a large response, and in the first season
the team consisted mainly of Scottish players! Regardless of the players'
birthplaces, the foundation of the new club caused tension. Local football
archivist Farnworth (1982: 33) notes: '*It is said that some families were so
divided on this issue that fathers ceased to speak to sons and brothers fell out with
brother.*'[4]

In later decades, and certainly when looked at from a Blade perspective,
family ties mainly determined an individual's subsequent allegiance. Some
have a father and/or brother who supports the city rivals, but this should
not be seen as the outward manifestation of some underlying family quarrel;
contrariness can play a part, and in thousands of cases allegiance has been
something accidental. Boys become followers of one or other of the two
clubs, and some go on to constitute the 'Hooligan Element'. Whether or
not they do this, any change of allegiance, once given, is out of the question.
Divisions based in football loyalty do not have their origins in correlates of
class, race, or geography. There is no marked difference in the localities
from which the supporters come. Unsurprisingly, there is a certain
clustering of support in the districts surrounding the grounds of each club,
Wednesday to the North, United to the South-East. Otherwise each group
draws support from every part of Sheffield and the surrounding villages
and districts. There is no correlation here between football support and
religious or political identity.

It cannot easily be argued that success in football competition is the
reason for the large number of loyal fans who flock to watch both United
and Wednesday. Historically neither side has been superior to the other
for very long; and neither has won an FA Cup or League Championship
for over fifty years. Recently Wednesday won the Coca-Cola Cup in 1991
and have been beaten finalists in that cup and the FA Cup in 1993. Overall,
however, the City has not seen much silverware, for United have not won

a thing for over seventy years. Considering this, the loyalty manifested in attendance figures is staggering, and from a population of half a million people the Clubs could attract a combined average of 50,000 per game when both were in the Premier Division in 1990–94, and needless to say they could pack Wembley Stadium (76,000) in 1993 for the United–Wednesday FA Cup Semi-Final. Of course, attendance figures are not just a reflection of the Clubs' footballing popularity, but to some extent are dependent on demographic factors and Council housing policies.[5]

Locating the Hooligan

Explaining why football is so popular is difficult. The historian, Holt (1989) relates the game to Geertz's (1973) idea of 'Deep Play', arguing that football was like a mirror for its spectators, it was he tells us, a: '...*celebration of intensely male values...where skill and cunning were valued, but hardness, stamina, courage, and loyalty were even more important. Fairness and good manners were not held in high regard'.* (173). Significantly, Holt adds that *'supporters never accepted the notion that the contests should be confined to the pitch'* (174). Things do not change, and across the past thirty years the match has been parallel to another competition between rival fans, although this is not one in which everyone wanted to be part of or witness. The obvious element in all of this is that it is synonymous with men, and that the game provides an access to male credibility. It is popularly believed that the concept of emotion and irrationality is a female trait (cf. Lutz 1988: 73–6), but when we look at football playing and spectating we can see how it allows men to act with the same emotions. Even though a century ago women were observed at Bramall Lane in numbers (Mason 1980: 171) cultural mores say that football is a *'man's game'*. Boys were and still are taken to watch *'the lads'* at the match by their fathers, grandfathers or other male adults. Later their attendance with male peers in what was a significant life-stage is taken further when allowed by guardians to go to away games. Certainly in the period of 1960 to 1990 women supporters were a 10 percent minority at Bramall Lane. Attending in two's and three's as teenagers, or in later years accompanied by boyfriend/ husband, the pervading local male attitude has been that women know nothing about football and should keep quiet. Football is *the* arena wherein men can hold opinions on everything, enact various levels of emotional turmoil and shout at the TV with mates. Of course, women can similarly do all these things but their opinions and emotions will never be considered by male fans as described above as deep and meaningful.

When masculinity, muscle and fantasy are combined with location, sporting prowess and social history, the result is thousands of football fans. Out of these come a few hundred who are fanatical about the game and its players, but who are equally prepared to construct their own off-the-pitch contests with rival fans. Believing what they do is for the good of the club and, for the most part, is morally correct (so long as the actions are within established parameters), the hooligan is a part of a crowd, and is often unknown and unrecognisable until certain actions categorise him as Hooligan. By the same token, many thousands manifest aspects of behaviour that, were they to take them further, would earn the condemnation of others.

What needs to be noted at this moment is that all these participants were football fans and were immersed in the game because of their local cultural upbringing. None was using the Club simply as a vehicle for gratuitous violence. What is also very significant is the fact that, as there is no specific criminal offence of 'Hooliganism', any research process needs to examine the *concept* of the Hooligan and how it is sustained through the interaction of the definer and defined (cf. Erikson 1962; Becker 1963). The term covers both those arrested and charged, and the fan with no criminal record who nonetheless has had behaviour and qualities conferred upon him. The crucial element here lies with the audience, which defines by coding the various behaviours (age, sex, class, occupation) that are 'known' to characterise a particular deviance. Once the act is defined and interpreted as deviant, as Kitsuse (1962) argues, the deviant can be accorded 'appropriate' treatment, both verbal and judicial, by conforming members of society. Moreover, the 'negotiation' of justice is significant here, in that who or who is not defined as deviant can depend on the various policies arising from the demands of bureaucracies, politicians and the media. The ensuing involvement of agencies of social control acting to enforce what is seen as culturally permissible results in the boundary maintenance mechanism of stigmas and the degradation ceremonies of the court; as well as providing arrest statistics and the construct of a 'Social Problem', that has produced a variety of theories from academics, police and other commentators.

The Anthropologist's Task

Because football hooliganism is a public scenario, there is never any shortage of witnesses to various events. That so little academic research has ever sought to witness these events at first hand illustrates an appalling lacuna. Such a detached approach may possibly be explained by an intellectual arrogance that suggests that some form of compromise would be achieved if its inquiries were extended beyond the secondary interpretations of the intelligentsia. What has previously been prepounded by way of explanation can be summarised in the following four theses:

1. According to an analysis that combines elements of anthropology with history and social psychology football hooliganism consists of dramas of ritualised and relatively harmless *'aggro'* performed by young men within 'rules of disorder' and, via a football-terrace, hooligan career-structure (Marsh, Rosser and Harré 1978; Marsh 1978a, b). This latter procedure has hooligan statuses and promotion structures that depend on demonstrations of character. The participants involve themselves in ritualised displays with patterned behaviour containing elements of message, moral approval and disapproval, encompassed in symbolic displays which are 'orderly to an almost absurd extent' (1978: 24). To an outsider it might look anarchic, but for these authors who base their research on interviews with the participants and video surveillance of the terrace scenarios, the issue is one of 'con-spiracy'. Seeking excitement away from the routines of work and school, the terrace action enables danger as well as heroes to be constructed. Such aggro, the authors concluded, is an illusory threat to society, and should be seen as part of an innate aggression manifest in all societies in different ways. Subsequent researchers questioned whether fan violence is really so ritualised and harmless. Others sought psychological perspectives of mass gatherings, blaming various: possession, imitative learning, and the notion of 'issueless' riots.[6] None could offer an argument as interesting as Marsh et al.

2. Football hooligans to structural Marxists are far more sinister than the last group of authors suggested. Explanations of football hooliganism by this perspective have a long pedigree. In the 1970s many authors, high on theory but always short on evidence, saw hooliganism as some sort of attempt to reclaim the 'magical' camaraderie and intimacy of a lost working-class system of traditional communities (Taylor 1969, 1970, 1971; Hall and Jefferson 1976; Cohen and Robins 1978; Robins 1984). Brief ethnographic detail was supplied by Phil Cohen (1972, 1976) and Clarke (1976, 1978) who added a new dimension of 'inter-generational conflict' reflected in the social and physical separation of young fans from the late 1960s onwards. For Clarke the issue was also one of lost tradition, because young men no longer inherited traditional controls on their behaviour and intervened in the game via their own spectacles of confrontation (see also Critcher 1979). One sub-cultural group in particular, the skinheads, were

apparently pursuing the 'downward' option of masculine, lumpen-prolatariat style. To academics like Sheffield-born Ian Taylor (1969, 1971a and b, 1976, 1982, 1987, 1989) the composition of the hooligan ranks changed from one based in sub-cultural resistance to one that should be seen in the light of a crisis in capitalist hegemony. Drawing upon the work of Stuart Hall *et al.* (1978) and the examination of 'mugging' as a moral panic, Taylor by 1982 presumes that the football hooligan forms part of a lumpen-proletariat prone to fascism whose violence has been underestimated and who needs controlling because having no revolutionary potential, his main function is frightening onlookers into voting for right-wing policies. Later in the decade a reader can see how what the academic left once considered revolutionary, and even termed them 'the last proletarian resistance movement', is now despised. Later Taylor (1987, 1989) has two sub-cultural rumps to feed the ranks of the hooligans: the underclass and the upwardly mobile and individualistic. To end their 'untutored masculinity' the author recommends moral education in citizenship in a planned and modernised society. Discussion about Ideological State Apparatus was quietly omitted.

3. Britain's self-appointed sociological experts in this field combine the meta-theory of Norbert Elias's (1978a and b and 1982) Civilising Process with ideas of Ordered Segmentation taken from a 1960s Chicago-based analysis of ethnic street gangs by Gerald Suttles (1968 and 1972). Thus a reader can choose from a variety of publications usually co-authored, but ultimately captained, by Professor Eric Dunning at Leicester University (see Dunning *et al.* 1984, 1987, 1988, 1989, 1991, 1994; Dunning and Elias 1986). The argument contends that the hooligan participants are from the lower echelons of the working class – the 'roughs' for whom uncivilised behavioural norms manifest themselves most visibly in a love of violence, be it against each other or a variety of 'outsiders' (Elias and Scotson 1965). Such an ethos makes the pro-white, anti-immigrant stance and potential violent marches of the far-right political movement attractive. Having values different from the rest of society, the rough working class are both unincorporated and suffer a positive feedback cycle from peers and their womenfolk, who expect violence from them. Constructing enemies from neighbours, during the week they 'typically fight each other' (1984: 14). They will at times, however, combine forces against a perceived greater 'outsider' enemy provided by visiting football fans or will join on a regional level against, for example, London hooligans. Media amplification around the issue has consequently ensured that more 'roughs' are attracted to football for the violence it offers; that violence then becomes more instru-mental. Thus evolved in the 1980s what they term 'superhooligan gangs' with 'members' and 'leaders' who plan 'complex strategies' and wear

specific clothing (Dunning *et al.* 1988: 179–80). Yet, despite ten years of research, these authors have nothing to add of empirical evidence regarding such gatherings. Moreover, we need to ask if the media can remake the hooligan (1988: 11), surely it also can provide for the promotion of civilised behaviour. From such ideas research grants to the tune of hundreds of thousands of pounds are awarded and testimony at Government inquiries into football hooliganism permitted.

This 'Figurationist' paradigm combines history and sociology in explaining social dependency networks (Elias 1978, 1982). The historical foundation to the Civilising Process combines ideas of divisions of labour, economic systems and the state monopoly of violence. Correlating these ideas with an analysis of courtly manners (Elias 1983), the author can conclude that there has been a diminuation in peoples' toleration of incidences of public violence. The concomitant control of the body and bodily functions originated in élite court societies and permeated to the lower orders and were sold to them as a ceremonial and civilising process. Adopted by the bourgeois and the 'respectable' middle class, those who indulge in public violence and displays of the body were, and remain, the antithesis of the 'respectable'. They are the 'roughs', i.e., the uncivilised outsiders. The small matters of genocide and world wars are apparently explainable by something called 'decivilising spurts'.

This history is combined with the application of a theory created in the ghettos of Chicago. The Leicester researchers see a similar structure evident in 'lower-class' housing estates in Britain. To support their theory, readers receive a laughable ethnographic account of life in such a milieu (Murphy, Williams, Dunning 1990: 129–66). A reader gets to learn something about 'the lads' from a Leicester council estate. Unfortunately we never see them at or near a football match. We do learn that their behaviour is stereotypically that of the lower class 'rough' male. Presented as supporting evidence, a reader is offered statistical evidence, some of it compiled by a government inquiry (Harrington 1969), or by other academics (Trivizas 1980), or via an attempt by their researchers to go amidst English fans when playing abroad (Dunning *et al.* 1988: 190; Dunning *et al.* 1991: 470–4). Their main evidence, however, is a product of statistics compiled on a group of fans by a TV documentary maker.

Chronicling a historical account of disorder at English football games throughout the century, the authors accept that disorder and violence and football have gone hand-in-hand. The violence, however, they claim is the preserve of the 'rough' working class; how they can deduce this from newspaper reports is not explained (cf. Clarke 1992). Regardless, the post-1960s football hooliganism apparently came at the same time as a 'decivilising spurt' that produced wider social inequalities. As the 'respect-

—tied in with the media's role

able' left the football ground intolerant of and abhorred by the growing violence, the consequent media coverage attracted others from the 'rough' working class to join the hooligan cohorts. To add to the confusion, the authors move on to consider the 'general crisis of identity' experienced by adolescents who are in some sort of rebellion against their parents (1991: 475). This does not fit their earlier suggestion that hooligans *have values different from the rest of society*' (Dunning *et al.* 1988: 204–12). It also seems at variance with their whole theory of enclosed socialisation taken from Elias's work, for they argue that a violent inheritance is transmitted to further the instrumental pursuits of hooligans, but we are not told how. Then they later explain (Dunning *et al.* 1993: 34) that there are 'roughs' among the upper and middle classes who are in the hooligan cohorts, apparently drawn to it by the attractions it can offer for their organising abilities and because it offers an outlet for their homoerotic feelings (1989: xi, 1991: 475). It is all terribly confusing. The pre-1993 position posits a picture of sub-cultural isolation which implies hooligans are outside the dependence network of work and education. Dunning *et al.* later posits that their theory never hypothesised notions of class segregation, despite the fact they proposed programmes 'targeting' communities that produced the hooligan, and recommended changes in the British class system as a cure for the hooligan problem!

4. The pronouncements of the police receive more publicity and greater credibility than those of the academics, and are willingly promoted by the media. Since 1986 the police have conducted 'Dawn Raids' coloured by exaggeration and institutional self-interest on suspected hooligans, and sold a script via stage-managed court cases and press releases (see Armstrong and Hobbs 1994; Armstrong and Young 1997). Imposing a suppositious quasi-military hierarchical structure on hooligan groups, the police have gained the audience of elected politicians, and have never had their ortho-doxy challenged by academics. Consequently, a reader can find in the Home Affairs Committee document *The Policing of Football Hooliganism* (1990 and 1991; Appleby 1991) the testimonies of a variety of police organisations detecting a 'Mafia-like command system running football violence in Britain' with official statuses of General, Lieutenants, Armourers and photographers who 'prey' on innocent supporters and who are motivated by 'outright wickedness'.

An incontrovertible 'institutional' truth contends that there has been an arguable change from the 'normal hooliganism' allegedly witnessed only two or three decades ago to the degenerate vision of the 'pathological' that now presents itself. Inevitably this has required the imposition of a regime of punitive sanctions, accompanied by a rhetoric that is always presented as serving the interests of deterrence. That many of these measures can be seen by the public at large, yet fail to gain condemnation, says much about the way the 'hooligan' identity has been proselytised against. Few can even begin to contemplate the support of an alleged hooligan in the face of a detractor's vision of his condemnable actions, for the law requires and shapes the evidential and semantic boundaries, while the public vision is directed by the police and focused through the media, who are served up the court case, the sound-bite and the public relations presentation. Approaching the issue from a different political perspective, the voluble opinions of anti-racist groups have similarly publicised how football hooliganism is an instrumental activity involving recognisable manipulators with a wider political and criminal agenda. Whilst given huge publicity, little in the way of hard evidence or detailed ethnographic accounts have been forthcoming. Such an opinion has its attractions, orchestration by the sinister few is easier to comprehend than mass participation beyond hierarchies. Such social fodder, it would appear, is awaiting exploitation by the socio-pathic Fascists (cf. Robins 1984; Cohen and Robins 1978), and no academic challenges what is an unlikely alliance of the political hard left and the police.

For those seeking a different viewpoint, there is no shortage of hooligan-related literature for an interested reader. Recent years have seen former participants pen their hooligan memoirs (see Allan 1989; Ward 1989; Brimson and Brimson 1996a, b). Such accounts reveal the ecstatic appeal for participants and are generally good, albeit occasionally prone to hyperbole and self-promotion in places. Others have tried to straddle the gap between journalism and more serious narrative, and have produced noteworthy accounts around the issue (Hopcraft 1968; Elms 1989; Hills 1991); yet others have produced accounts which combine fact and fiction. King's 1996 work presents a reader with a most brilliant 'novel' of the London-based hooligan scene. By contrast the supposedly factual account of Bill Buford (1991), translated into 40 languages, is a self-aggrandising journey amongst fans who obviously wondered why this 40-year-old American was in their midst. The author in pursuit of fitting in with his subjects admits to pushing two pensioners down a railway station staircase whilst abusing them, such was his supposed method acting. This confused man produced a poor book that was more fictional than a novel; Buford fortunately did not spend too much time with his hooligans, and the account is more about narcissistic contemplations than about the 'thugs' apparently representative of 'a country of little shits'. With this state of play the question could be raised as to what else is there that a reader needs to know on the subject? If they will bear with me I believe what follows is different, combining, as it does, first-hand accounts with a theoretical explanation.

Dramas, Fields and Metaphors

What participants in events labelled 'football hooliganism' are engaged in is essentially what Victor Turner (1957) termed 'social dramas'. Research, I believe, should follow the Turnerian thrust, which argues that:

> to analyse satisfactorily even a single social drama it is necessary to place it firmly in what may be called its field context, to give a preliminary account, whenever possible of the history of the field context, of how the kinds of groups came to be where they are and what accounted for their present mode of relationship. (Turner 1957: 90–1)

Varied hooligan events are created by the meanings and structures that Blades and their rivals bring to the occasions. Such gatherings renew and, at times, create new values and norms; and these events and their symbolic form, as Turner acknowledges, can be altered and manipulated. Turner's interest here was in norms and rules of conduct and how these could be changed to serve various ends depending on the situation; and because, as he states: *'in any society one is likely to find a large category of disputes where argument is mainly concerned with the question of which of a number of mutually conflicting norms should be applied to the undisputed 'facts' of the case'.* (ibid.: 147)

Bearing the above in mind, I hereby declare my interests, which are in 'meaning' and 'motivation' located within a neo-Weberian perspective of *Verstehende* sociology – trying to think oneself into the situations of the people one is interested in, remembering how Evans-Pritchard (1951) stated that the anthropologist's fundamental aim was to investigate classifications, in this case the 'Hooligan'. This combined approach involves recognising social and historical phenomena as beyond any single or simple identifying cause and trying to make sense from the social actors' viewpoint. As an end-product I attempt what J. Van Maanen (1988: 103) terms the 'impress-ionistic' style of ethnography, whereby the unfamiliar is presented to an audience 'seated ringside', whilst concomitantly trying to ascertain what are the actors' intentions and conscious choices within the class structure. This has been acknowledged by Leach (1954), Bourdieu (1977), and Abrams (1982), who suggests that the relationship of action and structure is 'a matter of process in time' and that such research must show the actor making decisions in complex circumstances (xiv–xv). And what a reader will find is that the Blades are a combination of *articulations, actions* and *behaviours* in various situations. Strauss (1969: 32) argues that a problem for research is that: *'Under certain social conditions a man may undergo so many or such critical experiences for which conventional explanations seem inadequate, that he begins to question large segments of the explanatory terminology that has been taught him'* (ibid.: 38). This is a crucial statement. Football hooliganism cannot really be 'explained'. It can only be described and evaluated. Analysis must attempt to describe the nature of this complex contestation and its construction within specific male milieus.

For the purpose of this book the following two chapters – the rest of Part I – examine a variety of social dramas over varying periods of time, inviting the reader to witness the Blades in action.

Notes

1. The term 'Blades' is older than the football club. Its first recorded citing occurred in 1882 during the 'Sheffield Riot', wherein a Salvation Army Temperance rally was attacked by a gang of muscular pugilists hired to disrupt the march by 'publicans' who owned drinking dens. The young 'thugs' were called the Sheffield Blades (*The Star*, 31 January 1979). The term 'Blades' was a journalistic cliché attached to *any* team from Sheffield at one time (akin to speaking of the men from 'Steel City'). As such, no club can claim to have originated the term. Ironically, Wednesday were originally nicknamed the Blades and United, founded later, were like any team from Sheffield at the time, known as the Cutlers. When Wednesday moved from Olive Grove to a new ground at Owlerton (close to their present on at Hillsborough), they lost the nickname 'Blades' and became known as the 'Owls'. United then became known as the Blades (cf. Farnworth 1982; Clarebrough 1989).
2. The origin of the term 'Pig' is, inevitably, the subject of dispute between the rival factions of the city. Fans of Sheffield Wednesday claim copyright going back decades, the origin being, in their opinion, the proximity of the United team's red and white-striped shirts to rashers of bacon. Fans of United claim that Wednesday, having taken a nickname from the animal kingdom (i.e. the Owls), it was only natural for them as rivals to seek the lowest and dirtiest animal to replace their chosen one.

3. Football has developed to the detriment of other sports in the city. After football the most popular active participant sport is Cricket, with the region having, in the early 1990s, eight Divisions consisting of 14 teams each. As good Yorkshiremen, Sheffielders are keen to follow the progress of their county teams, although the chance to watch them is limited. For eighty years cricket shared the Bramall Lane ground, and could attract crowds of 15,000. This link ended in 1973 when United began to build a new stand. Since then the city has never had a top-class venue for cricket matches, and although the county team play three to four games a season in the city they play their major games elsewhere in the county.

Participating or spectating in Rugby League never caught on in Sheffield. Explaining why is difficult. For some the argument is obvious; with Sheffield inventing organised football there was no need for its populace to seek recreation elsewhere in other forms. Other theories suggest that mining migration patterns might play a part. The argument is that miners in search of work moved from the North East to South Yorkshire (the North East is a football stronghold with Rugby nearly non-existent). Whereas migrants to the West Yorkshire mining towns and Rugby strongholds came from the Rugby stronghold of Lancashire. That said, Sheffield does have a professional Rugby team in Sheffield Eagles founded in 1984. In Rugby's First Division in the mid-1990s, they were never a strong team and for years were nomadic finding a home ground hard to come by. After playing at Bramall Lane, Chesterfield FC and Owlerton Stadium they eventually made their home in the Don Valley Stadium. On a good Sunday afternoon they could attract an average of 3,500, and it was ten years before a Sheffield-born player made the first team. The absence of Rugby Union may be explained in class terms; basically Sheffield has no male public school to provide a subsequent men's team. What Rugby Union there is in the city is played almost exclusively by the University student and in South West middle-class areas. Many players who represent the two city teams, Sheffield and Sheffield Tigers, are not natives of the City.

The significance of Boxing in Sheffield is difficult to evaluate. There is no written history whatsoever. That said, I think it fair to say that despite the labouring industrial-based masculinity, it was not a big sporting past-time in the city. This is a surprise considering how contenders often arise often out of poverty. The 'days of the hungry fighter' in the 1920s and 1930s produced very few local contenders or champions. There was Johnny Cuthbert, British Featherweight Champion in the 1920s and Lightweight Champion in the 1930s. In the preceding decade Gus Platts was the British Middleweight Champion.

In the late 1940s Henry Hall became British Welterweight Champion. The next champion took 30 years to arrive in the shape of Errol 'Bomber' Graham who, in the 1980s, was British and European Light Middle-weight Champion. Graham also held the British Middleweight title as did his stablemate Brian Anderson, and though both men boxed out of a Sheffield gym, only the latter was born in Sheffield. The former was actually from Nottingham. The local-based British Bantam-weight champion of the 1990s 'Prince' Naseem, became the British Lightweight Champion in 1994 and World Featherwieght Champion in 1995. Sheffield-born, Naseem was of Yemeni parents, and all the post-1980 contenders were trained by an Irishman. Despite the small number of participants in this sport in the city, since the Second War it has been massively popular as a male spectator event. That said, most watch it via TV coverage and only a few thousand per year ever attend venues.

After football, the biggest spectator event at one time was Greyhound racing. Available three nights a week at one of three stadia, crowds of up to 10,000 were common. However, the two remaining stadiums in the 1980s barely attracted a four-figure attendance in a week of events. Recently various entrepreneurs have tried to promote modernity, via USA style razzamatazz indoor sports. As a result the second most popular spectator sport in the city in the early 1990s was ice-hockey. Sheffield Steelers were founded in September 1991 by a Spanish-based businessman. Joining the National League, the sport attracted crowds of up to 8,000 and averaged 3–4,000. At one time, this made for the highest attendances for the sport in Europe, and the Sheffield Arena venue was able to create an ice-pitch for the games. The crowd was attracted not just by athletic achievements but by the whole 'package' of USA-style flashing lights and DJ-orchestrated chants. The North American influence was enhanced by the fact that most of the teams were Canadian, with some Czechs, and the players were promoted, via the local press, for their good looks. Consequently probably a third of all crowds were adolescent girls.

More recently again North American entrepreneurs have attempted to start basketball in the city, and the Sheffield Sharks team was created in July 1994. Financed by money from the US and managed by an Australian with a team mostly drawn from the States and Australia, occasionally they attracted crowds of a few thousands to their Ponds Forge city centre location. A year later saw American football arrive when the Sheffield Spartans played five matches at the Don Valley Stadium. The crowds were numbered in the hundreds, the event advertised as a 'fun-filled day for the whole family', and apart from the game itself, entertainment was offered from a pop band, cheerleaders and fireworks. Admission costs were slightly lower than for a football game.

4. The first city 'derby' match took place in 1890. The following season the clubs met twice and supporters of both sides produced funeral cards announcing the death of the rival side. After United had won 5-0 at Bramall Lane, cards were produced which read *'In loving remembrance of the Sheffield Wednesday football team ... who were safely put to rest ... at Bramall Lane.'* A month later United lost 4–1 to Wednesday and a new card was on sale which said, *'In pitiful remembrance of our idol, the Sheffield United football team, who departed their football life, struggling to the end'* (Clareborough 1989: 23). The bitter rivalries were epitomised in these football matches, described by Farnworth (1982) as violent affairs which produced many injuries to the players.

   Historian and club archivist Clarebrough (1989: 17–21) tells of hostility between the two clubs founded on accusations that United were trying to poach Wednesday players. No doubt this was exacerbated when in 1890 United undercut Wednesday's admission charges, and the fact that, at the same time, several Wednesday players joined United. Matches between the sides were violent occasions. One game in 1892 saw players leap into the crowd to fight spectators before forty police restored order (ibid.: 23).

5. In the early part of the century United had numerically larger support owing to the central location of the ground – near to large firms and densely populated working-class districts (Fishwick 1989: 34). Then, when the Hillsborough district underwent massive council housing development in the 1920s, this brought Wednesday thousands of actual and potential supporters. Today this is Sheffield's most densely populated district. United fans claim these massive estates around Hillsborough explain Wednesday's larger attendances. However, United fans assert that they are numerically larger within the city boundaries than Wednesday, whom they claim attract more outsiders from townships north of the city and from the nearby town of Barnsley.

6. One which is worth addressing, is the idea of whether disorder around football matches is an 'issueless' riot. The theoretical problem here is the one posited by G. Marx (1972) that argues that when collective behaviour is manifest how do we ascertain which circumstance has an issue and which one it is? (Pearton 1986; Guttman 1986; Smith, M. 1976; Gaskell and Benewick 1987). Applicable to this theory is the recent British school of thought emanating out of a University in Sheffield that talks of 'Flashpoints' as a prerequisite for crowd violence. Despite a funding brief to include football hooligan disorder in Sheffield in the 1980s, the

researchers were unable to find any examples of football hooliganism in the city or come up with a theory to explain hooligan events bar the vague line of it being 'issue-less' (Waddington, Jones and Critcher 1989; McClelland 1989; D. Waddington 1992). Despite a funding brief to research into a variety of public disorder issues in Sheffield, the authors state in their 1989 work that the football hooligan angle was abandoned because of the 'low level' of this disorder in Sheffield (Waddington *et al.* 1989: 14). In later publications, Waddington criticses my work and me (1992: 133) because of my proximity to my research subjects. The same author fails to mention that my proximity caused him in 1984 to request that I find him a dozen hooligans to interview for his project. My refusal to provide such research subjects may explain his later jaundiced opinion of my work.

The most recent psychological approach to the subject comes from Kerr (1994) who collected newspaper cuttings and assembled them together around something called 'Reversal Theory'. Drawing on an idea originating in the work of Apter (1982) this theory purports to examine ideas of boredom in everyday life and pleasurable arousal to combat it. What we receive is presented as an *'innovative psychological explanation of why soccer hooliganism takes place'* (X). This is all done in a conceptual framework which, *'... examines neither the individual nor society and keeps both on the hook'* (43). Yet, we learn that whilst fans and supporters attend matches purely for the enjoyment of the game hooligans attend for aggressive and violent behaviour (XI), and that football teams are merely 'flags of convenience' for them to manifest violence against other fans, police or members of the public (5). This sits uncomfortably with Kerr's attempt to understand human motivation and the *'complexity, change-ability and inconsistency of the individual's behaviour and experience'* (16). The theory is ultimately about the state of mind of the person at a specific time, and the crux of it all is the 'metamotivational state' (30). The book's aim is to unmask these states, but is not achieved. And as he promotes the idea of risk-taking as arising from a condition of boredom, Kerr does not explain where this state of mind arises from. Some, however, become 'delinquent' (never explained or defined) in their pursuit of 'paratatic dominance' (39). And whilst some are merely seeking risk and novel experiences, others are psychopaths – particularly the 'hardmen and superthugs' (39). Such theory is the product of an author who has lived abroad for nine years and never once given an example of any event around a British football match. A reader could validly presume he had never been to one as part of the research.

Chapter 2

Nine Weeks 1987: Unexpected Visitors and Close Relatives

It was Taff's idea that Blades should meet in the Suffolk Arms at Saturday midday. From past experience Blades anticipated Plymouth would have around 200 ordinary supporters – not 'Their Boys' – and therefore of no consequence. More importantly, West Ham were also in Sheffield to play city rivals Sheffield Wednesday and were expected to bring 3,000 followers. Amongst these would be a group of youths (maximum a few hundred) calling themselves the 'ICF', short for 'Inter-City Firm', a hooligan gathering given or adopting this name around 1982. No Blade knew what time they would arrive, or their mode of transport, or whether they would be able to avoid the police road-blocks on the motorway or the police waiting to capture them outside the railway station and escort them directly to the ground. If they did outwit these they could then present themselves in the city centre and confront Owls, who were duty bound to be waiting in expectation. Amongst the thirty Blades in the pub this Friday night, none had mentioned what they would actually do if the ICF were seen, for the choice was basically whether to talk to them and make them welcome or attack them. In their previous two visits Blades had done both![1]

Not that antagonism was the only of Blade existence. Far from it. In all the ten pubs along London Road the Blades were welcomed by the proprietors, be it on Friday nights or on match-days. Frequenting mainly The Lansdowne, the Blades were well known to regulars. With landlords and regular clientele, 'the lads' were generally very well behaved, though occasionally rowdy, and would usually move on to another pub within thirty minutes. Local residents were always to be found in the pubs at such times, and no Blade ever bothered them. In fact such socialising epitomised the egalitarian nature of much of the City. London Road ran through an old working-class district that still housed small steel workshops on side-streets. Subject to redevelopment since the late 1970s, the area saw new rows of terraced houses standing alongside old ones and three high-rise tower blocks nearby. It was a multiracial area, and the pubs always had a mixture of white locals sitting alongside Caribbeans, Asians, Irish, and the occasional Oriental with no obvious antagonisms. The pubs varied in clientele and décor. Some were considered 'poorer' than others, some were better decorated; some, mid-week, would be full of bank and office staff from nearby shops and businesses, whilst others housed the lost and lonely, content with pints and memories. On weekend nights after last orders many of the youthful crowd frequented a nearby nightclub, 'The Locarno'. Others preferred town-centre discos; some went to nearby restaurants or home. Along this street individual Blades were relaxed and secure and came and went as they pleased.

Whilst such socialising was par for the course, one particular Saturday saw a break with tradition in pursuit of a mission as Blades made their way towards the Suffolk Arms. This was known to Blades as a transport workers' ('bus drivers') pub, as it was next to a large bus depot. Blades had never met on a midday 'turnout' here before. However, Taff's suggestion was seen as sensible, because the pub was situated a few hundred yards from both the railway and bus stations. A more obvious pub to meet in, directly across from the railway station, was not used because many thought that, with the expected large following of West Ham fans, the landlord would either close the pub or operate a 'restricted door' policy. Another pub frequented on occasions (but not this one) was The Stamp. Located in the bus station, it had held gatherings of Blades since the mid-1970s, and in the mid-1980s the landlord welcomed the Blades both before and after games. On this specific day, however, Blades reasoned the Owls might have gathered within, and would almost certainly have greater numbers. Discretion was therefore the better part of valour.

Information of sorts added an edge to the day's proceedings. A rumour had gone round the pub the night before that the Owls had 'summat planned', a generic colloquialism understood by all Blades to mean that their city rivals had violent intentions towards Blades. Blades summarised such intended hostility with the statement, 'Pigs are supposed to be coming down', i.e. from West Street, literally downhill, to London Road. In the Friday night revelry, no one took the warning seriously. After all, during the previous few months Blades had spent nearly every Friday and Saturday expecting such an attack, and few had materialised. There was no good reason why an attack should occur this time. George, who had brought the message, was a voice in the wilderness, though his informant was a good mate, one of the Owls' 'main men'. His previous message had resulted in a fight along London Road; but though reliable in the past, no one thought him worthy at this moment.

By 12.30 Saturday morning, ten Blades were sitting in the Suffolk Arms. Gordon, always capable of evaluating and summarising, stated what the others knew was the truth: *'They* [i.e. the remaining Blades] *all said they were comin' last night; now they'll either be still in bed, still pissed up or 've gone straight to London Road.'* He then announced he was going to 'have a scout round', i.e. drive around the city centre to look for large groups of youths, and left on his own. Gordon soon recognised a group of Owls and became anxious about the direction they were taking. Driving ahead of the group, he recognised some of the Owls' Top Men amidst a wider group of peers, and quickly realised a hundred Owls were walking down 'The Moor' shopping area to seek out Blades on London Road. Driving ahead to The Lansdowne, Gordon found only one Blade, Seamus, who returned with him to the Suffolk Arms, where twenty Blades were now gathered. They finished their drinks and each climbed into one of four vehicles. On the advice of Marvin, they drove to a street adjacent to London Road, where it was agreed to 'park up' and walk, via the back streets, to The Lansdowne, hopefully to recruit more Blades and get 'tooled up', i.e. obtain missiles in the form of small bricks or planks of wood from nearby demolition sites.

A game of hide-and-seek was evolving. The Owls, having arrived 15 minutes earlier, realised no Blades were about, and, having walked the length of London Road, then gathered in The Queen, had a drink, and then walked back towards The Lansdowne. By coincidence the rival groups met; Blades walking along an adjacent street could not see Owls along London Road. A warning was relayed to the former as they approached the junction outside The Partridge by one of the bar staff standing on the pub doorstep. He discreetly gestured and pointed to his right implying that they should go back. However, Blades had no time to act on this advice, as the 'front men' of the Owls became visible. The rivals literally walked into one another.

Such scenarios can only end in fight or flight. Blades chose the former, and then were persuaded into the latter course of action. Although vastly outnumbered, the Blades had spread out across the street and on to the nearby petrol station forecourt, picking up various 'missiles' lying around. In a half-minute 'stand-off' verbal threats and insults were exchanged by some, whilst others stood in the ritual manner that is typical of a hooligan confrontation – bouncing about on the balls of the feet, arms flailing and wearing intense facial expressions. The impasse was broken when Blades took the initiative and ran at Owls, who backed away, although out-numbering them three to one. Seconds later the Owls, to a crescendo of 'Get 'em', ran at Blades, and they in turn had to 'back off'. It was now missile time: Gordon threw a fire bucket full of sand taken from the garage. As it landed harmlessly Owls ran towards him. Another Blade, Greg, then set off a fire extinguisher, also obtained from the garage. This action was countered by an Owl's throwing a small brick, which struck Greg on the nose. The Owls then ran *en masse* at Blades, causing them to retreat 200 yards down London Road back to the relative sanctuary of The Lansdowne. Once inside they gathered round the front door, awaiting an incursion. One Owl ran at the door, but quickly retreated on meeting Blades armed with pool table cues. Some Blades then ran via the back door into the car park and began throwing anything they could get their hands on at approaching Owls. In this small-scale scenario two Owls were felled by Parker via blows from a snooker cue he had requisitioned. Then, to a shout of 'coppers', all combat ended. A police transit van appeared, containing four officers, as the Owls walked back along the same route. No one was arrested. The Blades stood outside the pub with the landlord, cursing 'The Pigs'. One Blade, Barry, assured him they would avenge the attack, and a couple informed the inquisitive policemen that '*It wo' Wednesday.*' However, despite knowing many of the Owls' identities, Blades did not reveal their names to the police. Greg required six stitches in his nose.

Blades knew of only one appropriate response. That said, it had to be done properly and in the correct circumstances. Those who arrived later to hear of the incident were as angry as those who were there, but could only show their solidarity by swearing and cursing the Owls as they tried to salvage some credit. Some argued that, although they had been vastly outnumbered, they could claim to have 'backed them off twice' or 'had 'em wobbling'. Moreover, they had prevented them from entering The Lansdowne. Rationalising the motives of the Owls also provided some relief. Every Blade considered that the Owls were duty-bound to confront West Ham, and that they had distracted themselves from this task by coming for Blades was considered a negation of that duty. It was agreed the Owls were 'obviously scared of the Londoners', and had used an attack on the Blades as an excuse, a face-saver. Blades who arrived later brought the reassuring news that West Ham fans were 'all over town' and were 'just walking about as if they owned it'. The idea that Blades should immediately go up to where the Owls would be, The Bell, for a revenge attack was suggested but dismissed. Blades knew the Owls had a full turnout, and the United turnout being poor (sixty at most) for their own, inconsequential, match was insufficient to launch a realistic response. Besides, Blades argued that the police would be 'swarming all over the town now', and so a tit-for-tat fight would not be practicable. Everyone went off to the match and saw a United victory.

With Blades in three sides of the ground there was no central control or method of circulating information. This was just as well, for despite 3½ hours passing since the Owls attack, Blades had no plans as to how to gain vengeance. Instead, when the match ended (at 4.40 p.m.) Blades drifted towards The Lansdowne and waited outside it in the winter night. By 5.00 p.m. they numbered a hundred, and there was still no plan and nobody knew what to do. In such a situation Blades look towards a 'core', recognisable by their regularity in confrontations. However, these 'core' Blades had no plans! Some were quietly arguing that with the others – non-core – now tagging along, the job would be harder. After all, with so many strangers, who knew who could be relied upon? That said, they all realised that no one could tell the others to go away. It was in this shambolic situation that, at 5.10 p.m., the rag-tag collective under the rubric of 'Blades' began walking towards the city centre. The intention of the core Blades, plus some who were occasional in their 'front-line' commitment, was to descend on The Bell, as it was believed the Owls would be in there by now. However, as the mob of a hundred silently but hurriedly ran towards the pub, they realised their mission was in vain; for it was closed! Thwarted, the Blades walked on to The Stamp. Once inside, the majority were prepared to sit and wait, while others took it on themselves to drive or walk around 'scouting' for a sighting of the Owls. Shortly after 6.30 p.m. the Owls were found in The White Rose, a city-centre pub. Two Blades in a car, Gordon and Bernard, had not been deliberately 'scouting' for the Owls, but ironically had been walking around hoping to meet some of his Owl mates for a drink. He had seen the Owls (but not his mates), and told inquisitive Blades they were in The White Rose, a neutral pub in the city's football loyalties. About forty Owls were inside, standing towards the middle of the room.

The 'sussers' (for so such activity was known in hooligan circles) drove back to The Stamp. On entering, Gordon announced, *'They're in t'White Rose, let's go and give it 'em.'* He immediately departed, though his words were not a command, and anyone could have refused the suggested course of action. Every Blade followed, without threats, cajoling or urging. Their ages ranged between 17 and 30, and included many who had not been involved in hooligan activities for years. Some were considered very peripheral to Blade fights. Roughly half had not been involved in any act of hooliganism for over a year, some had *never* before been involved at all. All the same, a seventy-strong group walked quietly and calmly to a small pathway on a natural route between the two points. The only manifestation of organisation arose when those at the front began walking more quickly, causing those behind to shout 'slow down' and 'let's stay together', reasoning that if the Owls were waiting they would face the whole Blades mob and not 'run' the front-runners. This made sense, and the leading

Blades stopped, so that a compact group walked to, then waited along, narrow, dimly lit passage close to their destination.

A plan of sorts took shape. Without consulting anyone, six core Blades, (including Gordon, Dom, Jim and Limit), told the rest they were going to 'get 'em out' by running to the door of the White Rose and standing outside, taunting. The rest were to remain hidden in the darkness of the passage. When the Owls came running out in pursuit of the six as expected, the hidden group were to run around the corner, and in Gordon's words, '*steam into 'em and hammer 'em*'. The six then ran up the street out of sight. Meanwhile, those in the alley were told by a Blade standing on a nearby wall to 'crouch down' and 'keep quiet', adding the command: 'No fucker run.' Maurice, the Blade giving these orders, had rarely been out in the last three and a half years. He was an 'old lad', aged 27 and married with a wife and child. His Blade days were sporadic, and he had never done any leading or organising with the Blades. Yet, at this moment, Blades followed his advice and that of the younger Shane, who shouted 'Everybody get a rock.' Only a few acted on this, and they were easily obtainable from the soil of the nearby municipal flower-beds and gardens. One Blade, Pear, pulled a council litter-bin from a street lamp-post. Another pulled a wing mirror from a nearby car. Everyone crouched, peering through the foliage and darkness.

About 40 seconds later the six Blades were again visible, 'bouncing' backwards, obviously inviting the out-of-sight Owls to come towards them. On seeing this waiting Blades ran *en masse* across the road chanting 'B-B-C' ('Blades Business Crew': see Chapter 3 below for the origins of this sobriquet). The Owls ran back into the pub and bolted the door, seconds before the pub's two main windows were put in by a hail of stones, soil, and hands wrapped in gloves and scarves and plastic litter-bins. In return, Owls threw glasses, bottles, ashtrays and stools, which Blades retrieved and threw back in. In passing, it is worth pointing out that those punching windows (two characters, Beef and Liam) had taken *no* part in Blade–Owl scenarios in the previous two years. The former was an 'old lad', who in the early 1980s had received a three-month prison sentence for being drunk at a match and charged with threatening behaviour. The other was a young West Indian only occasionally out with Blades. Here they were 'front-lining', at great risk of injury and subsequent arrest; yet they *never* subsequently did anything comparable. Neither were ever subsequently arrested for Blades activities.

There was no way the Owls would leave the pub. Likewise, no Blade was going to be first in the door to face forty of them. However Blades had to be seen to be willing in their pursuit, and, as no police had arrived, three Blades, Tom, Billy, and Ralph, took turns to launch flying kicks at the pub door. After twelve running kicks the door collapsed. Tom picked it up and threw it in at the Owls! Blades broke into the ritualistic chant of *'Fight, fight wherever you may be/we are the famous BBC/and we'll fight you all whoever you may be/coz we are the famous BBC.'*

An interesting impasse was now created. Normally, the police would arrive at such a city-centre incident in about a minute; but this time for some reason it took them five minutes. This caused problems, for after throwing missiles and chanting, the Blades did not really know what to do; and since the Owls would not come out, there was not much point in hanging around. However, because the police had not yet arrived, Blades did not have an excuse to run away, and had to begin the process all over again. Thus chants of 'BBC' were sung again, and threats were repeated. In total some three attacks were launched on the pub, and by the time the police arrived some Blades had actually begun to walk away. And though seventy were present, only around a third were responsible for the missile-throwing and damage. The majority were spectators.

The police finally arrived in a patrol car containing one PC, who drove into the group at speed. An officer grabbed the first Blade he could as he got out. Blades left in all directions, some at full speed. Others – such as the older fans and those regularly involved in hooligan scenes – knew from experience that in police eyes running is tantamount to an admission of guilt, and whenever possible walked slowly away. For those leaving the scene a place of refuge was needed, and a few walked into the two nearest pubs and ordered drinks. Some walked a mile to The Lansdowne. Some went straight home. Others entered the places and pubs they knew police were least likely to search. Later police arrested a core blade in the bus station, and a peripheral Blade. Four other peripherals were arrested next day and charged. No-one knew who had given their names.

The same evening, a couple of miles up the road, Bud was celebrating his engagement, and both families and friends were to meet in a hired venue. Bud being a popular lad, many Blades had decided to stay out after the match and go to the celebration after having a few drinks. Approximately twenty Blades who had been outside The White Rose went to the 'do'. All now had to show an alternative side of their characters to a different audience, and had to talk to girlfriends they had arranged to meet there. Other Blades arrived who were ignorant of the evening's events, and when alone or away from girlfriends were told of the incident. They showed enthusiasm, and congratulated those who had been there. Generally, the

brief mentions there were regarding the incident centred on two aspects –
what the police would do, and what the Owls would be thinking. It was
expected the police would be furious. For twice in one day they had been
nowhere when a large-scale disorder had occurred. Blades also realised
that those arrested would no doubt face a serious charge, probably of affray
(carrying the risk of a heavy sentence) in later weeks.

Over the next week there was no United match and no mass Blade
gathering, and it was not until the Friday following the attack that forty
Blades gathered in London Road pubs. At 10.15 p.m., after a trouble-free
pub crawl, they returned to The Lansdowne and were shocked to find three
Owls there. One was the one Owl arrested after the attack on The White
Rose. Another was one of the Trio, whose last visit to this street had resulted
in him spending two days in hospital (see Chapter 3). No one recognised
the third Owl. Blades looked towards them, and the 'arrested' Owl broke
the silence, asking *'Any o' you lot outside t'White Rose last week?'* Holding an
empty glass behind his back, Luke walked over, stood eye to eye with him,
and replied *'I was, why?'* The Owl did not offer violence or hostility, and
sensing this Taff intervened by putting his arms around Luke and
encouraging him to drop hostilities, which he did. As the Blades seemed
not about to start a fight, the two Owls joined their mate, and Blades who
knew them (Gordon, Fagin and Taff) began talking and sat down at a table.
The crux of the Owls' visit was to ask Blades not to 'grass' any Owl up to
police. One had been arrested and police were inquiring about the names
of others. Such a request was entirely within the code of ethics that such a
group operated by, and the three Blades assured them of their silence and
said they expected the Owls to do likewise. They knew they could not truly
claim to speak for hundreds of others, but had to make a claim for the
honour and virtue of their colleagues. Onlooking Blades were somewhat
shocked by events. Some watched the Owls' facial expressions to see how
scared they were; others like Nick, Alan and Hank asked rhetorically *'Are
we gonna do 'em, or what?'* Nobody answered and nobody acted. Any violent
intentions were quashed when, shortly after closing time, six PCs arrived
and demanded Blades finish their drinks and get out. A harassed landlord
thanked everybody for their custom and apologised for the behaviour of
the police. The three Owls were escorted to the door by Gordon and left
unmolested.

The police officer in charge of The White Rose pub damage enquiry had
another serious incident to deal with in the early hours of this same evening,
when an argument on a late bus from the city centre resulted in two youths'
receiving slash wounds. This had nothing to do with football loyalties, but
was the result of a knife being produced during a fight between two groups

of youths from different districts of the city. The assailant was an Owl who gave himself up to police on the following afternoon, after a lunch-time drinking session in his village with some Blade mates who had not gone off to watch United play.[2]

Some who intended going to United and Wednesday matches a week after The Lansdowne–White Rose disorders never got there. Early on Saturday morning one of the three Owls who had entered The Lansdowne the night before, together with a Blade well known to police, were arrested for questioning and identification purposes. Later in the day the Blade told others the police had promised that if he came up with names of Blades involved they would allow him to attend matches again (believing him to be the leader of the Blades, they arrested him whenever he tried to enter a game), and had left him a contact telephone number. On the same day three Blades coaches were travelling to watch their team at Grimsby. At 10.00 a.m. one of the coaches operated by Skip was stopped by the police at the usual departure point. This occurred in a most dramatic manner, for the coach had travelled literally 20 yards when officers in four police vehicles, having watched passengers boarding from a discreet distance, raced to the scene and forced the driver to make an emergency stop. In the sudden silence a sergeant boarded, and instructed everyone to keep their hands by their sides and to stay still. The coach was searched by a dozen officers, but no weapons or alcohol were found. However, two passengers were arrested because their names corresponded to those on a police wanted list. Every passenger had to give his name, address, date of birth, occupation and address of workplace. (The same applied to the driver, despite his being 58 years old.)

Within viewing range, The Lansdowne Blades' coach was due to depart from a lay-by outside the Polytechnic Students' Union. Running his first coach ever, Nick had booked with a firm not previously used by Blades, and had told the operator he wanted it for an excursion to Cleethorpes seaside resort. In essence this was the truth, for Blades always went to the resort, a mile or so from the Grimsby ground, though not to paddle but to confront the local lads – an event that always took place on the sea front. On the way to the departure point two of the travellers, Hank and Titch, learned from the occupants of Skip's coach that the police were after two people in particular, one named Fletcher. Blades waiting at Nick's coach were relieved, for no one knew of a Blade by that name, and it immediately became a source of jokes. By 10.30 a.m. it was time to leave, for they had waited long enough for 'Fletch'.

Less than one mile into the journey this same coach was stopped and surrounded by six police vehicles. A sergeant boarded and spoke melodramatically into his radio, saying *'We've got them, this is them .... the Barmy Army.'* Blades stifled a laugh at this reference to a now-discarded term they had once used between 1979 and 1982. Whilst ten Constables searched the coach (again finding nothing) others took personal details, and Nick was questioned in a police car by two CID officers. Shown a photograph of an older Blade (not aboard), Nick noticed a list of surnames and nicknames and recognised many. One individual personality police particularly wanted to know about they held a photograph of. This was a peripheral Blade named Tufty. The fact that he was 32 no doubt provoked in police minds the notion that he was some sort of orchestrator. Later in Blades' discussions the list was thought to be significant, for to the Blades it meant that there was a police informer within Blades' ranks. From the coach seven passengers were detained, two because their names were on a wanted list, and five others because their home addresses were in the direction of the bus route on which a non-football-related slashing had occurred the previous night. None of the seven was sub-sequently charged. Twenty-five minutes later the coach resumed its journey with its stunned passengers – for Blades this was an unprecedented form of police enquiry. For the next hour alibis were concocted amongst those who had been outside The White Rose – i.e. roughly half the bus's complement.

Grimsby had been a regular fixture since the late 1970s. Being next to a seaside resort, it was a popular away trip for Sheffield fans, and Blades always had a lunch-time drinking 'session' in Cleethorpes. The local lads met there as well, and a fight usually broke out around 1.00 p.m. Blades had invariably 'run' the home turnout, who were 'game' but insignificant in the Blades' eyes. The pub they met in was known to many; however, Blades would start their session about half a mile away and 'work [drink] their way up', until, tired of the anticipation, they would throw down the gauntlet by walking towards 'Their Boozer'.[3] This was a truly ritualised procedure, and both sides knew the score. The arrival at Cleethorpes brought a dilemma, however, for when Their Boys appeared (as they always did) what were Blades to do? Fighting on this February morning after the raid on the coach, Fats argued, would be playing into the hands of the police. Others, particularly Alan and Jim, argued that it was out of the question for Blades to avoid a challenge. Around twenty-five Blades sat on the sea front, with only half a dozen wanting beer at this time of crisis. A dozen Rotherham Blades arrived in Louis's mini-van. They were told of the morning's events and seemed stunned. Twenty minutes later the local lads could be seen in the distance. Blades remained where they were. Seeing a police transit parked nearby, Barry even told the officers of the impending trouble and suggested police turn the locals away. The police drove towards them, the locals retreated, and the Blades continued to chat. Two locals avoided the police, however, and walked through the group unmolested, for with the police nearby they knew they were safe. Blades laughed and made sarcastic remarks.

At 2.00 p.m. the fifty Blades made their way to the ground around a mile away. A similar number of rival fans were waiting nearby, outside a pub. Two police transits followed the Blades, and the two groups 'shadowed' each other, walking down the same street on opposite sides of the road. Two of the locals shadowing the Blades from across the road thought the presence of police offered sanctuary for their gestures and insults. However, they were unaware that one Blade, Bernard, had crossed over. Discreetly, he punched one on the nose, causing both to run away, and Blades to cheer. The police remained unaware of these proceedings. Moments later, as a challenge, the Blades silently crossed over, and 'Their Lads' stopped in anticipation. Walking shoulder to shoulder amongst them, Blades then broke into a spontaneous round of applause, with sarcastic shouts of 'More!' and 'Well done', and personal insults were exchanged, but not blows; for the police were still nearby. Such a reception for rival fans was unique for Blades, and was never repeated again. Why it took place this time was purely contextual. Fear of the police was combined with contempt for rivals that required some form of release, but one that would not lead to arrest. A minute later, however, the police drove away; and, on seeing this, Their Lads, who were slightly behind, ran at Blades, and a scuffle began. Three home fans were knocked over by punches; the rest ran away, one into a nearby tree, knocking himself unconscious. The police returned, the Blades continued their walk, and a few home lads stood over their prostrate colleague.

There were other non-violent scenarios to be performed, with other players adding to the cast. Three more confrontations took place in the next 15 minutes. Joined by thirty Blades from Max's coach, the now-enlarged Blade group walked three times into rival fans gathered nearby and applauded them as they backed away. Max's coach had not travelled directly to Grimsby or Cleethorpes. As usual, they had stopped for a session in a small town about ten miles away, and then jumped off the coach near to the ground to have a 'walk round' – a euphemism for seeking an opportunity for a confrontation. During this 'walk round' not a single blow was struck. Neither was there any trouble in the ground, during a match that United lost 2–0.

Nor was there trouble after the game, and most of the 1,500 travelling fans boarded one of ten coaches and four mini-vans and awaited a police escort. Suddenly, two plain-clothes police officers from Sheffield appeared along with a local uniformed Superintendent, and boarded The Lansdowne Blades' coach. Everybody on board was now placed under arrest, on a charge that was said to be 'likely to be manslaughter or murder' because of the unconscious and hospitalised local who had run into the tree. The Rotherham Blades' van was also 'arrested', and the two vehicles given an elaborate, seven-vehicle, blue-light police escort, complete with motorcycle outriders. Blades could not believe this, and those involved made up alibis. The opportunity for police melodrama was not wasted, and on arrival at police HQ thirty officers formed a human circle around the coaches as Blades were taken off one at a time with a two-officer escort to a charge room (a distance of 20 yards). All were locked up, interviewed and released two and a half hours later without charge. In the interim period the youth had regained consciousness, and refused to make a complaint to police waiting at his bedside. Before being released each Blade was photographed twice for 'police records'. The coach driver had waited, although he would have been well within his rights had he gone back to Sheffield without the fans; and in appreciation Blades held a collection that brought him £20.

Elsewhere hurried discussions had taken place. On his release on the previous day, Gordon had phoned one of the Owls' top lads, who he knew from playing football with, requesting he and the Owls drop hostilities, the matter being 'too risky' because of the police activity. The Owl was prepared to do this, but said he had no control over others. This was true, for likewise Gordon had no control over Blades. The Sunday after the arrests, after a lunch-time drink on London Road with half a dozen other Blades, Taff was driving home when he saw two well-known Owls. On his offering them a lift (which they readily accepted) they laughed on learning where we had been drinking; after all, they explained, they had just been drinking with a dozen Owls, and had contemplated taking a mini-van to attack Blades they knew would be in there. They thanked Taff for the lift and went home. There was no revenge attack, and nothing happened between the factions over the next couple of weeks.

Nine weeks after the attacks on The Landsdowne and The White Rose, United played at Hull. Promotion, though mathematically a possibility, was probably beyond the team's capabilities, and this Easter Bank Holiday kick-off was set for 3.00 p.m. The proximity of Hull (70 miles by good road links) ensured a large following from Sheffield. Travel arrangements had been discussed in The Lansdowne, but remained unresolved, until Jap and Ray, along with Jade, volunteered to hire and drive a van. By 9.00 a.m., some thirty Blades had met on a pub car-park two miles out of town, which was chosen to avoid police scrutiny, yet still allow all to reach it with ease.

By 9.30 a.m. the hired furniture van had 32 occupants (29 in the rear), and was followed by three cars containing more Blades. Not everyone in the van was acquainted, but this was immaterial, for as Blades they were all pals together.

The usual procedure followed the arrival at Hull around 10.45 a.m. The van and cars were parked up, and after a half-mile walk to the city-centre precinct, some fifty Blades found a pub – the choice being dictated by necessity, for it was the only one open. Jade suggested buying tickets in a stand known from previous matches to be the place where 'Their Boys' sat, and after collecting names and cash he and a few others went off to the ground to buy the tickets. The plan was left there: there was no further discussion on tactics and no mention of violence, for it was certain the police would be out in force and the chances of a fight were negligible. However, the idea of a Blades presence in this stand would constitute a trespass, a challenge and an insult.

There was now time to kill and drinks to take before the action that was anticipated, for sooner or later it was expected 'Their Boys' would locate the Blades and attack through the pub door, or hurl missiles through the windows. Some left the pub on reconaissance, and as the remainder anticipated running out to face rivals with whatever missiles came to hand (bottles, ashtrays, glasses), a general restlessness ensued. Many moved away from the windows, as they would be the first thing to get smashed in any attack, and Blades were now standing, wandering around, and talking in slightly nervous expectation. An attack or a shout to action was clearly anticipated, when the unexpected happened, and three men came into the pub and entered an adjacent room. Blades immediately sussed them out as policemen, and when three Blades faced them in the room pretending to look for friends, they were able to return with the confirmatory news that they were indeed 'coppers', and two were from Sheffield. This caused surprise and bewilderment, for plain-clothes police from Sheffield appearing in the same pub at an away game was a unique experience. Were they trying to infiltrate? Or simply out to follow Blades around all day? Five minutes later the three came through to the room the fans were collected in, and the eldest (from Sheffield), said 'Good morning', smiled sardonically, and stood at the bar. The level of conversation dropped to a whisper, for no Blade knew what to say.

This same officer then broke the silence. (I will call him Clouseau, a name he subsequently became known by to the Blades, because of his droopy moustache and eyes, which they thought resembled Peter Sellers' as 'Inspector Clouseau' in the Pink Panther movies.) He said *'We know what you've come for, you've come for a big fight with that lot outside.'* After a moment's silence Gordon said, *'No we haven't, we've just come for a drink and to see t'match.'* Clouseau smiled, adding *'For me you could all go out and have a big scrap, but I can't let you do that.'* The younger Sheffield officer then said he was the Football Intelligence Officer for United, and a United fan. As the two sat and chatted with whomever would listen, Blades moved around; some would sit with one officer and then move to listen to the other. A few remained silent, pretending not even to notice the two. A dozen remained at the other side of the pub.

Boggy and Shane then addressed the question of 'The White Rose' and 'Lansdowne' arrests to the younger of the Sheffield officers. He said the police had a list of names (nine United, six Wednesday), and would be *'nicking everybody'* within the next two weeks; all would be charged with affray, and *'everybody will be looking at 18 months' imprisonment'*. Asked which United fans were to be arrested, the officer claimed no knowledge, saying United were being dealt with by another station. He then named two Owls, both familiar to the Blades (neither of whom was subsequently arrested), and then a nickname, explaining that the police were looking for this particular individual. This nickname, which all Blades were familiar with, was very close to that given to one of the Owls 'top boys'. Boggy changed the subject, asking, *'Have you got Fletch yet?'* Blades could scarcely conceal smirks when the young officer replied, *'No, but we'll get him.'* Four more joined in this 'wind-up', one saying *'He doesn't come up that much any more.'* Harry added *'He's an Arsenal fan, he's the top lad, organises it all.'* Another one said, *'He's a cockney, in his late 20s.'* The young officer sat earnestly nodding his head.

At 1.00 p.m. the Hull officer phoned for a double-decker bus to take Blades directly to the ground, announcing that all were to stay in the pub and board at 2.15 p.m. In the meantime he encouraged everyone to *'have a few pints and enjoy yourselves'*. Everything was going as planned until 1.30 p.m., when eight of 'Their Boys' walked in. Blades fell quiet; and Bobby deliberately barged into and stared at one. The Hull police officer quietly told the eight to get out, and as they did they walked a gauntlet of effeminate 'oooh' noises from Blades. By 2.15 p.m. all but five Blades were aboard the bus. The five had managed to avoid the police by entering the female toilets. Outside, around thirty rivals watched Blades boarding. Blades gestured abusively at them, and then along the journey sang a variety of songs popular at the time: 'Itsy Bitsy Spider' and 'Weak In The Presence of Beauty'. Three uniformed constables in the bus thought this was being directed towards them, and began laughing. Finally came the Rolf Harris classic 'Two Little Boys', before Blades were escorted off the vehicles to sit in the stand.

The match was a non-event, a nil–nil draw, only relieved somewhat by facing out two Hull lads who had deliberately sat as close as possible to the Blades. When faced with four Blades sliding across empty seats to sit directly behind them, however, they had fallen over the front row of seats in their haste to escape. Honour satisfied, the four Blades returned to join their laughing colleagues. After the game, the police escorted the group to a street near the ground, and even gave the driver a lift to the van so that he could drive it to the rendezvous. As the van and other vehicles (private cars) departed in convoy, one policeman noted the registration plates for intelligence collation. The journey home was not as uncomfortable, as there were now only 26 in the van. Some had returned on Max's coach, others had seen mates with cars and gone home with them. But there was fun to be had. Firstly, a mock fight began, in which individuals were thrown into the middle and booted by dozens of others. (This, it must be said, was half-hearted and undertaken in good humour.) The van arrived in Sheffield at 7.10 p.m., and fifteen entered The Stamp, where Eddy noticed two Owls, one of whom he had chased some nine weeks previously when he had waved a bottle at Blades. Eddy told him and his mate to 'fuck off', for with their superior numbers Blades did not consider it honourable to start a fight. The Owls left, and an hour later Blades walked to London Road and enjoyed the night there.

Sheepshaggers and Daft Pigs: Acquaintances Renewed

Fifty Blades were drinking on London Road on the Friday after the Hull match. The topic of conversation was next day's match, for Derby County were the visitors, and victory for them would virtually ensure their promotion. This and the short distance (40 miles) meant they would bring a huge following. Blades estimated this at around 10,000, and wanted to confront the DLF (the 'Derby Lunatic Fringe' – a name first heard in 1984). Blades had searched unsuccessfully for 'Derby' for two years, for they had annoyed both Blades and Owls by unexpectedly entering Sheffield three times in six months in late 1984 to early 1985. On the first occasion thirty broke their journey home from a match and walked along West Street one Saturday night. A month later a hundred travelling to nearby Rotherham called into Sheffield on Saturday lunch-time and chased thirty Blades outside The Bell. Later in the day, following United's home match, sixty Blades waited outside the railway station for their return. However, dozens of police prevented a fight. In February the following year a Friday night match at Doncaster (14 miles from Sheffield) saw fifty Derby fans enter

Sheffield and again walked along West Street, only leaving when police escorted them to the railway station. Blades who were present re-told how Derby had shouted *'You couldn't get a crew up between you'*, meaning that Owls and Blades together were no match for them.

Blades were therefore duty-bound to gain revenge, and opportunities arose. In January 1986 United were drawn against Derby in the FA Cup. Derby brought 8,000 supporters, but Their Boys did not 'come in' pre-match. Afterwards, Derby managed a 'pose' around Sheffield, courtesy of a police escort: sixty of them left the ground and walked along London Road and into the city centre, and, knowing where Blades were gathered, told the police they had lost their way and were not sure where their vehicles were. The police then escorted them through the bus station and past The Stamp. Now the Derby fans suddenly 'remembered' where their vehicles were, and were given an escort back along the same route. Two-hundred strong, Blades watched this procession in silence as the visitors giggled at their own audacity. It was a superb pose, and the Derby 'lads' drove away shouting and laughing at Blades. This smart manoeuvre made Blades want to 'get' them all the more. Meanwhile, the Owls carried out a reprisal in April. Returning from a match in the Midlands, fifty stopped off at Derby and were 'sussed' by Their Boys. A large fight ensued in a town-centre pub, and although Blades' gossip had it that the Owls had been 'done', these efforts had been more than Blades had achieved. An opportunity for Blades to take the issue to Derby arose in October 1986 when United played Derby. A turnout of over 250 travelled on four coaches. However, the day was a débâcle, for the police 'captured' the coaches and escorted the Blades to the ground.

The arrival of Derby was therefore again discussed in The Lansdowne on this Friday night before the game. The 'plan' was to go to a district in the south-east and meet at a pub called 'The Alpine', situated on a road many fans from Derby would take *en route* to Sheffield. No one I spoke to afterwards was certain of the name of the originator. Derby's mode of transport would be crucial. For their most recent visit Derby had come in a fleet of vans and cars, and if this happened now The Alpine would be a likely place for them to rendezvous. Another important factor in deciding the Blades decision to meet here was the slim hope that they could possibly escape the attention of the police. As the Blades had never met here before, the police would not anticipate their plans.

By 11.30 a.m. on Saturday about fifteen Blades were standing outside The Alpine. Ten had been out the previous night; the others heard that morning where to meet. However, the plan ran into problems when at 11.40

a.m., a police transit van drove past, and then returned. A Sergeant asked *'What are you lot doing up here?'* One Blade answered *'Just having a drink.'* The Sergeant replied *'You shouldn't be up here on match-day'*, probably because the pub was so distant from the ground. The police stood around for 15 minutes, and the Blades went quiet, neither side talking to the other. The police left, but the plan had been 'sussed'. More Blades arrived, but stayed only briefly on being informed that 'coppers were about'. The 'plan' now was to 'see where everybody else is'. A convoy of six cars left the pub for The Lansdowne. Thirty 'core' Blades then decided to 'walk about', presuming others would be in city-centre pubs. Ten were in The Stamp with Nick and Shane, who were usually found amongst the core. They had totally disagreed with the idea of going to The Alpine, Nick declaring *'No matter what you do, you can't get away from t'police.'* Two of the most astute Blades, they had not wasted their time on the excursion.

Minutes later the wandering Blades spotted a group of Owls looking down from a multi-storey complex (that Owls were present was only because their team was away to Luton, who had banned rival supporters to prevent hooliganism.) Blades doubled back and ran up the stairway, hoping to catch them by surprise. The ten 'Owls' saw Blades on the same level and walked away quickly. Some Blades began running, causing the escaping Owls to run across a dual carriageway. Police vehicles arrived, and a shout of 'coppers' saw everyone stop running and start walking in an orderly manner. The police drove past, and the 'Owl hunt' lost its impetus. Jade then suggested everyone go to a district about two miles away on the same road as The Alpine, but nearer to Bramall Lane. The idea was to meet at The Red Rose, where Jade reasoned the Derby 'lads' might now be. The police, not expecting this move, would be outflanked. His idea was accepted and everyone left. Most caught a bus; others took taxis.

Moments later, five Blades (Gordon, Titch, George, Flint and Boyle) who had earlier played football for United's Supporters Club against their Derby equivalents and missed the morning's events, wandered into the city centre. As the four Blade footballers approached the High Street they saw a group of ten Owls. One passed comment, and hearing this, Gordon 'bounced' towards them. Some knew Gordon and his fighting ability. This and a willingness in the other four to fight caused one Owl to plead *'We don't want no trouble . . . your lot have just chased us all over – we've only come out for Derby.'* The Blades contemptuously left them and continued their search. When they met others in The Lansdowne on their return from the Red Rose, they gleefully recounted what they considered the cowardice of the

Owls. The latter pub had been a disappointment, though the landlord and bar staff were pleased to serve them, and, with the majority occupying an outside beer-garden, the profits were good and regulars were unmolested.

For the police, this day was a 'high-risk' match for potential 'Trouble'. Police on foot and in various vehicles were out in force from midday, and alongside uniformed officers there were plain-clothes police, some riding in unmarked vehicles; others were on foot. The afternoon was one of glorious sunshine. Groups of Blades stood outside various London Road pubs. Around two hundred were outside The Lansdowne and though they were neither singing nor indulging in horseplay, nor intimidating anyone, the police decided to act. Ten officers from a transit van decided that everyone should go back inside the pubs. And as it approached The Lansdowne, the transit picked up speed and drove along part of the pavement, causing various Blades to take evasive action to avoid being struck. Those who they considered were not moving fast enough were pushed; those without drinks were ordered off to the match. One particular PC had a special trick of clutching a bunch of keys: sticking them out between the fingers of his clenched fist, he would 'jab' Blades in the base of the spine. No Blade retaliated.

As the match started a hundred and fifty Blades sat to the front left-hand of the South Stand. They were quiet and making no gestures or verbal threats, when a dozen police arrived and told them to 'shift' or 'fuck off'. All moved quietly as directed. Twenty minutes later, and despite not a single Blades' chant, forty uniformed police came and sat around them. Twelve others stood looking in. This heavy uniformed presence was enhanced by 'Clouseau' (mentioned above), who was directing a cameraman to photograph the Blades. Another three plain-clothes officers were near him, using binoculars. Suddenly, exasperated by a refereeing decision, one Blade shouted disapproval. After threatening him, an officer decided to sit next to him for the rest of the match. During this match a few Blades laughed at a youth aged about twenty of 'normal' appearance who was sitting watching them and scribbling notes on paper. I would see him regularly in the city-centre shopping precincts, and presumed (naively) he was a sociology student. Blades told me he was just a 'nut-case' who had been to special school and hung around town all day. After the game he ran away as Blades were dispersed by police, shouting incoherently before bursting into tears.

With the match over, Blades made their way out. A scuffle occurred when three Blades chased a similar number of Derby fans about to board a mini-van near Bramall Lane. One Blade was arrested, then released seconds later.

In his late twenties, this man was known as 'Dummy', on account of his being deaf and dumb. Outwardly 'normal', he was fashionably attired and frequented city-centre pubs, and was a devoted follower of United. Twice in the 1985/6 season he had been arrested for chasing rivals. When this happened Blades would make furious protests to the arresting officers about his disability, as Dummy made noises and waved his arms. He was always quickly released by officers who would stand about looking embarrassed whilst Blades walked away smirking at their complicity, roaring with laughter later at the re-telling of the tale.

As was the norm, most Blades drifted back to the Bus Station area, and waited outside The Stamp. Some stood outside a chip shop on an elevated part of the car-park complex. This acted as both a post-match feeding post for hungry Blades, and a vantage point over the railway station as an early-warning location for the presence of rivals to Blades. On this occasion the chip-shop was the wrong place for Prince, a well-known black Blade. Four West Indians approached him, and one punched him in the face, whilst another threw him to the floor and kicked him. A sovereign ring was wrested from his finger, and the four left. In spite of twenty Blades' being present, no one helped him. In The Lansdowne, half an hour later, Prince looked solemnly at the floor, and told how the incident was over an accusation he had 'grassed someone up', and added disgustedly that a Blade colleague had walked off and left him. No one else criticised the Blade accused – who wasn't in the pub anyway – the only comment came from Fagin, who, listening in, merely said *'Them Rastas don't muck about.'* Everyone laughed at this, including Prince.

By the time the group had been in the pub for an hour, a general restlessness could be noted. At 6.45 p.m. the phone by the bar in the poolroom area rang. The caller was Nick from The Stamp where, he said, sixty Blades were gathered. Nick wanted to ask if Blades in The Lansdowne were 'coming into town'. He told Tono, who had been first to pick up the receiver, which pubs he and the others intended to visit, and this information was then passed around. In the next 10 minutes individuals asked each other *'Are we goin' up, then?'*, a rhetorical question eliciting an affirmative reply of *'can do'* or *'not bothered'*. On this occasion a glance around the pub showed the Blades had a good 'turnout' and were strong enough to face anything the Owls could assemble. For, of course, one of the main purposes of going into town was to seek a possible confrontation with the Owls. Once everybody had finished their drinks a drift towards the door became inevitable, although some older Blades stayed in The Lansdowne. By 7.30 p.m. this group had located the others in The Boulogne, where around seventy Blades were watching a beer race between Tom and one of the 'alecarts' – a term used to describe a dozen older, peripheral Blades who were usually the worse for drink both before and after games. Tom won, for he could down a pint in three seconds.

Of those that remained, one group listened to Nev recounting how a 'Derby car' had been turned over after the match. To him it was an example of Tom at his best (Tom was elsewhere at the time) *'straight into 'em, questioned one of 'em, then over wi t'car'*. Tom had indeed 'sussed' out a parked car carrying five Derby youths. Asking them *'Where are you bastards from?'*, their silence had confirmed they were Derby fans. As more Blades surrounded them the four ran away, and one jumped into the driver's seat and locked himself in. Nev explained he had then kicked the side window and broken it, and Tom and two others had turned the car on its side. Others helped push it on to its roof. (No one knew at this point or even weeks later whether the Derby fans had sustained injuries.) The four other Derby fans had then returned, and one struck Nev on the head with a stake of wood. The attack was ended by the arrival of an 'old woman', who ran across the road screaming to Blades *'Leave them alone'* and *'Stop it.'* Blades had then left.

Blades later entered The Golden Egg, a popular disco pub with two rooms and two bars where groups of Owls often met, and which was consequently known as a 'Pig boozer'. Most Blades ordered drinks at the front bar. Those who went in the back found to their surprise that 'the Pigs' were in – fifteen were seated in a corner. Within seconds every Blade stood in front of them, blocking any exit. There were glasses, bottles, and ashtrays in abundance, all potential weapons. Amidst the silence Gordon said *'Any of you who don't wanna get 'ammered, walk out o' t'door wi me nar'*, an invitation no Owl had time to take up as Blades engulfed them. Three Owls standing at the bar asked of two Blades they knew 'Is it gonna go, or what?' Such moments are embarrassing. For though they contextually hate Owls, such Blades do not want their Owl mates 'done' by Blade colleagues. Pinkie, for example, knew many Owls, and even drank regularly with them, and he now sat among them hoping to defuse the situation. Moments later Gamble, another Blade, did the same.

It was at this point that the lack of leadership showed. Parker took the initiative and began generally threatening Owls; specifically 'offering out' three, saying *'C'mon, just you and me outside, now.'* Other Blades did the same to other Owls, but none took up the offers. Parker referring to the Blade–Owl incident nine weeks earlier, said sarcastically, *'You thought yu were reyt fuckin' hard coming down London Road and smashin' up t'Lansdowne, 23 of us 150 of your . . . that's really tough.'* He then asked each Owl individually if he had been there. Only one admitted he had been, and could scarcely avoid this admission, as many Blades had seen him. This was used against the rest, Parker saying to them *'Only one of you's got guts to admit it . . . you've let your side down reyt.'* In the Blade–Owl context it is considered reprehensible if, confronted, you claim not to have been present, or you acquiesce to a rival's command. Finishing his tirade, Parker walked away, saying *'If anyone of "ours" gets hammered when out on his own by your, you're all dead.'*

In principle, no Blade present disagreed with thumping Owls. Many had in the past thumped (or been thumped by) them. But the debate here centred on the question of style, for the Owls were outnumbered three to one. Because of this, Gordon said to Blades *'Leave 'em'*, adding for the Owls' benefit *'They're not worth it'*, and *'Don't drag ourselves down to their level ....* *We're Blades, we feyt fair.'* 'Victory' in such fights came only when there were equal numbers of combatants, or if the Blades were outnumbered and still 'did' them. Three core Blades, Alan, Shane and Eddy, along with Gordon were normally the most eager to fight Owls. Eddy, normally at the front of fights against Owls, had reserved his threats for one specific Owl, who in a previous confrontation had made a racist remark about his being black. Moments later, one of the Village Boys, Bone, mistaking Pinkie for an Owl, told him he was going to 'get killed', whereupon Pinkie thumped him. Other Blades intervened and calmed Pinkie down, and the matter went no further. Minutes later Bone admitted his error (saying he thought he was talking to a Owl), and was prepared to let the matter drop. At this time the Blades were approximately 60 per cent Sheffield regulars, 10 per cent Sheffield occasionals, and 30 per cent Village Boys (half occasionals, half regulars). No one knew everyone who was with the Blades, or who had come with whom: hence the mistake over Pinkie.

Although Blades had these 'cross-cutting ties' with various Owls, which limited aggression, there were still old scores to settle. The Blades divided into three schools of thought. One group, a dozen strong, acted as pacifists, taking the moral line of *'We're not Wednesday and they're not worth it.'* An identical number were militants, and took the approach *'Fuck it, let's do 'em, they'd do the same to us in t'same position'* (these were Village boys plus two Townies). The third, most numerous group (all Townies) had no strong feelings and would join in any ensuing fight, but were prepared to walk away if no fight started. Basically, no one knew exactly what was the 'correct' thing to do. A sense of virtuous superiority then seized those who had no friends amongst the Owls. Two Villagers, Des and Tom, announced to the 'Sheffielders' *'You shun't socialise with the bastards, we don't talk to any of 'em.'* This was counterproductive, for it only served to make the Sheffielders later remember that Des had stayed in the pub earlier in the season, ignoring the 'call-out' when others were outside fighting visiting fans. Six Sheffielders, Eddy, Alan, Gordon, Shane, Ross and Greg, announced they were leaving. Outside Eddy said *'I can't believe we left 'em [Owls] alone.'* Seconds later, by coincidence, the six passed one of the Owls' 'top lads', who was out with his girlfriend and unaware of the scenario. *'I don't believe it, fat fuckin' Marco'*, Eddy exclaimed, clearly audible to the man in question, and he shook his head as he walked to the pub, as if ashamed of his inactivity.

Outside, the Blades, having once again joined forces, began walking to West Street. Des criticised 'Townies' for not *'backing us up'*, and quietly told his mates he was going to 'start' with the Blade who assaulted Bone. Pinkie made no further mention of the incident. Gordon, sensing trouble, approached him, saying *'Stick wi' us . . . if anyone starts we'll back dee up.'* Ginger, one of the Village Boys, stated *'We should have fuckin' killed 'em'*, and Greg, a Townie, added, *'If that'd been us sat there we'd be picking glass out of our faces now,'* both comments summing up the frustration of the occasion. Eddy, sensing things were getting out of hand, said *'If they could see us now they'd be pissin their sens, Blade feytin' Blade. What's up wi' us?'* Tom helped matters by shouting *'We're all Blades, that's what matters.'* The recriminations finished. The group walked past The Bridle, a well-known Owls pub. The landlady locked the door. An attempt then to enter The West End failed when two bouncers refused entry. Blades walked on to the next pub, which did not have a strict door policy. Inside, two Villagers took it upon themselves to entertain, helped by too much beer. Tom began shouting occasional insults at other drinkers who passed through the room to go to the toilets, and even ridiculed the landlady. At times he was witty, but at others could be offensive, though he never encouraged violence in his fooling around. His mate, Mark, then took up the baton and began telling a joke to everyone, but had the punch line stolen by a Blade who shouted it out before he had finished. Mark threw a half-pint glass at him in what was actually a gesture of anger. The glass hit the wall and smashed, and most Blades laughed – some more nervously, in view of the fact the glass narrowly missed them. By now the Townies were viewing the antics of the Village Boys with a certain resignation, and, as might have been anticipated, their actions brought in the police, who arrived followed by the landlady. A sergeant ordered Blades to 'get moving', and within a minute every Blade had left the pub. Access to another pub would now be difficult, and police might no doubt following time-honoured tradition 'nick a couple' as an example to others and to calm them down.

It was now 10.00 p.m., and the group began to split. Some went home, others to pubs. Fifteen Townies entered The Rochester and saw some of the Owls they had humiliated earlier, who seeing them approach retreated and closed and locked the pub doors. The Blades entered the premise via the back door and, surprising the Owls, Parker approached them, saying *'We've decided we're not gonna leave ya, we're gonna do ya.'* One Owl remonstrated that they didn't want any trouble. Parker continued his bluff, and took two metal 'Owl' badges off two of them, throwing one across the floor and dropping the other in an Owl's pint of beer. On seeing the Blades, two Owls had entered the women's toilets. Gordon told a couple of girls to go in and tell them it was safe to come out, and, as they did, Blades laughed and clapped. The two sat down quietly, providing Blades with a 'laugh' both at the time and in later weeks.

Meanwhile, two Village Boys, one being Bone, had entered The West End with two girls. A group of Owls were in the pub and, recognising Bone from The Golden Egg, one of their 'Top Lads' challenged him to fight. Bone pointed out they were only two strong and he had a 'bird' [girl] with him, which should have provided a truce in the circumstance. The Owl suggested a 'one-on-one' [fight] outside, and Bone agreed. However, as both walked towards the door the Owl turned and began the fight in the pub. In the brief ensuing scuffle Bone was on top, but was hit from behind by a glass. On seeing the blood the challenger refused to fight on, the assailant who had wielded the glass wrapped ice-cubes in a beer towel as a compress, and apologised by saying his action was totally 'out of order'. An ambulance was called, and Bone required ten stitches. Two police CID officers entered Casualty at the hospital and asked Bone to name the youth. Bone refused, and justified his actions to Blades a week later, saying he would prefer 'to sort it out' himself.

The sight of the ambulance at the pub attracted three Blades walking to a nearby nightclub. Nick, Jim and Mel were furious and began shouting at the Owls: *'You've fucked it now'* and *'That's the last time we ever let you off.'* Enquiries as to the identity of the culprit produced only the response: *'a lad in a brown jacket'*, and, from one Owl *'We know what you're gonna say . . . "We left you alone and you did one Blade" . . . it's not what it seems, it wo' stupid.'* The three Blades went to the nightclub, where they met two other Blades (Bee and Lionel) and Pinkie, with a couple of non-'football' mates and Paul, who had been out all night. There were also fifteen Owls, known to the Blades as the 'Stocksbridge Pigs' after the township in North Sheffield they came from. The peace lasted an hour, and after a 'staring match' between two youths from either faction, one of the Owls threw a glass at Mel. He responded and, backed by Jim, Nick, and Paul, grabbed two Owls, kicking them to the floor and challenging the others to fight. The bouncers grabbed

Jim, Mel, and Nick, and threw them out. The three waited in ambush, Jim holding a piece of wood he had pulled off a fence that still contained a couple of nails. Minutes later the Owls came out in a mob, but the three ran at them, shouting threats and 'fronting them'. One of the Owls threw a bottle, which missed. A police transit arrived, and Jim and Mel were arrested. Both were found guilty on charges of threatening behaviour, and both received a £300 fine, with an additional 200-hour community service order for Jim. Mel had been in England only twenty-four hours having spent the previous year working in Australia.

Nick subsequently bumped into Boggy and Dene on their way to catch a bus after leaving another nightclub. He told them of the night's events, and the three began a 'Pig hunt'. Shortly after, they saw six Stockbridge 'Pigs' and, taking the initiative, invited them to fight. Three ran away. Only one stood his ground. In the opinion of the Blades he showed 'game', an opinion that encompassed their expressions of respect. However, this respect did not prevent them from knocking him to the ground, kicking him as he lay there, and then taking his shoes and throwing them into a building site. At this point an example occurred that showed the power of Sheffield women to intervene in fights. A young woman ran over, demanding Blades leave their victim alone; the Blades left, but not without a few insulting words directed at both the Owl and his saviour. The Owl walked away in his stockinged feet. It was not a fair fight by anyone's definition, but an action considered permissible because in Blades' eyes hours earlier a Blade had suffered a similar injustice at the hands of the Owls.

The following Saturday evening twenty-five Blades were out on London Road. They had not travelled to United's away game on the South Coast, as it was too far for an end of season 'nothing' (i.e. inconsequential match). Around 7.30 p.m. the third pub they visited was The Golden Egg, in which there were six Stockbridge Owls. Bright, a Blade who had been passive the previous week, told the Owls to *'get out'*, adding *'We're not gonna do yu, but tell your boys we're about.'* This time Joss intervened. Whilst a Blade and out with Blades, two of the Owls were his mates. A renown fighter in both Blade and Owl circles, he stood in the middle of the impending confrontation and threatened to 'kill anyone who starts'. Nobody started and then the pub's bouncers intervened and prevented trouble, telling the Owls to leave and Blades to order drinks. One of the fifteen Owls who had been in The Golden Egg the previous week came to the door minutes later, and told a Blade mate, *'The Wednesday are on West Street and we're game as fuck.'* Along with his elder brother, this Owl was known as one of the most 'game' of them all. The Blades drank up quickly and walked on to West Street, but finding no Owls, entered The Nottingham. Some stood by the door watching the road. Minutes later an Owl was spotted 50 yards away. Parker approached him on 'reconnaissance', and turned a corner to see forty Owls standing outside The Rochester. He called to the rest, who came running; however, as the two factions confronted each other a police van appeared. Despite this, Blades walked towards their rivals, two of whom came forward 'fronting up', whilst the rest stood near the police van. The confrontation was mostly verbal, though one Owl punched Eddy repeatedly in the face. Eddy offered no resistance, except to comment that better punches would be required if the Owl hoped to 'drop' him. Gordon was furious, and shouted at Eddy to hit him back. Eddy rationalised his passivity later, saying he was aware of the police presence and so did nothing.

The two groups walked towards West Street with police on foot and in vehicles between them (two more transits and one police car had arrived). At times rivals were literally feet from each other, with the messenger shouting *'We're game as fuck.'* Blades replied with shouts of *'Do summat then, we're on your Manor.'* The two groups paraded along West Street until police decided to escort Blades to London Road. At this stage, with three transits and twenty officers, the police now outnumbered Blades. Realising this, a couple of officers began taunting them, saying *'Not so tough now you're outnumbered are you?', 'Reckon you're good enough now?', 'Fancy your chances then?'* A Sergeant began kicking Blades' heels; Alan was tripped three times by him, and mumbled something in protest; the Sergeant then asked him three times *'What did you say?'* Each time Alan carried on walking, silently. The Sergeant then arrested him on a charge of being drunk and disorderly. The remaining Blades were escorted to London Road, and police then drove away to another incident. Alan was, in fact, unusually sober that night, having joined the group late, and was about three to four pints of beer behind the others. Nevertheless, he pleaded guilty in court a week later, thinking it better that the city-centre constables should not be prejudiced against him next time. He also knew the fine would not be more than £50. This is a familiar argument Blades use to explain a 'guilty' plea to a minor charge, reasoning that 'going not guilty and winning' might lead to the police having a determination to bring further charges against you until one is successful.

Two weeks later Blades discussed the events of that Saturday night. The 'glasser' was rumoured to be 'not a real Pig', but simply a mate of the fighter. If so, another element had entered proceedings – the Outsider who was ignorant of the 'rules'. Hostilities were promised from other quarters too. Eddy had a revenge of his own to take on the Owl who had hit him outside The Rochester. And yet another Owl was due to be the object of vengeance for pocketing Tono's designer sunglasses when they fell off in the same incident. Bone, the glassed Village Boy, also wanted a 'one-to-one' with his attacker if and when he was found. These confrontations settled nothing, but simply carried the seeds of further trouble.

In total ten youths were arrested for their part in the attack on The White Rose – nine Blades and one Owl; curiously, though, no one was arrested for the attack on The Lansdowne. Of the nine Blades, three had previous convictions for football hooliganism (all for threatening behaviour). Three of the four who pleaded not guilty had no previous criminal record. What began as a charge of 'threatening behaviour' for four of the accused was changed four months later, when all ten were charged with serious public order offences of 'affray' and 'unlawful assembly'. Before the trial, six Blade defendants had, via their barristers, agreed to plead guilty to unlawful assembly on condition that affray be dropped. On the fifth day the jury returned 'not guilty' verdicts on all charges on the four defendants who had pleaded 'not guilty'. The six who had pleaded guilty received 240 hours of community service orders and were ordered to pay £150 each to the brewery who owned the pub. Justice Crabtree was correct in telling the court that the 'real villains' got away scot-free. Due to structural faults The Lansdowne pub was closed in late 1987 and demolished a few months later.

Notes

1. In May 1985, whilst most Blades were in Brighton for their match there, Dom remained in Sheffield, and on Saturday morning waited at the railway station and, wearing his Blade's badge, introduced himself to the arriving West Ham fans, whom he stayed with for the course of the day. He guided them through the city centre to where the Owls would be waiting. Here West Ham confronted the Owls and chased them off. In return the Londoners bought him beer and paid his admission for the stand at Hillsborough. Later in the day Timmy, who had been working on a Community Service Order scheme as part of his punishment for a hooligan-related conviction, went to Hillsborough for the second half of the match and sat with the West Ham fans, talking to them and laughing at the Owls nearby, who were shouting towards him saying that he was 'dead' for his complicity. The following season in October, for the next visit of West Ham, United were away at Plymouth. Few Blades travelled the long journey. Instead, around twenty met on

the morning of the match and, on seeing West Ham fans come out of the railway station, ran out and after a brief confrontation succeeded in chasing about a dozen of them back in before police arrived and arrested two. After the fight Blades were proud that it was they and not the Owls who had turned out for West Ham, and, having shouted that they were Blades in the confrontation, thought this would obviously be taken back to London as proof of who were the 'Top Lads' in Sheffield. Walking into the city centre a few minutes later, Blades saw a group of seventy Owls arriving and, on seeing them, made sarcastic comments along the lines of 'Where've you been?', 'We've done your job for you' and 'Too late.' The police in transit vans were nearby, and so the rivals did not come to blows before Blades entered one pub and the Owls returned another in the High Street.

2. Whilst such an act was rare in Sheffield, this particular Owl, aged in his mid-20s, had used a knife before, and had slashed two rival fans in a pub fight in the mid-1980s. He was never arrested or prosecuted and remained with the Owls, some of them glad he did what he did in the circumstances (they were outnumbered and cornered).

3. The two sets of fans had met in different circumstances in 1984, when fourteen youths were charged with serious public order offences; and a prosecution was brought by the Metropolitan Police and British Transport Police against six Blades and eight supporters of Grimsby Town after the faction had been involved in an altercation on Euston Road, London that spilled on to the platform of St Pancras railway station. The Grimsby fans had travelled to see their team at Crystal Palace, the Sheffield supporters to see theirs at Brentford. A total of thirty-six Grimsby fans travelled in one coach; a dozen Blades had travelled in a mini-van. Both groups were staying in the West End for the evening, and planned to return at around midnight from the pre-arranged departure point of King's Cross railway station. The origin of the incident occurred earlier in the night, when in a Covent Garden pub words were exchanged between individuals from both sides that ended with the vague threat from a Grimsby fan of 'We'll see you later at King's Cross.' Therefore when the Grimsby fans did attack them on the way to the mini-van they were heavily outnumbered and had to fight their way to the van and, when surrounded, fight again. The incidents took place on a Saturday night at approximately 11.30–12.00, nowhere near a football ground. The end result of the two-week trial was that all the Sheffield supporters had cases against them dismissed owing to lack of prosecution evidence. Of the Grimsby fans, four were similarly discharged. Three, however, received Community Service Orders, and one received

a nine-month custodial sentence. During a visit to Grimsby in October 1985 Blades had received a chant of 'St Pancras' from the Grimsby lads, but had 'run' the home lads before the match, and so they met the chant with whistles and derision. The day ended with Blades running 'Their Boys' along the promenade of a nearby seaside resort and throwing two they caught over railings into the sea. The two waded out to howls of derision from the watching Blades.

Chapter 3

Nine Years 1985–1994:
Waiting for Wednesday

The origins of the outbreak of a period of intense hostility occurred over a packet of crisps in The Lansdowne pub on London Road. This involved black and white youths, but race as such was unimportant. One October Saturday night in 1985 around 9.00 p.m., a mixed-race Blade noticed one of five Owls (three of them black) staring. A sarcastic and over-polite offer to share his crisps was refused with an accusation from two of the Owls who knew him that he was a 'trouble-causer'. An invitation extended by one to fight Yifter was accepted, and Yifter followed three Owls (referred to as the Trio from here on) outside. Once outside, the three then offered to fight the audience of twelve younger Blades, and a fracas ensued in which nine white Blades fought the three older Owls. The Trio were muscular and better fighters, but in a brutal outcome they were laid out, with one unconscious from a chest burn (the result of being struck by a distress flare fired by a Blade). One other needed hospital casualty having been knocked unconscious. Blades felt the Trio got what they deserved, for they were older, 'harder' and showing off in a Blades pub. Owls saw things differently, their injuries had to be avenged.

Repercussions soon followed: within days the Trio had somehow obtained the names of some of their assailants. The first victim of Owls' revenge arrived at the Blades' departure point to an away match a week later minus a tooth. The Trio had assaulted him in a city-centre disco on the previous night when he was out with his fiancée. This appalled Blades; for, in their eyes, a woman's presence rendered it inappropriate for men to be settling scores. Matters escalated beyond match-day, and hostilities shifted to Sunday morning amateur football. A few Blades who had formed a football team had met in the city centre at 9.30 a.m. to rendezvous before an away game and were chased by a dozen Owls on a similar gathering. Twice in the following weeks four Owls, none of whom were involved in the Lansdowne incident, came to their match venue looking for two Blades in particular who were principally involved in the attack, and, pre-match fights and chases across the pitch involving half the team ensued. Blades also heard the Trio and Owls in general were trying to establish where certain Blades lived and worked. Thus it was thought they were considering taking matters to the doorstep, or even the workplace.

Meanwhile, events on London Road sowed seeds of further conflict when in late October some twenty Blades fought fifteen youths in The Lansdowne. The latter were dressed in jackets and ties (the dress requirements for the nightclub across the road) and were out on a Friday stag-night, and began singing football songs in favour of Wednesday. The result was one concussed and another with a broken jaw. To the Owls this was out of order, for this group of Blades had attacked a group distinguished by their attire, which said they were not 'hooligans' and therefore not 'game' (a couple in the group were later discovered to be United fans). Blades disagreed: they were Pigs singing Pig songs in a Blades' pub. The Owls were rumoured to be 'coming down' in numbers to 'sort it out' once and for all.

Blades did not take the rumour seriously at first, and as a result only twenty-five were on London Road in The Partridge on a Friday evening in November. The phone rang. It was Billy informing his Blade mates that he and his girlfriend had seen fifty Owls leave a pub and walk towards London Road. This warning was timely, for 10 minutes later the Owls entered The Lansdowne and began menacingly looking for youths with Blades badges. The Landlord threw them out, and, as they left they realised their opponents were 300 yards away outside The Partridge. Owls ran towards Blades, who spread out across the road, and when they were only a matter of a few feet apart the Owls stopped. One white Blade, Binz, took the initiative and ran into them, arms flailing, causing two Owls to fall. Then Des, a black Blade, wielding a small cosh, levelled another. The Owls backed off, and moments later ran away. The chase lasted half a mile, with the majority of Owls seeking refuge in The Rosebush. However, three were caught. One of mixed race was allowed to run away after a few punches, mainly because many Blades knew him (even so, he sustained two cracked ribs). Two others (both white) were beaten to the ground and kicked. One was saved from further punishment by two black women in their early 20s screaming at Blades and pulling them away. Almost ironically, and unbeknownst to them at the time, their brother was with the Blades. The other Owl lay unconscious, and his condition worried Blades. Some tried to revive him but failed, and then scattered on hearing police sirens. Twenty minutes later Blade front-runners who had regrouped found Owls in The Rosebush. The latter showed willingness to resume the fight. An agreement was reached when one Blade shouted that Dom, another Blade, wanted a 'one-to-one' with an Owl. The Owls agreed, but as the two squared up another twenty Blades appeared and put paid to this decorum. The Owls ran into the city centre, with pursuing Blades screaming threats. Police vehicles arrived, and Blades disappeared into various pubs.

The expected turnout for the Owls' revenge on the following Friday saw a congregation of some eighty Blades of great diversity. Alongside eight 'skinheads' (a generic term the mainstream Blades used to describe three British Movement sympathisers) and other shaven associates (not all sympathisers to their politics), were eight black youths, two sporting 'dreadlock' hair. Although natural enemies in one context, tonight they were colleagues against a greater enemy. Of the eighty, six had weapons. There were four wooden bats, one hospital crutch carried with a heavily bandaged knee as 'justification' should the bearer be arrested for using the crutch as a weapon, and a car aerial. These were thrown behind the pub gaming machine when four police officers entered, looked around, said nothing and left. And though they had clearly expected company, the men who entered at 8.45 p.m. astonished the Blades, for the visitors were the Trio. In the silence, one asked for a Blade by name (unaware that he was close by). Another, seeing a Blade he knew from other circumstances, kicked him, saying sarcastically *'Come to do us, have you?'* In the silence that followed Errol, a black Blade, walked over to the three. Recognising him and knowing of his fighting ability, the Trio stopped as he said: *'Any trouble tonight and I'm with these lads'* (i.e. the Blades). After a minute's silence The Trio left unmolested, despite the quiet urgings of some to 'rush' the three. The pub then continued as before, for no one quite knew what to say or what was an appropriate course of action.

A large police presence was visible, patrolling London Road on foot and in vehicles. This was obviously meant to be a visible deterrent, for police claimed in the local newspaper that they had been tipped off about the impending trouble. As a result, Blades could count eight transit vans, two patrol cars, two dog vans, and uniformed officers walking in pairs, as well as four plain-clothes police. Ironically, Blades located Owls by overhearing a police personal radio, for as uniformed officers again entered the pub, a radio message told them that a large group of youths were walking towards a specified street. Blades surmised the Owls were making for the pub on that road, and went there minutes after the police left. When the group was within 100 yards of the pub a police transit drove towards them, causing many to retreat. Those who continued (about twenty-five) stopped on seeing a video camera pointing out of the van doors. Strangely, the vehicle then drove away. This was the cue for Owls to come pouring out, for Blades to run at them, and for missiles (taken from pubs) to be thrown. Owls then ran back into the pub; but one did not make it, and was beaten to the ground, though not badly hurt, as he walked away a minute later.

Police in three vans arrived seconds later. Two Blades were arrested, and two later required stitches in bloody head wounds caused by truncheon blows. Police searching the Owls in the pub discovered a couple of milk bottles with petrol and a funnel – crude 'petrol bombs'. One Owl was arrested, and next day two more were detained.

The events of the night were not over yet, however; although the Owls' mob was out of action owing to police activity, Blades noted the Trio were not with them. At 10.00 p.m. they were found with another well-known black Owl in a pub behind London Road. Two Blades walked in, leaving another twenty outside. Eddy, a Blade of mixed race, walked directly to the four and stared at them. One asked *'What's your problem?'*; he replied *'You are.'* This was followed by a volley of beer glasses, which caused him to back off and South, his Blade companion, to be struck in the eye by a missile. This required stitches, and meant he was to lose part of his sight permanently. The four then ran to the door where Blades had gathered: two Owls were pulled out and one was punched to the floor by Sean and hit with a plastic litter-bin by Pear before police arrived in four vehicles, twenty-five strong. The police struggled one Blade to the floor and another struggled with police in the rear of a police van – in both instances I believe the police were executing their own form of summary justice. Other officers shouted threats as, truncheons drawn, they chased Blades leaving the scene. A total of nine Blades and Owls were arrested. Of the three Owls arrested for possession of the petrol bomb devices, two, aged 19, were given sentences in the High Court of three years' youth custody.[1]

Neither policing nor judicial tactics proved a deterrent. The Trio continued their hunt. Finding another Blade they suspected of being one of their assailants a few days before Christmas 1985 in a city-centre disco, they accused him of 'being there'. One held him, while another punched him. Had it not been for a packed bar and club officials, the Trio's revenge could have been worse. Blades were furious, because they considered that three on to one was bullying and, furthermore, he was ten years younger, and out with friends in a non-football context. To make matters worse, returning from an away match in January a coachload of Owls alighted on London Road and entered Blades pubs. Few Blades were in. None was assaulted. Owls informed those who were there that they were after two named Blades. Sensibly, these two kept a low profile for a few weeks, believing time would heal the rift and their pursuers would tire of looking for them.[2] With the season ending, the pair reappeared in a match tailor-made for Blades to put one over on their enemy. Being in separate divisions, United and Wednesday teams rarely met. However, there were always benefit games between the sides, and these, for a section of the fans, were an occasion for scenarios that benefited only themselves.

Testing Grounds: Testimonial Matches

It was announced that United and Wednesday were to meet in May 1986 for a testimonial for one of United's players. Blades gathered in The Lansdowne from 5.30 p.m. (for a 7.30 p.m. kick-off), presuming that Owls would be along West Street about one mile away. Blades, searching in cars, located them there at 6.30 p.m. Some, particularly the young lads, argued for *'goin' up and givin' it 'em'*. Others had older heads, and pointed out that with police in vehicles on nearby roads, to walk towards West Street would result in being 'captured' (a term used to describe being arrested or forced to turn back or do as police demanded). The Owls, it was reasoned, would have to pass on their way to the ground, and then *'When they walk past we'll run out and kill 'em.'* The younger Blades were against this enforced inactivity, arguing Blades must go to them, otherwise Owls might later claim Blades were scared, or be able to claim to have brought the fight to them. This impasse lasted 20 minutes, until a decision of sorts was made and a furious younger Blade, Limit, shouted *'All t' Young Lads are goin' up, anybody who wants to, come nar.'* Bud blew a whistle and shouted *'West Street by t' back door.'* Without further argument everyone walked silently, spread out over 70 yards along both sides of the road.

Predictably, police vehicles began following, but allowed Blades to walk to the Owls' pub, whereupon the Owls ran out to confront Blades. At this point dozens of police appeared, including five plain-clothes officers in a car, four on horseback and two in dog vans, who chased the main mob of Blades for over half a mile, arresting and beating two who had begun to throw stones towards their vehicles. Those who avoided the police then regrouped and, joining up with some of the main mob, faced the Owls 15 minutes later along London Road. However the large police presence prevented a fight, and after 100 yards of fans 'posing' and posturing with police separating the factions the police forced Owls down one street to the ground and Blades down another. In the 10,000 crowd most Blades went on the Shoreham End Kop to prevent an expected Owls' incursion, though fifty sat in the South Stand in expectation of a simultaneous incursion of Owls. The Owls entered this latter area and, escorted by police, sat adjacent to Blades, who glared and shouted abuse at them. At half-time the Owls left, whilst Blades remained in the ground until the end of the match.

By 9.30 around 150 Blades were back gathered in The Lansdowne, a whistle was blown again and a shout of *'back whacks to town'* was heard. Nobody knew who shouted the instruction or blew the whistle. That did not matter. Those who wanted to could now go with the flow. The 'plan' was to walk to the city centre via small side roads and avoid police. The group walked into the city centre, twenty minutes later finding the Owls expectantly packed into an alleyway. Three distress flares fired into them did not budge them, nor did another Blade's small wooden bat deter those that could see him. The fact that Blades were also numerically superior did not budge them. Their 'main men' were holding items taken from nearby roadworks, and another had a cosh. Bottles thrown from the Owls' ranks landed harmlessly, as the reflection against the neon street lights provided an early warning system. Despite Blades' taking the fight to them and running at the Owls the latter's refusal to move meant that having 'fronted' Blades they had gained a momentum, and when the Owls eventually counter-attacked, Blades backed down and eventually ran. The Owls chased them, making whooping noises.

There were two Blade casualties, an Old Lad and a young peripheral. The veteran was Benny (aged 33) who had always refused to run from the Owls and subsequently had the reputation and wounds to prove it. Despite not having been in a Blades' turnout for a year, having 'retired' from hooliganism, he had arrived specially for this event. Wielding a cosh, he had run into the Owls, who had beaten him to the floor. He was rescued by Gordon who, also using a cosh, had struck two of his assailants. Sporting a bruised eye, he wandered away shouting that Blades were '*shit*' and he would never turn out again. A younger, peripheral Blade was not so fortunate. Seeking refuge in a nearby pub he found his entrance blocked by a pub doorman, and cornered Owls then 'jumped him'. He sustained a broken leg and a small wound on his back believed to be caused by a craft knife, which required stitches. Blades were devastated; some went home immediately, others slunk off into various London Road pubs. The group did not meet throughout the summer. Vengeance had to be pursued and status regained. Four months later another match provided the opportunity.

For the Monday evening September testimonial at Wednesday's Hillsborough ground a 'turnout' of seventy Blades met from 6.00 p.m. in The Stamp. At 7.00 p.m. the Owls were located in an area they had never used before, in a pub along the main approach road to the ground. With numbers down to fifty (some tired of waiting, and went to the match) Blades took a back street route to this pub (a distance of two miles) and thereby avoided police. Some armed themselves with small rocks, pieces of wood and the odd piece of metal reinforcement, though not all obtained missiles. Sensing that some amongst them were not committed to the forthcoming action, Gordon spoke loudly and rhetorically, saying: '*Anyone runs tonight, and we'll remember who they are.*' Neither he nor anyone else elaborated, but all got the message. Approaching the pub Pear took it upon himself to go ahead along to check the Owls were still there, as the rest stood on top of a grass bank. This was a sensible strategy, for if Owls were in, they would have to run out of the pub and up a hill. Their missiles would therefore probably not touch Blades, and Blades could 'steam into 'em'. The strategy was in vain: the Owls had left, so Blades entered the pub and over a drink began to reflect that the Owls might return afterwards, when they could then ambush them.

Blades then did something they had never done before, and that would never occur again – they made 'petrol bombs'. Two Blades contributing 50p each went to a petrol station to buy petrol, which was poured into four milk bottles produced by two others. Another two found old cloth, which provided the incendiary wicks. Another lent gloves, so that no fingerprints could be found. Two others assisted: one helped buy the petrol, and the other lent a coat so that the 'bombs' could be carried inconspicuously. Soon after they were made, the police entered: a Sergeant said he knew they were Blades, and if they did not *fuck off into town* they would be arrested. Under a two-van police escort Blades were forced to leave the pub and walk towards the city centre. However, on passing a housing complex, Barry had the idea they could lose the escort by running into it, and could meet later in a specified pub. Thirty made the dash. Those who remained were left by police on the outskirts of the city centre with a warning to *get off home or get nicked*. Soon they met with the others as arranged, Sean and Greg still carrying two of the devices, as they had done throughout the police escort.

At the rendezvous drinks were ordered. The devices, placed under a table, caught the attention of one of the young bar staff. Ray noticed the attention and rescued the situation, saying, *'You haven't seen them bottles and we won't wreck this boozer.'* The barman moved on to serve elsewhere. At 9.30 p.m. the restless group left, with the plan of ambushing the expected Owl opposition. The main group would hide in an alleyway off the main road the Owls were expected to walk along, whilst two Blades, Timmy and George, would offer themselves as 'bait' by standing alone on the street under the glare of street lights whilst Blades hid in an alleyway ready to ambush Owls. The only street light in the alleyway was smashed by a rock thrown by Tonno. Blades then waited. The plan worked: one of the Owls' Top Lads, walking 100 yards ahead of their mob, ran towards them shouting threats. When he was only yards away and about to be a target for a rock from Timmy, a police van arrived, causing Blades to run up the alleyway, their plan effectively ruined. Five minutes later a police transit van appeared and the officers jumped out and chased Blades. Inadvertently this action led Blades to the Owls.

The latter had made their way towards The Bell on the High Street. Blades, fleeing police, ran into High Street, saw the Owls and began chanting 'B-B-C', whereupon the Owls, gathered and posturing, prepared to fight. In the melee the two 'petrol bombs' were thrown, the Owls – numerically superior – although unaware of the nature of the missiles, ran. Neither device exploded or caused injuries, for the throwers had thrown them deliberately short of any target as they later told Blades. An hour later police forensic staff gathered pieces of broken glass, and as he boarded a bus to go home, a core Blade was arrested. Days later another Blade was arrested and charged. In court two officers claimed to have seen the latter throwing milk bottles at police vehicles. He was found guilty and fined £300. Three other officers had apparently 'seen' the former leading an attack on 'youths'. He was more fortunate, and was found 'not guilty'.

What was significant in this incident was that the forty Blades developed an attitude of virtuous superiority. They had 'turned out' and 'done' the Owls, and a few weeks later they 'confirmed' the name of the Blades Business Crew – the BBC – by creating badges and making 'calling cards'. The Owls responded in kind; and they too created a name for themselves – the Owls Crime Squad (OCS). Chants of 'O-C-S' and 'B-B-C' were to be heard around Sheffield city centre for the next ten years.

There was nothing organised, regular or inevitable about the Blade–Owl vendetta. Matters could go quiet for months, only to resurface in a multitude of incidents that would produce a perceived wrongdoer and a subsequent desire to teach the perpetrators a lesson. At times over 1986 nothing happened for weeks; then two incidents broke the uneasy 'peace' at Christmas. First, Bud, in a city-centre disco with his girlfriend and another couple, was subject to an assault by one of the Trio, who recognised him from the attack on them in the previous year. Then, in the city centre on Christmas Eve at lunch-time, Bud's attacker was seen. Anticipating the Blades' revenge, he pulled out a cosh and struck a Blade, causing a small head wound. Other Blades kicked him as their attack felled him in a shop doorway. A security guard pulled him into the store, locking the doors. However, his parcels of shopping did not go with him, and became Blades' Christmas presents.

Publicity and the BBC: 1985–1997

The BBC 'began' life in September 1986. In origin the inner clique consisted of 12 Blades who attended the same school and most frequently fought Owls in 1986. From a wider core of around sixty, this group decided the pubs on London Road were the nearest and liveliest area, even though most lived over two miles away from The Lansdowne. That said, any Blade with free time was welcome, and newcomers to London Road or those travelling to the match came to regard the BBC as a semi-permanent gathering, which is precisely what it became. The term 'BBC' first appeared on a 1985 leaflet advertising a coach being run to a south-coast away match. The original name was the subject of light-hearted arguments for the following six months among four Blades. The name was considered to be a good one: no 'leader' imposed it, and no one gained status by claiming to be its originator. Following the adoption of the title 'BBC', metal lapel badges appeared; a Blade had 120 made to his design, which borrowed from the club motif, substituting the white rose and scimitars for the skull and cross-bones beloved of piracy. This produced an immediate £90 profit, and six months later another 150 badges made a total profit of £200. Sold in Blades' pubs to anyone, *'even little knobheads'*, I even saw two teenage girls wearing them at a match. Thus these items were not worn to celebrate some form of hooligan credibility, but were bought and worn by anyone with a spare pound coin.

Blades generated other paraphernalia in response to media publicity involving artefacts created by other supporters, and between 1985 and 1987 produced and circulated 'calling cards' and leaflets circulated in and around Blades pubs for six months.[3] The most lasting one, produced by two young Blades, reading *'Congratulations, You Have Just Been Tuned in by the BBC'* was considered the best (i.e. the funniest). In hopes of receiving publicity (and notoriety), the cards were even pushed through the letterbox of *The Star* and sent to a national tabloid; but the ploy failed. Six months later the cards were no longer spoken of, and were destroyed because of a fear of a police raid. Blades now realised that their possession could be used against them in any court hearing, though, contrary to what the media reported, they were never pinned on to beaten rivals. Ironically, the few occasions that rivals did see them was when they were exchanged in peaceful circumstances for other fan cards, or were left on away-ground terracing.

Prior to the appearance of the cards, leaflets were made and circulated by three different Blades. Two were produced a few weeks prior to the long-anticipated home fixture against Leeds in March 1985. In an earlier 'away' fixture Blades had 'done' Leeds' lads, and it was expected they would be out for revenge (see Armstrong 1994). The first leaflet, made by an old lad , called on Blades to be out in force, and to all appearances carried instructions to meet in a specified pub, The Sussex. Such information was redundant, for Blades already met in three neighbouring pubs in the city centre. The following week another leaflet was produced by Barry. The message again was an encouragement to 'turn out' for Leeds, as well as a suggestion that the day of circulation would afford Blades the chance to 'get' Derby lads, who, it was thought, would be passing through Sheffield on the way to their match. To assist in publicity, two Blades, both with jobs involving travel, stopped on their journeys in Leeds. In the knowledge that Their Lads gathered in certain pubs before games, the leaflets were pasted on to the toilet wall. On the morning of the match Blades headed for The Sussex would have found two policemen standing at the door. However, by 12.00 noon Blades were in one of the usual three pubs laughing about the red-herring that had been effectively laid in The Sussex leaflet. In reality, the leaflets never tried to arrange violence or rival gatherings, for they stated the obvious, and the suggestions they promoted were to be ignored, but were considered funny.

Around the same time some of the respective Blade and Owl factions took their opposition to their increasing levels of abuse in the messages on their T-shirts. The messages they sent were often obviously violent; yet the origin of the garments suggests caution should be used in interpretation. The shirts were produced by a Blade printer and illustrator; but his assistant was an Owl, well known to Blades as one of their Top Lads. Although having a conviction for football hooliganism, the Blade was not part of the 'core'. However, he attended matches with his elder brother, who was a 'core' Blade. The three men so divided on match-days regularly drank together, and on such occasions would dream up designs. Thus, the Owl helped to develop the Blades' design, and a few weeks later the three would sit together as this Owl drew his reply for his group's shirts. Blades' designs proclaimed the inability of Owls to hold their beer, to pull women or to fight; and to assist this degradation the designer used 'The Adventures of Bertie Blade', borrowing a cartoon character from the Sheffield *Green 'Un* sports paper, with origins in the 1940s. Bertie Blade had changed somewhat, and took on a resemblance to the 'Desperate Dan' cartoon character from The Dandy comic. With an exaggerated bristling chin, strong arms, and stout chest, he was thus a parody of masculinity, and a joke not a role model. In his adventures, an exaggerated masculinity was emphasised, in which he attracted young women, drank large amounts of beer, and would fight and beat the best. Inevitably the antithesis of these attributes in the strip cartoon was the character of Ozzie Owl, who epitomised a vision of Wednesday's less than human status (Figures 1 and 2). The messages in reply from the Owls were simple – Blades were masturbaters and should be murdered, and to have a terminal disease was preferable to any change of allegiance (Figures 3–6). The intentions of these entrepreneurs was more to provoke laughter within each group than to encourage fights between them. The makers sold the garments in pubs along London Road before home games. Costing £5–£7, each design came in one (large) size, and between sixty and a hundred were sold. Their Owl mate did a similar sales promotion before Wednesday matches, and their customers were aged between 16 and 40. A profit margin of nearly 60 per cent went into their three pockets. I never heard of fights arising from these offending T-shirts. Not all who bought such garments were Blades or Owls, for some were mainstream United and Wednesday fans.

It Just Needs One: Personal Issues: 1987–1993

Whilst mob-vs-mob fights between the Blades and Owls were the norm, there were occasions when individual Blades (and Owls) held centre stage. Even when the two groups confronted one another the outcome could be an agreement for one from each faction to fight a 'one to one'. Such scenarios illustrate two aspects of the drama. First, that personal issues could (at times) take precedence over the wider issue. Second, that the factions respected the rules of 'one-to-ones', for the fight did not escalate, and the groups essentially fought by proxy. In late 1987 and early 1988 arguments between rivals, inevitably over accusations of bullying or 'mouthing off', saw amidst dozens on each side a Blade *'offer out'* an Owl. The two left the city-centre pub to find a *'quiet place'*, usually a car park, to *'sort it out'*. Onlookers from both sides gathered, shouted encouragement, but were not to intervene until there was an obvious winner, whereupon – acting as judges – their intervention saved the vanquished further pain and implicitly declared a victor. In the space of six months, one Blade, Bobby, was twice involved in such a scene with the same Owl. He rationalised his motive as *'I just don't like him.'* The first fight ended prematurely and amicably after a couple of minutes because of a fear of a police arrival. The second, weeks later, involved a walk of 400 metres, where Bobby, stripped to the waist and surrounded by Blades and Owls, promptly lost the fight! No Blade criticised him, for he was *'game'*, a *'good Blade'*. The Owl was similarly said to be game and acknowledged to be the better fighter.

Impasse and the cessation of hostilities between Blades and Owls could last weeks or months and have no great rationale. In 1987 from the time of the smashing of the windows in the two pubs to Blades again confronting Owls was a nine-week period in which nothing happened. Then events of the night of the confrontation resulted in various fights between the two sides over the next four weeks. The summer was quiet; and then, with the beginning of the football season in August, Blades once again went walking along West Street looking for the Owls. Twice they found them, but no fight took place: once Blades stood over and laughed at the group of ten Owls they found, and another time realised half the opposing group knew some Blades quite well, and so a fight was not considered appropriate. Hostilities then ceased between August and the early part of December. My question as to why this happened produced various replies, ranging from: *'They're not worth feytin' any more'*, or *'They're useless'* to *'Everybody knows each other now.'* On one occasion in September six Blades, including Nick, Shane, Jim, and Mel, walked into The Bell and, finding thirty Owls gathered before their home match, showed them photographs that featured the two mobs confronting each other!

At the same time Blades and Owls still spoke of how *'it only needs one to start'*, for both sides understood that a misdemeanour by any one of them could renew hostilities. Such a person would be regarded by the others as the *'silly bastard'*. He was the one who, when the groups were both in pubs together, would tire of the inactivity, and without consultation or attempting to attain a consensus, would throw a glass, or threaten, or accuse the other group, and thereby 'start' a scene. Over the years individuals on both sides were guilty of this. At other times it was words spoken that provoked fights.

One incident in December 1987 held all the ingredients for trouble and provided plenty of material for repercussions. After six weeks of quiet, twenty Blades on a city-centre pub crawl entered a disco on West Street. Along the way, talking to, commented how 'quiet' matters had been recently, but cautioned, saying *'It only needs one.'* To the Blades it was one of the Owls' Top Lads, who on seeing the Blades in the club came over to them, calling them *'wankers'* and suggesting that in fighting ability they knew *'fuck all'*. In response Nick punched him, other Blades kicked him and other Owls with him until the club's bouncers sorted matters out. To the Owls, the Blades were bullies; but the Blades the Owls subsequently breached codes of honour. In the attack one Blade had hit the Owl over the head with a bottle (fortunately this did not cause serious injury). Five days later, out on his workplace Christmas outing which took in West Street, one of three Owls recognised the Blade assailant and without warning headbutted him, causing a serious nose injury that required an operation. Blades were disgusted, for there was no warning, and the attack, which took place in the company of women and older men who had no connections with football, was cowardly. They conveniently forgot that the attack on the Owl was not honourable in the eyes of their enemies. The Saturday night hostilities resumed over January–February of 1988.

Then for no apparent reason events calmed until one Saturday in May 1988. This was the last match of the season for both Clubs. Blades returned from their nearby game within an hour of the final whistle, and the Owls had remained out after their home game. No message or invitation had been passed between the groups; but, working on shared assumptions, both realised the others would be out in large numbers, in keeping with the traditional Sheffield last-match-of-the-season celebration. Taking the back route from London Road, eighty Blades arrived at 9.00 p.m. in a pub near to West Street. After a half-hour wait half a dozen Owls, all well-known to Blades, walked through the door. The Owl who had been beaten in December in the disco (addressing no one in particular) said *'Forget it, lads'*, adding that police had entered another pub where the main mob of Owls were drinking and had arrested four *'for nowt'*. Some Blades talked with the Owls, though the majority looked on silently, another core Blade then entered and, on seeing this Owl, looked bewildered; the Owl recognised him, for after all they were familiar. However, the previous time they had met the Blade had been swinging an iron pole grabbed from a nearby builder's skip, and the Owl had replied by throwing lumps of building rubble. The latter's question of *'What wo' up wi' de' other week?'* was met with a similarly rueful remark. The two managed a grin, and then parted and talked to their respective factions. The Owls remained in the pub unmolested; the Blades walked to a pub across the road.

At times group disorder could lead to subsequent personal vendettas. One memorable incident involving Blades and Owls began in September 1991. The Blades were part of a Sunday football team training on a recreation pitch near a pub which two of the top Owls drank in. Noticing who they were, whilst on their way to have a Sunday lunch-time drink, they rang around and gathered thirty Owls within an hour, and then walked over to the training session. Realising that not all the players were Blades, one Owl shouted: *'All them who's got nowt to do wi' it fuck off, now.'* The message was understood by the six Blades who, telling their colleagues to leave the scene. As some departed, others fetched golf clubs from a car boot and handed them out, and the Blades, stood in a group swinging them at oncoming Owls, but quickly realised the odds were too great and ran in all directions. No one was caught by the pursuing Owls, but the humiliation had to be avenged. Meeting at 7.00 p.m. that night the six, with two more (including Noel), travelled in two cars to the pub an hour later. With faces concealed by scarves and, in two instances, balaclavers and armed with four baseball bats, the Blades broke two pub windows and turned over pub tables as they pursued four specific Owls. One was struck by a bottle thrown by Noel; the Owl's injury required four stitches. Honours evened, the Blades left within two minutes. The police executed a dawn raid the next morning and, at 6.00 p.m., eight Blades were arrested, taken into custody and questioned. No one was charged (only four of those arrested had actually participated). The issue died down. Meanwhile, police made public their belief that the disturbance was drug-related because markets were being fought over.

The Owl that was glassed eventually came looking for Noel two years later. To add insult to injury Noel had, in a subsequent Blade–Owl pub confrontation, assaulted him again. The Owl made inquiries and discovered where Noel could be found. Each Friday Noel, his non-Blade mate and their two girlfriends would, after having a drink, enter an Indian restaurant in an area renown for the popularity of a nearby Shabeen. The pursuing Owl brought an entourage of ten mates. On entering the restaurant he revealed a small baseball bat, so Noel requisitioned kitchen utensils and his mate beer glasses, and the Owl and his mates were backed out of the door. Then their nightmare began. These white boys were in the wrong area and attacking the wrong person – Noel was popular with the local black youths, and within minutes the Owls were pursued by twenty of them. One young Owl who fell had to suffer the ignominy and humiliation of having a black Blade standing over him offering a wooden bat to a sixteen-year-old mate and laughingly tell him to 'bash his first pig'. After a few blows the Owl was allowed to run away. No one ever came looking for Noel again. Likewise Noel never sought out the Owl.

Match-day Manoeuvres 1989–1993

This never-ending Blade-Owl saga was about 'winning'; but 'winning' was not always a matter of violence. There were other shows and indications of power, whose various outcomes saw constructs and excuses used by either side to explain various courses of action. Thus, at a pre-season friendly match in 1989 when 200 Blades turned out for Owls, the latter did not show, upon realising that the thirty who had turned out would not be much use. Instead of searching for them, Blades enjoyed a drink and went home claiming victory, in that Owls were scared. A year later (1990), on the occasion of a mid-week fixture (a Wednesday player's 'testimonial') Blades could not be bothered to go to Hillsborough, and there was no turnout from them. The Owls, no doubt, would claim they had intimidated Blades to not appear.

Twice in 1990 there were matches between the sides; the first was a pre-season friendly played at Bramall Lane. On a glorious August Saturday 250 Blades gathered along London Road. Owls meanwhile had met in a council estate pub three miles from Bramall Lane, and from it one of their

Top Lads had phoned The Partridge, asked for a top Blade by name and invited him to bring Blades to meet them there. Informed of Blades' position, number and state of mind, the Owl promised instead to be down soon. They did not arrive at the pub, because Blades, knowing of the bus routes and arterial roads and anticipating their route, saw their arrival; and the 'call-out' produced a mass, silent half-mile walk to the pub the Owls had entered. Blades approached the premises over a grass wasteland, and were therefore clearly visible. On seeing them approach, the Owls ran out, stood and fought toe-to-toe for about half a minute, and then backed off and 'ran'. Seconds later police arrived and chased the combatants away. Blades had 'won,' no one had got hurt (hardly a punch had connected) and no arrests were made. What was memorable was the sight of a large black youth with the Owls past whom many Blades ran in pursuit of other Owls until Dene, one of the top Blades, had the courage to thump him and knock him over. One Owl who stood his ground was one of the Trio. Facing assaults from four Blades, he was rescued by Gordon who, holding him in a necklock, steered him to space where he could run away. Weeks later he sought Gordon out and thanked him in person.

Blades went to the match; the Owls missed the game, but instead went to various pubs and met up later in the day at 8.30 p.m. with two hundred Blades who had entered a city-centre pub. From their rendezvous in pub a few hundred yards away, Owls attacked without warning – so swiftly, in fact, that only fifteen Blades could get out of the pub's doors. As missiles taken from the Owls' gathering-point rained on the door, the rival factions screamed mutual threats; and amidst the mêlée one Blade was felled by a wooden bat before Owls were sent scattering by a Blade's rottweiler dog, and backed off further when a young black Blade of fighting repute floored one of the Owls' Top Lads (who was also black) with one punch. This had an effect on the other Owls who contented themselves with shouting threats and breaking two large windows of the pub before having to flee upon the arrival of police. The prostrate Blade and another semi-conscious Blade both needed an ambulance. Blades vowed vengeance; but this did not come that night. Owls retreated to the pub on the council estate where they had met at lunch-time. Blades remained in the city centre.

Both sides claimed victory that day. A few months later, Blades turned out for an insignificant midweek Cup match at Hillsborough. Such was the football passion in the city at the time – with United top of Division Two and Wednesday doing well in Division One – that 32,000 people attended. Of these, two hundred were Blades, who met in the city centre, then moved to the University area of town and finally walked to Hillsborough aiming to avoid police. The Owls were not around before or after the game and, after wandering the city centre, Blades went home claiming a moral victory, illustrating once again that supremacy and reputation did not always require a violent contest.

Furthermore, even when contests occurred, these were so multifaceted that it was open to debate as to who had won the day. When both teams finally found themselves in the same Division in 1991/2 and the first Sheffield derby in 14 years took place, the factions knew a good turnout was necessary. Police forced a Sunday midday kick-off and an all-ticket entry policy to limit the potential for trouble around pubs. But regardless, Blades fought Owls outside a city-centre pub the night before the game; and on the morning of the match Blades met in two pubs that opened early (illegally). There were, however, no incidents before the match. A confrontation did occur at the coffee bar in the South Stand, for which thirty Owls had bought tickets. Moments before kick-off half a dozen Blades, realising who they were, exchanged punches with them before police appeared and surrounded them. Afterwards, although a hundred and fifty Blades met and remained in the city centre all afternoon and evening, the Owls were not found.

A brief incursion and a city-centre fight after the match contested the issue at the mid-week return fixture six months later. This produced 22 arrests and a disturbance in the ground as thirty Blades entered the Wednesday end. Surprisingly, this was not a deliberate ploy to provoke trouble (albeit they knew their presence was unlikely to cause social cohesion), they had bought tickets for this part of the ground because the allocation for the United end had sold out. When United scored the first of their three goals they cheered, and scuffles subsequently began with furious Owls before the intruders were rounded up by police and ejected. After the match skirmishing occurred between rival mobs along the roads into the city centre. The largest fight took place two hours after the game, near midnight, outside a nightclub when forty Blades confronted and 'ran' around fifty Owls. Two of the latter who did not run quickly enough were kicked repeatedly before Blades left them. Once again Blades claimed a victory.

The 1992/3 season again saw the Bramall Lane fixture played on a Sunday, this time in the afternoon. Kick-off was at 2.00 p.m. (which, in contrast to police arguments of less than a year previously, allowed everyone to have a drink). Blades met along London Road, and soon discovered Owls were a mile away. The latter took the initiative and, via the back streets, appeared close to London Road at 2.45 p.m. What could have been a large-scale mêleé was prevented by police on foot and horses escorting the Owls to the ground. Nothing happened in the ground. Nothing happened afterwards either, and Blades contented themselves by claiming the Owls had hid behind the police and brought the issue to a head, knowing full well most Blades would be in the ground at that time. The Owls claimed they had done their job of taking the matter to the Blades front door and the Blades should have made more of an effort to find them later.

London Calling: Local Faces in Distant Places 1991–1993

One Blade–Owl event defied all previous procedure and protocol. In 1991, a hundred and fifty Blades were in a North London pub three hours before an FA Cup fixture at Chelsea. In the previous fortnight a regular core Blade had received a series of phone calls from a youth with a London accent informing him that he would be *'sliced up'*, and that Blades would be *'killed'* on the day of the cup match. Unaware if this was a 'wind-up' by fellow Blades or a serious threat, the Blade refused to respond to the caller's requests to 'name a place' where Blades and Chelsea could meet. On the day of the match, in a pub Blades often used when in the Capital, the phone rang and the same caller asked for the Blade (and another by name), telling the two of their impending fate and where he and his colleagues were (a pub half a mile away). Simultaneously a Blade saw an Owl across the street. Sensing the Owls were gathered nearby, the Blades walked towards the specified pub and spread across 70 yards. The seventy waiting rivals were spread across the main road: one brandished a knife, one fired a distress flare, and one was squirting a liquid from a plastic lemon container. And though a few Blades began fighting, the sight of the knife and the unknown liquid was too much, and Blades 'backed off' to the sanctuary of their pub. This was then attacked and windows were broken, before the sound of police sirens sent the Chelsea mob scattering. Amidst the anger and rancour of being 'run', the mystery behind the phone calls was solved, for two well-known Owls were with Their Lads. Wednesday were also in London that day at Arsenal. However, these two had not 'turned out', but had joined Chelsea mates – a product of friendship established at England matches – and provided phone numbers based on knowledge of Blades' addresses and where Blades would be before the match.

Revenge was soon to be gained. The Chelsea fans and Owls had sensibly run when police arrived; however, they ran too far. Catching a tube at the stop beyond the incident, they were on the train when the Blades boarded it, having been ushered out of the pub by police. Three minutes into the journey one Blade noticed ten of the Londoners and their Owl mates in the next carriage, and at the next station stop the train doors were forcibly held open by a dozen Blades as dozens of others rushed to the one carriage and administered a somewhat riotous revenge. The end-product was a ten-minute beating of a heap of bodies, the arrival of two dozen police, the cowed presence of a few dozen frightened fellow-passengers, and (amazingly) at the end of it all, only one rival with a concussion and head wound. All the victims of the beating walked away, albeit one of them needing assistance. However, Blades all agreed that they could not claim a 'victory' under these circumstances, just a satisfying retribution. Two weeks later, in a Sheffield nightclub, one of the Owls chatted about the incident with four Blades he recognised, unaware that two of them had punched and kicked him in the mêlée on the tube.

This event had repercussions, as the Londoners attempted to get revenge. Over a year later United hosted Chelsea in the season's final game. Rumour abounded that Owls would combine with the Londoners. On the day, the hours before the match were incident-free. Afterwards Blades found forty Chelsea fans with ten Owls in a pub about a mile from London Road. Over two hundred Blades entered the nearest pub, whilst two Blades, Gordon and Declan, went on reconnaissance. Whilst they were gone the landlord demanded that the group leave (which they did), as police in vehicles and on horseback arrived. The Blades were then told by police to return to London Road. They did.

Meanwhile Gordon and Declan, having walked into The Tavern wearing Blade badges, talked to Owls (who recognised them) and Chelsea fans who silently stared. After 10 minutes of amicable chat, the Owls discreetly advised the two Blades to leave – which they did, fearing that some Chelsea fans were about to end the period of hospitality to strangers. Three hours later (9.00 p.m.) Blades found the Owls and their new-found Southern mates in a city-centre bar, which fortuitously happened to be one the Blades had fought the bouncers of sporadically for over a year. Blades could now kill two birds with one stone, and knew that their football adversaries knew what to expect on this night. A hundred Blades who gathered at the door were met by the pub bouncers who, armed with CS gas spray and bats, beat the front men back. Police arrived in force and arrested (and charged) eight Blades. That was the end of events. The Blades who faced a charge of affray in court all walked free as the case against them was not proven.

The next time United played at Chelsea nothing happened: the turnout was very poor, not through fear but because of the time of year – winter – and the low league position of the United team. When both Sheffield sides competed at Wembley in the FA Cup Semi-Finals, however, Chelsea turned out a forty-strong mob who gathered in London's West End in expectation of meeting the Blades. The latter, though, were either homeward-bound or in North London pubs. The time after that was the occasion United were relegated from the Premier Division. Whilst there were 3,000 fans from Sheffield there was no large-scale trouble before or during the game. Two brief confrontations did take place at a nearby tube station and in a pub in London's West End, but this involved more mainstream United fans (not Blades) and their Chelsea equivalents. The Blades never got another chance to confront the Londoners, as the teams played in different divisions for the next four years.

Bouncers, Batsmen and Blades 1991–1993

First of all, Blades had nothing *per se* against the occupation of pub and night-club door security, i.e. 'bouncers': indeed, some Blades were bouncers, and many had mates employed in this role. Second, Blades did not object to their presence, and were often glad of restrictive door policies. Third, most bouncers were locally born and known by name and reputation, and were often respected for their fighting abilities. Others, however, were considered with contempt, and were said only to be so employed to satisfy some basic male instinct for power and authority in glamorous surroundings. For Blades out socialising matters could be complicated when one of their members came into conflict with such bouncers, when the usual principles would apply; the bouncers were accused of bullying, and would have to be taught a lesson, and frequently the bouncers had football loyalties or friendships with the Owls. Blades would come into contact with police, and via the latter with the media, whose reporting omitted the complexities.

The pub-football identity issue got even more complicated in the early 1990s when pub and nightclub security, United footballers, and the Owls all combined to provoke the Blades to act, in their opinion, righteously in order to punish what they perceived to be bullying. The origin lay in two separate incidents. One involved Mick and Kenny, out with their wives one night, all of whom were refused entry to a nightclub by the bouncers. Perceiving the refusal to be unwarranted and rude to their wives, the two Blades vowed vengeance. A further issue hastened their desire when months later a Sheffield-born former United player was assaulted by the same bouncers. The player, who had recently been transferred to a local team, was out with two non-Blade mates. In his leisure time and when not playing for the team, he would socialise with some Blade mates and sit with others at the match when injured. He was on crutches at the time; and, to Blades, this was a case of appalling bullying. Moreover, since he was both a popular player and a mate of the Blades, this matter needed avenging. It must be said that the assaulted player had no part in subsequent matters, for Blades took it upon themselves to 'sort it out'. Their response occurred a few weeks later when sixty Blades who had stopped out after a home match walked to the club at 8.30 p.m. to seek out the offending bouncers. Around fifteen of the latter saw the group approaching and closed the doors, sensibly ignoring Blades' shouts to come out and fight.

In subsequent months the pavements outside the club and a nearby pub which was controlled by the same bouncers until the club opened its doors saw various ritualised 'set-to's' between bouncers and Blades. The latter would, in various numbers, walk slowly past the former, mobbed together elevated on the pub's stairway. Invariably a police van, alerted to the movement of dozens of young men, would be following or be parked yards away from this flashpoint, with officers watching but not obviously intervening. Such ritualised hostilities were limited to verbals. The ritual however turned to disorder in November 1992, when a hundred Blades left a city-centre pub they had gathered in after a match and stormed both the front and back doors of the pub the bouncers were working in a pincer movement. The bouncers fought back and, as police arrived in half a dozen vehicles, Blades fled. This time eight Blades and three bouncers were arrested as ten police vehicles blocked both ends of the road and attempted to arrest anyone fleeing the scene. Of those charged only two were found guilty on minor public order offences. Incriminating evidence of the affray could have been afforded by the pub's surveillance camera above the entrance; however, one Blade sensibly covered the lens with his jacket as the confrontation began.

The sparring continued, and on a Saturday in November 1992 seventy Blades walked past the pub at 10.00 p.m., but avoided conflict with a dozen bouncers (some holding small wooden bats) because of police vehicles parked nearby. Inside, however, two groups of Blades remained unaware of outside events. The bouncers, still armed with bats, demanded they get out. Others received different treatment, and were sprayed with 'mace' (a toxic substance capable of debilitating a victim by causing extreme eye and nose irritation). One in their group was a United player, coincidentally also encumbered by a broken leg and crutches. He and his mates left the pub with eyes streaming. Though they were unwilling to divulge what had happened, Blades surmised from experience and were not impressed. Soon after, on Boxing Day, having returned from their game at Manchester, thirty Blades had a drink on London Road. Two days later they were to learn the bouncers had expected an attack on the pub that night, and in anticipation had wooden bats ready, and, even more provocatively in the Blades' eyes, had allowed thirty Owls entry to help repulse Blades. Worse still, the Owls, they had heard, had been allowed free drinks. Why they should be so favoured was attributed to the fact that some of the bouncers were Owls, whilst others had Owl mates.

Police attempts to keep the city tranquil elsewhere, however, were not always successful. Some police activity, it could be argued, only served to sustain conflict. In late 1993, Blades believed the Sheffield police exacerbated issues between these bouncers and themselves. In some undisclosed fashion it seemed police dossiers were given to some bouncers in city-centre bars and discos. This followed a number of altercations involving Blades and bouncers of another disco-pub who had teamed up with Owls. These dossiers consisted of mug shots with name, age, and district of residence. It did not take a genius to connect details from the telephone directory, and match a surname to a district. As a result six Blades received threatening phone calls, and one even had a crude 'petrol bomb' device thrown from a passing car at his house. The callers to the others told them how they knew where they lived and that they were going to 'kill' them. Blades had no idea who their callers were, although it was known that such dossiers had been photocopied and had been passed on by the bouncers to their Owl mates. One old, retired Blade lived in the same district as a younger Blade with the same surname, and the former's response to such bewildering calls was to inform police. Another victim of the calls was the wife of a Blade, who also told police of the nature of the messages. Word got back to whoever had made the calls that tracers had been placed on these phones, and the calls ended.

Blades settled an issue at another pub the same year. Out on a workplace 'piss-up', a Blade, the worse for drink, was assaulted 'without reason' by the bouncers. After the next home match twenty-five Blades walked to the pub and stood at the top of the staircase which led into the premises. One Blade entered, to find the pub contained only four bouncers, and asked for the bouncer he wanted to 'see'. When he appeared he was assaulted, which was the cue for the others to run in. The other bouncers were thumped before seeking refuge behind the bar. A few stools were thrown at the optics and a few bottles broken before the Blades left. The last man to leave shouted *'You know what that were for.'* As far as Blades were concerned, justice was done. At this point the matter ended as quickly as it had begun, for Blades now felt they had made their point. Police were never called, and the newspapers never got to hear of this fracas.

A year later, in 1994, another group of bouncers entered the fray, without any obvious reason in the Blades' opinion. They had regularly allowed Blades into their pub for over three years, and the two groups got along fine. Then, for no particular reason, they barred entry one Saturday night. Words were exchanged around the door, as were a few punches. The following Saturday whilst up-town a dozen Blades found the same bouncers had joined forces with others from other pubs, with which they had also had no argument. These twenty-five collective guardians of social tranquillity, however, made what proved to be the mistake of gathering outside a pub, some armed with baseball bats, and threatening the small group of Blades. A few phone calls and half an hour later Blades were seventy-strong and outside the pub, and in the ensuing fracas the bouncers were 'run' into it. One who did not make the door was knocked out with a punch by Sean. Later in the night Mick and Timmy, knowing the bouncers quite well, asked them for an explanation. A good one was not available. The two Blades warned them that whilst they had gathered twenty-five for this special occasion, they could gather a hundred and fifty every Saturday. Consequently there was no further trouble from this source, and once again neither police nor journalists witnessed or propagated this incident.

Bad Debts and Bouncers: 1991–1993

In 1991 two local black entrepreneurs (peripheral Blades) hired a club for a private 'rave' night and paid a sizeable deposit. The club management reneged on the deal (allegedly because of police pressure on them, because they feared drugs would be sold at the event); they cancelled, but did not return the deposit. As a result, the two in seeking redress not only fought the head of the agency who supplied the bouncers to the club, but repeatedly challenged other bouncers and threatened the club management. Their fighting ability worried many bouncers, to the extent that some refused to work the door any more. However, neither brought other Blades into the conflict; Blades joined in as a result of a subsequent dispute which had a dynamic all of its own. The similarity of this to earlier scenarios stemmed from the actions of the management and was assisted unwittingly by police. To avoid local complications the management began hiring a new security team bussed in on Friday and Saturday nights from the city of Nottingham 35 miles from Sheffield. In their first few weeks this well-paid 22-strong group, no doubt fed intelligence from their management and police sources, set out to show who was boss, and having been given mug shots compiled by police assaulted a few recognisable Blades inside the club and challenged 'the BBC' to 'have a go'. Many Blades were only too happy to oblige, and did so on four occasions, which produced large-scale disorder and casualties.

The first incident occurred in April 1992, when the bouncers barred entry to the club one Friday night to some Blades, having allowed others to enter – a procedure assisted by a police officer well known to Blades, who at 11.30 p.m. stood across the road from the entrance and nodded or shook his head towards watching bouncers as various Blades sought entry. Soon after the officer left, Blades outside the premises, aware that some of their numbers had gained entry, believed a tactic of separation had been implemented and that what would follow was a violent assault on those inside. As a consequence the twenty Blades stormed the door, but were kept out when the bouncers locked it.

The next occasion, on a Friday night in the summer of 1992, arose out of a challenge issued from the same bouncers. After a night in the city centre Blades walked to London Road, and outside the nightclub twenty-five faced up to similar numbers of bouncers, recognisable in their red tracksuits. Events were violent but over quickly, as the bouncers, armed with small wooden bats, repelled the Blades as they stormed the door, and the matter ended within two minutes when police arrived and once again chased Blades away, arresting two as they fled. The next came in the autumn of 1992, when twenty Blades fought bouncers inside and outside the club foyer. During this mêlée one Blade fired a distress flare at bouncers gathered around the foyer door, and another released an anti-rape spray (Mace) device. This had unexpected results, as the club's three hundred patrons had to be evacuated, and three people (two of them bouncers) needed medical assistance as a result of inhaling this substance. As a result of being captured on a surveillance camera inside the club foyer four Blades were arrested and faced serious charges.[4] One had charges dropped at the committal stage of proceedings because of insufficient evidence; the other three appeared at Crown Court, two under the Firearms Act and for affray, and one solely for assault and affray. Eighteen months later all three were merely fined, having pleaded guilty. Their anticipated custodial sentences were not realised; one was doubly grateful, having changed his plea from not guilty to guilty so as not to be in custody and thus free to watch United play Wednesday in an FA Cup tie.

One final fight between this same group of bouncers and Blades occurred on an August night following the first match of the 1993/4 season. At 10.30 p.m. a group of fifty Blades walking past the club and shouting threats towards their adversaries, were suddenly faced by twenty bouncers. Some carried wooden bats, and another carried a bin-liner full of empty beer bottles, which were subsequently thrown at Blades by six of them. The challenge was accepted, and in the ensuing fight one Blade was beaten unconscious with a wooden bat wrapped in a plastic bag and taken to hospital Blades were initially 'backed off' by their stronger opponents, only to regroup and chase their adversaries back into the club foyer. When police arrived the issue was more or less over, but their enquiries began when they walked 200 yards up the road and entered The Partridge pub, where the Blades had retreated and where an argument had begun over the rights and wrongs of the fight and who had 'bottled it'. Into this stepped fifteen police accompanied by two Alsatian dogs, and took, what appeared to me, a very heavy-handed approach. The result was that Blades and other local drinkers not involved in earlier proceedings fell in heaps as they tried to avoid canine fangs. A furious pub landlord bawled at the police to get out, and after two minutes the police left, abusing the Blades but without making any arrests. Their enquiries at The Locarno were more fruitful, and a bystander (a retired solicitor) informed them how the bouncers started the fight and of the weapons they had. When police asked to see the surveillance cameras, which would have recorded events immediately outside the door, they discovered they had conveniently been turned off. Three bouncers were arrested and one was charged, but in Crown Court the judge dismissed the case, stating that the guilty party was the Blade Business Crew and that police should be arresting them, not bouncers.[5] Soon after this the Nottingham firm ceased to be employed.[6] Blades previously banned were allowed back in, and the two entrepreneurs received their money.

Notes

1. In his summing-up the judge, Justice Hunt, said

> *You both went off to get the petrol and together you assembled these devices and, having assembled them, you concealed them in a bag and moved them to where*

supporters were assembling in various licensed premises. There had been previous trouble between the supporters of Sheffield Wednesday and Sheffield United, and you were both aware that there was to be trouble in the future . . . each of you told the police that you would not have had the 'bottle' to use them yourself. I am sure you genuinely believed that. Caught up in the emotions of football fanatics it may well be you may have been carried away by the adrenalin pumping around in your systems. Even if not, there would have been others there who would not have thought twice about using them and each of you accepted that. This is a case where I have to have regard to the public interest rather than to your personal circumstances as individuals. The courts have got to let it be known that the manufacture of petrol bombs for use in disputes between rival football supporters or indeed in any other ways by people with real or imagined grievances will of necessity lead to an immediate custodial sentence of some length.

Another youth arrested after being found carrying four of the devices pleaded guilty to possessing explosive substances with intent to endanger life. He was sentenced to 18 months' custody in March 1987.

2. The two Blades were never 'found' by the Owls. Two years after the event one of the two was cornered in a pub by one of the Trio, but 'talked his way out' of this hostile situation by claiming complete innocence.

3. Such calling cards were not only meant to be informative but to be menacing, and had been used for more violent ends than football hooliganism. During the Vietnam War, US helicopters dropped leaflets on Viet Cong areas that read 'Congratulations, you have been killed courtesy of the 361st. Yours truly Pink Panther 20' (Knightley 1975: 387). Closer to home, cards bearing the message 'The Boys are Back in Town – 40 Commando Royal Marines' were scattered around the Irish Republican stronghold of South Armagh by British soldiers (*The Guardian*, 22 March 1988).

4. The footage of this incident was given to a regional TV news programme by police. Shown twice in 1996 the highlights gave no indication of the precedence to the foyer fracas nor offered any greater analysis than to permit police to state how awful the 'BBC' was.

5. The same Judge achieved national notoriety the previous year when jailing a 24-year-old 'graffiti artist' for five years for criminal damage. Provoking both strong sympathy and condemnation from different quarters, this South Yorkshire man was the subject of various editorials in *The Star* and dozens of letters to the editor, both condemning and supporting the sentence. Owing to the agitation of a pressure group, the young man was released and his sentence reviewed. In a speech to students at the University of Sheffield in 1996 the judge blamed the early release on the protestations of 'trendy lefties'.

6. In July 1993 The Locarno management sought the renewal of its entertainment licence; the police objected, citing 'disorder and drugs' in a letter to the Licensing Justice. Furthermore, they wrote, *'the doormen are reluctant to cooperate with police'* and the Management were not taking *'firm control'* but delegating the day-to-day running of the club to door agencies (*The Star*, 22 July 1993). The Licensing Panel extended the licence, but only for two months. When the next application went through the Courts *The Star* reported how the police had searched the premises and found *'baseball bats, wood scaffold poles, and snooker cues behind the reception desk'* (26 October). Four months later journalist Michael Land described the club as a *'haven for football thugs, hooligans and drug use'* and wrote that *'a man sustained serious injuries in a football thug brawl'* and a passing bus had its windscreen smashed and a club bouncer was arrested. Other events recorded were that the club manager (aged 34) was attacked by two masked men after the club closed and that armed police accidentally shot one of the club's cigarette machines following up a report of an armed raider (*The Star*, 28 November). The club's licence was not renewed, but a new management reopened the club the next month and attempted to attract a more student-oriented clientele.

Part II

Fighting the Hooligan:
The City Fathers

The hooligan was no one's friend; he faced prosecution assisted by police and media constructs that sought to personify him as an embodiment of the most violent and reviled of public phenomena. In any court of law an issue as well as a defendant was in the dock. In the case of hooliganism the issue was always public morality and its control. The hostility against the hooligan was both personal and collective: a main purpose of the Court is to take a single action and persuade us that it is an enduring characteristic of the actor. In 1991, the concept of a 'proper' response to Blade (and Owl) behaviour was promoted in *The Star* (10 May 1991 and 22 November 1991). An advertisement suggested to readers that they should apply to become magistrates, while at the same time asking if various activities angered them. Hooliganism was one of the categories listed; so that it might be argued that the imposition of the law and sentencing of Blades was reliant on the emotion of anger and the explicit principle of exacting vengeance. We should therefore first look to those circumstances surrounding the events so far described and others which preceeded them that in the absence of first-hand experience presented a particular type of account to an unknowing audience, and then to the way in which fans were made subject to official and unofficial police action.

In the words of Smith (1993) no landscape is innocent; scrutiny will reveal the intervention of various authorities, and their implicit link to wider social relations. Put another way, the history of space is also the history of power (Foucault 1980) and, when football grounds and city centres are examined, one sees how the powerful aim to deter those who would indulge in disorder by instilling in them the certainty of detection, backed up with a regime of punishment. This is nothing new; moral regulation of the carnivalesque is as old as the British police (Storch 1976; Cohen 1979; Brogden 1982) and in their behaviour, dismissed as irrational and pathological, the football hooligan, an icon of working-class masculine mores, has become the contemporary enemy of rational recreation. As Cunningham (1980: 91) noted, such an enemy in the past was not idleness or 'aristocratic dissipation', but popular culture and its accompanying emphasis on 'drink, on spontaneity, on emotional involvement, on physical contact'. The 'enemy' remains the same today. The police would respond in their time-honoured manner by stressing their prudential and pastoral role. The contest would be publicised, politicised and polemicised.

Chapter 4

Media Accounts: Impartiality and the BBC

What is 'Truth? said jesting Pilot, and would not stay for an answer

(Francis Bacon 1985 [1625]: 61)

Information about football hooliganism in Sheffield came from the city's two daily newspapers. In 1986, the more serious, business-oriented *Morning Telegraph* ceased publication, leaving the city with the more 'popular' parochialism of *The Star*.[1] This paper, published six evenings a week and with a circulation of around 100,000[2], also produces the Saturday evening sports paper, *The Green 'Un*, devoted to local football and sport. Ironically, one of the earliest 'factual' information reports came not from this local source but from a national tabloid in 1973. So prolific were football hooligan confrontations in the City during the 1970s that Sheffield United topped a *Sunday Mirror* 'League Table of Shame' (4 May) arrest figures league, with 276, Wednesday coming third, with 258. Readers of the tabloid would believe incidents of large-scale disorder were happening at Bramall Lane, and they would be right. Locally, however, the media, although headlining the issue, did not emphasise the violence of the conflicts so much as the degree of *disorder* encapsulated around football hooliganism.

The Extent of 'Hooliganism': Local Sources and Knowledge

Historically various police officers were always allowed to give an opinion on the topic at the behest of journalists. The most authoritative documentary evidence for decades has been the *Annual Reports* of the South Yorkshire Constabulary. To judge from this source, taken in isolation, the issue has not been considered too serious, for there have been relatively few references to it across the 30 years 1966–1996. The first mention came in 1968, when the Chief Constable merely made the observation that: *'The year has brought another disconcerting social trend to the area, that of open public disorder with hooliganism at and around football.'*

The following year, the Chief Constable noticed an improvement: *'A pleasing aspect of the year has been the reduction of incidents involving hooliganism at both football grounds in Sheffield. The provision of extra police personnel in the vicinity of the grounds and in the city centre following matches brought about a considerable improvement in behaviour and resulted in the prevention of wilful damage and nuisance.'* The 'improvement' continued over the next few years: *'It is pleasing to report the improved behaviour of football supporters throughout 1971 . . . there were no offences of wilful damage and nuisance on the scale of those experienced two seasons ago.'*

This 1972 *Report* further noted, in relation to football, a *'marked decrease in the number of incidents of violence and disorderly behaviour during the year'*. Stranger still is the fact that, despite mass brawls at both Bramall Lane and Hillsborough between 1973–80 and high-profile media coverage of events, there was no mention *whatsoever* of these disturbances in the Chief Constable's *Reports* of those years. The next mention came *nine* years later in 1981. Then, the Chief Constable reported, not the violence of fans, but the disorder and logistics problems they created, which implied a serious problem in relation to his establishment:

> *I doubt if the Football League's programme would be sustainable without the commitment of large units of police manpower to certain matches. That commitment is not just to prevent disorder in the football stadiums, but to patrol nearby areas to ensure that the local residents and business people can live or ply their trade without being molested by chanting and often drunken 'invading' supporters. The police service is not organised to hold large number of officers as a permanent reserve to deal with public disorder. The reserve which is created must come from the man on the beat. The more frequently we are called upon to deal with incidents such as the city-centre problems, and unruly spectators en route to football matches, the less time officers will spend patrolling residential estates.*

One implication might be said to be that hooligans were a problem because they deflected the police from their 'proper' task. No further report singled out specifically football hooliganism for special mention. From 1981 the *Reports* always contained a brief section on football, but very little comment amidst the arrest statistics presented.

Unfortunately for analysis, police-compiled sources did not always tally. In Sheffield in the late 1980s, according to figures compiled by the ACPO Chair of the Football Hooligan Committee, there were 90 arrests from total attendances of 395,519 at Hillsborough, and 60 arrests from 223,960 spectators at Bramall Lane in the 1987/8 season. These figures are very different from those publicised in *The Star* (17 November 1988), which, though not revealing the source, presumably came from the Sheffield police:

	1986/7	1987/8
Sheffield United arrests:		
In the Ground	40	50
Outside the Ground	10	24
Sheffield Wednesday Arrests:		
In the Ground	122	105
Outside the Ground	38	21

Just to add to the confusion a reader could cite arrest figures produced for the Football Trust, which partly funded the policing costs of football matches and showed the following:

	Year	Arrest	Ejections
United	1986/7	53	41
	1987/8	60	52
	1988/9	50	98
	1989/90	97	196
	1990/1	91	177
	1991/2	95	48
Wednesday	1986/7	101	98
	1987/8	90	62
	1988/9	80	172
	1989/90	80	172
	1990/1	64	80
	1991/2	159	88

So, what do the above figures tell us? A possible interpretation suggests that at Bramall Lane hooliganism had declined to almost nothing (50 arrests) by 1989, after a rise by one-fifth in 1987/8 (60 arrests) over the previous season. At Hillsborough hooliganism in 1989 was similarly declining (80 arrests) compared to the two previous seasons (101 and 90 arrests). And then we could argue that in 1991/2 the 95 arrests at Bramall Lane and 159 at Hillsborough suggest the 'bad old days were back' or whatever cliché came to hand. The figures provide us with nothing to base an argument on because we have no idea who was subsequently charged, or what charge they faced, or even the circumstances of the arrest.

One way of measuring the extent of hooliganism in Sheffield might be to look at police arrest statistics as specified in the same *Reports*:

Season	Arrests	Attendances
1983/4	750	Crowd increase from 201,000 to 1.4 million
1984/5	863	
1985/6	693	From attendances of 1.189 million
1987/8	710	From attendances of 1.192 million

As is evident, however, such figures are vague, for they provide no breakdown among the five South Yorkshire grounds, nor the number of visiting fans, nor *any* circumstances of arrest. If the proportions of arrests to attendances are taken at face value, one could argue from the 1986 *Report* that the phenomenon was 'growing'. Conversely, it is 'declining' if we looked at the absolute figures compared to those of previous seasons. The 1988 *Report* suggests a 'growth' in the problem, but the percentage arrested was still no larger than in the previous season. In a nutshell, it would be naive to base any argument on any such source, and this does present us with a phenomonological problem: namely, not only do we not know the extent of hooliganism, but we also do not know whether it is growing or receding.

Local Media and Local State 1966–1977

Football hooligans are believed to be appallingly violent. That said, early manifestations of the phenomenon did not worry the local press or fellow fans too much. In response to the earliest Blade outbreaks on the terraces at Bramall Lane, older 'respectable' fans declared to the local press their willingness to identify and report miscreants. This report was instigated by concerned fans, and journalists then took up the initiative with the first local 'special' hooligan report in *The Star*, appearing in April 1967. Journalist Len Doherty reported incidents of disorder and damage without sensationalism or condemnation; but later there was a shift in reporting, and from April 1972 until the end of the year *The Star* regularly encouraged the disapproval of the football hooligan by making various related issues front-page news.

The media evidence presented around football hooliganism in the late 1960s strikes a contemporary reader as almost quaint. In 1968 *The Star* reported the unlikely scenario of 200 Blades, *'hands linked'*, running through a city-centre subway trampling flower-beds and knocking two pedestrians over (30 September). The following month a small unsensational article reported that forty windows had been broken near the Bramall Lane ground. The damage was blamed on United fans, but no indication of the circumstances was given. Earlier in February 1967, *The Star* reported that on the evening before the United–Wednesday match at Bramall Lane, Wednesday fans had painted slogans on walls outside, and called this *'One of the worst incidents of pre-Derby match hysteria the Bramall Lane ground had ever known'*. In April the following year, *The Star* reported gangs of Blades and Owls youths had fought and chased one another and trampled on flower-beds outside the Town Hall after a match. Then in September a youth was arrested for leading a large group of United fans through an area in the city centre called The Moor while singing, waving a bottle and looking for Owl fans. The following month *The Star* told of trouble after a Wednesday–United match at Hillsborough, caused by 500 youths running down a street.

Let us look at what was happening that was newsworthy. Disorder *did* occur on a large scale, and in April 1972 fights in and around Bramall Lane between United and Newcastle fans resulted in 54 arrests. Days later, 30 arrests were made during and after a match against Manchester United. Missiles had been exchanged across rival factions on the kop and local shops and homes had had windows smashed. For the moment, such incidents were only back-page, and amazingly the same fans were even praised by police following this day of disorder for their *good* behaviour! (4 April). Two days later front-page headlines described rivals at the same match exchanging missiles such as bottles, golf balls, stones and bricks; and this was true, for I was there. Months later matters were much the same, and the first week of the 1972/3 season illustrated the scale of the disorder. The headline '18 Sheffield Soccer Rowdies fined £990' detailed how, at a match two days previously between United and Newcastle, these 18 were part of a total of 83 fans arrested. A further 54 miscreants were reported in court next day. Weeks later, the visit of Chelsea produced 41 arrests. Then two weeks later again (2 October) front-page headlines reported 68 arrested in an account of fights between Sheffield and Manchester United fans, and quoted the United chairman as asking Magistrates to 'hammer' the troublemakers. The stark facts are that in three matches at Bramall Lane a total of 192 fans had been arrested at a time when police were fewer in number both inside and outside the ground than they were a decade later. Nor did they have the assistance of segregation measures, surveillance techniques and special public order police squads. Despite all this, the reporting was not particularly hysterical; rather it was factual and moderate, and the police and political responses reported did not seem to be particularly perturbed.

Many hooligans read such reports, but they had no deterrent effect whatsoever, because things were no better in 1974. A match between United and Manchester United in March resulting in 48 arrests, with fights in the ground and damage to city-centre shops requiring a specially-convened court to deal with the accused. When the same Manchester fans visited Hillsborough in December, 113 arrests were made (30 were juveniles), 60 people were reported injured, and 11 needed hospital treatment, although the most serious case was of a broken jaw. The match was even delayed following a pitch invasion. One hundred police on ground duty had to be supplemented by 80 reinforcements to control elements of the 35,000 crowd. Once again the local press began to set the agenda: the following day *The Star*'s editorial called for fences to be built around the ground and identity cards to be issued to all supporters. Still, the issue did not go away, and by 1976, 350 police officers were on duty for the 'all-ticket' Sheffield United–Manchester United match in August, the highest number ever for a football match in the city. They did not contain fights in or outside the ground.

However, the issue and the response were gaining a momentum that was to become the norm. In February 1976 front-page headlines in *The Star* told of '*Vandals on Rampage at Blades Ground*' and of how four turnstile doors were opened and slogans painted on the wall of the ground by four youths one Friday night (7 February). This was hardly a rampage, but was sufficient to add to the growing moral panic.

Petitions, Politicians and Pontificators: 1977–1979

Local public opinion manifested itself in neighbourhood activism against the football hooligan in 1977. A symbiotic relationship between local fears and the media need for a story saw *The Star* articulate the circumstances and fear and demands of these people and the events they were a response to. In March, front-page headlines such as '*Streets Besieged in Fans' Battle of Bramall Lane*' described after-match fights between Blades and visiting Nottingham Forest fans. Two policemen needed hospital treatment – one after being hit by a brick – and a Blade sustained a broken jaw. Nine arrests were made, and windows of nearby houses were broken. A local vicar organised a residents' petition presented to and, in turn, signed and presented by local councillors to the Council and Club. Signed by seven hundred, it demanded a month-long closure of the ground after every major act of hooliganism, more police protection, and compensation from the Club for damaged property (6 April). The following day news came of another petition, signed by 1,400 Hillsborough residents fearful of the impending visit of the then notorious 'Red Army' hooligans from among the 25,000 Manchester United fans expected at an FA Cup Semi-Final versus Leeds, who had similarly notorious supporters. The media, playing the role of anticipators, informed their readership how local shops were boarding their windows and that most pubs both in the area and in the city centre were not opening.

National politicians were brought into this local issue. The then Minister of Defence and Sheffield Labour MP, Fred Mulley, told a resident in a letter he made public that he would visit the next match at Bramall Lane and discuss matters with Ministerial colleagues (cf. *The Star*, 21, 25, 31 March 1977). Another Sheffield Labour MP, Martin Flannery, MP for Hillsborough, asked the Home Secretary what could be done to alleviate the *'sheer terrorism which is part of the football scene'*. The City's transport staff decided to boycott the route to Hillsborough, fearing that they themselves were in 'grave danger'. In the Hillsborough ground, a three-metre-high fence was erected in front of all of all terracing, only to be pulled down by Liverpool fans in the disaster of April 1989. A full-page article in *The Star* (21 April) described the fear of local residents and of nervous young housewives on Librium because of fear of attack.

Such anticipation needed a climax, and the match-day produced an emotive front-page headline, 'Cup Invaders Put Hillsboro' Under Siege', together with a photograph of young fans under police escort from their transport to the match. The Monday edition had the story it needed and wanted, with a front-page report compiled by *five* journalists describing how the day produced two Manchester fans stabbed by 'Sheffield youths' in the city centre, 93 arrests (70 for being drunk and disorderly and 23 for possession of offensive weapons, assault, theft, or using forged tickets). Thirty windows were reportedly broken around the ground and hundreds were involved in running fights. That said, no further details of the woundings were available, nor was there any discussion of the possibility that police pro-active tactics had been responsible for the arrests. What was more newsworthy was that local residents had asked for other semi-finals to be played elsewhere, and that the local Police Federation had called for a ban on Leeds and Manchester fans coming to Sheffield (26 April). A copy of the petition was sent to the Football Association, and they responded in August with an apology.

After all this, local councillors and local police came together to discuss an issue that by now had become politically and financially sensitive. The following month, the City Council Police Committee debated whether *ex gratia* payments could be made to residents whose property was damaged as a result of this match. The question they had to decide was whether 21 residents' claims, totalling £387, could be compensated under the 1886 Riot (Damages) Act. They voted against it. The issue was then debated by the

Labour and Conservative group and the Magistrates' Committee; again they decided locals could not be compensated. The full debate was never publicised or reported on; but the issue was serious, for had the claims succeeded the police would have had to admit that there was a 'riot' they could not control. Had they done so, the local Council would have faced a bill, possibly of thousands of pounds. There were no further details of the debate, just the fact that they had decided there had not been a riot, however much the media hyped the story. No riot had taken place – and that was official!

The recommendations of a group consisting of city councillors, local residents, police, and football administrators were then publicised in *The Star* (29 September). These, it was said, sought: legislation that would allow them to ban any sporting event in the county that they believed might lead to violence, stiffer sentences for hooliganism, and for talks to begin between the Council, licensees and magistrates with a view to banning the sale of alcohol on certain match-days. The concerned parties were not united, however; and on the next day United's Secretary accused the Council of being rude for not consulting them! The Chairman of the Working Party replied that the Club would be brought into discussions at the next stage; but if there was any further stage, then it took place without media publicity, for nothing more was heard of the group.

For the next two years hooliganism barely merited a mention in the local press bar the procedure of listing the names, ages and addresses of those facing charges in the courts. Seemingly, in this period, September 1977– May 1979, both local papers lost interest and police sources did not want the issue publicised. Certainly, there was a reduction in disturbances in the football ground that was clearly due to structural changes and police tactics; but there was still disorder before and after matches on the streets.

The 1980s: Confusion and New Clichés

The new decade provided a new genre of media accounts of football hooliganism. Gone was the combination of the descriptive account of events with the names and addresses of the arrested participants after their court appearances. In their place came dichotomous reports and enquiries into the changing manifestations of football hooliganism. On the one side were the intermittent informed academic accounts of the perspectives and styles of young fans. On the other were the reports of police and media, which apparently reciprocally inflated each other's conjectures on the sinister forces and individuals behind hooliganism. This transition to a more pathologically-oriented analysis did not, of course, occur overnight; but it left residues of confused and contradictory accounts about the scale and significance of the phenomenon and the identities of the hooligans. What will concern us below is how the increasing dominance of a hysterical coverage of local hooliganism further disorientated the city fathers charged with maintaining public tranquillity.

The more one reads the more one could be confused as to the nature of the beast. A 1980s reader could compile a confusing impression of Blades from various *national* media sources. The *Sunday Times* in September 1983 described football hooligan scenes in Sheffield and elsewhere, with one ex-hooligan of United quoted saying he left the scene when *'they began using petrol bombs'*. Other sources accorded United fans the title of very well-behaved fans, and in 1984/5 they were the winners in a 'Top of the Kops' competition organised by the *Daily Star* national tabloid. In 1991/2 United followers were the *Sunday People*'s best-behaved supporters, and a trophy and £1,000 were given to the Supporters Club. Yet in the month following the first award 'Blades' were listed as one of the top ten hooligan groups in England and Wales by the broadsheet Sunday newspaper, *The Observer* (12 June 1985), and the publicity given to Blades in the local media in 1991/2 belied any notion of their being the country's best-behaved supporters. The question, then – how can fans be both well-behaved and notorious hooligans? – is easily answered: it all depends on which newspaper one reads!

Closer to home, various commentators disagreed not only about the behaviour of Blades but about their numbers. In 1983 the United Chairman, Reg Brealey, in a local radio debate, considered they *'had a dozen'* who would *'make a mess of things'* (Radio Hallam, 22 November 1983). The following year local police, in the person of a Superintendent Sumner, could tell *The Star* of United's *'500 troublemakers'* who were *'highly organised'* (19 November 1984). On the same day, in the city *Morning Telegraph*, a police super-intendent called them one of the worst sets of supporters in the country, following a day of football hooligan incidents: he did have something to be concerned about. My own experience of the day started off, following a four-year pattern, by meeting with two hundred other Blades at a city-centre pub. On three occasions before 1.00 p.m., expectant Blades had chased Manchester invaders away through the city centre. Later a hundred Blades walking close to the ground confronted fifty rivals before being chased away by police. An hour later a dozen fought thirty visitors outside a pub. Blade reinforcements continued the fight using missiles obtained from roadworks. After the game scuffles broke out and two visitors' cars were overturned, one with five youths in it, causing one to receive treatment for a leg injury Two policemen with drawn truncheons who tried to clear Blades from surrounding streets were themselves chased the length of the street by a hundred Blades (Blades were more surprised than anyone!). They were rescued by colleagues both mounted and on foot who, with truncheons drawn, then 'ran' the Blades! There had been mass chasing in the High Street, cars overturned, and policemen getting 'run' by Blades shouting *'Kill the Bill!'* Something had to be done.

One of the things done was the production of a special report. And as fans continued to confront each other, so politicians realised the futility of just condemning, and decided to consider other forms of prevention. The Deputy Chairman of South Yorkshire County Council, Trustee of the national funder of anti-hooligan measures, the Football Trust, and Vice-Chairman of the Yorkshire and Humberside Regional Sports Committee, co-authored a 1984 report titled *Football Violence: The Metropolitan Viewpoint* (published by the Association of Metropolitan Authorities). This recommended councils' 'targeting' the communities that produce the hooligan, repeating in this the calls of the fashionable football sociologists of the day. Which parts the authorities would target in Sheffield or South Yorkshire was not specified; and the idea also prompts a question as to what this 'targeting' would involve. At all events, regardless of the report, no scheme ever 'targeted' Sheffield hooligans, and Blades and Owls continued their ways.

Political rhetoric was forgotten until the next major publicity occurred a year later, following a fixture that provided opportunities for political posturing as well as a chance to show how the media could construct stories. To give *The Star* its due, there was a story to report, for the day *did* have potential for large-scale disorder, and violence was anticipated in revenge for events at Leeds six months earlier, when Blades had taken the fight to their Yorkshire rivals. The participants were to be numbered in the hundreds, and four hundred Blades met in pubs in expectation of their Leeds equivalents' arrival before the match (see Armstrong 1994). As they 'patrolled' Sheffield for four hours, police sealed off the city centre to visitors by controlling all transport routes. What disorder there was initially occurred in the ground during the match. United took a 1–0 lead, and Leeds fans began breaking seats and throwing them on to the pitch. Blades replied, throwing seats (and one crush barrier) over the fence to show their willingness to compete in the same scenario. One policeman was helped away after being struck by one such missile. Elsewhere, in the stand one Blade fired a nautical distress flare at a group of Leeds fans. The dangerous magnesium-generated device hit the roof of the stand and landed harmlessly amongst other spectators. The game was played in a hostile atmosphere, with police drawing truncheons. Twenty strong, they charged the Leeds fans as they pulled in unison at perimeter fencing, threatening to pull it down and all the while trying to avoid blows to their fingers from police truncheons. After the match three hundred rivals clashed in a one-minute running fight a quarter of a mile from the ground. The events were the most extensive acts of football hooliganism in the city in the 1980s, and resulted in 34 arrests, but no reported injuries. In fact, there were none around the game involving rival fans.[3]

After the Leeds match, local politicians and police got together and agreed to 'smash' the hooligans. The Deputy Chairman of the South Yorkshire Police Authority, Brian Flannigan, stated he would meet the chairmen of all the county's clubs *'to stamp out this terror once and for all'* (*The Star*, 29 March 1985). The following day readers learned that a new Council Sub-Committee with *'strong spending powers'* was to be formed to give the police as much help as possible in smashing the folk devils of the 1980s *'drug pushers and soccer rioters'*. In August the same year *The Star* reported a 'crisis meeting' on football hooliganism between senior police chiefs and council officers. The Police Authority Chair, George Moore, described the meeting as *'extremely productive and fruitful'*, adding that they had examined plans to break up large groups of fans by using stadium enclosures, and to make some matches all-ticket. They had also discussed the possibility of installing closed circuit television surveillance in the ground. This was the last the public were to hear via the media of any local political debate on the issue of football hooliganism.[4]

Safety Valves: Labour Reconsidering

Not all politicians were in concert with the police vision of events. Joe Ashton, a Sheffield-born Labour MP (and Director of Sheffield Wednesday) has had a chequered and confusing career in relation to his pronouncements on the subject. As far back as 1973 he suggested his own method of solving the hooligan problem. Thus, *The Star* (16 November) reported his argument *'We need some bobbies with truncheons to deal with the lunatics on the Kop.'*

Yet in the period now under discussion he was one of the few political voices of dissent. As a member of the House of Commons Select Committee on the Policing of Football Hooliganism, he took a large part in the Commons debate on the Football Spectators Bill in October 1989. Addressing the House, he explained that every society needed an outlet for violence, and that if football did not exist something similar would have to be invented to replace it. His logic was that chanting and *'harmless behaviour'* at matches prevents crime. The reason the USA has a terrible crime problem was, he asserted on who knows what evidential basis *'the absence of a collective sports outlet'*. Offering, in effect, a neo-Marxist analysis, Mr Ashton explained that societies required an *'opium for the people'*, particularly the masses, the young unemployed or those in monotonous work. And, he suggested, whilst they have football to *'believe in'* they would not turn to *'the IRA, drug peddling, muggings, or armed robbery and everything else they had in America'*. Arguing he was *'not defending the hooligans'*, he said *'there would be much more hooliganism if football did not exist'*. To support this, he cited Britain's small towns, which see fights when pubs close, and *'lager-lout areas where there is no football team to provide a safety valve'*. Taking a socio-historical approach tinged with autobiography, Mr Ashton then recalled his time of National Service, but of course pointed out that neither this nor wars exist any more. What does remain, he said, was a surplus energy in 18–20-year-old males, who, by linking arms on the Spion Kop at the match and singing, could *'get rid of that tribalism . . .* [as] *a very good and necessary safety valve'*. Mr Ashton confessed to having been *'involved – innocently – in punch-ups in the past'*, but hastily added that *'hooligans must be eradicated'*. In pursuit of this aim, he went on to praise the funding by the Football Trust of the video cameras used to survey and arrest fans (*Hansard*, 30 October 1989: 123–6). And although his speech was reported in a small article in *The Star*, significantly no editorial comment was made and no headline was given to it.

Elsewhere, a post-Hillsborough realism temporarily infected local political thinking on football hooliganism. In 1989 this influenced local politicians to use a language and voice criticisms they had not dared to in previous years. Thus the Labour MP, David Blunkett, addressing the House of Commons, demanded a change in police attitudes towards football fans. Another MP for the city, Pat Duffy, spoke of football's *'structure, greed and psyche and its contempt for ordinary working-class lads'* (*The Star*, 18 April). A few weeks after the Hillsborough disaster, football hooliganism and Blades were back in the media. The final Saturday of the football season produced a few fights, one of which involved Blades, and alongside half a dozen others made national TV news headlines. Blades in the seats spilled on to the pitch towards the end of their match at Bristol, and spectators witnessed *'Nuns'* and *'hippies'* (it was promotion day fancy dress carnival) chasing rivals before the police controlled matters. Later in the day a small group of the two hundred Blades and United followers staying in a seaside resort got into a minor scuffle that resulted in 27 arrests (one mini-van containing 15 Blades was detained) and the event was described in the House of Commons by Tory MP David Evans and in many national newspapers as '*a riot*'. On Monday David Blunkett, quoted in *The Star*, called them a disgrace to their club, their families and the City. On the way to the courts on Monday morning, the local media were out in force recording the fans' entry. All pleaded not guilty to the blanket charge of unlawful violence, and all charges were dismissed. No media recorded their acquittal.

Inventing Enemies

Incidents that did not involve Blades could, if there was a football connection, be made to involve Blades by the media and police without supporting evidence. In April 1986, fifty Millwall supporters stopped in Sheffield on their way home from Leeds. One was taken to hospital unconscious at midnight after a city-centre fracas misadventure, and died five days later. *The Star* (4 April) reported the incident as arising out of a '*violent flare-up*' between Millwall and Sheffield United fans. Later *The Star* reported the man's injuries had been sustained following '*clashes between rival gangs of youths*' (7 April), i.e., no longer explicitly football fans. Blades dismissed the report, for they knew nothing about it. A month later, however, *The Star*'s back-page headline screamed 'Blades Lives in Danger – Police' (3 May). This described Scotland Yard's fears that United players' lives could be at risk, since Millwall fans '*were believed to be intending to avenge the death last month of a supporter who died in Sheffield – by ambushing the Blades' team coach*'. The team and supporters were advised to travel on a specified route to the match at Crystal Palace in South-East London, six miles from Millwall, who were at home on the same day. Blades thought the possibility of an attack remotely plausible, but had no plans to cope with such a situation. The Metropolitan Police took the 'threat' seriously, and escorted all coaches to and from the ground and stationed two transit vans of officers at both Charing Cross and London Bridge stations from 1.30 p.m. to 5.30 p.m., with instructions to look out for a planned confrontation between Millwall fans and the Blades. Not a single Millwall fan was seen by Blades or police.

This did not end the more fanciful media invention inspired by actual football-related violence. In November, twelve Millwall fans travelled to Sheffield after their game in the Midlands. After drinking in one district, they had driven to another near to the motorway and became involved in a large-scale fight. The evening was initially friendly, with the Londoners mixing amicably until one pulled a knife on a 17-year-old local in a pub toilet and demanded money. Soon sixty youths became involved in an affray, and seventeen were arrested (including all twelve visiting fans), although no one was seriously injured. No Blade was involved. Reporting the incident two days later, *The Star* recounted the death of the fan in April, adding, without evidence, that *'since the incident, Millwall fans are known to have made threats against Sheffield United and Wednesday supporters'*. Of course, the source of these claims was not given, and although I searched for months for any evidence of this, I am certain that neither Blades nor the Owls knew of *any* such threats. After a court case in February 1987, *The Star* reported the prosecution evidence, that the twelve were on a *'vendetta visit seeking a clash with Blade supporters'*. Nine Millwall fans and two Sheffielders were jailed for three months on a charge of threatening behaviour. One Londoner also received a two-year sentence for robbery. At the next fixture at Millwall in March 1987, Blades expected Millwall fans to seek to 'avenge' both the death and their fellow supporters' gaol sentences. That said, Blades did not propose or prepare anything, and neither did they find Millwall fans waiting. In fact nothing happened! Thus it seems that, contrary to a year of press reports, not one Blade had struck one Millwall fan or vice versa, and the construction of violent rivalry by the press and police was seemingly without supporting evidence.

Reporting of Intra-Sheffield Hooliganism 1986–1989

A series of fights around pubs in the city centre between Blades and Owls in 1986 provoked a response from the Chief Constable, who said he was *'angry and worried'* and wanted to *'stamp out this terror once and for all'* (*The Star*, 29 March 1986). The factions fought on regardless until May 1986. After a quiet summer, hostilities resumed with the football season in September 1986. However, it was not until some eighteen months later that police announced measures to mount what a front-page report in *The Star* headlined as a 'Crack Down on Drunken Thugs'; it described *'vicious clashes between Blades and Owls'* as a major reason for the disturbances (17 April 1988). Soon after, *The Star* publicised the formation of a six-strong, plain-clothes police squad to be located in problem pubs (8 May 1988).

Even so, Blades and Owls still regularly chased and fought each other, though their activities were not reported. This was, perhaps, because a football connection was not recognised when, for example, a pub fight between Owls and Blades was reported in *The Star*'s front page as an unrelated incident, *'Scores of drunken youths smashed glasses, tables, and chairs in a saloon-style brawl . . . 30 youths fought in the bar'*. The pub manager described how *'hundreds of customers jumped up on a balcony to escape the fight'*. There was still exaggeration, of course: having been present, I saw what really happened. Six Owls *were* in the pub, and around twenty-five Blades walked in. One Blade, wanting one of the Owls for a previous assault, challenged him to a fight and then attacked him. Two Owls then produced small baseball bats, and in the ensuing fight two Owls received head injuries. The only ones jumping over elevated areas were Owls and Blades, provoking twenty bystanders to take cover. A glass collector (someone employed to bring empties back to the bar) was struck by a glass thrown by a Blade, his arm wound needing twenty stitches (*The Star*, 20 February 1988). Although it had mistakes, the media account exhibited a minimum of hysteria.

A similar event happened in the following month. Twenty Blades out on a Friday night went into a city-centre pub. Shortly afterwards, fifteen Owls entered and a fight began that lasted two minutes. Missiles were thrown, windows were broken and one thrown glass stuck in a wall. An Owl, struck by a beer glass, received face wounds that required stitches, but this was not reported in *The Star* (7 May 1988). However, the report did tell of panicking customers *'trampled'*, and *'screaming women showered in broken glass'*. The pub manager described how a dozen youths had entered the pub and *'immediately attacked a group of customers'* in a fight that lasted 15 minutes and caused damage of £450. That same night, both plain-clothed and uniformed police had followed Blades, but were nowhere to be seen when the fight began. They arrived after the event, and must have later alerted the newspaper. Again the account was close, but not factual, for it overstressed the involvement of innocents. Similar incidents could always provide the necessary hyperbole. One made a front-page story, under the heading 'Havoc As Soccer Thugs Blitz Pub'. This occurred when Blades attacked Owls in a pub. Damage to the pub was estimated at £3,000 and four people (two innocent drinkers) needed treatment for flying glass (21 November 1988). Blades broke four windows and the factions exchanged missiles; and two bystanders were struck by broken glass. This time the article was brief and factual.

Six months later a special report on Blades appeared. The police seem to have furnished the reporter with most of the details and 'facts', and in May 1989 *The Star* published a photo of three police vans and half a dozen vague figures of the night outside a pub under the headline 'Just Another Saturday' and the sub-heading 'It's Fight Night for the Soccer Thugs'. Journalist Nigel Morris then gave readers a 'Diary of Shame', an itinerary of events, seemingly police-produced, that 'showed' that vicious pub brawls and fights between rival fans in the City were on the increase. The itinerary, at times, was factually wrong, for a fight in a city-centre pub described as being between West Bromwich and Owls fans was mistakenly reported.

The aggressors were not Owls, but, in fact, were Blades. When pressed by the media, there seemed little that those close at hand to the incidents could find to shock. The above fight (with West Brom fans) merely led to the visitors' being escorted to the station. There were no casualties and no complaints from the landlord. When asked, the landlord of another pub had no complaints against the Blades, despite an alleged 'fact' in the report that both he and his doorman had been recently locked out by '300 Blades thugs' and had sustained a 'wrecked pub'. What *had* happened on that particular night was that, at 9.00 p.m., a hundred and twenty Blades were inside enjoying a drink when the *police* suddenly closed the premises and demanded they all leave. Later, Blades gathered outside a pub near West Street, but were again moved on by police without incident. According to the same report, the previous week the 'Blades Barmy Army' (a *nom-de-plume* between 1979 and 1982!) apparently 'wrecked' a pub near West Street. The police allegedly ejected this group, but again there was no complaint from the landlord about the reported wreckage, mainly because there was none! The same night the paper tells us that another fearful landlady rang police on seeing 'youths massing'. And though it was true that police ejected Blades from her pub, the report, of course, fails to mention they had been very good customers for half an hour before fear overcame her profit motive.

Further on in the piece a police sergeant was allowed his say, positing that Blades and Owls were *'detestable thugs'* who were *'vicious but uncomplaining'*. This contention was based on the point that one Blade had made no complaint about a head would he had sustained, despite the fact that this needed stitches. Police tactics, the sergeant declared, were to visit pubs known to contain the groups and walk around looking at everyone: *'We do not intimidate. It is just a case of showing the thugs we mean business'* (12 May 1989). We might consider, even when cliché and condemnation is expected in such circumstances, whether there could be any other group in a large city such as Sheffield whom the police would feel free to use such language about, or to discuss with the press in this manner, without the fear of incurring a disciplinary offence of 'descreditable conduct' or some similar charge?

A few years later the Blades were allowed to state their case. In an unattributed article in March 1993, the Blades were described by a Bolton police superintendent as having been involved in an orchestrated attack on a Bolton pub. The account described how a pub had been *'wrecked'* after Blades goaded locals into a fight, having entered *'two well-known Bolton supporters' pubs'*. The truth was that seventy Blades returning from a match at Blackburn stopped off at Bolton. This was not a planned event, but a spontaneous decision, although they did then go in pursuit of Bolton lads who, a year previously, had entered a Sheffield pub *en route* home from a match at Rotherham, and a minor skirmish occurred. In Bolton, Blades entered the first pub they saw outside the station and asked where 'Bolton's lads' could be found. The reply was 'at a nearby pub'. Blades walked there and met resistance from twenty-five locals, many sporting skinhead hairstyles. A fight broke out and the two main windows of the pub were smashed by missiles thrown by Blades. Police arrived a minute later. Blades left the scene and boarded a train. Police who escorted them to the station were not too distraught about the events, telling the Blades that the pub was used by British National Party sympathisers and that the fact that it was damaged and its regulars frightened was no bad thing. There were no injuries and no Blade was arrested. A leading Blade phoned *The Star* telling the journalist of the attack, and giving an account that was deliberately journalistic and exaggerated, speaking of *'numerous injuries'*, and saying *'The pub looked like a bomb had hit it.'* On the other hand, the same Blade stressed that the 'BBC' had an *'unwritten code'* and were made out worse than they are, because, in truth: *'We don't go around hitting just anyone and we don't use weapons . . . we pride ourselves on our code of conduct and we class ourselves among the five top teams in the country.'* This was an interesting example of news-management and an isolated example in which those normally without a voice had a chance to represent themselves.

As might be expected, the police were always selective in the presentation of reality that they used, and in what they told the media about controlling the football hooligan. From my observations, police tactics changed with the month and the match. Sometimes they were seemingly low-key and almost uninterested; at other times they appeared to create arrests. Two matches played in the same year illustrate this: before one Wednesday–United fixture in April 1993, in a small article a few days before the event, *The Star* informed readers that police predicted a *'trouble-free match'*, which would, a superintendent declared, be *'treated like any other game'*; though he admitted they had a *'contingency plan'* to deal with any trouble (21 April). Six months later the police presented a new face. Under the heading 'Thugs face crackdown', reporter Paul Whitehouse informed readers of a police plan to 'get tough' on hooligans at the Sheffield derby at Bramall Lane the next day, when senior officers declared *'tearaways . . . [would be] increasingly likely to end up behind bars as police patrols deal firmly with any trouble'*. Furthermore, *'the yobs'* would be banned from Bramall Lane *'as police struggle to improve life for ordinary fans'*. Quoting the 'South Yorkshire Football Liaison Officer', he writes: *'It is a change of policy. They are not going to get moved on anymore. We have been, and are, taking steps to*

make sure they get their just desserts. It will continue until they are finished . . .
It will be done properly and above board, but if they don't stop on their own we
will make them.

What was not subsequently publicised was the dubious and controversial police tactics on this day. There was a small confrontation near the
ground between rival fans before the game. This was easily dealt with by
police, without a punch being thrown, and the match itself was trouble-
free. However, as around four hundred Blades made their way into the
city centre after the game, eight mounted police, along with police vehicles,
galloped and drove at the unsuspecting fans at the rear. This naturally
caused dozens to run away. However, four other mounted police at
the opposite end of the road prevented their escape. Meanwhile, plain-
clothes officers hiding in shops were directing events over personal radios.
Blades remonstrated with their assailants and for their temerity five
were arrested and charged with being 'drunk and disorderly'. Blades also
alleged later, that when a hundred of them appeared at a city-centre pub
they faced a wall of thirty officers, including four mounted police. Behind
these were three transit vans containing more officers, and as they
approached the pub they claim, police shouted and challenged them, calling
some by name and adding the insult 'wanker'. When Blades did not take
the bait, some officers seemingly began pushing them, and within a minute
four were arrested. Two were tripped by pursuing officers, who then asked
them *'Did you tell me to fuck off?'* The Blades again claimed that they had
not done so, but were still arrested and charged with being drunk and
disorderly. The day's events retold by police in a press release were
publicised in *The Star*, and a one-sided account became available through
the media.

Citing a court case in the Magistrates' Court that day, the article reported
prosecution evidence that told of sporadic disorder between 8.30 and 12.00
p.m. both in London Road and West Street between rival groups of fans.
This culminated at 10.00 p.m. in a fight outside a London Road pub that
allegedly made the street impassable for the general public. This was not
the case. The fact of the matter was that Blades and Owls had *not* been
involved in *any* sporadic disorder, and the 10.00 p.m. fight was nothing to
do with football or Blade–Owl antagonism. It occurred between two groups
of drinkers, and was the result of two men fighting over a long-standing
local family feud in which two Blades in a group of fifty got involved, being
friends of one of the factions. The Court that day witnessed some fascinating
procedures; for a start, only 21 of the 34 arrested were charged, and of those
charged, 14 were on the minor charge of breach of the peace. As for the
'"bloody" battle of London Road', with the road blocked surely there was

a good case for riot, affray or at least unlawful assembly; but no such charge was brought. The road was however blocked by police vehicles! A further three defendants were charged with being drunk and disorderly, one with threatening behaviour, one with violent disorder and two with assault on police. The latter accused were in their early thirties and had nothing to do with Blades. They were in the area when the trouble arose, and were in the pub when the fight began. Both resisted arrest. Finally, one youth running away without paying for a meal in a London Road restaurant was charged with breach of the peace, but became one of the match-day arrest figures. Thus football hooliganism was again redefined, and the phenomena now included the crime of 'not paying for onion bhajis'.

Notes

1. *The Star* has not been noted for accuracy or restraint. Front-page headlines following the fire at Valley Parade, Bradford, in 1985 blamed the tragedy on 'organised hooligans' from Bradford and Leeds. They had no evidence, and did not retract when the Government-appointed Popplewell Report (1986) concluded differently and ridiculed such a claim. In 1989, after the Hillsborough disaster, *The Star* was the first newspaper to give headlines (18 April) to police-concocted stories of Liverpool fans storming the gates in an organised attempt to gain illegal entry to Hillsborough and then stealing from and urinating upon their dead and attacking rescue workers. Even *The Sun* later apologised to its readers for running a similar story. *The Star* did not.
2. *The Star* had a circulation of over 160,000 in 1985. By 1994 this was down to 90,000 and what was once a broadsheet became a tabloid.
3. Other processes worth recording relate to the ability of police and press to construct a reality that was passed on to its mass readership, and of which the hooligan participants were ignorant. One such incident occurred in 1985, following the Leeds match just described, when out of the blue came a report that football fans had beaten up a pensioner. Four days after the match (27 March) a photograph of a 70-year-old man was accompanied by an article headed 'Soccer Thugs Hurt Former Head'. The former headmaster, readers learned, was *'knocked unconscious amidst . . . mindless violence'* after the match. His wife, allowed to explain her story, described rather differently how *'a group of youths bore down*

on them from the opposite direction and knocked them for six and trampled on him'. After informing readers that he had received the MBE for helping underprivileged children the piece ended by saying that the police were investigating the matter. A few months later the man died. And reporting his death *The Star* (27 September) made further reference to the supposed attack: *'Earlier this year he was knocked unconscious . . . when he was set upon by youths.'* An alternative reading of events could be that, after the match and anticipating trouble, groups of police were directing departing fans this way. As a result of this, tempers frayed, and a huge confused crowd built up. When Leeds fans began pouring out at the same time, rivals began exchanging insults. Fifteen police then drew truncheons and, followed by four mounted colleagues, charged the Sheffield fans. People naturally ran, and it was in this panic that the man was knocked over – in no way was it an attack. In fact, two Blades picked him up, and older supporters comforted him as he sat on a nearby wall. Meanwhile nearby police were furiously condemned by older fans for their inept tactical manoeuvring. Whilst the old man would not have been knocked over if fans had been locked in loving embraces, we need to ask if the journalist had checked his facts. However, it was a good story, with little chance of a contradictory reply, despite two Blades' sending factual accounts of the incident to *The Green 'Un*'s letters page.

4. This was a subject the police and politicians agreed on; other public order issues were fraught with problems. Previous public order funding had not always been made know to the local police committee. In 1979 *The Star* reported the existence of 'secret' police in the city 'revealing' that South Yorkshire had six squads of riot officers trained in riot control. This information came from a confidential document circulated by police to members of the Police Authority requesting more money to provide 70 riot shields for *'police support units in public order situations'*. The report said 50 shields had been bought the previous year, but the request had not mentioned any specifically trained squads. The Assistant Chief Constable explained the units had been in existence for ten years, and were there to support local police in a number of situations, adding: *'We use them at football matches for instance'*. No member of the police committee knew of the existence of such squads (*The Star*, 1 February).

Chapter 5

The Forces of (Public) Order

'duty at the local football match offers the action of a fight, you can, as one of the PCs put it, have a right "punch-up", it should be pretty good'

(Simon Holdaway (1983) *Inside the British Police*, p. 137)

In April 1989, Hillsborough Stadium became world notorious as the place where 89 Liverpool fans were crushed to death on the Leppings Lane terraces minutes after an FA Cup Semi-Final was underway. The subsequent enquiry, headed by Lord Justice Taylor, had to fend off the idea that somehow hooligans were to blame, and the disaster provoked Sheffield police to cover-up their responsibilities for events that occurred. The enquiry eventually recorded that a build-up of fans at the turnstyles meant that the kick-off should have been delayed. But this was not done, and the police panicked because of the crush of fans and ordered large gates to be opened. This allowed fans to spill into two pens which were already full to capacity. Senior police officers in the ground control tower 40 yards away with the benefit of sophisticated, expensive and much publicised closed-circuit TV surveillance, made a decision, requesting police dog units to stand in front of the eleven foot high fences to deter fans from moving onto the pitch. Some officers responded to fans' attempts to scale the fence and escape the crushing by striking their hands with truncheons. The subsequent report by Lord Justice Taylor did not mince words. His Interim Report (August 1989) was scathing of police tactics. The officer in charge *'froze'*, the tragedy arose out of a *'lack of leadership'*, and Senior officers were described as *'defensive and evasive'*. South Yorkshire Council's supervision of safety measures at the ground were described as *'inefficient and dilatory'*, and despite police-press propaganda concerning fans' inebriation and cabilistic movements Taylor found they were not to blame. The event which took fifteen minutes would make headline news for the next eight years. The Final *'Taylor Report'* in 1989 called for a change in policing attitude towards football fans, stating how police saw each match as a 'battle' to be won.

Meeting Force with Force

The response of police towards controlling and curtailing those perceived
as hooligans in Sheffield was often based on intimidation and violence.
Tactics in the early days told only of procedural steps taken in accordance
with Government directives. Thus, in 1969, the Chief Constable of Sheffield
announced that trouble around football matches had been reduced by
officers being strategically placed along approach roads to the ground to
stop vandalism and control mobs of up to 150 youths (*The Star*, 29 March).
What was never publicised was a police procedure in the 1970s whereby
miscreants were held against walls as beatings by police officers were
administered, often in full view of match-goers. Another tactic memorable
because of its brutality that was used at both Sheffield grounds consisted
of two PCs holding an offender's arms behind his back and 'running' him
down the terracing steps. Near to the perimeter wall he would be released,
offering him little or no time to throw his arms forward as protection. These
fans, led out with bloody faces and in a semi-conscious state, were a
sobering message to others. This tactic was no longer in use by the late
1970s, although beatings of those arrested in police stations or police
vehicles were often claimed. Another controversial local police tactic was
made public by Sheffield-born Labour MP Joe Ashton when, in a House of
Commons debate on crowd safety in 1974, the electorate learned that a
'popular penalty' for those arrested at Sheffield games was for police to drive
them out and dump them on the moors on the outskirts of the City. The
tactic was denied by two police superintendents in charge of the two city
grounds (*The Star*, 9 February), and this seemed to satisfy the journalists
and quell any call for a political inquiry. However, in local male circles it
was widely understood that this was a common practice.

An innocent public might well believe that no punishment was too harsh
for hooligans who sought violence against innocent fans; but the reality
was that across this era, on many occasions the only disturbance at Bramall
Lane was between visiting fans and the Sheffield police. Indeed, fans could
often be more sinned against than sin themselves, and could expect little
or no sympathy from the public. This was epitomised in April 1978 when
a police officer was fined £100 for assaulting a visiting fan. The supporter
was struck by a 21-year-old, 6'8" officer, and sustained a bloody nose. The
case received massive publicity, and the sum of the police officer's fine
was sent in by well-wishers. Blades of course knew, as good hooligans,
that the police had the task of preventing their activities, and that few
politicians were ever going to take their side in arguments with the law.

This understanding meant they were powerless and knew it, which limited their intentions in interactions with police.

From the late 1970s and throughout the 1980s and 1990s, Blades faced the specialist public order Tactical Support Groups, who were quick to arrive at scenes of disorder in transit vans, when their presence would always cause the combatants to scamper as it was claimed, if caught, they would inevitably face arrest or abuse or unofficial and unrecorded police punches, in a street-clearing exercise. This tactical 'sweeping' operation required that those who had gathered be chased and dispersed. The Blades knew this, and from the late 1970s to the late 1980s awaited its inevitability after many home games. Indeed, often it seemed that hundreds of other youths also anticipated and enjoyed the action it provided; and I suspect that many of the police enjoyed it too. In effect each episode became a form of choreography, where the performers tried actually and metaphorically to avoid tripping or standing on the toes of the other side and their contemporaries. Thus, when hundreds of youths were walking from the Bramall Lane ground after the game – usually along either Shoreham Street or Arundel Gate and after pretending to look for rivals – the arrival of mounted police cantering behind them and for some inexplicable reason often shouting threats, caused those at the back to run. This would create a 'domino effect', which, at times, saw a couple of hundred start running away. And this had an influence on other police; for those in vehicles, on seeing this surge, would drive at full speed to the front of the 'chase', alight from their vehicles, and confront the now decelerating mob with the application of pushes and punches. What might therefore appear to an onlooker as a mob with a specific intention and direction, was usually no more than a police-created panic. These ritualised scenarios were understood by both sides. The police cleared the streets around the ground. Blades at the same time had their bit of action to recount to mates later.

More importantly, the police having dogs and horses with few or no opportunities to use them, the match was a good opportunity to train them for the ever-expected serious disturbance. From the late 1960s, on match-days, Blades were also subjected to the public order specialist with four legs, and police Alsatians were occasionally unleashed and allowed to leap at fans. Blade garments have been torn by canine fangs, and twice in ten years Blade skin was pierced, causing minor injuries. As a deterrent their effect was immense, for they caused all Blades to cower in their presence. However, these beasts occasionally showed an impressive impartiality, and in 1993 I saw Blades cheer as one that was clearly out of control bit a police officer.

From the 1960s mounted police were always present, and always feared and disliked by Blades. From 1991 they were also present in the city centre on the eve of the local derby game, and all too often appeared to be used with total disregard for safety, whilst the large truncheons their riders carried were often used with unnecessary vigour on Blades. Their galloping tactics seemed to have only one aim – to clear the street. At times in the 1980s Bramall Lane saw fourteen mounted officers at home games; yet such a cavalry unit was unnecessary. After escorting visiting fans from railway stations and coach parks they presumably were in the ground in case of a pitch riot, but were never needed in this capacity in fifteen years (1980–94). A couple of times they trotted in front of the Bramall Lane End when uniformed colleagues were making arrests, and in effect were a visible and physical, if over-dramatic, deterrent.

Police construct 'sites of danger' (see Holdaway 1983: 39) and then arrive at such places forewarned and forearmed as to how to deal with situations. From the late 1980s police were able to demand that pubs close before and after games around the Bramall Lane ground. The assistance offered by Home Office Circular 68/1988, which reminded police that under the 1964 Licensing Act they could close licensed premises on 'high risk' match days in areas where serious disorder was expected, was supplemented by 'requests' for London Road and city-centre pubs not to open their doors until 7.00 p.m. on some Saturday evenings, to deny Blades a place to rendezvous. The most drastic of these actions occurred when United played Wednesday on a Sunday midday fixture in 1992. On this occasion senior police requested that all pubs within a two-mile radius of the ground remained closed. Police rationalised this policy as being a way of preventing possible trouble, but it simply annoyed regular drinkers and the pub landlords, who saw their pubs closed and their tills empty. Moreover, policing policy in regard to ordering pubs to close was never consistent, for onlookers would sometimes witness two pubs on London Road closing at 2.15 p.m. or 2.30 p.m. while, 50 yards away, others were still allowed to serve. Police policy was apparently aimed at those pubs where they believed the hooligans were, seemingly unaware that they could, if they chose, walk a few paces and drink elsewhere. It seems they were also unaware that some licensed premises always ignored such requests, so that there were pubs that were ostensibly closed on match day but were open via the back door for those in the know. Police impositions therefore displaced Blades but did not defeat their gatherings.[1] Across the research period it seemed that Blades were always in the 'wrong' place according to the police. Whether outside a pub or walking peacefully to the ground, they could be subjected to hostility from foot patrols, or from officers in vehicles or on horseback. Police vans would sometimes arrive and stop abruptly, with the drama heightened as officers piled out, slamming the doors. They would then approach, looking as mean as possible, and begin pushing the fans. If a Blade protested, the police would infer prior knowledge of violence, or an intent to cause trouble, and threaten or arrest some of the young men. And if this was protested at, then those who complained might later be denied entrance to the match, or be arrested at that location.

Paying the Bill

Until the 1980s there was little national co-ordination or central political attempt to regulate the cost and style of policing at football grounds. Each force decided how many officers would be needed to police a match, and the number was a matter for the Chief Constable. His power was embodied in the 1962 Royal Commission on Police, which stated: *'He is accountable to no one, and subject to no one's orders [for the way he] settles his general policies in regard to law enforcement and the concentration of resources, on the method of dealing with disorder'* (quoted in Northam 1989: 143).

In practice the numbers on duty and tactics used were generally a product of agreement between the Football Liaison Officer (Football Intelligence Officer in some forces) and the Senior Officer in command of match-day operations. The football club, as a private company offering paying customers entertainment, has a duty to ensure safety, and to this end the Local Authority license the ground, where stewards and police are in attendance to uphold the law and maintain the peace. The Audit Commission's evaluation of policing costs suggests there was no easy way of determining how the police charges were reached, for they differed around the country. Such costs are ratified by the Police Authority for the area under Section 15 of the 1964 Police Act, and rose (nationally) 11.5 per cent in 1987/8, 22 per cent in 1988/9 and 47 per cent in 1989/90 (this last figure representing a rise that was seven times the rate of inflation and eight times greater than police wage increases). In 1989/90 the national cost of policing football was put at £6.7 million, compared to £4.1 million in the previous year, and saw some 5,000 officers on duty each weekend in and around the various grounds. The cost was expected to rise to £7.5 million in the following year according to figures

released by the Football Trust, which paid £2.5 million of the bill. It was
this expense that caused the Sheffield United chairman to challenge the
legal position.

Capitalism, which Hall *et al.* (1978) and Taylor (1982) see as behind the
ploy that set up the fear of Hooliganism, was personified in the person of
Reg Brealey, the Sheffield United club chairman from 1981 to 1995. A multi-
millionaire and helicopter-owning director of 23 companies, this Tory-
supporting member of the Church of England Synod was a capitalist *par
excellence*. Yet he was never super-critical of Blade support, and was far
from being in league with policing philosophies. He alone of the football
club chairmen challenged the police right to decide how many officers
should be present at the matches. The club was in debt, yet had to foot a
very substantial police bill that they alone would decide upon. This meant
that the more police were present, the deeper into the red the club went.
Ironically, the police stance received strong support from local socialist
politicians – who might have been thought to be against the forces of an
oppressive legalistic machine. However, in this case I believe it was a
situation of Locals and Labour, versus an Outsider and a Tory – in this
instance it was an establishment figure who, for once, failed to exaggerate
the issues.

In late 1983 Brealey challenged South Yorkshire Police Authority's
legal right to charge for policing at football matches, arguing that since
the Club had not requested policing, no contract existed between them.
Besides, he argued, the issue was a public order matter, and therefore
policing should be free. He also claimed he could quote figures to show
that the costs in South Yorkshire were higher than anywhere else in the
country. In response, the police threatened to close Bramall Lane ground
if they considered it to be inadequately policed, and a game scheduled
for 30 January 1984 was under threat of having to be played behind
closed doors.[2] An impasse followed, and by June 1985 United were in debt
to the Police Authority to the tune of some £122,000. The matter went to
the High Court in February 1986, with Brealey telling how he proposed
employing a lone police spotter to watch for trouble. This officer would
alert others on stand-by outside the ground, and the club would only pay
for police called into the enclosure. This somewhat bizarre proposal had,
not surprisingly, been rejected. After a hearing lasting a week, Brealey lost
the case and the Club was ordered to pay £71,500 to the police for their
presence at the ground. The judge stated police duty at the match
constituted 'special police services' within the meaning of the 1964 Police

Act, and added *'if the police attend in order to enable the match to take place, then I consider a request to be implied'*. Brealey decided against an appeal to the House of Lords, and was left with a £400,000 debt to the Council and legal fees.

The early 1990s saw policing join the other social services that would come under Government scrutiny in its political thrust to cut public expenditure to the bone. And as policing football was costly to the public purse, it became just one more area that the monetarist thrust of politics identified as being ripe for action in relation to privatisation. In February 1991, South Yorkshire police announced that their overtime budget was to be reduced by 20 per cent, as part of an attempt to meet Government criteria for cut-backs. The Chief Constable and his Finance Officer, announcing the cut, spoke of a total overspend on their budget of some £200,000, part of which was a result of United's new status as a First Division team. A report sent to Divisional Commanders advised the 'utmost economy' in overtime use, because a shortfall of some £73,000 had occurred over the original estimate set for the year (*The Star*, 6 February 1991). Along with this, the police planned to classify all matches as 'duty time', when officers would get a re-rostered rest day in lieu of overtime payment. The political nature of such events saw local MP and Wednesday director Joe Ashton become involved, making the claim that police were rewarding themselves by choosing the times of kick-off.[3]

In May 1991 it was announced the cost of policing football in South Yorkshire was set to rise by 50 per cent on the previous season, with planned progressive changes over the next five years. This would mean that United's policing charges would rise from £74,000 in 1990/1 to £379,000 by 1995/6. No doubt much of this was rhetoric that was part of the struggle between central government and the clubs and the changes the former were making in relation to police funding. However, like all other clubs in the 1991/2 season, United hired a private security company to steward the Shoreham End and the perimeters of the pitch. Based in Slough, 'Extra Staff Special Events' provided up to 100 stewards (male and female) who were polite and recognisable in red tank-tops and were paid £5 per hour – a considerable reduction on the hourly rate for police officers. The presence of these stewards provided by a private company was inevitable, given that in 1994 the Police Authority announced it would increase its charges by 80 per cent on the previous season as a result of a Home Office directive to recover the full costs of policing (*The Star*, 22 August 1994).

Crime and Punishment

Reaction to hooliganism invariably focused on finding some perceived appropriate law and punishment to fit the crime. The legal process was not short of measures. That said, even in the 1990s hooligans were often charged under the 1361 Justice of the Peace Act with the minor matter of 'breach of the peace'. Following an assault, the charge would generally lie under the Offences Against the Person Act of 1861, though fans could also face more recent legislation, such as the 1936 Public Order Act updated by a 1986 Act of the same name which gave magistrates the power to impose fines of up to £2,000 and/or imprisonment of six months, and a 1977 Criminal Law Act that established new maximum penalties for many 'hooligan' offences – common assault; obstructing police; possession of an offensive weapon; and insulting, abusive or threatening behaviour. All were punishable with a range of fines and maximum prison sentences, but also carried the possibility of a Community Service Order (CSO) as an alternative to imprisonment. The idea was to deprive the offender of leisure time, instil a sense of discipline and force offenders to make reparation to society. In this situation the 'hooligan' could find himself painting, carrying out minor repairs or digging for community causes for the old and infirm. The philosophy was intended to show the miscreant a positively viewed cultural activity that might offset his earlier negative behaviour; but many of those sentenced in this way I knew remained involved in 'after the match events'. Their CSO supervision usually ended at 4.00 p.m. which meant they could be at Bramall Lane or around the railway station in minutes!

The use of more serious charges, particularly that of affray, against fans was obvious from around the mid-1980s, and the first occasion it was used against the Blades related to events without any football connection, after a city-centre stag-night for a core Blade in September 1983 ended in a large-scale fight. Around twenty-five fans entered a nightclub, where one of the leading Blades had a gold chain stolen by a bouncer. In the ensuing fracas one Blade received a fractured skull and eleven were arrested and subsequently charged with affray. A bouncer who had wielded a pick-axe handle was charged with grievous bodily harm. Following the court case in October 1984 two Blades were jailed for 15 months, five received 15 months' youth custody and four were found not guilty. The bouncer received an 18-month sentence. Blades all believed Sheffield police had used this charge as a means of getting back at Blades who had been a source of irritation to them for the previous two years, and the police admitted as much to those under arrest. However, it is more than likely that affray was a logical charge to prefer, for it meant they could avoid having the impossible task of framing individual charges of assault or wounding that they would not have been easily able to prove. But if the police hoped that this would act as a deterrent, they were to be disappointed. From the late 1980s onwards Blades faced more serious charges on a regular basis. Yet there was no more serious violence perpetrated then than in the previous decade. Most of the more serious charges of affray were preferred following fights in city centres *en route* to matches, or after Blade-Owl fights in Sheffield in the evenings. Yet Blades were remarkably successful in contesting affray charges, with 26 charged (20 in Sheffield and 6 elsewhere) and none found guilty between 1989 and 1994.

On top of this there were always those extra legal irritants. When arrested fans could be on the receiving end of two forms of instant, informal punishment. By delaying release after arrest in what might be described as 'preventive custody', the police seemed sometimes to keep fans until the match ended to avoid further trouble, and did this by making enquiries and the paperwork surrounding an arrest take a few hours longer than might be expected. As a result, those fans arrested even some hours before the game could often miss the match; and this was particularly annoying when they had travelled perhaps 200 miles or more. Prolonged detention could also mean fans might find the coach home had long since gone, and face the prospect of a hefty rail fare, with perhaps a long wait for a morning train. In the circumstances, some fans hitched or took a cab; but a fare of £100 for this form of transport was not unknown. Another method of 'punishment' from the late 1960s came with the imposition of restrictive bail conditions which saw Blades who were arrested and charged after city-centre fracas given bail conditions that barred them from one mile of the city centre, with the Town Hall being the defining centre. Then again, in later years police operated their own tactic of 'holding' when they arrested *en masse* known Owls they believed were out to cause a breach of the peace. One Saturday night in December 1994 14 Owls were arrested as they walked along West Street at 10.30 p.m. and held until 4.00 a.m. before being released without charge, with the tactic publicised in *The Sheffield Star* (19 December) as necessary because, police reported, they were on their way to an impending confrontation with Blades and feared a public disturbance, adding *'Usually innocent people end up getting injured in this sort of thing.'*

Inevitably, there were also unofficial measures that stood well beyond and outside the criminal justice system. These, nevertheless, were forms of control, for many require crime and its occurrence to have a face and a name. Thus we can see elements of what Braithwaite (1989) defined as *Shame* operating as a form of social control and informal sanction. Without doubt a fear of various types of extra legal consequence can occupy the minds of plaintiffs and be just as effective as any formal or legal punishment. This was particularly the case in the 'world's biggest village', where the evening newspaper's crime reporting seemed to consist of little more than publishing the name, address, age and charge preferred against some accused. This would be supplemented by a few sentences from the prosecution case (the more dramatic the better – regardless of the fact that the defendant might later have the case dismissed or the accusations might be proved to be false), and could occasionally be accompanied by photographs of defendants leaving the court.

Blade Cabalism: 1988 and Beyond

Another response to the ever-changing pattern of hooliganism occurred in the creation of new police statuses. The role of Football Liaison Officer (FLO) was established in Sheffield in 1980, with a primary duty of liaising with counterparts in other forces whose football supporters were due to visit Sheffield, and vice versa. For each occasion the FLO would produce a report that estimated the size of the crowd, the method of the visitors' transport and the likelihood of disturbances on the basis of recent information and past matches between the two clubs. The FLO role was superseded in the late 1980s by the quasi-military position of Football *Intelligence* Officer (FIO), whose brief, from 1990 onwards, was to 'target' serious and persistent hooligans, thereby complying with the new 'intelligence-led' policing philosophy of the 1990s. In relation to Sheffield United this role was initiated by a Police Constable in 1988 (an officer in his late 20s who remained in the position until 1997): he would gather 'intelligence', which was then collated by the National Football Intelligence Unit (NIFU), later to be subsumed as a department under the National Criminal Intelligence Service (NCIS) in London. Working with him at home and away games between 1987 and 1992 was Bramall Lane's 'community policeman', who policed the neighbourhood as well as policing every home match. Initially, on away match duties, they would wear civilian clothing, but later chose to wear uniforms. The two officers, plus two others who sometimes travelled with them in the late 1980s and early 1990s, were well enough known for Blades to refer to them as 'our coppers'. But they were disliked and distrusted and the target of much ridicule and gossip. Contact between these observers and observed was invariably restricted to mutual visual recognition and occasional muttered abuse. Whilst the police knew who Blades were and built up dossiers that they photocopied and sent to various forces, they had no real contact, bar watching those they targeted, and thus no true *idea* of what Blades did or were likely to do. Media pronouncements, however, suggested that times they knew more than the Blades did.

One characteristic of police thinking in Sheffield from the mid-1980s corresponded with what their colleagues were saying elsewhere, inferring that, if people did something as a group, then they must have some coherent command structure with an ultimate leader. Perhaps the most striking example of how their anticipations were less than accurate can be shown by events following the Hillsborough Disaster in 1989. At the subsequent Taylor Inquiry the police lawyer spoke of 'concerted action' to enter the ground illegally, adding *'the notion of a plan by some to foment difficulty and disorder cannot be easily dismissed' (The Star,* 14 July). Later, when faced with criticism of their tactics, the Sheffield police argued back by inventing evidence of crowd motivation. This failed because they had no real evidence and, like everyone else, they only knew what had happened in the ground. This, it seemed, was a classic case of assuming what you set out to prove.

The police tactic of the mid-1980s onward was to 'find the leaders' and arrest them, in the belief that the headless remainder would then be incapable of subsequent action. From early 1984 Sheffield police began to make public their impression that the Blades (but never Owls, for some reason) were highly organised. After one Saturday of disturbances, *The Star*'s 'crime reporter', Dick Taylor, under the heading 'Organised Terror by Soccer Hooligan Mob', wrote: *'An organised gang of troublemakers are bringing terror to the terraces of Sheffield United, a police chief revealed today . . . they are to be banned, by name, from further United matches . . . police have identified which pubs they meet in before matches to plan violence. And they have detailed information about their tactics'* (19 November 1984).

The possession of this detailed information did not stop further disorder or even come to fruition in, or end the need for subsequent, court cases. It was not until some four years later, through court proceedings reported in *The Star,* that the police dignified this construct of an organisation with a name: the Blades Business Crew ('BBC'). During the third day of a Crown Court trial in January 1988 where nine Blades and one Owl appeared following a city-centre affray, the Prosecution Counsel told the court of the 'BBC's' characteristics: *'it was out to cause trouble at home and away matches . . . its sole purpose is attacking buildings, causing violence and trouble at matches . . . not genuine supporters.'*

Soon after this, another organised sub-group was created when, in March 1988, seven youths at the Crown Court on a charge of violent conduct were alleged to belong to a newly organised entity. The defendants were accused of being 'founder members of a [then] newly-formed group called the "Baby Blades"'. Yet the term the 'Baby Blades' was a passing joke: a silly name arising out of a comment made one Friday night when an elder Blade laughed at the up and coming young element. Of course there was no such organisation or organiser. In the dock the same four young lads who had pleaded guilty had just started drinking with the Friday night crowd (three others were local youths who just happened to be in the pub when the fight with the Owls started).

The BBC was then given more sinister motives encompassed in a hierarchical system that had at its core a command structure. In March 1991 the 'BBC' were to achieve regional notoriety, when *The Star* published police-gathered stories that contained few substantiated truths. A front-page article (11 March) told how three pub landlords in the vicinity of Hillsborough stadium had voiced concern to police that they would be 'targeted' by Blades before the forthcoming Sheffield Derby. An article under a front-page headline, 'Police Get Tough on Soccer Derby Thugs', told readers how police had uncovered a *'sinister plot by the Blades' Business Crew hooligans'*. The 'plot' was also revealed on regional TV news, and so millions learned of the 'BBC' plan. The police had 'found' this story; the media published and broadcast it without question – yet not a single Blade knew of the plan, and I can verify this, for I was with them, and there was none.

Journalism then became investigative, but only when carried out in the company of police. In July 1992 Sheffielders learned more about the 'BBC' when a centre-page article by journalist Martin Davies, 'Trailing the Blades Business Crew', was accompanied by two photos. One was of two PCs standing in the darkness; the other, taken from 200 yards, depicted forty young men drinking outside a pub. A Chief Inspector tells of a 'tip-off' about impending trouble concerning the 'BBC'. These, we learn from Davies, are *'a rag-bag of yobbos, ostensibly supporting Sheffield United, who need booze to give them bottle for violence'* (7 July).

This 'rag-bag' had recently 'rioted' in a city-centre pub, caused 'aggro' on The Manor Estate (this is a reference to the fight with Owls mentioned in Chapter 3) and had now turned their attention to the bouncers of The Locarno (see Chapter 3). The police tell the reporter that, having been banned from this venue, the 'BBC' had fired a distress flare through the window, and that police strategy on this evening was to provide a visible uniformed presence supplemented by two mounted police. The Chief Inspector added by way of causation that *'there is a substantial drugs element behind public disorder'*. The journalist confirmed this, stating *'the trouble is part of a struggle for territory'*, without any precise indication as to what he meant by this. So, how evil were the 'BBC'? A couple of police ruined the construct somewhat, for Davies quoted one as saying: *'As soon as they see a bit of blue they're off.'* His colleague added that stag-nights give more trouble, and Davies added his own words, saying that they [the 'BBC'] *'seek safety in numbers, attacking people on their own, or wading* en masse *into pubs'*.

How such violence was motivated was then made public, as was the police intelligence about them. Front-page headlines in 1993 in *The Star* announced 'Blades Thugs on Secret File'. Journalist, Bob Westerdale, using police sources, reported five Blades were on a National Criminal Intelligence Service Football Hooligan Unit 'soccer thugs' list. These allegedly constituted the 'inner sanctum' of the 'BBC' – *'an organised gang of thugs hell-bent on fighting rival supporters'*. The Unit, we learned, *'knows the name of each man and even who their leader is'*. Quoting a Police Inspector recently seconded from Sheffield to the London-based Unit, he tells us: *'There are around five United followers who revel in the planning and execution of violence against other followers. They have about 25–30 others who are also willing to follow them and do the actual fighting.'* The principal troublemakers were apparently aged between eighteen and twenty-seven, and had jobs. And whilst Wednesday also had their 'Hotheads', they did not have individuals who *'regularly plot atrocities'* (10 August). The uni-directional flow of power ensured that only the police could dictate and define what the 'BBC' was. Knowledge was an institutional prerogative; contrary opinions were simply wrong.

Surveillance: The Enemy Within

A basic problem for police was that they frequently arrived at hooligan incidents just as they were ending, and therefore could not catch Blades 'at it'. However, they realised that if they could capture the occasions of disorder and conflict on celluloid, then they would have evidence to make serious charges stick. Thus from the mid-1980s police began to scrutinise and photograph Blades' movements, both inside and outside the ground – sometimes overtly, but much of the time covertly. Some of the technology used was obvious and advertised, and was paid for by private enterprise, as when Sheffield United were given a £25,000 grant by the Football Trust to install fifteen CCTV cameras. In 1989 the Football Trust donated £30,000 to South Yorkshire Police to purchase *mobile* video cameras to monitor fans. They then paid for self-congratulatory adverts in the club programme over the next nine years that told of the good work the cameras had done. Trust posters that spoke of the potential of the technology were also displayed at the ground. Despite the all-encompassing nature of this electronic scanning the police escalated the surveillance, and Blades watched as from 1989 to 1994 three officers (or civilian personnel) operated a camera from a TV gantry. From 1991 they in turn were supplemented by three plain-clothes men who located themselves opposite this camera in a cordoned-off part of the John Street Stand, with yet another camera on a tripod. We might ask: what wild and unimaginable villainy was this overkill intended to prevent? For as the account shows, hooligan activity was negligible; and as with the increasing use of police helicopters to control football crowds, we might ask what is the cost of this technology, and what is the ultimate aim of it all?

Later again, the FIO would be seen on match-days with a small hand-held camcorder held to his eye as he videoed anybody he considered dubious and later spoke their names into a dictaphone. Other mobile surveillance cameras were placed in premises in the city centre and London Road premises (both commercial and residential). These were requisitioned by police to gain vantage points to record the comings and goings of Blades, the obvious aim being to build up a dossier and hopefully capture them *in flagrante*. Much work went into this, and by the 1990s there were some 350 mug shots of Blade suspects held in one Sheffield police station, some taken whilst the individual was under arrest, and the rest a product of covert surveillance cameras in the streets or at vantage points in the Bramall Lane ground.

Surveillance was subsequently combined with intelligence-gathering to become the leading mantra of police targeting from the mid-1980s. From 1987 onwards the move to combine surveillance, intelligence-gathering and targeting saw payments to inform becoming part of the techniques of control. Blades in police custody for various matters would be offered cash for information, with inducements ranging from £25–£100 as the norm. Another incentive offered was to reduce some possible charge a Blade faced, by 'having a word with an officer in charge of the case' or the custody sergeant. This held out the possibility of a 'binding over' instead of, perhaps, a prison sentence or fine, or might well reduce a charge of supplying drugs to one of possession. No doubt some took the bait, and many in custody were urged to put names to pictures, for the police wanted data on those they had photographed for their intelligence systems. The problem with this was that many Blades were only known to each other by nickname; but even this was sufficient for police purposes, as they sought to fill out their dossiers with 'street-names' and other information, such as 'drug user/ dealer', 'new member', 'leader'. The combination of police intelligence and surveillance enables a process of demonology (Virilio 1994: 234).

Surveillance apparatus ranks and differentiates because, whilst photography has no identity, it is invested with power relations (Tagg 1988: 63). Like Foucault's prisoners, those watched are the object of information never a subject for communication (1977: 210). Blades had no opportunity to dispute what was held against them, and the police did not wish to hear that their intelligence was wrong.

The Better Team – Right On Their Side?

The two groups – hooligans and police – shared some cultural background and some of the same social spaces; some police officers who attended the match had been at school with Blades, and certainly both groups shared the city centre. As a result, many knew who Blades were, and where they lived. In return, Blades would sometimes acknowledge this shared circumstance. Other officers knew Blades as a result of a previous arrest situation, and this was ironic in that it sometimes worked to Blades' advantage. For example, I witnessed occasions when officers (perhaps because they even liked some individual Blade) would discreetly advise particular Blades to leave the scene when they knew their colleagues were 'after them'. At other times the more elderly officers would recognise a Blade as the son of a neighbour or friend, and this could cause those Blades to make themselves scarce lest their parents be told of their activities or be warned in an informal, off-duty situation of the path they were treading.

The idea that policing football is dangerous can be offset by asking what activity is so well anticipated, with specific kick-off times, an enclosed and controlled stadium, surveillance in depth, and specified routes of travel and control of access, as well as large numbers of young, fit officers to contend with any trouble? And even when Blade and Owl confrontations occurred away from the match, they took place in city-centre venues around weekend licensing hours when the greatest concentrations of police could be found. It must therefore be stressed that Blades were not in contest with the police, for the law ruled the streets, and, like all the young men in the city, they were well aware of the fact.

Blades accepted the tactics of the police, however irritating, and though indeed scared of facing serious charges they were not antagonistic to police, nor did they perceive police behaviour to be entirely antagonistic. They accepted the job of the police was necessary, but thought it legitimate to sidestep police opposition. In fact the police were regarded fundamentally as the hooligans regard themselves – i.e. as for the most part 'normal', though some were seen as having a stereotypically violent disposition. They expected that any question they put to police would be met by sarcastic remarks or abuse, and that any failure to comply with police instructions would produce threats. Faced with non-violent police officers, Blades would react with comments that even expressed a degree of admiration: *'reyt good, their coppers'* or *'sound'*, i.e. fair in their treatment, in that they had escorted Blades away from a confrontation without making arrests, or in that they policed the day without resorting to threats and violence. Mind you, by the same token, if the police showed too much *naïveté* they were seen as *'soft'*, *'dizzy'*, *'slack'*, *'daft'* – *'They ain't got a clue'*, and *'Don't know what it's all about.'* Blades were always prepared to accommodate the vagaries of police demands, and, in return, they thought police should permit them to indulge in a degree of performance.

As knowing agents Blades realised the politicians were more often than not engaged in the pursuit of hearing their own voices, and would condemn them out of hand. They also understood that the magistracy consisted of figures whose decisions were often made at a whim, depending on their mood, and that this often depended on what they might have read in the media. Thus, to Blades, the law was an arbitrary entity, with an end-product in those arrest statistics that can be used to support rhetoric and political positions – but that often deny reality. Furthermore, even as the newspapers portrayed Blade life as a form of shame, and the courts tried to reform them through the 'degradation' process, we can note that any such attempt depends for its success on the actors' acceptance of the labels they are being given. Blades did not accept that what they had done was shameful or wrong.

Notes

1. In January 1990 an FA Cup quarter final against Manchester United was re-scheduled to a Sunday midday kick-off. With Sunday licencing hours fixed at midday there was to be no opportunity for fans to drink. However, there were profits to be made, and the back doors of pubs were open from 10.00 a.m. throughout the city. Four pubs near the ground were raided by police, and all four licensees lost their licences. All bar one lost their jobs (he was retained, as his 21-year service was highly regarded by the brewery). Yet on the same day eight police officers were drinking at 9.30 a.m. in a pub near West Bar police station, and

were actually thrown out by uniformed colleagues (*The Star*, 19 June). This was made public by other landlords in disgust at what had happened to their colleagues. After an internal police inquiry it was announced on the front page of *The Star* in November that the seven PCs and one sergeant were all off duty, and all were drinking either coke or orange juice. No action was taken against them or the landlord.

2. Solicitors acting for the Council were reported to be seeking court action to ban fans from the ground unless the Club requested sufficient policing on that day. The Police Committee then gave the police the authority to issue a writ in the High Court for £51,000, which they claimed United owed them in back payment. An arrangement not specified publicly was made between the two sides, and the match was played with police in attendance. Subsequently a working party of representatives of the Club and the authority was established, which resulted in a method of calculating charges that was reported to give an annual saving to the Club of £50,000 – seemingly, policing costs were negotiable. In February 1987 the dispute was heard in the Appeal Court: United lost. Speaking in *The Star* (20 March 1987) Brealey described the decision as 'devastating', adding 'I look at this judgement and feel we are one step away from the way things are done in the Eastern Block.' Strong words from a contributor to the Tory Party, but prophetic all the same for the later police action against football fans in England.

3. A Police Federation spokesman said that this would be denuding the streets of policemen in mid-week, and morale would plummet through their losing a holiday (*The Star*, 25 March 1991). The change did not win the sympathy of local-born MP and Wednesday director Joe Ashton. In the same year he suggested that times of matches were decided by police to reward their members by letting them get home early, yet claim a full day's overtime (Home Affairs Committee 1990: 273 and 154).

Chapter 6

Narratives Negated: Maximum Control of Football Spectators

They fight by shuffling papers; they have bright dead alien eyes; they look at our labour and laughter as a tired man looks at flies. And the load of their loveless pity is worse than the ancient wrongs, their doors are shut in the evening; and they know no songs.

(From 'The Secret People' by G. K. Chesterton 1927)

For over a hundred years professional football matches have provided (and still provide) gatherings of collective identity that have no parallel in Sheffield. Nothing else could ever regularly attract the up to 50,000 who stand or sit in the city's two professional football club grounds for two hours in the open, usually in winter. This attraction offers no material or financial gain to its devotees, who constitute an audience seduced by an unscripted drama wherein every motion is open to appreciation or question or ridicule, and one that often ends in happiness but frequently in disappointment for them. It is an enchanting dramatic activity in which standards can never be hidden nor the audience deceived (cf. Bromberger 1994). This love of football and the practice of football support is due not merely to the game's spectacle or practice but, in Bromberger *et al.*'s (1993a: 117) argument, its 'dramatic qualities', which he equates with the 'genres of theatrical production', providing a unity of time, space and action that favours the communion between players and spectators. Support, then, is a compulsion born sometimes of aesthetics and at other times of a love of watching and commenting accompanied by the chance to validate (or invalidate) social relations. Such an activity also permits various antagonisms to manifest themselves, in what Bromberger *et al.* (1993a: 133) calls 'ritualised warfare'. Regardless of any theories postulated, football 'fandom' produces people who are generally neither totally rational in their thinking nor polite in their expressions.

Boorish to Bourgeoise: Changing Audiences

Football support in Britain was and remains a leisure-time activity in which men manifest emotions they are reluctant to show elsewhere at other times. Via a shared enthusiasm they hug, dance and sing unashamedly in each others' company – actions largely avoided elsewhere in their daily lives. That said, the commentary is not all virtuous; the football crowd, in the words of historian Hopcraft (1968: 179) is *'always going to have more vinegar than Chanel'*; and grounds have always reverberated to a witty, ribald and/ or abusive narrative directed towards players, match officials and rival fans. For decades fights between rival fans were part of the match-day occasion (see Hutchinson 1975; Mason 1980; Fishwick 1989) and the match was thus (and remains) a focus of male entertainment in more ways than one. Some fans, particularly from the 1960s on and consistently from the younger (late teens to late twenties) element, have manifested behaviour and in unison used words that were to many other match-goers threatening or offensive. This was a form of participation not witnessed in the 1940s and 1950s, and since the 1960s the football authorities and police have done all they can to curb, curtail and criminalise this excess. What further disturbed the authorities was that it was the same people who fought with rival fans who did most of the singing, so that the conduct stigmatised as 'football hooliganism' was thus manifested in both actions and words. And hence, when there were no actions to police, words became sufficient grounds for arrest and criminalisation and thus for sustaining concern with the 'hooligan problem'.

That football clubs can influence, and therefore are responsible for, their fans is a basic premise of the Football Authorities (FA Rule 31). Consequently came the belief that somehow the football club itself could curtail hooliganism, whatever its manifestation and however it was defined. But after twenty-five years of not being able to eradicate this indefinable, the football authorities sought solutions in words that politicians heed. Two political buzz words of the 1980s became the proposed means to curtail the excess of some fans – 'Community' and 'Family'. The latter was to become the icon of post-1979 Tory social policy, and concomitantly the ideal gathering that the football Authorities sought as its audience. The ideas around 'community' were vaguer; somewhere, it was postulated, a hooligan-producing community could be 'targeted' with a view to preventing the lads doing what they did. Advertising was used in an attempt to combat hooliganism: posters were displayed around the grounds, paid for by private business advising fans on how to behave. Significantly for any law and order debate, morality was even put out to tender when private business paid for a variety of surveillance cameras for the sole use of police to watch and record football fans and, via print-outs of profiles, to build up databases both local and national. For over ten years now the profits of the 'Spot The Ball' and football pools gambling competitions under the aegis of The Football Trust have assisted in the surveillance and criminalisation of fans – all without a whimper from sociologists, the media, or politicians.[1]

Probably the most prominent accompanying change was the professional clubs' promotion of women, be it in women's football teams, or in encouraging them to spectate, in some cases at certain clubs by stressing the availability of match-day child-care facilities. Support for such schemes came from the highest political levels: the Government-commissioned inquiries into the game in the 1980s considered the role of women in football as 'essential' (Popplewell 1986: 40), but mainly as a means of altering the behaviour of some of the men in the crowd (cf. Taylor Report). This theory had the support of the police (Home Affairs Committee 1990) and of Britain's 'expert' sociologists at Leicester University, who recognised the need for women in the football ground to 'civilise' the males that curiously they had previously stated had created the hooligan in the first place. In a Catholic sense the visitation of virtue as epitomised by femininity and motherhood would cleanse the polluted sites. The fairer sex was idealised in terms that defined them as the opposite of brutish men. Another crucial step in image-making was to gain control of the way the game was portrayed to a wider non-attending public. Thus favourable TV coverage was negotiated when in 1986 the football authorities forbade TV companies broadcasting matches to broadcast any obscene chants.

Because abuse was often part of the chants beloved of fans, chanting became criminalised, with the assistance of a variety of moral entrepreneurs. Campaigns were begun, both in other European countries and Britain, to 'Kick Out Racism'; and the definition of 'Racism' widened, so that abusing rival players for whatever reason and with whatever words was included under this term. At the same time, hoping to appeal to a new audience, from the late 1980s the game sold itself through new television channels and went cap-in-hand to multinationals for sponsorship. Multinational marketing campaigns used famous footballers to promote their merchan-dise in combination with a political message of toleration for all peoples.

The standard response in the 1990s to any form of abuse towards rival players from rival fans, British media pundits, politicians, and those who pontificated on the game was hyperbolic outrage. Two of Britain's major clubs, Manchester United and Leeds United, even installed their own club 'hotlines', where fans could inform (anonymously) on fellow fans who swore during games: the latter faced being banned from future entry. Earlier, in 1987, the West Midlands police introduced (without consultation) a 'code of conduct' for fans who attended the six grounds under its jurisdiction. This included a *ban* on chanting and gesturing, which would on occasions see dozens of fans arrested at a single game. With fights no longer occurring in the ground, a new form of 'violence' was publicised and policed – that of words and gestures: the definition of 'hooligan', like that of 'racism', was ever-widening, as the authorities realised that the personnel and technology in the ground were largely ineffectual in preventing the pre-match and post-match hooligan scenarios. As these events began to be publicised as highly organised and led by sinister forces (cf. HAC 1990), the chants too were given attributes never afforded them before.

Oaths and Truths

The sinister nature of chanting at football matches was central to police public order ideology as epitomised by the organisation in charge of public order policy. In 1987 David Phillips, then Assistant Chief Constable of Greater Manchester and Chair of the Association of Chief Police Officers (ACPO) committee responsible for public order in Britain, explained to a conference on the subject how football hooliganism manifested itself. Apparently it was attributable to 'the crowd', which provided malevolent individuals with immunity from arrest and produced 'a volatile mix, capable of ignition' particularly when sound levels were high enough to cause 'mass paralysis'. Aware of how this inertia was possible, the hooligans apparently deliberately organised chanting and mass clapping because: '*the hooligan wants to be part of a large group, he is a would-be leader, a sort of "warlord"; when he hears chants in unison behind him it gives him feelings of greater power*'.

Without supporting evidence, Mr Phillips concluded that 'the most violent are those that do this chanting'. It should come as no surprise that over the next eight years police at most grounds arrested hundreds of individuals who were considered to be trying to begin chants. Regardless of whether there was any factual basis in such claims, the police *knew* the real motive – it was written down in a document dissseminated by their professional hierarchy. The South Yorkshire police hierarchy certainly believed in the malevolence of chants, and told the local media what they knew. According to them fans in one area could send messages via chants to others awaiting such signals for them to begin to cause trouble elsewhere (*The Green 'Un*, 30 March 1985). Fortunately for the rest of the crowd, the police knew what the chant was. Whether the hooligans did was never revealed.

Gradually police began to alter the ground, both to facilitate speed of access in apprehending offenders and to make policing easier by making groups of spectators smaller and more uniformly categorised. These processes were an attempt by police to produce, via surveillance, what Foucault (1977) has termed the 'docile body', i.e. one which does not participate in its surroundings or only does so in a way controlled by power. In 1985 Sheffield United were given £25,000 by the Football Trust to install closed-circuit television (CCTV), and five years later, in May 1990, the police refused to supervise matches until a new control room was built to allow for further CCTV monitoring, and stated that no matches would take place until it was built. Thus was created a situation where every spectator was visible to the discipline afforded by surveillance, in the shape both of privately-hired stewards and uniformed police who spent the whole game looking into the crowd, and also simultaneously of technological surveillance provided by a police-operated CCTV system. No one in the ground was anonymous any longer.

To assist the visibility that police surveillance required the ground was changed structurally. From the mid-1980s, when the hooligan shifted their location from the terraces to the stands, even seating was taken out, as the police decided which areas were 'no go' for young men and extended 'sterile areas' separating rival fans. In fact in every season between 1982 and 1990 the club lost potential revenue as the police extended their 'no-go areas'. The club was even harder hit when the ground capacity of 44,000 in 1985 was reduced to 31,000 in 1989 following the Hillsborough tragedy, and two years later reduced by a further 25 per cent to accord with new local authority guidelines. Fans could now watch in a 'capacity crowd' with plenty of room around them to swing the proverbial cat, and in the consciousness that three times their number had once stood where they were now.

Not that the police needed it (existing legislation was adequate), but to expand police discretion, further legislation was introduced to try to control fans and curb excess of any type. Some legislation came with the idea that alcohol was the root cause of hooliganism. Thus the Sporting Event (Control of Alcohol, etc.) Act 1985 barred entry to fans under the influence of alcohol and banned the sale of alcohol in the ground from any point that gave a view of the pitch! In the following year the 1986 Public Order Act provided for 'Exclusion Orders' that courts could impose on those convicted of 'hooligan-related offences' that would bar them from entering football grounds for various lengths of time. Later came the Football Offences Act of 1991, introduced by a Private Member's Bill following the Home Affairs Committee (HAC) inquiry into the policing of football hooliganism by a select group of MPs. This made the chanting of indecent or racially offensive words, as well as entering the field of play, a specific criminal offence, even though in their submission to the HAC the police in the shape of ACPO stated that the law as it stood was adequate to deal with hooliganism. Regardless, everybody had to be seen to look busy, including the clubs, who had to act in order to pre-empt others' acting for them.

House of Cards: Pre-empting Politicians

Politicians had earlier preceded this type of legislation by attempts to bar fans from entering the ground by law or by the declarations of the club management. A total ban on visiting supporters was suggested by a *Daily Mail* journalist in 1985 to Mrs Thatcher during a post-Heysel meeting she called with selected sports journalists. The principal initiator of such measures was David Evans, Chairman of Luton Town FC (later to become a Tory MP), who, in 1985, implemented an identity card requirement for the Luton ground following disturbances there involving Millwall fans. People with an address within a 20-mile radius of Luton would qualify; away fans were allowed only as guests of local fans. The Government eventually planned to control behaviour by legislating that fans should be licensed to enter the ground via identity cards, which would be confiscated if the holder misbehaved. A Parliamentary White Paper, 'The Football Spectators Bill', planned to introduce the scheme in the 1990–1 season – a proposal made with little regard for civil liberties and every regard for political populism. Football clubs would have to pay the costs, estimated to be hundreds of millions of pounds. This ill-thought-out proposal was dropped when politicians realised it would never be workable. But it did have unexpected uses.

The identity card proposal not only provided for clubs to alter the structure of their grounds, but more significantly, gave some an incentive to raise admission costs. The really significant effect of this Bill, however, was that, with the threat of ID cards hanging over them, the Football Authorities attempted to put their own house in order. This had begun years earlier, when in 1987 the Football League imposed on all clubs a ruling that 50 per cent of grounds should be reserved for supporters who had joined 'membership schemes'. Consequently, Sheffield United designated the South Stand and John Street Side as 'Members Only': in this way those who stood or sat here (areas adjacent to rival fans) could, if police so decided, be barred from entry, or refused membership. To join, supporters completed an application form, and then paid £1.25 each in return for their very own card and identity number. Applicants were warned on the form that those 'whose presence on the ground is a cause of danger, nuisance or annoyance to other spectators' would be removed. By 1991 membership cost £3.00, permitting a card-holder to take in three guests. The scheme did not affect hooliganism one iota – by the 1980s hooligans no longer sought each other in the ground.

Following the Taylor Report in 1990 (re-echoing the suggestion of the inquiry of Justice Popplewell in 1985/6), all Premier and First Division grounds had by 1994 to be all-seated.[3] The drawback was that this would cost the clubs £500 million in renovations (some respite was offered in 1991, when the Chancellor of the Exchequer reduced betting tax on the football pools, thus enabling £135 million to be made available for funding ground charges over the years 1992–7). Thus the nature of football spectating was changed for ever – what had sufficed for a hundred years had to go; owing to seat allocation, rarely would a group of friends ever be able to attend together, having gone along to the match on a whim. Owing to poor design, many spent the whole game in a yo-yo-like squat in order to see; the rear five rows of the Shoreham End Kop were found standing the whole match long, despite the continued (and irritating) efforts of stewards to insist that everyone sit. No longer able to move elsewhere should the opinions or words of a fellow spectator trouble them, their response was to complain to stewards, who were under instructions to warn the perpetrators of their misdemeanours, and, if they persisted, either to eject them from the ground or, if they feared causing an escalation of the trouble by doing so, to bring in the police to do the ejecting. Such attempts at discipline could occur hours and even days later: fans of Sheffield Wednesday were even visited *at home* to be lectured on their language by police or the club's Safety Officer (invariably a retired senior police officer), who had used the club's database on season-ticket holders to ascertain where they lived.

The Possibilities of Participation

The basic problem was that the football audience was predominantly white working-class males who were not always aesthetically pleasing and expressed opinions that were not always politically correct: but this was their way of *participating* in *their* club. The newly fashionable game and its corporate-inspired world had to do something to change this procedure. One solution proposed in the FA-commissioned *Blueprint for Football 1991* (produced by the Henley Forecasting Centre) was to appeal to the middle classes and pitch admission costs to suit their income, thereby pricing out the 'lower orders'. Consequently, the cost of attending a match from the mid-1980s rose way out of proportion to any constructs of inflation or the 'cost of living'. At Bramall Lane charges varied with the section of the ground; but where seats replaced terracing prices were raised immediately. In fact, over the ten-year period 1982–92, the price of a season ticket for anywhere in the ground rose nearly *300 per cent*, while if one paid separately for each home game the rise was 380 per cent. Following promotion to Division 1 in 1989 fans found admission prices on the kop had risen from £4.40 to £6.00, and the maximum price of seats was £11.00 (raised to £12.80 in 1991/2), although owing to the classification of the visiting teams into 'A', 'B' and 'C' categories, seat prices varied with the visitors' crowd-pulling potential. Thus, for all the 'right on' talk about 'Community', when successful the club did not reward their supporters from the local community in any way, but milked them for as much profit as possible.

Football clubs can provide rich megalomaniacs with a constituency without any controlling mandate. From such a position a nobody can become a somebody with regular access to the media, and it was upon football supporters that some could attempt their own ideals of social reform. The man who was to depart under a cloud of criminal investigations from his role as United's Chairman in 1995 was, at the beginning of his reign, regarded by the fans as visionary. In the 1980s, with gates declining and debts growing, having just taken over as Chairman, Reg Brealey inherited a club with financial problems (see Clarebrough 1989). As an astute (and very rich) Lincolnshire-based but internationally renowned businessman he could imagine what might be possible financially if only the inhibiting image of some fans did not obstruct his projects, which could otherwise 'rescue' the club (and his pockets). Thus Brealey set out producing, promoting, and marketing United as the 'The Family Club'. What followed over the years was a concerted publicity effort using the image of a family club, which at times featured stage-managed photographs and insincere clichés in merchandising brochures of 'The Caring Club' and 'The Friendly Club'. There was no stopping such publicity: by the 1990s both city clubs stressed the concept of Family, which was multifunctional but neatly side-stepped a reality in which women were employed at each club only in a serving or ornamental capacity, with their representation as spectators being only about 10 per cent of the total crowd.

Regardless, to encourage the attendance of the young and accompanying parents, Chairman Brealey in his first season periodically gave away hundreds of free match tickets to schoolchildren, and introduced a 'Family' ticket (reductions on child admission with an adult ticket). There was more to his scheme than profit: in 1982 Brealey outlined his intentions in *The Sheffield Star* (10 August), explaining that 'The Family Club' was crucial to the club's publicity, because *'the family is still the most important unit in our nation'*. As a contributor to the Tory Party and member of the Church of England General Synod, Mr Brealey possibly saw in football a chance to amend the social breakdown that his favoured politicians were creating: *'We live in difficult times, and Sheffield as much as any city: perhaps more than most. Families are under pressure. There is the recession, unemployment and the associated social problems. We see football as a great safety valve, and making our Club the Family Club is, I feel, a contribution we can make.'*

The desire to attract a family audience resulted in the creation of segregated 'Family Enclosures' in nearly all League grounds in the late 1980s. At Bramall Lane the left-hand side of the South Stand (2,000 seats) was sold in promotional leaflets as a 'safe and well-segregated area' with its own catering and toilet facilities (which was not true, as they shared them with everyone else in the stand), for which one needed a Family Enclosure card, originally costing £2 (£10 for adult and £7.50 for children by 1994) to gain access. The leaflet that advertised this stated that this 'ensured' that no unruly supporters could mix with the 'vast majority of well-behaved families and individuals'. The enclosure area was sponsored initially by Pannini, a company that produced photographs of footballers to stick into an album given free to all members. Later, in 1990, a sponsorship deal saw a deal with the Co-op supermarket until the multinational burger chain McDonalds took over the mantle of the 'Soulful Corporation' in 1994. Unless young fans joined the Family Enclosure Scheme they (and their parents) had to pay full price regardless of age, which meant in 1992 a minimum of £9. Visiting fans had to pay £14.

The same Mr Brealey altered the nature of spectating at Bramall Lane. Grandiose structural schemes in the early 1980s aimed to convert the football ground into a 'leisure village', but came to nought because of his politics and the City Council's bloody-mindedness and refusal to grant planning permission. However, he was able to categorise fandom. For ninety years, paying the admission fee at the turnstyle had been the supreme level of fandom and enthusiasm. Not any longer: the turnstyle-paying punter was to become the ground-level category in a supporters' pyramid. In July 1981, Brealey established a variety of supporters' schemes: one was the Travel Club, which organised coaches to away games. Individuals who joined were given a membership card with a photograph, withdrawn if they misbehaved, thus making them ineligible to travel. This gave to fans the illusion of 'membership', but with the threat of exclusion. Concomitantly, to attract wealthy supporters he began the 'Executive Club': an annual subscription bought a car-parking space adjacent to their upholstered and (in some cases) personally-named seat. They could enjoy the exclusivity of their own bar, with admittance restricted by the presence of a uniformed commissionaire – lesser fans drank in the Social Club next door – and dependent on a dress code that insisted on men's wearing ties and prohibited denim and training shoes. Having appealed to The Family and to those aspiring to the middle-class status of 'Executives', the next step was to make the match-day dialogue appropriate to the ideal type of The Family or to the corporate dinner-table. How this was to be done was lost in a dispute the Chairman had with local politicians and police (described in Chapter 5).

The outcome of the aforementioned dispute was that with policing costs set to rise another 50 per cent in 1991 United, like all other professional clubs, hired stewards from private security agencies, who were three times cheaper than the police. Instructed to watch the crowd constantly for 90 minutes at fixed points, they would warn any miscreants of their behaviour physical or verbal, and inform police of persistent offenders. The relationship between the two sets of guardians of morality, old and new, was not cosy; the police had no love for these low-paid uniform-wearers, and stewards did not take too kindly to police not always being forthcoming with assistance. In the confusion over what was appropriate conduct and prohibited words stewards claimed to fans that they were acting on police instructions, while the latter claimed they were working to the demands made on them by the club, and the club could wash their hands of responsibility, arguing that they had no control over the police. Those who used swear words or whose behaviour could be defined as rowdy were closely watched by the human eyes of stewards and police, whilst in the operator's room up to half a dozen police officers observed via cameras, recorded and made facial print-outs of individuals and groups who sang and made gestures in response both to events on the pitch and towards rival fans. Via the lenses the police could decide who was 'prolonging celebrations' and therefore liable to 'provoke disorder', and then order uniformed officers at ground level to arrest or eject them.

Drinking Man to Renaissance Fan?

Academic analysis has read into the chants various degrees of nationalism, regionalism and socio-political antagonism, but Redhead's (1986) analysis does not hold water with Blades chants. Instead, I feel we can 'read' them, as Archetti (1992: 219–21) does, as vehicles to: dramatise and exaggerate gender; create tension; provoke nostalgia; show endurance in the face of defeat; provoke ridicule; and, at times, provide intimacy. Manifested in chants are themes of sex, death, group identity, love and hate, where real men are contrasted to weak ones, and, drawing on Eco (1984), spectators turn participants, becoming narrators encompassed in transgressions of etiquette. What troubles the Authorities is that images of violence, sexuality and profanity are brought into the public discourse, a moral order is stated, and people and events are classified and evaluated. The message does not have to be true, though it must provoke a reaction; but the reactions were not always ones of humour or limited to match-goers.

What was witnessed in response to the above was football clubs and police attempting to purify the ground of the very words that were, ironically, permitted in cinemas and even assisted in winning national awards for literature and film productions through their contributions to the portrayal of social realism. The Sheffield Police Federation meanwhile defended their members' use of the same language against edicts from their higher officers,[4] whilst willingly arresting people who used the same words at the match. From the 1960s, societal attitudes have become increasingly liberal towards sexuality, the body, and language; the exception, it would seem, is when such words are used by football fans. Whilst some chants might contain obscenities, they also constituted the only point at which spectators could at times assert their opinions and perhaps even exert some influence over the club management. Others contain words that are meant to be offensive by attributing feminine characteristics and general incompetence to fellow men. Such accusations, dressed up in imagery and metaphor, are part of a decades-old ideology – a collective consciousness, in fact, that will not disappear simply because politicians pass new laws to criminalise the opinions it embodies.

Carnival Curtailed and Criminalised

By the early 1990s that labelled as the 'Carnivalesque', i.e., chanting, singing and dancing with accompanying artefacts (cf. Giulianotti 1991a), was banned by some clubs. The reason is not that hard to find – the football authorities cannot abide the carnivalesque because it is prone to disorder; they must therefore control or curtail it. It is easier to control by preventing in the first place; and thus everything joyful was stamped upon. The police took the lead, and decided fans could not hold items such as banners, or flags, or inflatable toys. At some grounds even the joyful waving of sticks of celery to an accompanying song was banned.[5] At Bramall Lane neither celery nor inflatables took off. Instead, balloons were the chosen item. This began in the 1991/2 season, when one middle-aged fan bought 5,000 red ones and gave them to turnstile operators to give to United fans before the Sheffield derby. So spectacular was the effect (they were blown up and released as the team took the pitch) that for subsequent matches over the next five years various fans bought balloons by the hundreds. Some police forces, however, prevented fans entering the ground with them. They had either to let them fly away or burst them. Whatever some fans carried with a view to displaying in the ground could be interpreted by police as 'provocative' to other fans. Thus, a Union flag with the words 'Sheffield United' written on it was barred. At other times they were banned because, in the 'market-speak' police borrowed from the clubs, they 'might obstruct the view of other customers'. In the new world of football and marketing such items could, if draped around the ground, obstruct advertising hoardings: absent businesses could thus, in this new football world, dictate the paraphernalia that fans carried.

Some artefacts that fans carried were undoubtedly *dangerous*. Others, regarded by the police in this light, were merely spectacular.[6] Fans knew that these two classes of item were different; the police treated them as the same. Thus, anyone possessing anything that burned or made smoke was liable to arrest. One such incendiary was a nautical *distress* flare occasionally fired by Blades in the 1980s hooligan confrontations. However, the *luminous* flares held by dozens of United fans in the 1991–4 seasons were of a very different variety. Whereas the distress flares were fired, travelled a distance, and could maim, the luminous flares were hand-held, and after emitting smoke and a brilliant light (in this case reflecting the club's colours, red) burned out. Police could not tolerate these items, and at Bramall Lane deployed special observation teams with cameras on tripods to try to capture on film the people who lit them. The 1991–4 seasons would see *three* plain-clothes officers waiting in front of the Shoreham End, to jump to life when a flare was lit and begin photographing. Their job was made difficult by the habit fans had of passing the flare along the seated rows: short of arresting up to a hundred people police could do little! However, police found the excuse they needed to advertise the appallingness of such carnival when a compliant media publicised the iniquity of such items following a game at Nottingham in May 1993, at which an eight-year-old received burns as a luminous flare was passed around. Days later police warned fans via *The Sheffield Star* that arrest would be the consequence of holding or possessing such a device. The United Club Secretary reinforced this position days later in the match-day programme. Ironically the same programme praised the atmosphere the fans created with accompanying photographs of massed and jubilant United fans – complete with the aforementioned lighted flares.

The Purified Community

In view of all the various epiphenomena visited upon the football crowd, the aim must surely be to prevent unscripted participation. This will please those who seek a 'non-sexist, non-racist' fortress-style football ground containing mutually appreciative consumers. But if football is seen as a reflection of society, why should football be devoid of prejudice? Such emotions have engendered and sustained the game for decades. The corporate vision that now dominates football seeks to deny manifestations of fanatical support, preferring an Enlightenment philosophy that regards local bonds and traditional attachments as synonymous with ignorance. Progress, as manifest in bourgeois-defined ideas of good manners, will emerge through impartiality and universality.

Maybe the fact that football is now a multi-million business means that its image is more important than its fans; but this is a problem. As a product it can be marketed only in the moment of production as spectacle. Given great fan loyalty to the product, the management enjoys the luxury of the monopolist producer. The management, however, is in a paradoxical position. In the future the greatest source of income, it is assumed, will come from the consumers as families (who may have no great product loyalty). To build up this future support management must be prepared to disadvantage the most loyal and dedicated fans – i.e. working-class males – and, like politicians, concentrate on marginal voters. However, fan loyalty is loyalty in opposition to other clubs – hence the chants antagonistic to others become the greatest public manifestation of that loyalty. What we can thus see is a process that in a Marxist sense regards the fans as there to be exploited using Weberian notions of rationality.

In this new world football clubs will in the future (as has already begun in some grounds) have to orchestrate chanting or even play recordings of chants over the tannoys to provide 'passion' and 'atmosphere'. As Eco (1986: 19) would argue: *'We are giving you the reproduction so you will no longer face any need for the original.'* The police and football authorities have largely achieved what Bourdieu and Passeron (1977) would term 'the enslaving violence of the agreeable', in which the product is presented to the 'customer' (no longer a fan) as if it were a hamburger. As the need for consistency and conformity becomes the order of the day, and as the 'McDonaldisation' of wider society (cf. Ritzer 1994) gallops ahead unheeded in British society, the paying match-day customer is promised a commodified leisure experience for the family that will not require him or her to think or worry about any form of 'pollution' from the unsightly. Controlled by panoptical CCTV surveillance, the aim is to make discipline automatic: behaviour is normalised, with the audience reacting in a manner predictable to the point of docility (Foucault: 1977). That seen as detracting from the norm produces a ranked and separated hierarchy of individuals, as the body itself becomes the site where power is exercised and the 'deviant' is arrested and criminalised. All the time the authorities assure us of their righteousness in defeating the icon of evil – The Hooligan.

The Football Authorities are pursuing what Sennett (1970 and 1977) terms the 'purified community'. The 'city' he argues is seen by many as a disorganising influence on life, and those that fear it become self-obsessed, particularly over the primacy of privacy and self-enhancement over public life. With this comes an intolerance of difference, a fear of change, and a society afraid of difference, which is 'willing to be dull and sterile in order not to be confused or overwhelmed'. From this ideology 'The Family' becomes the refuge from diversity for parents to hide their children and themselves in. The only hope, Sennett argues, is to break down these barriers and use the diversity of networks available in the city to live fuller lives, and at the same time reduce our concerns for status and challenge the facelessness of bureaucracies.

The fact that 'Hooliganism' is a growth industry is not necessarily reflected in the numbers of its participants, nor by their frequency of appearances on the streets. Rather, the expansiveness lies in the way institutions think, for, as Foucault (1970) showed, institutions overcome individual thought and straitjacket minds and bodies. In the event, an ever-expanding set of antagonists becomes imperative, for, as Douglas (1987: 92) persuasively argues:

Institutions systematically direct individual memory and channel perceptions into forms compatible with the relations they authorize. They fix processes that are essentially dynamic, they hide their influence, and rouse our emotions to a standardized pitch . . . Add to all this that they endow themselves with rightness and send their mutual corroboration cascading through all levels of our information system. No wonder they easily recruit us into joining their narcissistic self-contemplation. Any problems we try to think about are automatically transformed into their own organizational problems. The solutions they proffer only come from the limited range of their experience. If the institution is one that depends on participation, it will reply to our frantic question:

'More participation!' If it is one that depends on authority, it will only reply 'More authority!' Institutions have the pathetic megalomania of the computer whose whole vision of the world is its own program.

Notes

1. The Football Trust was founded in 1979 and chaired by Lord Aberdare, the former Minister of State for the Department of Health and Social Security. The Deeds of the Trust made particular reference to promoting measures that would control or suppress unruly behaviour in relation to football. In giving dozens of police forces *mobile* surveillance cameras the Trust did not specify they were only to be used on football hooligans.
2. The law defined chanting as repeated words or sounds made 'in concert with one or more others'. If individuals shouted alone they could be prosecuted under the 1986 Public Order Act – for using 'obscene and foul language at football grounds'. The 1991 Act had a very low prosecution and conviction rate. When one considers that annually over 5 million people attend professional league matches, only ten were convicted under the Act of 'taking part in indecent or racialist chanting' in 1993, which was double the number of 1991, but half that of the previous season.
3. Popplewell regarded all-seater stadiums a 'sensible idea', with reservations because of 'the idiosyncrasy of football fans' (6.16). For the ignorant he expanded: *'If seating is provided for them they may well tip back the seats and stand in front of them; then stand on the seats; and finally rip up the seats and use them as weapons'* (6.16), an attitude reminiscent of initial middle-class responses to the idea of baths for working-class houses: they would surely, it was argued, be used as coal repositories. However, authority was added to the all-seater scheme in July 1989 by football's world-wide ruling body, FIFA. An edict stated that as from 1993 all 'high-risk' matches (i.e. those in which the attendance would contain over 10 per cent of away fans or there were over 3,000 persons attending who were considered high-risk) could only be played in all-seater stadiums.
4. In April 1992 *The Sheffield Star* told of a meeting of senior police officials in the city who raised concern about their constables' use of bad language. The order to them was to avoid such words. An unnamed

detective was quoted, stating that the 'edict' would not alter anything, and that swearing was a way of 'letting off steam – we are no different to anybody else'.

5. Around the same time that it became a criminal offence to swear at a football match the guardian of children's morals ordained that such words might be permitted in celluloid performances. In January 1989 a new censorship rating of '12' was proposed for the film and video industry by the British Board of Film Classification. The Board had recently stopped giving films 'PG' ('Parental Guidance') certificates if they included the words 'shitting' and 'arse-hole', and now considered that the word 'fuck' did not require a certificate restricting the audience to those of 15 and upwards. The Board's director, James Ferman, explained *'It's lunatic that 12, 13, and 14 year olds should be stopped seeing such an otherwise suitable film because of one word they probably hear every day'* (*The Independent*, 27 January 1989). In 1991 the British Standards Council Report, *A Matter of Names – The Limits of Broadcasting Language* reported that use of the word 'fuck' was not objectionable as long as it was justified by the drama and occurred after 9.00 p.m. A few years later the Booker Prize for Literature was awarded to a work by James Kelman that included over a thousand 'fucks' in the text, and in the same year the box-office success of the year in cinemas was 'Four Weddings and a Funeral', with a censor rating appropriate for 15-year-olds, which began with ten 'Fucks' before any other dialogue.

6. In November 1993 a man in his sixties was struck and killed at a match by a distress flare released in the ground at the end of a Wales–Romania World Cup qualifying game at Cardiff. This one-in-a-million incident was the product of one man in his mid-thirties releasing the device, not at any particular target, nor indeed in a particular direction.

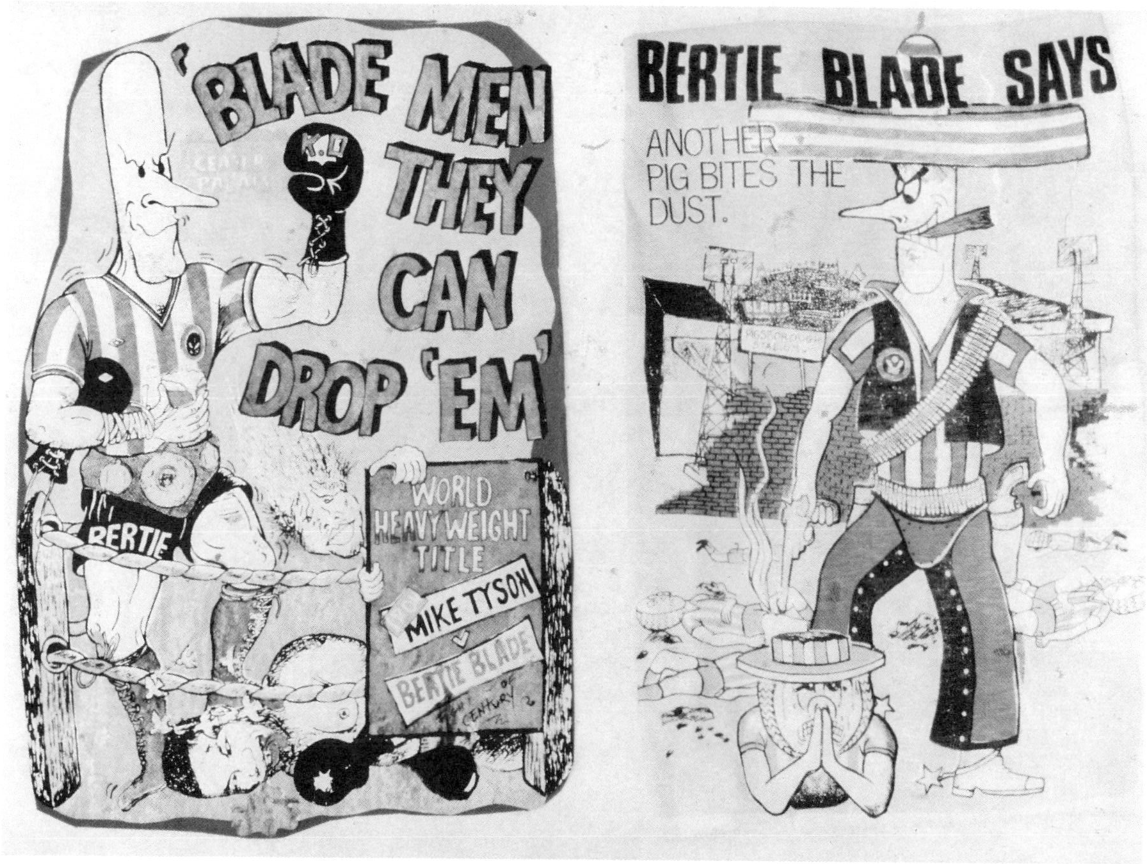
'BLADE MEN THEY CAN DROP 'EM'
K.O
BERTIE
WORLD HEAVYWEIGHT TITLE
MIKE TYSON
BERTIE BLADE
BERTIE BLADE SAYS
ANOTHER PIG BITES THE DUST.

Figure 1.

I'd Rather Have
AIDS
Then be a Blade

Rock Hudson

Figure 2.

Figure 3.

Figure 4.

Figure 5.

Figure 6.

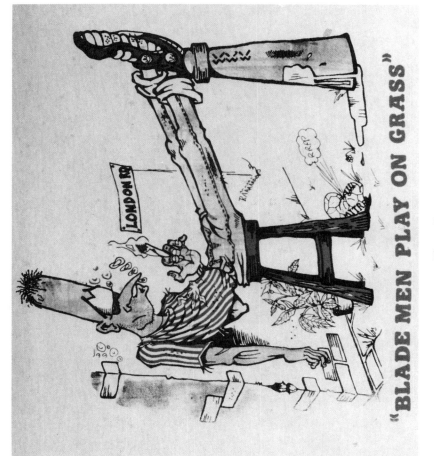

"BLADE MEN PLAY ON GRASS"

Figure 7.

Figure 8.

Figure 9.

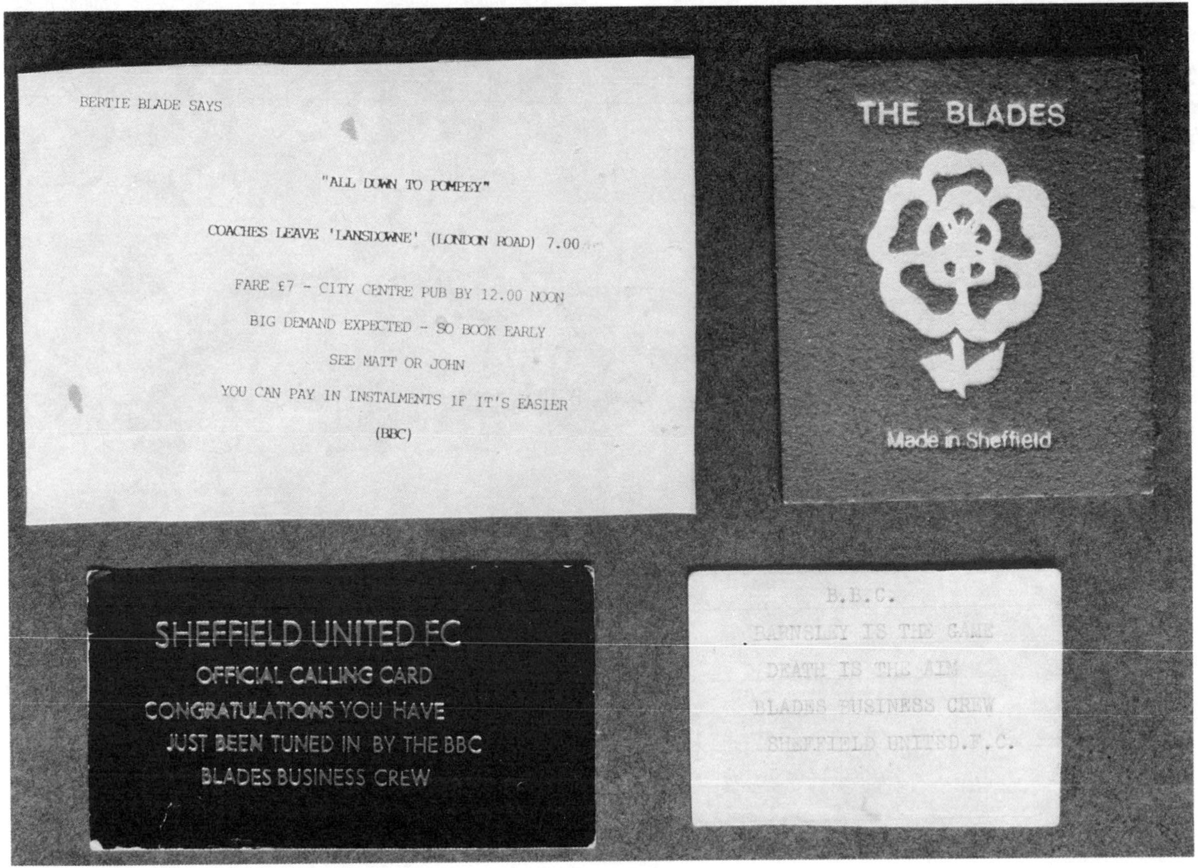
BERTIE BLADE SAYS
"ALL DOWN TO POMPEY"
COACHES LEAVE 'LANSDOWNE' (LONDON ROAD) 7.00
FARE £7 - CITY CENTRE PUB BY 12.00 NOON
BIG DEMAND EXPECTED - SO BOOK EARLY
SEE MATT OR JOHN
YOU CAN PAY IN INSTALMENTS IF IT'S EASIER
(BBC)
THE BLADES
Made in Sheffield
SHEFFIELD UNITED FC
OFFICIAL CALLING CARD
CONGRATULATIONS YOU HAVE
JUST BEEN TUNED IN BY THE BBC
BLADES BUSINESS CREW
B.B.C.
BARNSLEY IS THE GAME
DEATH IS THE AIM
BLADES BUSINESS CREW
SHEFFIELD UNITED.F.C.

Figure 10.

Part III

Evidence Meets Theory

Integral to the performances that encompass so much of the   _.ttus
are notions of 'correct' masculinity and comportment. In _..ost of these
notions participants are schooled in the local male cultural background,
whilst others are there to be learnt. As we will see, some enact performances
to teach a lesson; yet others, at times, are themselves disgusted onlookers.
The resulting issues, broadly encompassed under the notion of 'style', is a
combination of clothes, posture, gait, conversational topics and opinions,
and the threat of, or actual execution of, physical violence. Habitus on an
individual level provides a cognitive and motivating structure that helps
categorise and predispose situations. It is essential to recognise the sociation
of a Blade style, for in its *collective* dimension as *group presence*, via
symbolism, it creates an identity outside any notion of class (see Ricoeur
1967; Chambers 1986).

Chapter 7

'A Damned Bad Place'?: Sheffield[1]

Immorality among young people seems to be more prevalent in Sheffield than anywhere else . . . The younger generation spend the whole of Sunday lying in the street tossing coins or fighting dogs, go regularly to the gin palace, where they sit with their sweethearts until late at night . . . here and there cards are played, and at other places dancing was going on, and everywhere drinking . . . crimes of a savage and desperate sort are of common occurrence

(Frederick Engels (1892) *The Conditions of the English Working Classes in England in 1844*, p. 231).

The link between the hooligan participant and the socio-economic environment is often assumed to be strong, but academic research does not offer a reader much in the way of empirical evidence. Whilst Robins (1984) talks of 'satellite cities' and hopeless inner-city environments, he does not explain how the environment provides the motivation to join the hooligan cohorts. The Leicester sociologists simply speak of uncivilised outsiders from estates to which civil society has not penetrated. Then, with Taylor's (1989) postulate that hooligans come from two rumps – the 'underclass' of traditional workers (and non-workers) and the upwardly mobile and individualistic bourgeoisified workers – one begins to wonder which young man is *not* a potential hooligan? What this chapter seeks to show is that the relationship between environment and action is rather more complicated than an emphasis upon the determining role of social class allows. Other social factors are significant in the generation and manifestation of football hooliganism. These include three of considerable importance: local ideals of appropriate masculinity; youth styles; and shared consumption patterns; in short, the main constituents of the 'habitus' defined by Bourdieu (1977: 82–3) *'a system of lasting possible transferable dispositions which, integrating past experience, function at every moment as a matrix of perceptions, appreciations and actions'.*

Manner Beastly, Customs None?

For those who consider football hooligans as 'Outsiders' beyond the realms of civil society it is of note that the city's populace as a whole has been considered thus, and has frightened many an onlooker for decades. In 1861 one observer was provoked to state how the city was *'as devoid of the decencies of civilisation as if it was in the Dark Ages'* (quoted in Pybus 1994: 144), and forty years later another could comment: *'If not viciously criminal beyond the average . . . the Sheffielders were yet a turbulent race, very apt, whether with or without reason, to express their feelings by riot'* (R. E. Leader (1902) 'Reminiscences of Old Sheffield', quoted in Bean 1987: 29). When not rioting, its residents were prone to accusations of sedition and savagery, and, during the French Revolution, renowned for 'ignorance and disloyalty' and having a population that *'works for three days for large wages then drinks and robs for the rest of the week'* (quoted in Wickham 1957: 62). A century later, a Royal Commission was convened to consider the violence surrounding what became known as the Sheffield Trade Union Outrages (1867) (see Pollard 1959), and which led Engels (1892: 231) to comment on the city that *'crimes of a savage and desperate sort are a common occurrence'*, for there were both violence and incivilities surrounding the local political arena. Decades later Orwell (1937), in *The Road to Wigan Pier*, described the Sheffield populace as *'troglodytes'*. The same era heard Garvin (1932) comment that elections in the city in the late nineteenth century were some of the most savage and disorderly of Victorian times.

Though the above-mentioned issues were often overtly political in their nature, there were always personal matters to sort out. Throughout the nineteenth and twentieth centuries frequent violence occurred when pubs closed their doors. The most serious pub violence was the product of a gang vendetta over the control of gambling and the 'pitch and toss' rings of the early 1920s. The 'Gang Wars', as they became known, are still remembered in oral history and achieved national notoriety, earning Sheffield the title 'Little Chicago' (see Sillitoe 1955; Baldwin and Bottoms 1976: 48–50; Cockerill 1957: 88–95; Bean 1983). The vendetta produced brutal clashes, during which participants were slashed with razors, and one was even murdered. The police responded in kind, and a 'Flying Squad' established to smash the groups spoke a metaphoric language that local men understood when they met force with force: men convicted of murder were hanged.

Violence obviously continued in the post-Second World War period, although little is chronicled. Professional criminals exist, originally regarded as synonymous with entreprenurial scrap metal dealers and in recent decades with drug distributors. More recently, after the arrival of the Tory Government in 1979, high levels of violence were manifested in the traditional police and working-class male battlegrounds on the picket line (cf. Geary 1985; Wiles 1985; Scraton 1985). The violence demonstrated by grown men against police and some strike-breakers during the 1980 Steel Dispute (see Brownlow 1980) and the 1984 Miners Strike was of a very serious nature (cf. Fine and Millar 1985; Jackson and Wardle 1986; D. Waddington 1989). During the latter over 850 pickets were injured (and 220 police) in a year-long operation that cost the South Yorkshire police £40m and involved 1,700 arrests. Significantly, there was an absence of local condemnation of these acts from many quarters, be they the man-in-the-street or local politicians, in contrast to local reaction to the Blades' football-related activities, which are roundly condemned, particularly by local politicians. And thus, whilst violence is a fact of life in this city and region, it was only a way of life for a tiny minority.

Recruitment of the Hooligan

It is perhaps relevant to consider the absolute levels of football hooligan participation in the City. By the 1980s, the population of the city was around 530,000, in a South Yorkshire Metropolitan Borough with a total population of 1.3 million. The 1981 census figures suggest there were some 73,800 residents between the ages of 16 and 24, whilst those between 25 and 34 years numbered some 70,100. Given that around 50 per cent of these would consist of the female population, this leaves a rough figure of some 70,000 males between 16 and 24 years of age. We can immediately see from this that the vast majority – perhaps 95 per cent or more – were not football hooligan material. The question this generates, then, is: what is distinctive about those that make up the ranks of the Blades and the Owls? Or, put another way: what was it that militated against all those others joining in and behaving like Blades? What research is asking, essentially, is whether there are obvious differences between the hooligans and the other young men in Sheffield.

For this discussion it must be stressed that in many respects, until the mid-1980s, the working-class population of the city was not totally fragmented and fractured. The city and regional population had, and still has to a degree, homogeneous patterns (see Buckatzsh 1950; Hampton 1970; Corfield 1982: 102–3), and life in the city has many small-town features that seem to impose a common culture on its inhabitants. Interests are primarily in local neighbourhood matters, and many Sheffielders proudly call their city 'the world's biggest village' (cf. Hunt 1956; Holt 1986: 138; Burns 1991: 63). A sense of neighbourliness does prevail, so that the city traditionally had a low rate of suicide and mental illness compared with other places of similar size (Parkin 1971). In a sociable culture, ignorance is not a virtue, and people gossip employing a narrative culture with strong use of metaphor, irony and understatement. News spreads via the streets or through the drinking that occurs in the Working Men's and Social Clubs and pubs, which still today constitute the main form of social life for citizens of all ages. Like a village, Sheffield has a definable boundary (it is 15 miles across) and is not part of a conurbation. The city has never been a cultural backwater, and believes it has a strong sense of civic decency (see Wickham 1957; Inkster 1976).

Sheffield has had a continuous politically radical history involving, at times, tends of thousands of its inhabitants (see Donnelly and Baxter 1976; Mather 1959; Rowbotham 1976; Pybus 1994). Industrial production responsible for building the city relied on masculine strength and endurance, based as it was on both skilled steel-producing artisans and a factory/coal-miner proletariat. Both occupational cultures shared a sense of admiration for the skilled and strong male, many of whom in their leisure time played as hard as they worked. The former were self-employed on piece-work, and chose their hours in their small workshops, working when demand required it, and when the water was not frozen over or they were not suffering the effects of over-imbibing on a 'St Monday'. The latter have a reputation for heavy drinking that goes back a century, no doubt founded in a realisation that in such a dangerous environment their next workday could be their last. This combined with a political radicalism when downturn in demand saw economic depression and the growth of Chartism (see Mather 1959; Rowbotham 1976; Donnelly and Baxter 1976). In any sociopolitical analysis, Sheffield was and remains one of Europe's most proletarian cities, a bastion of Nonconformism and Methodism with tinges of Puritanism (see Hey 1976).[2]

Mid-nineteenth-century economic changes saw a shift from a dependent artisanry to a factory-based proletariat. This communitarianism produced a politically conscious workforce that has shown in various industrial disputes that it was not to be dictated to. Both the population that worked in collective industries and the artisans shared many socio-economic habits, and there was and remains an egalitarianism and a suspicion of the 'boss', or those who 'set themselves up' to be something they are not. The city was the first headquarters of trade unionism (see Pelling 1963: 70; Howard 1976: 59–73) and the first city to elect a Labour administration in the 1920s.

In this kind of environment male friendships were often a product of common experience and economic necessity. Today, manufacturing work has all but disappeared (see Westergaard *et al.* 1989; Lawless 1990), and for men in service jobs or without work male friendship – even those founded in football identity – can become an end in itself. Yet despite the economic difficulties and consequent poverty,[3] the electorate has not turned to any ultra-extremist politics. The city and region still return, as they have done for many decades, some of Britain's biggest Labour majorities and negligible votes for right-wing parties.

Theory and (Sheffield) Data

For the majority of Sheffield citizens, even in the age group of the participants, hooligans are considered 'Them', and somehow different from 'Us' by virtue of what they do and what is reported more than by what is known at first hand of the participants. There is, of course, the dualist concept of Us and Them, which is more than a simple question of class categories; but it cannot be argued that Blades and Owls come from any isolated class fragment. The argument of subcultural isolation in the lower working class does not really apply to districts of Sheffield that produced Blades, because, as Parker (1974) found in his study of 'The lads' of the Roundhouse district of Liverpool:

> the place is not subject to a homogeneous and linear socio-cultural milieu. It neither completely accepts the meaning of the dominant social order, nor lives by a completely distinctive subcultural blueprint. Instead we find a spectrum of viewpoints ranging from the 'respectable' law abiders to the street-corner delinquent. There is a considerable tolerance between these moral standpoints, and significant overlaps in certain matters. Such complexity leads us to challenge the sociologists' obsession with socialisation and the internalisation of distinctive norms of explaining delinquency in black and white fashion (1974: 113).

Local chauvinisms obviously exist; mental geographies betray prejudice that is sometimes based on class, and at other times based on vague ideas of culture, which have been recorded from before the First World War, when West of Sheffield fears were of both their lower-order city brethren and wild Irishmen (Gaskell 1976: 190). 'Them', in recent decades, are for some the inhabitants of the nearby towns of Barnsley, Doncaster, Rotherham, and Chesterfield, and mining and residential villages that are to be found around the city as suburban overspill or 'occupational communities'. Inhabitants of these districts and towns are regarded by city sophisticates as rather backward, and occasionally and stereotypically are referred to as 'hillbillys' and 'woollybacks'. Such districts and towns are regarded as having no attractions, and were it not for the existence of their traditionally lower-division and less-supported football teams most young male Sheffielders would rarely find any reason to visit them. The adjacent town of Rotherham, with 26 per cent of males unemployed and one family in eight dependent on income support in 1994 (*The Guardian*, 31 May), almost makes Sheffield seem affluent. Despite these negative stereotypes, neither Blades nor Owls particularly disliked their football teams, for these were considered too insignificant for Sheffield fans to worry themselves about. Yet Blades were also drawn from these areas, and so men who did not live in Sheffield would fight to 'protect' the reputation of the city, yet also fight for Blades and Owls against their city rivals.

Social status in Sheffield has been crucially dependent on housing, with roughly 50 per cent in council-owned accommodation. But this was a precarious status, because what in one decade was seen as status-conferring-housing could be stigmatising only a few decades later, owing to stigma imposed by 'problem families'. New housing estates were built in Sheffield each decade from the 1930s onward, each would produce a new form of living and result in families being moved from various areas designated as needing redevelopment. Some of these estates were built close to the city centre; others were ten miles away. As a result, one might claim to see the significance of local neighbourhood networks in the latter, and a possible identification with the city centre milieu for the former. Basically, any theory can be applied to an argument of the ecology of football hooliganism so long as one is selective in one's approach to the evidence.

Within the city, 'Them' for many working-class people are also those living on certain estates. Perceptions of class-structure significantly come from people's own particular milieux, and what is seen as 'good' and 'bad' in relation to housing districts is crucial to ideas of social status. Throughout the 1970s and 1980s, five council estates were notoriously known to house 'Them' (two are mentioned by Baldwin and Bottoms (1976: 12–26) in their study of crime in Sheffield) and were regarded as 'problem' estates by police, social workers and other city residents. Of three 1930s housing estates, one, Parson Cross, laid claim to being one of the largest council estates in Europe, and Wybourn (1,600 homes) had 24 per cent unemployed, 29 per cent of households single-parent and 79 per cent of households dependent on some form of state benefit in 1994. The Flowers Estate and the Manor Estate achieved notoriety by being regarded as homes to many 'problem families' and criminals. For some inexplicable reason two other large 1930s estates – Woodthorpe and Arbourthorne – do not merit the same stigma. Two early 1960s high-rise complexes of flats, Hyde Park and Kelvin, were of low repute across the thirty years 1960–90, and were considered high in crime and low in standards of personal behaviour. The former's reputation was established when a young girl was killed by a TV set thrown over a landing by a juvenile in the late 1970s, and even though it is now largely demolished, the name is still a source of derisory asides. The frequent appearance in court and in the local newspaper of offenders from Kelvin did nothing to combat common prejudices about the estate and its crimo-genic inhabitants. As a result Hyde Park was part-demolished in 1989 and Kelvin fully demolished in 1995.

Other districts attained reputations for other reasons. Just outside the city centre are Pitsmoor and Burngreave, which, in the past ten years, have gained a reputation for being 'mean'. In part this is due to the area's association with drug-dealing centred around all-night West Indian 'Blues' clubs. The high ethnic minority (mainly West Indian) population (nearly 25 per cent) and the presence of 60 institutions catering for clients ranging from battered women to probationers contributes to the stigma. There are further complications to be considered, however, for occupants of these estates and districts will regard only certain streets in the estates or landings of the flats as 'rough'. The possession of a 'reputation' will be attributed to certain neighbours, known colloquially as 'bad families', 'scruffs', 'rough arses', 'soap dodgers' and 'reyt 'uns' (cf. Damer 1974, 1992; Mawby 1979: 34; Coffield et al. 1986 for similar stories). A stroll round any stigmatised estate would show dirty, unkempt properties next to those of house-proud and outwardly 'respectable' families.

None of the males drawn from any of the above areas or types of areas were role models for the young men who constituted the Blades, though each could be acknowledged as being 'rough' or 'hard', or at times both. Indeed, it is significant for any discourse on the social background of Sheffield's football hooligans that few young men from the aforementioned five estates were to be found either amongst Blades or Owls. In fact only *one* Blade out of the core fifty (mid-1980s–1990s) was from such an area, although around fifteen Blades from the two hundred in the Appendix were drawn from the Pitsmoor/Burngreave estates. The fact that some were black surely adds a complication to any suggestion that hooligan identity is essentially based on white lower-working-class culture. The fact of the matter is that the Blades were *not* from Sheffield's 'inner city' or from the poorest and most deprived areas, nor for that matter from renowned 'rough' estates. In fact, as McClennan *et al.* (1990) argue, Sheffield's poorest districts by the late 1980s were actually on the *outskirts* of the city. Thus, to target the 'inner-city' communities in an attempt to stop hooliganism was always going to be a futile exercise; and whilst it may, *de facto*, be true of Sheffield that some of the poorest districts are on the outskirts, the precise location of such estates is not relevant to an argument concerning the level of deprivation from which hooligans come.

Mates, Status and Conformity

I would suggest Blades and Owls were not an 'Outsider' group of misfits within Sheffield, nor did they only find mates who were similarly inclined. All Blades socialised with non-hooligan mates, who would refer to Blades as being *'into football feytin''* or as a *'bit of a hooligan'*. These were not particularly condemnatory descriptions, for these contemporaries were generally more permissive of such actions than older generations – even though few could understand Blade motivation. Antagonism towards the football hooligan was often generalised, with hooligans ridiculed and reviled by older generations (especially football supporters) in terms such as: *'silly buggers'*, *'bloody daft'*, and *'idiots'* who should *'grow up'*. Publicity from media reports of court sessions is potentially shameful. There exists a folk wisdom that says: *'Good families do not turn out bad human beings.'* Consequently, there is surprise and indignation when a 'nice family' produces a football hooligan. The problem, however, is trying to establish by what criteria a good family is defined. Theorists might well argue that coming from a 'good home' would protect against becoming a hooligan. Yet in this contentious debate there is no proven causal link between delinquency and 'broken homes'. That said, the absence of family, or the reality of a family in which some young man was unhappy, could undoubtedly cause some to seek security in a pseudo-family or alternative friendship network. In consequence, the Blades could well provide this for a period of time, and this could be a positive side to the existence of this gathering.

So: who were the Blades and where were they from? Perhaps a good starting-point might be to see who was absent from their ranks. The middle classes and highly educated young men were noticeably absent, and this is not surprising, for the middle class have long pursued educational achievement and gained a geographic and social mobility as a consequence. Following football and 'hanging about' with lads was simply not on their agenda. In the decade of the research, I only came across ten Blades who had managed to acquire 'A' level exam passes; but this again is not surprising. Sheffield did not have a high percentage of school-leavers staying on to take further education. Yet by the early 1990s, no fewer than six Blades who had been regular combatants in the mid-1980s started university degrees under 'Access' courses, illustrating that some could capably combine Blade activities with academic pursuits later in life.

Blades and Owls were not the product of some particular occupational status. Though the majority were in manual occupations, these often demanded some skill: few Blades held bottom-of-the-pile jobs. The dexterity and ability to manoeuvre and manipulate the situation demanded in a diversity of occupations from scaffolding, mining, and shop-fitting to plumbing and demolition requires skills of command and a competence that many white-collar situations cannot easily match. What is notable is that many Blades were self-employed or controlled goods and information in positions of employment that could well have been in jeopardy had any bad publicity from some court hearing about hooligan matters come to light. And so an individual employed in some company or factory had much to lose. Many held positions as supervisor and foreman. Quite a few were self-employed in their various trades of plumbing, carpentry or building. Others were shop managers, gym-instructors, or self-employed drivers, and thus a cut above any idea of the hooligan as belonging to a wage-labour proletariat. Core Blades were generally 'doing well' in local occupational hierarchies, or were subject to boom and bust entrepreneural activity.

Those who were officially and therefore statistically unemployed were rarely sitting back bemoaning their hopeless situation. For a start, they had Blade company to socialise in, and in this network a multitude of opportunities to make money was available. Some of it was relatively harmless – moving rubbish for a fee, gardening, running a market stall, selling counterfeit clothing, acting as 'bouncers' in nightclubs. Other entrepreneurial activities were illegal – burgling, shoplifting, drug-supplying. Exactly where such activities fit into the Registrar-General's classificatory scheme is anyone's guess, although they provided high income at times. Once again research could be said to have drawn a blank, in that the employment patterns of Blades do not distinguish them from the majority of their non-hooligan peers.

Those Like Us?

Blades operated by a logic that was far more subtle and analytic than some sociologists would allow them. They knew from living in a shared space that the environment did not necessarily form the total person, and thus were forever making distinctions based on other, more variable criteria.

Blades came from all over the city; but particularly the South East and West, and from various villages outside the city boundary. Whatever their initial form of belonging, most Blades arrived as *individuals* at gatherings, particularly those who gathered on Friday nights. Their sense of inclusion became solidified as many original Blade mates were often no longer similarly motivated and dropped out. Hence the idea of an Ordered Segmentation principle was not applicable *intra* the group. Not for a minute would they consider themselves as an homogeneous entity, nor wish to be compared or spoken of in the same breath as those they sometimes stood and fought alongside. Some of this prejudice was geographical; and Blades often operated a mode of belief that spoke in a form of socio-geographic determination – albeit mainly in a joking context, but sometimes as a way of defining those they considered to be culturally unwise. Other forms of internal disagreement were based on variable perceptions of masculinity, and usually embodied in notions of style in relation to clothing and social activity.

Blades from outer-city areas present an even greater theoretical problem. Drawn from mining villages and suburban estates (both private and council) to the south-east of the city they numbered around fifty. Some of these – the 'Kivo lads' – were renowned in the mid to late 1980s, in the opinion of most Blade onlookers, as being just plain 'daft'. This opinion was elaborated via various comments, *'They piss on each other and think it's a laugh', 'They've only got to pass a pub and they're pissed up'* and the classic *'They're just football hooligans.'* In general, the core Townies regarded them with detached amusement, seeing them as victims of their tough talking, hard drinking, mining background; 'rough' lads, but definitely not role models. And whilst their behaviour was regarded as excessive at times, they were admired for regularly 'turning out'. They, in turn, acknowledged and even celebrated their 'otherness', and thought the Townies were more concerned with being *'cool'* and *'posing'* than with drinking and fighting. Despite this, these Townies and villagers regularly travelled and socialised together. Some of the Kivo lads turned out for the Owls in Benefit games, and occasionally on Friday and Saturday nights.

Conceiving of themselves as similar to Rotherham Blades and other villagers, they occasionally went to Rotherham for a night out, though the Rotherham lads discreetly considered them 'embarrassing'. Although all the Kivo lads were employed, a couple were forever on the look-out to save money or get something for nothing. When not drunk they were rational, reasonable, hard-working lads, who, in their locality, were considered neither as deviants nor as particularly 'hard cases'. Their 'otherness' was reserved for the occasions when they took on Blade identity, and the intimate nature of the small village meant everybody knew one another. These Blades would point out *'top lads'* in the village who they would not *'fuck about wi'*. In this setting they had equivalents to live with. This included Owls, and so the locality had a *modus vivendi* that did not include football fights. That said, when United played Wednesday in the 1970s, the two factions travelled to Sheffield on separate transport and sent warnings to each other as to what would happen if they saw each other *'actin' big'* later in the day. In 1994, the village saw a vendetta of tit-for-tat beatings occurring in pub car parks that were related to a local Blade–Owl hostility. This rumbled on for a year, but was of no concern to the Townie Blades. The latter, however, did involve themselves in other kinds of conflicts.

Was 'Race' an Issue?

The question of how good or bad race relations are in the culture from which Blades are drawn is one that must be considered before Blades and their equivalents can simply be dismissed as being violent racists. And thus the overall impact of racist behaviour in Sheffield as a whole must be explored. The Sheffield populace has little or no sympathy with fascism, for right-wing fringe groups have always polled a very low vote in both local and national elections. Significantly, the city was the only major conurbation in England to escape the serious consequences from the 'inner-city riots' of 1981. A protest march against police brutality by young people, primarily skinheads, even saw local Labour councillors amongst it. The police responded somewhat incredulously by claiming in June that such skinheads had injured 119 of their officers in 1981!

This absence of rioting might indicate that race relations in the city are relatively good, even though recent isolated disturbances involving Pakistani and Bengali youth with white counterparts in the south-east of the city do not bode well for the future. The immigrant population is small (about 4 per cent) numbering some 25,000 drawn from Bangladesh, Pakistan, the West Indies, the Yemen and Somalia. And though immigrants are found in density in half a dozen districts, there are no 'ghettos' (cf. MacKillop 1980) and newcomers are not (in my experience) regarded by locals as a 'threat' to employment. The Asians are employed mainly in small businesses, restaurants, taxi-driving and steel factories (often working long unsocial shifts in dirty conditions), and West Indians tend to be found in the service industries. This might be considered as evidence for discrimination – for it might be argued that immigrants had been kept out of the upper end of the labour market by racism, and there is probably some truth in this. In places, 50 per cent of the Asian and black youths are unemployed, compared with only 25–30 per cent of white. Yet children of the locally born unskilled white workers also end up in similar low-paid employment or are equally unemployed. In this situation and context it is important to compare race and class together.

I know from subjective experience that black and white youth mix well as football fans. Youths whose ethnic origin is Irish, Italian, Yemeni, Caribbean, and on one occasion Hong-Kong Chinese have attended the match and have been part of both Blades and Owls since the late 1960s, and neither set of supporters had a reputation for manifesting vocal racial prejudice or racial violence, or was renowned for being racist or anti-racist. Amongst the two Sheffield hooligan elements there was an imbalance, however, and by the mid-1980s there were definitely more blacks amongst Blades than Owls. The reason for this is not too difficult to establish, for those areas where the black population lived in greatest numbers were closer to Bramall Lane than to Hillsborough.

It is however a more complex matter than geography: also significant is the fact that Blades' gatherings in the 1980s contained more 'wide-boys', a category of entrepreneurs that increasingly included young black mates by virtue of the fact that many of them, unable to secure paid legitimate employment, moved into entrepreneurial activities. Thus Blades, similarly entrepreneurial, had opportunities to meet black lads, and they in turn had an empathy with their white equivalents that drew them to the Blades, many of whom simply were not representative of some part of the traditional concept of a working-class proletarian Sheffield youth. By contrast, by the early 1990s the Owls had only two black youths regularly within their core gathering, whereas the Blades could turn out some fifteen black or mixed-race youths in a regular complement of around a hundred men.

Owls and Blades have never been influenced significantly by right-wing politics, although there were individual Blades who belonged to Far-Right groups.[4] It was notable that two of the 'villagers', who attended a National Front march in Rotherham in the late 1970s, later developed a close, friendly contact with black youths amongst Blades. They were tolerant and relaxed in such company, and kept occasional bigoted remarks for black opposition players, when they knew no black Blades were in earshot! Across the late 1980s, only *two* members of the British Movement (later to become the BNP) were regularly amongst Blades. In Blade company these never promoted racist issues; their antipathy to an identifiable 'other' seemed to consist of hostility to Irish Republicanism and its sympathies. Indeed, on one occasion I saw one give £10 to a black Blade, telling him to repay it when he could. Two other Blades members of the National Front (NF) worked in a business that sported 'NF' stickers in their mess room. Yet black Blades occasionally dropped by and were welcomed with a cup of tea. Ironically the accusation of racism used so freely against the football hooligan was in turn used by those so labelled against those within their ranks who really showed this tendency; they were considered to an extent to be 'outsiders'.

Blades should therefore be construed as neither fundamentally 'racist' nor 'anti-racist'. Their antipathy towards public displays of racism ('Sieg Heil' arm salutes, racist chants, badges with symbols associating them with the Far Right) by occasional rivals was based on pragmatic rather than normative cultural values, and sustained the Blades' collective perception of their contextual moral superiority. Blades regarded such actions carried out by other fans not with deep political antipathy, but simply as *daft*. They knew such activity was not always a serious statement of political sympathy, albeit they knew very well that *some* fans were active in various Far-Right groups and that the England following held a number whose idea of 'patriotism' was beyond their definition. However, Blades generally ridiculed the semiotics of racism, which they considered neither funny nor clever, and certainly not something to which they aspired. For not only did 'Blade' identity cross racial and ethnic barriers, but non-Blade black youths were so similar in their cultural complexity that there was little for others to have to 'tolerate'.

Designations of Manhood

Any analysis of this area of masculinity needs to consider the complex relationships between the modes of thought it encapsulates and the specific experiences that the process of creating an identity can encompass. Inevitably there are pluralities of masculinity, and various assemblages of masculine style (cf. Moore 1988: 193–205; Brittan 1989), and so the tripartite approach to masculinity suggested by Cornwall and Lindisfarne (1994: 10) is useful in this context, for their vision contains material related to: notions of malehood, designations of manhood, and attributions of masculinity.

Transitions from boyhood to manhood were invariably work-related, involving rites of passage that invariably contained some well-intentioned horseplay and ridicule, wrapped around concepts of subsequent mutual respect and responsibility for the elders who would lead the young men into their new place in life. In return, the young men were expected to show willingness to learn from, and exhibit deference to the elders, and they in turn might take the novice out for his first pint in the local pub as part of a movement towards the adult life. These stages and this inheritance provided what some have called the making of a 'real man', and what others (critics) would call 'hegemonous masculinity'. Thus empowered, the youth took on the mantle of male authority, could attempt to show dominance in the domestic sphere, and – for those so concerned – seek via various social dramas to attempt to influence some areas in the public sphere as well. With the de-skilling of the workforce and the ending of exclusively male occupations the one surviving facet of masculine credibility that has come down to the current group of young men is the ability to fight, and via that ability to hold a reputation. Though not a material commodity, it is an asset that in some instances can lead to renumeration in pub and nightclub security. But, beyond that, it is an asset that can attain male respect, and it is this that is available in Blade gatherings and more than ever before unavailable in occupational cultures.

This idea of respect wherever groups of men are found is bound up with comportment and ideas of masculine honour and shame. For the young South Yorkshire male, and thus implicitly for the potential Blade, this process begins when he starts to attain an inner self-esteem and gain the respect of others, which is bound up and sustained by a currency that is a curious admixture of mates, money, cars and dealings with women or girls, and style, and fashion, and not being seen to be a 'mug', or being considered 'incapable' in the peer group, of not being too similar to men of his father's age, and in drinking, fighting, 'posing', being able to 'do the business', and so on *ad infinitum*. Perhaps the ultimate accolade, however, is to be simply regarded all round as being a 'good lad' in male company, neither a trouble-causer nor 'soft' (the antithesis of 'hard'). This 'enabling' masculinity is not equally available to all. Some talk a good fight and find those like themselves to mix with, whilst others 'talk shit', and others either tolerate or ridicule them. Some, often those sitting in the same pub as those participating in the above, simply have no wish to be involved in this form of male milieu.

Masculinity has its limits and its myths. Blades, like many other young men in similar contexts, are prepared to fight, or project a willingness to fight that stands as a proof of an undeniable masculinity. What can be said is that violent scenarios in the Blade world have three identifiable bases that were also practised by thousands of their peers and tens of thousands of their elders and forerunners, i.e., the honourable defence of women; the sustenance of the individual presence; and the support and defence of the collective. The first of these usually concerns a defence of any attempt to besmirch the name of a related woman, and is not just an honourable activity but an imperative. The other two depend largely on situation, in which options are considered and the levels of violence are open to debate. Although the term is open to a variety of interpretations, 'bullying' is censored (mainly via gossip, but in some cases by giving the bully a taste of his own medicine), and the use of weapons, particularly knives, in various scenarios and instances is considered, at times, unmanly and usually unnecessary and forgiveable only against those whose actions and motives are beyond the ideas of reasonableness.

Masculine competency in the eyes of other Blades was perhaps most visibly embodied in bodily comportment and 'hardness'; then in the ability to drink; then in sporting ability; and then in reciprocal banter – the main subjects of which were ridiculing other men and discussing men's relationships with women. Every opinion and joke was thus, in some way, critical and discriminatory, via such narration expectations of male and female norms were expounded. Women were not accorded equal status in all things; gender segregation was physical and philosophical; and homosexuality was an attribute at least derided and ridiculed by nearly all men and significantly by many women. For this reason, in the decade 1984–94 no Blade, if having homosexual leanings, ever 'came out' and declared them.

Obviously there was a diversity, firstly in how Blades met women and subsequently in how they treated them. But from a research point of view, most Blades were single. That said, a sizeable number continued their association despite cohabiting and even marrying. Some meanwhile rarely had 'dates'; others were 'boys about town' pursuing multiple liaisons; and others were separated or divorced, but were willing to try again. As in any male gathering of this kind, attractive women were always admired, be it in the role of pub strippers (*'dippers'*) or when in pubs passing the time; and in the latter scenarios a few Blades took their chance when circumstances permitted. At other times women would be the subject of ribaldry, for instance *en route* to away games, when it was not unknown for Blades to make lewd comments in pubs. These were meant not so much for the woman in question, but to impress their fellows and make them laugh. In essence the activity was ribald and suggestive, but was often (but not always) invoked against those who could handle it, and who were often as adept in its use.[5] However, comments made to a woman by a male who was not her boyfriend demanded of the latter retribution, and the only way understood was to demand an apology and, failing receipt of that, to proceed to violence.

Attributions and Negotiations: What a Man Should Do?

For many male altercations there was never any particularly 'good' reason given. Sheffield men (and many women) would no doubt rationalise these events as a life-stage ritual, and argue that if a fence were erected lads would gather either side, construct the other group as rivals, and attempt to climb over and thump those on the other side. It is true to say that lads of a certain age seem to be given a licence to behave like this by their 'community', as the parental upbringing often condones this, when small boys in their pre-teens will be advised to *'hit 'im back'* and *'be a man'*, so that an attitude of *'lads will be lads'* prevails. For many males scenarios begin with a realisation that other males are a threat by virtue of holding a different identity. With perhaps the exception of some in the middle-class south-west of the city, each school tends to regard its nearest as a rival, with pupils gathering at the end of term, when fights occur. Every school also has a fighting hierarchy, with a *'cock o' t' schoyl'* at the top whose status depends on the personality and abilities of the possessor of the title. But it is too simplistic to suggest that this simply produces some grim, age-based segregation and pecking order; some were happy to locate themselves in this hierarchy, while others did not join in such procedures. Violence and sport also came together in adolescent years, with inter-school football and ancillary hostilities featuring as teams met on the field and fought after the match. Concomitantly, youth clubs have long been the scenes of fights and masculine displays of prowess, whilst areas away from any institutional base such as the public spaces of shopping precincts, or bus stations, may see incursions of rivals from other districts to challenge youths 'hanging about'.

Other adolescent arenas for 'acting hard' are not so much spacial as temporal or transitional (see Mungham and Pearson 1976). The mobility offered by public transport since the 1960s has provided some with the opportunity to enact hostilities, so that a passing double-decker bus will see many adolescents looking up towards the upstairs back seat where the aspiring 'hard' lads gather. If 'looker' and 'looked' did not know one another, then a two-fingered gesture would often be exchanged, whilst on board fights with lads from other districts occasionally broke out. Transitional annual events could also provide theatres for hostilities, and the visit of the Fairground (*'t' Feast'*) to various districts was an arena to display juvenile 'hardness' or at least to 'look tough'. Such occasions could well see fights develop, involving lads who had 'come up' to the host district to fight local equivalents. The site of the fairground was not defended the rest of the year, but was action-facilitating for one day only, one that was loaded with a range of masculinity-enhancing activities for all ages that had nothing to do with 'Ordered Segmentation'.

It is only later, when violence can have greater consequences, with serious injuries sustained, that fighting becomes frowned upon. By the early twenties fighting was increasingly seen as silly, for, as various generations considered, by then a man *'should know better'* and should have other significant others to tend and turn to, like a girlfriend or wife and maybe a child. The youngster is now a man, and should ideally curtail excessive masculine wiles and *'grow up'*, *'get a steady job'*, and generally *'settle down'*. The pattern of this courtship leaves no place for any vision of a genderised 'positive-feedback cycle' in which women encourage their men to be violent, masculine types. Indeed, as will be shown, the opposite is usually the norm, for courtship was patterned by other cultural mores and male hardness was a fact that existed irrespective of the views of women.

That said, all violence scenarios depended on context, because *'attributions of masculinity depend on who throws the punch, who receives it and who is watching'* (Cornwall and Lindisfarne 1994: 14). These males between 12 and their mid-20s grow up being 'checked out' and 'sussed out' by their peers, a system and style of activity whose procedural origins are difficult to explain and that may well be incomprehensible to a middle-class reader. A youth regarded by others as manifesting masculine traits that are over-emphasised to the point of parody is known colloquially as *'showin' off'*, *'givin it big 'un'*, *'acting t' cunt'* or *'geddin' lairy'*, *'reyt big 'ead'* or *'wanker'* with a *'lot o' lip'*, who *'fancies hissen'* and *'thinks he's summat'* trying to *'start'*. If he is any of these or is generally *'flash'* in manner and dress, then he is in for trouble. He will usually be *'offered out'* – the term used to extend an invitation to fight. Challenges are rarely random, and, however tenuous, a reason is required. The most common is the accusation of *'starting'*, known colloquially as *'givin' t' eye'* or *'pikin' off'*. This is interpreted in one of two ways: sexual attraction or hostility. In heterosexual working-class Sheffield a male staring at another male means hostility and consequent trouble. If the starer is known to you and you have no desire to accept this silent challenge, then you look away. If the challenge is accepted, mutual staring is ended by one of the protagonists walking over to begin the formalised challenge. Before walking over, the challenger standing with his mates will usually have asked who his 'opponent' is. They can inform him of whether he's *'oreyt'* and a *'good kid'*, which may be sufficient for hostilities to drop. Alternatively he may be considered a *'wanker'*, or caution may be advised if the youth is believed to be *'hard'*, or *'can handle hissen'* or is *'a good feyter'*.

As mates they will reassure the challenger that they will back him up in case his opponent's colleagues *'start 'owt'*. If the 'aggrieved' is unplaced he can announce to mates his future intentions to *'sort it aht'*, or maybe that he is going to *'kill 'im'* (a figure of speech, not real intent). In the absence of an intended victim an aggrieved may well tell others: *'He's dead when I see 'im'* or *'I'm after 'im.'* Euphemism may be used also, so that *'I'm gonna 'ave words'*, *'That's it'* or *'I'm lookin' for 'im'* could be a veiled threat or just be an announcement of an intended verbal disagreement. Throughout conversations humour and violent imagery intermingle.

Should matters escalate, set facial expressions are assumed by the challenger for the benefit of the watching male audience, standing close by. The protagonist's challenge will then be on the lines of:

> *'What tha lookin' at . . . bastard/twat/cunt?'*
> *'Summat wrong?'*
> *'I'm offring de aht na.'*
> *'I think you and me ought to go outside now and sort it out.'*

The challenged has two options – to fight or back down. A man may take the latter course by *'talkin' his way out of it'*, in which case he may subsequently be accused of having *'bottled out'*, *'yiteoned out'* or *'shit 'imsen'*. In his defence the youth can be blunt and admit his aggressor would have 'killed me'. There is no disgrace in declaring that another man is a better fighter. Acceptance of a physical confrontation is equally formalised. A reply to the first question along the lines of *'not much'* or *'You . . . cunt'* or simply *'Fuck off'* means trouble. Fights should be 'fair' – that is, equally matched in stature and age. Weapons should not be used and onlookers should not join in. Breaches of this code are bullying; bullies need to be taught a lesson, and matters will escalate until honour has been satisfied. Violent acts can be justified later if the one who received injuries 'started' the issue, usually referred to by onlookers as *'mouthin' off'*. In which case most (often including the injured) will agree that he deserved what he got, because *'it wo' his own fault'*. Once revenge has been exacted the matter should be dropped.

As the adage has it, *'Tall poppies can get cut down; and a smack in the mouth can be a great leveller'*; and as many men would argue, there is sometimes a beneficial side to violence in *'calming'* a man down. However, an ability to fight does not automatically bring prestige or respect, for many Blades and Owls mixed in other social circles where this was not an important cultural consideration. Hardness should therefore not just be equated with that much-used but under-analysed term, 'respect', for the term really means nothing until put into a cultural context.

Given the absence of a condoning community, there was thus no single interpretation of the propriety of violent action within the locus of Sheffield and the hooligan world. Given this continually moving process there was never any 'positive feedback cycle' that would encourage the participants, for no one wanted a son to be involved in football hooliganism. Those who signed petitions against the activity in the 1970s, for example, were from the same working-class background as the participants. Again, there was a positive lack of feedback from women, and many Blades I knew were consistently badgered to 'retire' by their girlfriends and spouses, even though few of these knew the full extent of the extremes of their partner's behaviour.

Mad, Bad and Dangerous to Know?

What did it mean to be 'hard', and why did some aspire to be considered hard? And can we posit that local hard cases were attracted to the match because of the chance it offered for a fight? In truth matters are much more complex, and in the typology and mythology of masculine credibility, Blades and Owls have a small self-seeking audience. Elsewhere in the city and region every pub, estate, district and area has men who are renowned for their physical toughness. Some have a reputation for violence, to the extent they are accorded the title of 'hard bastard' or just plain 'mad', or in colloquial Sheffield, 'big hitters' or the 'real mesters'. But defining what behaviour is required to attain these statuses is difficult. Part of the problem lies in the audience, for there is no agreed definition of what constitutes a 'nutter' or 'hard man', and those in proximity to some renowned individuals are often able to subvert the mythology or stigma by anecdotal evidence that suggests the man in question has 'quietened down' or is 'not bothered any more'. Others, discreetly, might suggest to interested parties that the myth was built on sand and go on to recount some recent escapade to demonstrate this. Consequently 'hardness' is a difficult status to aspire to, and a precarious one to attempt to sustain, although some do in a variety of ways.

Actual violence, or the threat of it, or the avoidance of it, relies upon the competent masculine performance. For many years of their lives, working-class lads are dressing and comporting themselves to *avoid* various accusations and possible confrontational 'scenes' (see Willis 1977). A muscular male body, especially displaying a tattoo, signifies an aspiration to 'hardness', or at least a commitment towards certain standards. These tattoos, indicative of the wish to be considered 'outside' mainstream middle-class society, usually sport the names of loved ones followed by symbols of loyalty, depictions of violence, quasi-religious icons, and in some cases loyalty to football teams. I estimate that perhaps 50 per cent of certain groups of working-class men in Sheffield have a tattoo. Tattooing occasionally created an outraged response, but so long as such designs were confined to the arms and the back and were few in number, there was nothing 'deviant' in it. However, when tattoos proliferated or were extended to the neck or face, then the majority of Blades saw something in them that was almost a parody of masculinity.

But anatomy is not destiny. Destiny comes from what people make of anatomy, and, whilst big men and muscular torsos are desirable commodities in this male culture, not all of those with such physique want to fight. And not all such types are the 'hardest' in fighting ability. The mythology, however, has it that a 'big lad' will – because of his size – have the right qualities to punch. Blades tended to work on this principle, and would discuss lads they knew who were big and thus implicitly fearsome. But the quality that made a Blade was *'bottle'* in circumstances of street disorder not involving a one-to-one fight, and this quality was way beyond muscular torsos and tattoos. It was an indefinable attribute that some held for years and others experimented with, sometimes for only a day. This attribute was not a working-class inheritance.

Win or Lose, We'll Have Some Booze

As an occasion for heavy drinking and the occasional display of ultra-masculine behaviour, the pubs many young men gathered in, whether or not with a Blade identity, provide any control system with a considerable problem; and, given the historic association of pubs with amateur and professional football in the city, we can see that the game's correlates of masculinity and the celebrations of spectators and players will inevitably meld with excess alcohol use to create potential violence.[6] Company, place and context structure meanings, so that gender mix, and different social evenings and locations all generate their own specific style of drinking, and if need be subsequent fighting. The historic arena for youthful male hostility and violence has always been centred on the pub, and this has always caused the older generation much consternation. Whilst drinking in local pubs and working men's clubs has been a regular and, for the most part, moderate event for many decades, the major social event since the early 1970s for 16–30-year-olds is 'goin' up town' on a three-hour-plus pub crawl in the city centre's hundred pubs and (in 1988) fourteen night clubs. This is a change in behaviour since the 1970s, which influences this age group whether or not they are Blades or Owls. What is significant is that various generations since the mid-1960s have produced Blades: the argument is therefore that the Blades are a constantly mutating manifestation, reflecting in part some older local masculine traditions and others bound up with new youth cultures of consumption.

Crucially, Blades gather in leisure time, which in this culture traditionally means drinking time, and thus has caused many observers to see hooligan hostilities as a product of alcohol consumption. Furthermore, Blades gathered around the specific social event of the match, where the celebration of friendship was renewed in the only way that was culturally recognised – over a pint. There was nothing deviant in this, albeit such an opinion has to challenge those who adopt the Nietzschean idea that all prejudice comes from the intestine. Indeed, Blades were part of a culture in which 'drink' facilitated various male *rites de passage*. For tens of thousands of men, drink, pubs, and friendship are inseparable, and popular masculine wisdom permeates drinking practices – the best *'sessions'* (drinking binges) are always impromptu. Over-indulgence and its consequences are seen as part of growing up and are the source of boastful regrets voiced through various terms for incapability: *'blasted'*, *'wasted'*, *'para'*, *'pissed'*, *'bladdered'*, *'wrecked'*, *'rat-arsed'*, *'blindo'*, *'in a reyt tangle'*, *'legless'*, *'done it'*, *'out me 'ead'*. Men, it is said, usually drink when in a good mood to get into a better one. Thus, having a drink becomes inseparable from *'having a laugh'*; and so consumption is usually accompanied by a constant repartee of mutual insult, innuendo, ridicule (*'piss-taking'*) and joke exchange interspersed with serious narrative and, occasionally, collective singing, inevitably centred on football songs – Sheffield has no other oral or folksong tradition. The alcohol-induced pranks and statements are recollected and given weight because of their ability to have individuals *'rollin' about'*, *'creased up'*, *'on t' floor'* and *'hittin' t' deck'*. Such reminiscences invariably centre around occasions when much beer was consumed and a *'reyt laugh'* was had.

There is therefore a meaning to drinking that has nothing to do with being thirsty. There is barely a male social and leisure occasion that does not involve alcohol. Usually, the idea behind the *'session'* is to *'have a wobble on'*, to get *'a bit merry'*. Sometimes, though, the intention is to get very drunk in a hedonistic, excessive, carnivalesque pursuit. That said, for all the idealism surrounding these requirements there is no shame in a man acknowledging that his consumption capacity is lower than others; this is preferable to making a nuisance of himself. A few drunken acts may be excused, but the regularly incapable drunk who *'can't hold his ale'* is a burden, for his mates or others have a duty to get him safely home. Frequently, being incapable brings the stigma of being considered a *'piss-head'*, or *'beer-face'*; and this is a poor delineator of masculinity.

There are various social consequences surrounding this shared consumption pattern, which centre on aetiological meanings versus social effects. Most Sheffielders believe that *'when the beer's in the brains are out'*. Bellicose and argumentative behaviour under the influence is referred to as *'beer talk'* and *'fighting talk'*. Such claims or threats should be forgotten by all concerned the next day. Words spoken in a sense were excusable because of the beer. However, the excuse can become so formalised as to act as the prior disclaimer to intended action. Most fights occurred where most drinking took place; though some fights would be prearranged. Before the more temperate demand that such premises should be closed, however, it should be stressed that such premises and contexts have socially useful functions, for they act as a legitimate way of displacing tensions both at a community and at an individual level.[7] In Sheffield, and in many other placed in the world, a man *'sees'* and fronts an 'enemy' in the pub, and this is rationalised by the belief that others – particularly the family and especially the women and children – should not be brought into what is essentially a male matter.

As has been said, excessive drinking does not lead necessarily to violence, for the link is not so simple. Blades, for example, were the worse for drink on many occasions, but did not fight. At other times they fought without drink, and so the analyst can only say that the context of drinking produces greater changes in behaviour than the alcohol does. More important, though, was the fact that drunkenness was used to excuse a range of behaviour, be it considered unwise, reprehensible, or even admirable. So, with or without alcohol, Blades knew what their 'task' was, and what was the honourable response to various perceived insults, and most would attempt to accomplish this whether or not they had been drinking.

Youth and Crisis 1960–90?

A male concern with cavorting for peer groups is nothing new, and before football provided a locus for some there were other arenas in which to parade and provoke. Though many such practices had been prevalent amongst male groups for decades, what changed radically from the 1960s was the attendant rituals surrounding the rise of 'youth culture', and its association with the idea in the minds of others that there was a 'crisis'. What is also significant is the regional specificity of various masculine styles. What holds true for London may not be true for Sheffield and vice versa, so that much of subcultural theory has to be criticised for its unwillingness to challenge universals.

The concept of 'youth' is now difficult to address, as what was at one time presumed to consist in falling within the 14–25 age range is now a concept that it is problematic to define in terms of age. This is perhaps the crux of what being a Blade is – it is an attempt by some to play with and control in various ways individual identity. Consequently, the youth of the late 1970s and early 1980s need never grow out of what was previously considered 'youth culture'. With places to go and people to be seen with and in the absence of more constraining or significant identities, Blade identity was attractive to many even beyond their mid-twenties and early thirties, in spite of 'good' occupational status, incomes and mortgages.

One particular form of consumption associated with football hooligans' other leisure pursuits for decades was and is dancing. In the early 1970s and in an early 1980s revival, Blades attended 'Northern Soul' nights, following a music and dance form that remains under-researched. Known simply and colloquially as 'Northern', this youth cult attracted many football lads following midlands and northern teams. In these venues, the young men did not truly bring their footballing identity with them, for the 'Northern' night was reserved for a different type of male posturing that was based in dancing. However, hooligan friendships were made and provided the basis for visits and guesting at other hooligan venues. 'Northern Soul' venues were usually old dance halls in either deindustrialised urban centres, seaside towns or small towns on the periphery of conurbations. Those attending would partake in 'all-nighters' that moved their venues, so that there was no regular association of locale and place. Such events were the stylistic forerunners of the late 1980s 'rave' phenomena (see Redhead 1986, 1990).

By the early 1980s, performance and display needed neither music nor even a private venue. With the creation of pedestrian shopping precincts in the late 1970s a significant meeting-place for the youthful 'pose' was created in Sheffield's city centre, particularly in the Fargate shopping precinct. Youth and consumption thus became synonymous, as hundreds of youngsters aged between fifteen and seventeen gathered here. In 1984 one group known as the 'Fargate Trendies' emerged, adopting the name as a self-deprecating title that described their designer clothing and post-1980 'Casual' style fashion. Where and when the 'Casual' movement precisely originated is a matter of some conjecture. Locally the form and its associated styles can be said to have begun around 1981 – though football-related fashion rivalries *always* existed before the onset of the Thatcherite period. What happened after was that the fashion changed shape and colour.

Being cosmopolitan and a product of a media-generated imagery the casual 'style' was witnessed first-hand via the wider travel experience of various fashion 'leaders', and was not merely founded in local working-class culture. Around 1980 an observer at the football match would note the beginnings of what might be termed 'respectable-looking' Blades – groups of young men clad in designer jumpers, crew neck T-shirts, gold neck chains and designer sportswear. Hairstyles were generally short, sometimes with a 'wedge' cut (long thick hair on one side, shorter and thinner on the other). Clothing and fashion formats were borrowed from various middle-class arenas. The tennis club provided Tacchini, Fila, Ellesse, Adidas, Diadora, Robe di Kappa and Nike. The golf circuit was emulated with Pringle, Lyle and Scott and Slazenger jumpers, and Lacoste T-shirts. In winter the ski slopes provided inspiration for Berghaus labels. Later, the country set Burberry and Aquascutum jackets and scarves appeared on the autumn football terraces. That said, such garments were not accompanied by middle-class college-boy looks! The lads still had the *stare*, and a few – for the match – had practical 'walks' (known colloquially by their various overriding traits: 'shoulder-rolling', 'bowling', or 'stiff-legged'). By contrast with what happened in the earlier hooligan years, then, the lads became very unobtrusive in appearance and made little or no attempt to manifest an 'otherness', be it vocally or sartorically. Looking good now, they were critical and snobbish about their peers and rivals. But, the crucial element of Casual style was that whenever a garment was defined as being 'in', someone somewhere would decide it was not. The question by the early 1990s was really what designer label was *not* noted when the lads gathered.

A minimum sense of style was expected of Blades and was appreciated by many, even though there were those who never joined the fashion parade simply because its fluctuations proved too expensive; and so, within reason, a Blade could wear just about anything. Such fashionable clothing was expensive, and as a result some of it was stolen or was counterfeit. However, a considerable percentage was bought by young men, who, at this point in the 1980s, had employment, an expendable income, and access to easy credit. For those without such resources, a variety of entrepeneurial activities were available, be it shoplifting or manufacturing counterfeit designer goods. If the garments looked good, few wanted to know of their origin or quality.

More important, though, for any analysis of style is the recognition that casual style was practical and eminently sensible for three reasons. First, it was totally unlike the media stereotype of football hooligans, and so, through their skills in presenting themselves for a couple of seasons, Blades could avoid officialdom along their travels, yet be able to locate rivals by their similar dress. Then again pub landlords, both at home and away, who were wary of obvious football fans were not necessarily so concerned by respectably dressed young men. In other words, such style was non-threatening. Thirdly, such attire was sensible in football grounds, for it was comfortable, warm and sometimes afforded access to parts of the ground that the police and club officials would otherwise have denied to the stereotypical hooligan. Just as importantly, casual and sports-oriented clothing was conducive to running, be it from pursuing police or from rival fans. Generally, the clothing was enabling, as individuals had simultaneously to persuade the authorities of their honesty and respectability; convince rival fans of their toughness and a willingness to confront; and impress fellow Blades with their individual style. The absence of club colours in this genre implied to some critics that this gathering was non-team-oriented and therefore was parasitic upon the game; but this is an incorrect reading of events. All of these style-brothers were long-standing fans and enjoyed the action that match-day brought; but in this situation they were competing at another level off the pitch.

Style and Place: Drink and Dance

The Casual style was also significant in that it pioneered a collapse in one leisure demarcation, and facilitated easier access to some pubs and nightclubs. The fashion was 'midway' in that it was 'dressed up' but at the same time was not 'dressed down'. It was 'good', but could be worn without any feelings of self-consciousness in pubs considered to be 'dives', although it did not quite meet the door policies of part of the disco nightclub world of the early and mid-1980s that demanded a jacket, collar and tie, and proper shoes (cf. Giulianotti 1993: 21).[8] Post-1980 Blades thus found places to socialise that their predecessors would never have used, and they frequented the preserves of the University student and the musical *avant-garde* simply because a relaxed door policy and dress code almost ironically gave the new stylistic Blades access to locations that would have once seen the management flinch at the thought of having the 'appalling' Blades on the premises. The style and place also included new forms of consumption and excess. Alcohol was never dropped, but drug use became a norm for thousands in the city and hundreds of Blades.

The hedonistic culture that the concept of Thatcherite individualism and the idiom of 'self' let loose after the late 1970s saw a change in drinking habits, so that heavy alcohol use, late-night and all-night raves, and the use of the drug 'Ecstasy' (MDMA) and other drugs has produced behaviour that many of the local elders simply do not understand. In this post-traditional social world there are now not only prolonged weekend excess, but also midweek and lunch-time drinking sessions for those not confined by the discipline of labour that previously structured much of male identity.

That said, Blades were clearly never 'drug-addicted demons', as some of the media might like to suggest. Until the late 1970s marijuana was mainly confined to the city's University circles and West Indian 'Blues' and 'Shabeen' premises. The late 1970s saw the rise in popularity of 'Whizz' (amphetamine sulphate), particularly amongst working-class males. Inhaled ('snorted') via the nose or poured into a pint pot, mythology had it that the bad stuff floated, whereas good stuff did not. This was superseded from 1980 by recreational drug use, most obvious in pub toilets, where the sweet smell of marijuana competed with cigarettes and alcohol. From the mid-1980s no city-centre pub seems to have avoided the 'toilet camaraderie' that accompanies the clandestine 'skinning up' process of building a 'joint'. And though heroin could be found in the city, it was not used in the circles in which Blades mixed. Seen as a drug for 'losers' and those without the personal abilities to become a Blade, heroin was said to be found on 'sink' estates and in bedsit land, with the urban dispossessed, who were a long way removed from Blades society. A more fashionable and affluent section 'snorted' cocaine powder; but at £50 a gram, this was a substance beyond most of those in the lower financial divisions. And perhaps for this reason it was never passed around Blade gatherings.

According to some analysis (see Redhead 1990 and Hills 1991) the hooligans left their match-day pursuits to seek out another thrill: one remote from repressive policing and synonymous with the use of the drug ecstasy. Though this theory was propounded by Hills from a London viewpoint, we can analyse it with Sheffield in mind. Blades and Owls both had their own favoured venues for 'raving'. Up to a dozen Blades (not all were interested in the scene) would, on occasions, enter what was considered to be an Owl venue, and though they would indulge in the time-honoured pastime of staring out rivals, fights did not occur. This is not to say that the 'rave' scene suddenly turned hooligans into 'peaceniks'; rather, it coincided with a period when hooliganism both against Their Boys and Owls was going through one of its many changes, and was declining in frequency for a variety of reasons. It is opportunistic simply to link the two events together and find a causal relationship. For the problem with such an analysis is that it cannot account for any subsequent 1990s hooligan outburst – unless the theorists consider that the decline in raving at around the same time suggests that the party was over, and everyone could return to the fighting. The reality, of course, lies in the diversity that lies within Blade make-up, for a Blade could be a good raver and a good Blade at one and the same time, just as at an earlier period they had been good Northern Soul boys as well as committed hooligans.

Knowing the Hooligan?

There is a greater issue here that is challenging sociological orthodoxy. The cause of the problem is embodied by the questions of what to make of, and how to classify, the class affiliation of the Council-employed gardener who, two years later, was a company rep with car and expense account? And what of the two Blade miners, forced into redundancy, who became a publican and a computer operator respectively? What of the Blade florist who became a University undergraduate? Or the labourer who bought a van and now lives by carrying out property repairs? Or the entrepreneur who spends his summers in nightclubs in the Mediterranean, but winters in Sheffield stealing clothing? The issue then is to ask how sociology deals with and interprets these situations? For sociology's response to the complexity of the matter seems to be to merely provide what might metaphorically be described as a 'snapshot of events'. Long-term participation, I would argue, inevitably produces a more complex reading of the social process, and thus denies them their simple classifications and categories.

The true way of interpreting Blade make-up is to see it as an identity that is bound up in the common activities of male leisure, drinking and football enthusiasm, and that has these simple elements surrounded by symbolic, semiotic and cultural forms that give them meaning and resonance. It has no conscious notion of creating 'resistance' (real or semiotic) to some vision of hegemonic morality or lost community, and is multi-vocal to the extent it denies any simplistic labelling. Moreover, it is not established to exist in opposition to some other youth subculture. With the 'gear', travel, match-going, drinking and socialising, Blades are consumers *par excellence*, and in any debate around issues of 'Incorporation', Blades can certainly be said to achieve this on a commercial level.

⸢I will, however, argue for aspects of a socio-environmental causation, that, to an extent, is built around the production and sustenance of norms of masculinity and that condones some involvement in violence.⸥ These modes of thought and belief systems provide the templates for appropriate responses in specific situations. However, as in all behavioural forms, there remain areas of ambiguity, so that what would perhaps seem to be an ideal template for a specific response will simply not be responded to by some, even as others are willing to overstep the mark. Blades therefore operated their own social process, yet had values that were no different from the rest of society; nor did they show any disregard for conventional morality. It must be apparent, then, that social identity in this situation is temporary, age-specific, and forever being contested by the construction of particular 'others'. Sometimes this would occur and be lodged in the social; sometimes it would be focused on aspects of gender. For some, known as Blades and Owls, it was football-related.

Notes

1. King George III (1800) after visiting the city. Cited in Pybus (1994: 79).
2. We could ask whether it is perhaps correct to assume that working-class morality (in so far as Elias acknowledges its existence) is borrowed from or emulates the middle class? In a discussion on 'respectability' focused on Sheffield, historian Reid (1976) has argued it was a concept that arose from a working-class emulation of middle-class norms in the eighteenth and nineteenth centuries owing to the workshop system, and produced a 'deferential' working class in a hierarchical (not dichotomous) type of society. Nationally a different picture emerges, when another historian, Hill (1988), describes early nineteenth-century forces of religious dissent as both politically radical and having a strong strand of 'respectability'. Sheffield, having a long history of political and religious non-conformism in opposition to local élites, would therefore seem to fit this theoretical position. The protagonists of such non-conformism, as Hill (ibid.) noted, argued for the development of the separateness and uniqueness of working-class culture, regarding it as morally superior to that of the upper class. This view challenges the perception that the aristocracy and middle class sold the concept of a well-ordered and sober life to the working class. The Labour movement of the late nineteenth century, Hill

argues, stressed the necessity of a sobriety and diligence that was not so much an imitation of the middle class as something that came from within. Elias himself said as much (1982: 311–12), and notices in times of change that those lower in the social strata actually see themselves as superior, and exaggerate the perceived differences between themselves and the higher classes. Though working-class deference can be found, there is little to suggest that those in the lower socio-economic hierarchy over the past ten years wish to emulate their so-called betters. Indeed, we might ask who are these social betters and who are their social inferiors?

3. Even in May 1990 15 per cent of the population were described in a City Council report presented at an EEC Conference as living in areas of deprivation or acute poverty. This 15 per cent included 25,000 children. Whilst the unemployed rate had fallen from 16.7 per cent in 1986 to 10 per cent, the report described how this hid both a discrepancy between inner city (20 per cent) and outer city (5 per cent) and a growing gulf between skilled full-time and unskilled part-time workers (*The Star*, 18 May 1990). This 'blip' of recovery was over by 1992, when the Sheffield Council Economic Development and Employment Department found that unemployment in the city was rising faster in Sheffield than anywhere in Europe. With 20 per cent of the under-25s of the city jobless and a rate amongst men generally 30 per cent higher than the national average, the Council calculated the true rate of unemployment in the city at 17 per cent (over 43,000) compared to the Government's adjusted figure of 12 per cent (nearly 30,000) (*The Star*, 9 January). Three weeks later a survey showed that the electoral constituency of Sheffield Central (which encapsulated Bramall Lane) had, at 18.4 per cent, the highest unemployment levels of any Yorkshire constituency (*The Star*, 30 January). In October 1991 a report found that in one area of the city 4 in 10 households were dependent on state benefits. Across the city nearly 20 per cent of households were dependent on benefits and one in eight were unemployed (source: 'Poverty in Sheffield', produced by Sheffield Freedom from Poverty Campaign). In 1993 the Norfolk Park Estate, consisting of 3,000 houses, had one-third of its working population unemployed and six out of ten people dependent on state benefits (*The Star*, 15 July).

By 1993 15 per cent of the population (i.e. 72,000) suffered dire poverty. A Council-commissioned study identified 33 areas, some of which had eight out of ten families with children and no wage-earner. Since 1987 areas classified as suffering acute poverty had doubled. A sample of the 33 areas showed the following:

	Population	Unemployment Rate
Wybourn	3,750	53%
Flowers	2,482	52%
Kelvin	1,800	62%
Hyde Park	1,700	65%
Parson Cross	10,500	45%
Manor	5,000	63%

Source: Alan McGanley, 'Poverty and the Poor in Sheffield' (Sheffield City Council).

4. Two incidents, taken in isolation, could provide ammunition for accusations. In the mid-1970s, twenty Blades were approached by the then National Front Organiser for Sheffield. He requested help alongside 'his lads' against the Socialist Workers Party in the city. After buying drinks he suggested they walk with him to where the 'Reds' were selling Left-Wing newspapers. This single event was the full extent of Blades' involvement in the Far Right, and they were quickly disillusioned. As Benny, one of the twenty, explained: *'He didn't 'ave any lads, it wo' just 'im! We told him to fuck off an' never saw him again, except when he got into t' papers when he got thrown aht o' t' party for marrying a black "bird".'*

It took another six years before any form of Right-Wing activity was evidenced at the football ground. In the second case, two Unitedites briefly sold National Front newspapers outside the ground in 1982. This provoked the hostility of black Blades and other match-goers, and they were told to leave by police. They never sold the papers again. Their precise whereabouts during the research period is not known. One is believed to have become a Mormon; the other apparently left Sheffield.

5. One night in a seaside resort two girls were not too happy about meeting seventy Blades. Wearing high heels and mini-skirts and aged about 18, the two were subject to ribald comments before a drunken Blade, attempting to dance, became over-enthusiastic in his 'flings'. This ended with both girls in a small ditch that ran through the park. The girls returned with police; but a change of shirt concealed the Blade's identity. Many laughed at his actions; others said to mates it was 'not reyt'; but nothing was said to him. A year later, again at a seaside resort, two teenage girls after exchanging banter with twenty Blades were subjected to the 'bumps' in celebration of one's eighteenth birthday. During this she sustained torn shorts, which left her somewhat immodest. Apologising Blades held a 'whip-round', producing £7 and a new pair of shorts. Across ten years I did see some 'grope' women in pubs. In ten years there were four such instances.

6. In 1865, 11 out of 13 football clubs listed in a local directory had public house addresses (Golby and Purdue 1984: 168). In origin, Sheffield Wednesday played on a pitch belonging to the adjacent pub (Davey 1983). All Sheffield Supporters Clubs were founded in and had their meetings and departure points from public houses. The game then and now, for spectators or participants, remains the prelude to a pint. Each Sunday lunch-time, hundreds of Sheffield pubs witness sportsbags piled in corners whilst their owners conduct the post-match post-mortem over a pint. Appropriately, the most common pub name in the city is 'The Sportsman'.

Sheffielders' alcohol consumption has historic notoriety going back to the nineteenth century (see Engels 1892). Consumption was bound up with masculinity and manufacture. Beer drinking was believed to be fortifying for steel foundrymen and for cleansing the dusty throats of steel-grinders and coal-miners. A pub was to be found adjacent to nearly every factory gate, and apprentices – fetching beer for their elders – provided the next generation of consumers (see Davey 1983: 75 and 100). Out of the city's historical association with Chartism and Teetotalism the radical politics remain, but not the sobriety. That said, Sheffield-brewed beer is strong and, even today, is nationally renowned for this quality.

In 1991 a full-page article in *The Star* (5 February) announced that Sheffield was a 'Drink Problem City'. The evidence for this came from the Chief Constable's *Annual Report* to the city's licensing magistrates. Apparently Sheffield had Britain's fifth largest alcohol problem, because 1990 criminal proceedings for drunkenness showed a 13 per cent increase on 1989 (1,923) to 2,007. More facts and figures were compiled the same year. Readers of *The Star* (6 June 1991) were told of 25,000 people in the city with a drink problem. The claim, made by the Sheffield Alcohol Advisory Service in a publication *'Towards an Alcohol Strategy for Sheffield'*, stated that in 1990 2,067 people had been charged with being drunk and disorderly (+244 on 1989), and that offence was the most frequent one for the 21–30 age group. In 1990 Sheffield had 1,084 licensed premises.

7. At one time local licensed premises were the site of bare-fist fights (Davey 1983: 83–7) and could be said to have facilitated the gang wars vendetta.

8. An explanation of the Casual phenomena comes from Redhead (1986, 1991), who argues that the 'Casual' was a remake of the 1960s 'Hard Mod' (see Hebdidge 1979) that explored the 'upward option' of social mobility and added elements of 'Glam-Rock' to defy essential definition as it pursued exclusiveness. A better understanding of the 'Casual', I

suggest, comes from Giulianotti (1993): he introduces Bourdieu's (1984) idea of 'cultural intermediaries' alongside elements of post-modern theory. These intermediaries, borrowing from Featherstone's (1991: 5) argument, produce markets and distribute symbolic goods that serve to dismantle the established symbolic hierarchies. But who are these people? For Bourdieu it was the 'new petit-bourgeoisie', for Featherstone it was those in media, in advertising, and in the world of fashion and what he calls the 'para' intellectuals (ibid. 9). Thus we can identify the effects of the media as being influential in promoting and propagating the Casual style.

Chapter 8

Taking Kops and Posing: The Spatial Nature of Hooligan Contests

I maintain that there are few finer moments in life than when you step into an alien city centre en masse, *all dressed up ruthless, and watch those people stare.*

(Kevin Sampson (ex-hooligan), *The Face*, 1985)

In their own vernacular, football hooligan gatherings identify spaces as their *'manors'* or *'patches'*, either materially or symbolically. Yet none of these spaces is able to display the fixity – whether in terms of established boundaries or permanent ownership – that popular motions of 'territorialism' or 'turf' imply. Anthropologists know that space does not exist as an ontological fact. Space is specialised, endowed with meaning, and embodied with regimes of articulations, some of which can be inherently conflictual (cf. Lefebre 1991; Shields 1991). How a group locates or zones space results in its classifying and constructing a sense of place that will always contain social and horizontal spatial relations. At one level all spaces are resources in which personal and collective expressions of social agency, or impositions of power, are realised and exercised. At another, the presence of other spaces may be crucial at times, for they function as counterpoints in bestowing meaning (Bailly 1986: 83). As Sack (1986: 76) argues, control of space cannot be merely notional, but is synonymous with the exercise of power. Territoriality therefore does not exist unless there is an attempt by individuals or groups to affect the interaction of others. Analysis of Blade activities thus requires an examination of the nature of *locales* and *stations* in relation to the arrival and departure of the varying passengers who use them, and in this particular case, of the contestations of football hooligans. As Fiske (1993: 11–13) argues, *locales* are spaces that involve *'continuities between interior and exterior, between consciousness, bodies, places and times'* and, implicitly confront, resist or evade *'imperialisation'*. In contradistinction, *stations* are places *'where the social order is imposed upon an individual'* and self-constitution is denied. As will be demonstrated, the greater stationing of football grounds and the attempts to control resulting impositions (structural and procedural) encouraged counter-intuitive creations (i.e. agency) to provide for escalated levels of re-localisation.

'Come and Have a Go': Game On

In its origins football ground architecture reflected the ritual contest on the pitch. The home side had a preferred 'end' to play towards. Away fans, being in the minority, were expected to gather at the opposite end, where home fans of less celebratory and participatory status would be congregated. The pre-match toss of the coin would always (and still) see the United captain choose to kick into the Shoreham End in the second half of the match, thereby reflecting the game's cultural conviction that fans could be worth a goal or give their team a psychological lift. Thus began chants in support of the team and denigration of the other players and fans. However, not all such fandom was purely mechanistic in nature, and organic rivalries between fans emerged that were relatively autonomous to the game. With no segregation between the mid-1960s and the late 1970s, rival fans would attempt to stand on one another's 'kops' – the terracing behind each goal, populated in part by the young, rowdy fans, and generally the focus for the most vociferous and partisan. This competitive practice of 'taking' these ends became the *raison d'être* of a young hooligan supporter's actions (cf. Marsh *et al.* 1978; Ward 1989).

There was a symbiosis between the young male fandom and ground space, and at Bramall Lane the Shoreham End (United's kop) was defended in the early 1970s by the self-proclaimed 'Shoreham Boot Boys'. By the late 1970s these had become the 'Shoreham Barmy Army', a title adopted in various chants manifest as hundreds of participants gathered on the kop from 1.30 p.m. onwards. Rival fans would usually enter around an hour before kick-off, whereupon Blades would direct threatening chants at them, initially down the rear of the kop stairway, to the turnstiles the opposition were entering; then fight them as they attempted to walk up the stairs. Occasionally rivals entered quietly, and on a given signal (or when their team took the pitch) would begin chanting as they either walked towards or stood facing the Blades' 'mob'. The contest had begun. Fans caught in the middle of the impending confrontation would back away, thus creating a circle or 'hole' of empty space. Invariably, within half a minute, one side would begin the fight by rushing across the space, and wild punching and kicking would ensue. Though the procedure looked messy, its protocol was well understood by the participants.

The outcome might be complete victory for one side, signified by: the disappearance of opponents into other spaces, including the pitch; the postponing of further hostilities, to be possibly reopened by particular events on the pitch; or no genuine conclusion, usually as a result of police intervention. The visitors' aim was to chase the home fans away and occupy their area of terracing.[1] Alternatively, if Blades successfully repelled an encroachment, rivals would spend the match in the right-hand corner of the kop protected by police, with Blades surrounding and chanting at them. The defeated outsiders might then call it a day and climb over the low perimeter fence, and with a police escort, walk along the cinder track adjacent to the pitch to the Lane End, where most visitors were to be found. Their walk would inevitably be accompanied by chanting and gesturing towards Blades on the kop, who would reply in kind. Fellow fans would applaud them as they approached. This 'pose' was part of the day for many; the police disparagingly but knowingly called it the *'Hero's Parade'*, for the defeated visitors had been *'game'*, and had *'had a go'*; and Blades had a duty to do the same at their ground.

Impositions and Creativity: Structures and Agents

Obviously not all spectators wanted to be part of these disturbances, and such visible rivalry attracted easy political and media attention. For those who wished to take no part in such proceedings the football ground, at times, had become an intimidating place. Questioned by journalists as to the possibility of ground segregation, the club replied *'paying spectators must be free to choose their own positions'* (*The Star*, 13 January 1969). But for the alleged benefit of the game and public tranquillity something had to be done, and a shift in public order policing tactics was combined with structural additions. Four diagonal railing-style metal fences five feet high were erected along the back of the Shoreham End in September 1974. Two gates were built into the low perimeter fence, allowing police easier access to the crowd, and, at the back of the kop, a platform was built on which two policemen could stand, allowing a 'bird's eye' view of the 'mob'. At the same time police began to search fans as they entered the ground, which led to the banning of certain regalia, such as wooden poles supporting messages written on cloth banners, and heavy industrial footwear. At times (at some grounds), male adolescents under 16 without an accompanying adult were banned. Extra police were also used to control fans both inside and outside the ground, and from the mid-1970s their observations began to be supplemented by Closed Circuit Television (CCTV). Moreover, police also began standing at turnstiles, monitoring fan loyalties and directing visiting fans to a police-declared 'Visitors' End'.[2]

In this situation Blades had to be creative to continue their scenarios. Initially, they simply moved off the kop and gathered in an unusually shaped piece of terracing adjacent to the Bramall Lane End known as 'The Triangle', from where they would direct chants at nearby visitors. This began in 1973, but ended the same season when police closed the section to all spectators. In any case the number of Blades gathering there had become too great and a larger area was needed. From 1974 until 1979 Blades regularly gathered on the Bramall Lane End, and the 'Lane-End' mob was born, with the collective celebration of mental illness in their chant:

> *We're all mad, we're insane*
> *We're the boys on Bramall Lane*
> *Na Na Na Na, etc.*

This move meant that Blades could now confront rivals on the terracing, an area traditionally reserved for visitors. Moreover, the Lane End was relatively easy for a home fan to enter. One could hide overt football favours in the shape of the United scarf (*de rigeur* at the time) up a jumper or inside the denim jacket. And should police ask, your allegiance was definitely with the visitor's city, and if necessary you imitated the regional accent. Once inside, a ritualised gathering and movement was required that played to an audience across the pitch: to the kop, whose members knew what was happening. Having grouped on the uncovered section of the Lane End the Blades (when numbers were sufficient) would walk slowly but directly to terracing behind the goalposts, where the rival hooligan element would have gathered. Another, more dramatic, entry was for Blades to gather outside the ground, and then close to the kick-off to enter the Lane End terrace from the stairway and chant and wave scarves towards the Shoreham End. The wave would be returned as an encouragement from that End to their fellows to do battle, and cheers arose as the skirmishes began. The combatants' activities therefore provided entertainment for thousands of other uninvolved males.

Police Command, Club Obey: Extending Control

There were various debates about what affect this behaviour was having on the rest of the crowd. But something had to be done, and structurally this meant that Bramall Lane became the first football ground in Britain to have a police station built into it. Whilst this was convenient for both administrative and incarceration purposes, the realisation that an officer-presence did not stop fights saw the introduction of other administrative methods of crowd control. Thus, from the mid-1970s onwards, matches began to be given 'all-ticket' status, with the rationale that ticket restrictions would tend to deter ticketless fans from travelling to the match, and segregation would be ensured. Neither of course was achieved![3] In mid-1989 the Club removed fences at the back of the kop after the Hillsborough disaster, when police and fire brigade demands met with the agreement of the city council. This was rationalised in the local press as being *'in the interest of crowd control and safety'*, which, ironically, was precisely why they had been erected some fifteen years earlier. Those around the perimeters of the terracing were taken down the following year. At the same time police in various places, including (briefly) Sheffield, attempted to erect 'exclusion zones' around the ground. This checkpoint system helped reinforce the police pronouncements and constructs that the Hillsborough disaster was an organised attempt by ticketless fans to storm the gates to attain entry. Two other control measures were available: coding the match in the name of security and altering the time of kick-off (and sometimes the day). Whilst the former had been common since the 1970s, the categories changed but the criteria always remained in the hands of police – who would claim their intelligence was the only source of reliable knowledge. As for altering kick-off time and date, this had been done since the early 1980s. However, this cosy procedure, in which the Club obeyed police requirements, was challenged by the demands of live TV coverage, and in some instances, if money did not actually talk, it certainly was able to outbid the police requests.[4]

To stop rival fans gathering near to one another, police made various parts of the ground unavailable for spectators. The first 'no man's' area was created in the late 1970s when a small rectangular-shaped terracing joining the Lane End with the John Street Terrace was cleared of spectators after Blades had begun to gather there. This space was considered sufficient until 1984, when the prohibited area was extended into the Terrace by a few yards and a fence was erected. Over the next two years two further enlargements of this 'sterile' area occurred: the John Street area became one of the most intensively policed places in South Yorkshire between 1984 and 1992. During the early and mid-1980s, police were stationed in pairs at every entry gangway in the stand; dozens sat along the back row of seats, whilst others sat along the side. Twelve officers would normally stand among the Blades, although their numbers could be as high as forty. These would be in formation, standing side by side on the pitch perimeter looking in at Blades through the fences. Even before entering, Blades had to pass a dozen officers standing by the turnstiles watching for signs of drunkenness, searching them as they entered, occasionally threatening them as to the consequences of their behaviour and occasionally abusing Blades they recognised. Post-Hillsborough this became more intense, with officers even smelling the breath of fans and forbidding entry to those they deemed to be 'drunk'.

With all this attention an observer might have considered the area to have been a prior trouble hot-spot. Yet nothing could be further from the truth. In fact, the John Street terrace fence was breached by only two Blades in fifteen years, when, as a dare, both scaled it in the half-time interval. As Blades cheered, one then stood on the pitch dancing, until four PCs jumped on him. He was charged with threatening behaviour and fined £150. Minutes later his mate climbed the fence, ran across the pitch and sat in the stand. He was immediately arrested and ejected but not charged. Post-1990, with the removal of fences following the Hillsborough tragedy and the construction of a low wall and a wide gangway, the pitch perimeter became an easier conquest. Consequently, big occasions could witness United fans celebrating goals by jumping out of the John Street terracing and dancing on the cinder track. Visiting fans could similarly allow their joyful celebrations to extend to the cinder in front of the Lane End. On seeing this police would rush from all directions, probably fearing a pitch invasion. However, no fan ever went on to the pitch at these times, and seconds after they jumped out they would jump back into the terracing. However, unable to tolerate this breach of a boundary, some policemen would set out to arrest the celebrants with incredible enthusiasm. Some would even sprint to catch them and make the arrest.[5]

Blade Creativity: Stage One

The segregation of football supporters within grounds had three kinds of dysfunctional and unforeseen consequences. Firstly, the initial segregation of supporters tended to be spatially incomplete. Spaces such as toilets or food kiosks, traditionally associated with more decorous and pacified behaviour outside grounds, often remained accessible to opposing supporters, and thus became new venues for the contestation of rivalries. Although now infrequent, segregatory deficiencies (open spaces, unlocked gates, errors in police escorting methods) still occasionally became facilitators of brief, unanticipated conflict. Furthermore, the attempted stationing of supporters within designated sections of the ground could, on occasions, be purposively elided. Sneaking through a turnstile into the opposition's territory, purchasing blocks of tickets for alien or 'neutral' spaces to tease rivals, occasionally stealing complementary tickets left at collection points for the opposition's players, were effective strategies in evading control strategies. Thirdly, and more substantively, on the mundane occasions when segregation was effective *a priori*, the impositions against contact with rival fans and others were re-stylised, resisted and circumvented.

In the early 1980s the spatial semiotics of hooligan action were re-codified for this new era of segregation. The home 'ends' and 'kops' were largely abandoned by the hooligan element, to become the home for those dismissed by Blades in various terms of ridicule and masculine contempt, such as the *'shirts'*, *'cavemen'*, *'Christmas trees'*, *'canaries'*, or *'beer monsters'*, and for the category of *'loyal supporters'*, the non-critical term used for those who enjoyed a chant. No longer were rival fans as protective towards their opposing ends, as the visiting football hooligans would be funnelled into their traditional end at each ground, to be greeted and ritually mocked by the home hooligans, now ensconced in the nearest stand or terracing available. A repertoire of insults and appropriate responses developed as epithets and, very occasionally, coins would rain across the fencing. The intensification of masculine style within 1980s' football hooliganism partially resulted from such segregation. Rival mobs seated adjacent to one another provided captive targets for ceremonies of public degradation via chants of irony, sarcasm and scatology. An outside audience also came into play to a far greater extent, as the semiotics of the hooligan presence became spectacularised, not just at the ground, but also for national consumption through wider television cover. For those watching the TV coverage, the sight of rivals, dressed up and draped nonchalantly across ground seating and glancing contemptuously at one another, underscored the ground's spatial transformation from locales of territory to stations of semiotic resistance.

The police looked on at this often silent scenario: initially, as long as the protagonists were kept apart, they were usually happy; then post-1990 police began arresting for the slightest transgression of a morality they imposed. Segregation at this level necessarily ensured that the expectation of disorder within the ground was minimised. Subsequently, the non-combatant fans who had formerly been dismissed by the hooligan element were persuaded, as a result of their own ingenuity and the pursuit of excitement, to move into these pacified social spaces, if not displacing the hooligan groups, certainly matching them in numbers as they mocked opposing fans with improbable threats and match-related expletives. Partially reflecting the extension of the definition of football hooliganism to cover increasingly nebulous behaviour, police then came to stigmatise purely participatory fandom within the ground.

Sites of Disorder: Bramall Lane 1980–1994

Amidst this debate over policing numbers and hooliganism, no one saw fit to chronicle levels of disorder in order to be able to present arguments as to what might be considered an 'appropriate' level of policing. To fill this void this section attempts to consider this from a perspective of having attended most of the games in the past twenty years. We can begin by looking at instances where fans ended up *on* the pitch at Bramall Lane. Barring the few occasions at the end of games when incursions were out of spontaneous joy, the last time such an incursion occurred with consequences for crowd control was in May 1981, at the end of a match that United lost and that relegated them to the Fourth Division.[6] Two years previously, at the last match and on the occasion of United's again being relegated, this time to the Third Division, another invasion had occurred.[7] There were no other comparable pitch invasions between 1980 and 1995. And though fencing did play a part in preventing invasions, incursions did occur at the last matches of the season, when joyful fans celebrated successful results. Not all invasions were the result of hooliganism, some were joyful; but not all the onlookers knew the difference. In these ecstatic celebrations, of course, some fans were arrested, providing yet another statistic to 'prove' that football hooliganism was rampant.

If we were to demarcate the ground in this same time-period and analyse which locations were prone to disorder, we would find little to chronicle. The *Shoreham End* last saw sporadic disorder in April 1980 at a United–Wednesday League fixture, when a hundred Owls knowingly trespassed on the kop. This was easily brought under control by the police locking one of the diagonal fences to the rear of the kop, thus separating the factions. Later, a Cup match against Wednesday in 1981 and testimonial games in 1984 and 1987 saw brief scuffles brought under control by police in less than a minute, with Owls receiving a police escort to the visitors' end. In some two hundred League and Cup matches between 1980 and 1987, no Shoreham End disorder occurred until late 1989, when a hundred Manchester United fans were found to have bought tickets locally for the all-ticket FA Cup quarter-final. This was not an attempt to 'take' the kop, or even to fight, for they were escorted off, having declared themselves to police. Shortly before this match the Boxing Day fixture with Leeds saw forty visitors escorted off when they too were found to have circumvented the all-ticket arrangement. And in both cases the groups with tickets were not 'Their Lads', but simply a collection of fans of all ages (see Armstrong 1994). Thus the site that was the most populated and partisan produced less than six disturbances in fifteen years (1980–95) from around 350 matches. Of these, only the first produced injury to a participant, when an Owl was stabbed in the buttock. There were no reports of any injuries to police in this time.

Elsewhere, disorder was even more minimal. The *Bramall Lane End* saw only two brief disorders, both in 1984, which police controlled in seconds. In both instances six Blades entered the area believing away fans would not confront them. They were wrong. Ironically, occasional 'trouble' or disorder witnessed in this area was always between visiting fans and Sheffield police. The latter, in the mid-1970s, traded punches regularly on the visiting fans' terracing. Watching Blades cheered their efforts as they landed on the visiting supporters. But the only notable incidents in recent years occurred in 1985, when Leeds played at Bramall Lane, and six years later in 1991, when Chelsea were the visitors.[8] Statistically then, in this area of the ground, there were no *actual* fights between rival fans in the fifteen years (1980–95), other than a few stand-offs and posturing exercises and three outbreaks of police–visiting fan disorder. Elsewhere in the ground trouble was so rare that one is forced to recount incidents that in other circumstances would be barely worthy of mention.

Aftermatch Aftermaths

From the mid-1960s and through the 1970s fights and chases outside the ground were usually confined to streets and roads leading to the railway station and coach park, particularly Shoreham Street. In response to fights involving visiting fans and damage to their coaches police escorts of football coaches began in the 1970s. Escorts involving police motorcycle riders from the edge of the town to the ground before and after games were made easier when police demanded that visiting coaches did not arrive until one hour before kick-off. Those travelling on the 'Football Special' chartered trains were simply let out at the same time as the home fans to make their own way to their transport. Not surprisingly, in this era of free movement fights and chases were frequent. It was not until 1983 that Sheffield police decided to control access from the railway station regularly, and even then their policy seemingly varied by the week. Blades never attempted to attack fans in the mid or late 1980s who had travelled on the Special and were now under 'escort'. Such fans were not considered appropriate opposition; that said, some Blades occasionally shadowed this entourage when they realised Their Boys had travelled on scheduled service trains, and were using the escort (or had been forced to walk with it by police) *en route* home. This shadowing was a way of telling opponents they knew who they were.

Throughout the 1960s and 1970s visiting fans were always allowed out at the same time as home fans. Not surprisingly, there were regular fights in the streets around the ground. To curtail this, police changed their tactics from 1981, and held all visitors back for up to half an hour until the area had been cleared of all evidence of home fans. But tactics could change with the season, and with the police instructions given over the public address system towards the end of the game to visiting supporters. In 1984/5 these tended to increase rather than decrease the level of disorder, for the announcements said: 'Those visiting fans who wish to leave the ground now may do so. Those wanting a police escort will be given one to their transport if they remain in the ground after the final whistle.' In accord with this, the exit gates on the visitors' end would be opened fifteen minutes before the end of the game. And if Blades standing on the nearby John Street terrace saw 'Their Boys' move, they would leave and stand on John Street in anticipation, so that three times in that season post-match scuffles broke out there. At other times, having heard the message, rivals would attempt to leave the Lane End, but were prevented by police. There seemed to be no consistency. Eventually, by April 1985, visitors were being told over the public address system to stay where they were at the end of the game and await a police escort; they were no longer offered a choice. After being detained fifteen minutes visitors would be taken to coaches and trains, or to cars and vans parked in nearby streets.

Eventually this problem was overcome, and from the 1987–8 season visiting coaches were escorted by police vehicles directly to the ground, with the occupants shepherded straight to the turnstiles. Coaches then returned after the game from a designated coach-park to pick up immediately outside the ground. From 1990 police closed Bramall Lane to all traffic from 1.00 p.m. to 3.00 p.m. to allow visiting coaches to park, and then closed it again at 5.00 p.m. to allow all visitors' vehicles to leave the city centre in a convoy escorted by police. For those wanting security the day was completely safe. But not all visitors wanted their movements planned and curtailed.

Another route to conflict was provided by an area adjacent to the away end and London Road. This labyrinth of back streets built around terraced houses and small workshops was known to Blades as 'The Triangle', and its geography was defined by three pubs. Mini-vans and cars parked here were a problem for police and visitors. Such travellers were often from the hooligan element, attempting to avoid the impositions police had created around organised transport. And if Blades could not fight the occupants of these vehicles, the vehicle could very occasionally be damaged. A registration number was often a give-away, whilst a sun shield might advertise a garage in rival territory, or perhaps their fans might have been seen leaving it. If it was one used by 'Their Boys', news of where it was parked would be passed around the Blades, with the normal response being along the lines of *'might go up there after'*. This was neither a promise of action nor a suggestion to others as to the correct form of response. And knowledge of a vehicle did not bring an obligation on anybody to act.[9] Police gradually took control of this area from the early 1980s, and mounted police were introduced after the game, whilst police vehicles cruised the area more frequently. Then, from late 1986, police did not allow the away fans out of the ground until they had cleared the area. This was achieved by walking six abreast along various streets, effectively sweeping away lingerers whom they knew full well to be waiting for held-back rivals. As a result, after-match fights became a rarity: in 1986/7 there were only three such incidents. The 1987/8 season saw no incidents (mainly because visiting fans were inconsequential), and subsequently only one vehicle was damaged in the next seven years, as thwarted Blades did not bother to wait around the ground after games. When the change in the licensing laws permitted pubs to be open all day from 1988 Blades were inside various licensed premises minutes after the game. Only those who knew of the possibility of a confrontation with Their Boys bothered to roam the streets.

Blades Away 1968–86: Organised Violence or Pragmatic Responses?

Originally, in the 1960s, away travel was a collective event, with fans travelling by coach. After this, collectivity was enhanced when train travel on British Rail 'Football Special' excursions became popular. However, this brought incidents of 'train wrecking' and widespread public condemnation. Blades, like their contemporaries, sometimes indulged in train-damage, but such activities were limited and sporadic, with the last such occasion occurring in 1979.[10] Visiting fan coaches were also damaged on occasions, and though a rare practice in Sheffield, this did happen, usually after the match, when missiles were thrown as the vehicles passed. Occasionally a passer-by might suffer the incivilities of fans travelling to games; but the chances of a member of the public's receiving personal harm were slender.[11]

Such activities and ways of travelling were rather *passé* by the 1980s. Aware of public opinion, the supporters clubs' coaches banned the 'troublesome element' from travelling with them. And Special Trains were so tightly controlled by police they lost their appeal to both the hooligans and mainstream fans. But there were other unofficial ways of moving around. Between 1981 and 1983 Blades travelled by the scheduled inter-city 'service trains', on which 'block bookings' could be made. This entailed groups' buying similar tickets to the same place, and thereby obtaining them at a reduced rate. Cheap travel was later facilitated by what became known as 'Persil tickets'. These began as a commercial venture by a detergent company in conjunction with British Rail, but inevitably soon produced groups of travelling hooligans: mothers and girlfriends would purchase washing powder that carried special travel vouchers on the packages. These allowed two to travel for the price of one, and Blades would split the fare. The offer ended in 1983.

Soon after, various individuals began organising coaches that were not part of the supporters clubs' excursions. Such 'unofficial' coaches were not exclusive to the 1980s, for similar arrangements had been operating since the early 1970s. What was new was that these became the 'lads' coaches, and an established alternative way of travel. Blades referred to such coaches by various self-denigrating names – *'thugs' bus'*, *'early coaches'*, or the *'daft coach'* – and occupancy was limited to 'The Lads', who knew the risks the day held. The police, of course, had to 'capture' this vehicle, even as the Blades were trying to outsmart them in order to meet the waiting home lads; and so occupants boarded with the knowledge that the idea behind the day was a drink and a possible confrontation with rivals. These were the 'Early Crew', with a job to do before the match began, and travellers boarded by a self-selecting process, paid their own fares, and in return received a full day of risk. Risk had to be calculated, for no one wanted to suffer injuries at the hands of rivals. Between the mid-1960s and mid-1970s, with rather ineffective policing procedures Blades, like Unitedites generally, tended to be selective about away games. Some fixtures would see little away support, whereas places where Blades anticipated a lesser breed of hooligan to themselves would attract large followings. The informal hooligan 'League Table of Reputation' has a long history that is as manufactured and distorted as the phenomenon itself. Somewhat ironically, the increased efficiency of policing had the counter-effect of increasing the potential for hooliganism to a degree, by making it possible for many thousands to travel with little personal risk.

Another factor affecting forms of travel was the status of the football club. Playing small-town opposition in the lower divisions meant that a large gathering was not required, for the locals did not have sufficient numbers to merit a big turn-out. And so, from 1982 to 1984, with United in Divisions Three and Four, Blades often travelled in hired mini-vans. Dozens of such vehicles proclaiming a Sheffield address could be seen parked in streets around the ground, and this blatant advertising had its drawbacks. Home lads could let the tyres down, break windows and await the occupants' return. Following promotion to Division Two in 1984 Blades knew they would face some 'good' and numerically stronger home 'crews'. So once again coaches were considered preferable. To put the issue succinctly, police behaviour in part determined the choice of transport, but the reputations of rival fans determined the type of vehicle used.

Various individuals amongst Blades took responsibility for organising these 'unofficial' coaches. There were two motives. One was personal: financial gain for the organiser from the profits of the journey. But also, at a collective level, coaches removed the problems of 'getting there' for hundreds. There were obvious problems for an operator, in that few Blades knew fifty others well enough to create a regular entourage, and an informal network was thus required to fill the coach. This was facilitated by a post-1979 change in Blades' existence, when for hours every week they shared a common social space in the pub and were able to relay information. News of an intended coach thus became common knowledge, perhaps only an hour after the organiser had suggested the idea. Crucially, the role of coach organiser should *not* be linked to any notion of 'leader', for such excursions contained very little planning. In a parallel manner 'trouble' (whether on arrival or *en route*) tended to be unplanned and spontaneous, and, contrary to voluble opinion, planned violence was not the aim of the day.

Such travel was as much about male sociability in leisure time as watching the teams play. The day was built around the match, but the match was often peripheral to the day's events, which provided the chance to have a drink. Any trip within two hours' drive of Sheffield did not merit 'makin' a day of it', i.e. remaining in pubs in the vicinity of the match until late in the evening. The decision as to when and where to stop *en route* was usually taken by a consensus. Thus, in a sense, a coach, van, or car organiser when taking bookings took the 'will of the meeting'. He could choose a town and use this proposed 'stop-off' as a selling point. Alternatively, if enough people wanted to come 'straight back' he would drop the idea. It was all very pragmatic. There were various factors to consider. One was distance – a case of *'all travel and no drinking'* – or it could be a case of *'not on t' way home'*. Then again, the proposed venue might not be welcoming – *'Too posh'*; or be limited by a vision of its potential – i.e. *'it's dead'*. Others were avoided because of some perceived mystery – *'don't know much about it'*; and the winner usually had two main characteristics. One was distance – *'It's only an hour away'* – and the other was antecedents – *'We've 'ad a good time there before.'* At other times operators could attract custom by emotional and material enticements. The promise of porn videos on the coach TV would appeal to some, whilst the chance to *'have a drink, no worries about driving and no worries about some bastard seein' yu get out of yu car and kicking one of your panels in'* was often a vote-winner. At other times there was no apparent logic about the choice of transport.

Games in London traditionally meant a night in the West End, returning at midnight. Between the late 1960s and the mid-1980s, games in the Capital would require a 24-hour excursion for some. After a Friday night 'session', Blades would board the midnight 'Mail Train', arriving at 5.00 a.m. The group then found comfort in the 6.00 a.m. opening of pubs in the London Bridge vegetable market. Later they made their way to the vicinity of the ground, and after the match enjoyed the West End, with the day ending on the midnight train. In 1988 the late trains ended, and so did this twenty-year procedure. In London Blades got into fights with a variety of oppositions – sometimes around railway termini, and sometimes in West End pubs. Opponents were usually London hooligans *en route* to or from games in the North, or other visitors to the capital from the provinces. There was nothing inevitable about the recognition various crews afforded each other. Sometimes rival lads would happily exchange stories over drinks; other times they fought. It was interesting to note, however, that never once in the years 1970–94 did Blades combine forces with Northern lads against their Southern equivalents.

Like any other social group, Blades also enjoyed a trip to the coast. Seaside fixtures usually meant at least one evening and sometimes a whole weekend away, accompanied by a lot of drinking. Such excursions sometimes produced disorder at the end of the night with local lads, or other football fans who had decided on a similar venture. By looking at the fixture list Blades could deduce which fans might be calling in which town. Occasionally Blades expressed a desire for a fight, with the required ingredients being *'a good drink, a good feyt . . . then get home'*. What a 'good fight' was, varied from person to person. But for most it meant no injuries and no arrests; and at times they got exactly this. At other times places were avoided as being too risky, because of the potential for violence.[12]

Controlling the Nomads

Police monitoring of public transport routes for the arrival and escort of away fans has been particularly acute at train stations. In order to avoid 'capture', away hooligan formations responded, particularly in the early 1980s, with efforts to re-establish degrees of self-control by seeking alternative travel arrangements. Decisions over the method of transport chosen to particular away fixtures tends to depend upon the recent history, the success of prior transport methods, the reputation and reliability of those who set themselves up as transport 'organisers', and the likely numbers of those attending, relative to the kudos to be accorded the waiting rivals. The most popular method was the use of privately-hired coaches and transit vans. The visitors' selection of coach transport rather than rail had two major consequences. Firstly, the coach allowed a greater degree of spatial control regarding entry and 'fan' activities within the host/rival city. However, more importantly, via such transport the awaiting police escorts could be eluded, with the result that the visitors exercised a fuller autonomy in choosing pubs for pre-match congregation. Such venues may be decided upon beforehand, at the recommendation of more knowledgeable members of the party, and enable numbers to be swollen by those arriving by other means of transport. More commonly, coach travel served to collapse the distinction between disembarkation point and private congregational spaces, with drivers instructed to drop the party off at particular pubs, thus avoiding the public spectacle of 'fans' having to stroll an uncertain distance through the host city with or without a police escort. Secondly, coach travel enabled the construction of transient hooligan spaces along the main arteries linking the visitors to the host city. Other disembarkation points may also be found where confrontations can be sought with 'third party' forces. In contrast to the activities in the host city, these additional opponents need not have a football input, but may simply be any aggregation of young men gathered in a core space (public house, city-centre streets, market squares, motorway services, seaside promenades, nightclub car-parks). Importantly, when such confrontations do occur, they should not be interpreted as being instrumental variations on some sinister hooligan agenda. They are, instead, historical continuations of the male working-class tradition for revelry in liminal, recreational spaces that has long resulted in occasional brawls contained within the perimeters of the outsider–local antagonism.

With this background we can now examine what role individuals had in structuring the process. Beginning in the late 1970s with Benny and the 'Barmy Army', the lads' coaches changed operators and style over the decade. Whilst all occupants knew what they were doing when boarding, not all were alike and not all wished to be associated with Blades on other vehicles.

The Barmy Army: The Hooligan Buses

Benny, a 'core' Blade from the early 1960s beginnings to the early 1980s, was the first Blade to institutionalise the 'lads' coach', with journeys beginning in the 1979/80 season. The origins were simple. Benny, a 'troublemaker' in the eyes of various committee members of the supporters club, was banned from travelling on such coaches. As a devoted follower, he organised a coach of his own; helped by his mate Todd. The subsequent label 'Barmy Army' was given to his coach by the secretary of the supporters club, voicing his disgust. Benny and his mates adopted the name, and the 'Barmy Army' consisted of a 'core' from Benny's locality and others from all over Sheffield who had met via the match. To fill the seats, he would take anyone, with Todd collecting names at the previous home match. The point of departure was from the pub where Benny drank, and then the swimming baths in the city centre. Todd collected the fares, whilst Benny always sat at the back next to the emergency door. At other times the 'Barmy Army' coach originated in Rotherham. The late 1970s and early 1980s saw a large Blade gathering from this town, capable of almost filling a coach on their own. At times 20–30 Rotherham travellers would pick up their Sheffield colleagues and combine forces. There was no animosity between the groups, mainly because neither were homogeneously structured entities. The chosen coach company varied, but Benny preferred what he called *'bent'* drivers, whilst his claim to map-reading skills to avoid police has to be taken with a pinch of salt. Neither he nor anyone else knew what the police were up to, although the police did phone coach companies telling them what a nuisance Benny and his crowd were. Some firms then refused him further vehicles. The pair ran their last trip in January 1985, when Todd took a job requiring him to work alternate Saturdays, and a few months later got married. Benny 'retired' around the same time. When Benny was in his early thirties and still running coaches he was in no way involved in leading the young into violent confrontations. Indeed, his inactivity meant that younger Blades deserted his coach because of the lack of action. Not that anyone ever criticised him, for he was above reproach. However, many of his travellers were referred to disparagingly by the 'young lads' as *'Beerswillers'* and *'ale-carts'*, for they considered them more keen to seek beer than seek out rival lads (see Chapter 10).

The role of operators was then taken on by Taff and Marty, and these two branched out occasionally into more 'exotic' entertainment for their travellers – on one occasion providing a stripper, and on another providing a ready-rolled 'joint' of marijuana for everyone who boarded. Far from influencing subsequent behaviour, these two took the money, and then sat in the front seats. As Taff explained, *'What t' rest of 'em got up to either on t' coach or for the rest of t' day I couldn't give a fuck about.'* Their excursions coincided with the team's being in the lower divisions, so that another source of large-group travel was not considered necessary. This also meant that their profit-making excursions numbered only five.

Max's Lads and The Lansdowne Élitists

Promotion to what was then Division Two in 1984 rekindled the need for large-group away travel, and so a variety of operators saw an opportunity in what was an empty market. One such entrepreneur was Max, who whilst young and not a core Blade had a base of twenty mates that when added to could fill a coach. An enterprising youth, Max was only fifteen when he took his first coach of school mates to an away match. Four years later, in 1984, he began to run trips regularly. With the other operators leaving the scene at the time he filled a gap, and took coaches to 90 per cent of away games. Initially, his core travellers were drawn from the North of Sheffield, where he lived, and which was also his first pick-up point. In later years his core were from pubs he frequented in relation to residence and work. In the course of a season over two hundred Blades would travel with him; most of whom were aged between sixteen and thirty-five. All his travellers enjoyed a pre-match drink and most, but not all, were prepared to fight. Generally, however, Max's coach was not as 'game' as those run by Blades from The Lansdowne. This fact was acknowledged by Max and his core; but they considered their trips were more 'relaxed' and their coach contained a friendlier crowd. Whilst he travelled free, the profits made were channelled into an end-of-season 'piss-up' for all his regular travellers and to subsidise the travel cost on long-distance trips when demand was not so great. Such excursions also made the club money, because Max sold *en route* official lottery cards that gave the winners instant cash prizes and produced profits for the club.

Functioning at the same time as Max, and often departing from a pick-up only yards away, were coaches run by Bee. An educated and articulate Blade, Bee was well known, and could be considered a core Blade since the late 1970s. Seeing a chance to make money, Bee ran coaches to half a dozen away games over the next two years, before tiring of the hassle and putting his efforts into teacher-training college. Others took over; the young lads came of age, and with them came an attitude that they were the Blade vanguard and that no one who was not prepared to fight should be allowed to board. In truth, this aim was not realised.

The 1985/6 season saw Jim and Mel organise coaches to six away games. So popular were their trips, that for three games they ran two coaches. Coaches were hired from a small company in the residential suburb ten miles outside Sheffield where they both lived, and the two recruited in pubs before home matches and on Friday nights on London Road. For short-distance games they merely stated a departure time and place calculated to avoid police, and for this reason moved the departure from the city centre to the car-park behind The Lansdowne. All comers were welcome, and in anticipation of an overspill they twice booked a second coach on reserve. For one long-distance away game they took precautions against financial loss. As the journey required a 7 a.m. start, they anticipated that some individuals would let them down, and so, two weeks in advance, a leaflet was produced specifying the time, departure point, how to book and the cost. A non-returnable deposit was requested to cover non-appearance, and no one let them down. Their 'coaches' were involved in two large-scale fights, both of which took place in towns miles from the day's football events and opponents. On both occasions their was no pre-arranged plan to fight (I was a traveller on both journeys and can verify this). Their last trip ended in financial loss, an absconding driver and police attention following a fight with other football hooligans at a motorway service station; and they ran no further trips.

In the 1986/7 season South and Fagin managed four excursions. One trip saw the money 'disappear' between collection and paying the driver – nobody owned up as to who stole it. Another saw them hire a double-decker bus, only to watch in anger as some passengers pulled the stuffing out of ripped seats. Another trip was eventless and profitable; but their final trip resulted in a débâcle. Two coaches were hired for a much-anticipated 'walk round' Derby town centre. Over a hundred Blades gathered in The Lansdowne via the back door at 10.00 a.m. (the landlord having opened early as a favour), and boarded, only for an officious driver, alert to watching police nearby, to demand that those without seats get off. This threw arrangements into chaos, for as with all their excursions, they had recruited with book and pen and requested a deposit of £1. Those with 'names down' and money paid, both believed, had a right to travel. But problems arose when mates who had done neither boarded the bus. South and Fagin could no longer honour their promise; this brought a problem that showed how ineffective an organiser was when Blades would not do as instructed. In a dilemma, Fagin announced *'Anyone who ain't booked ged off nar.'* Nobody moved, and knowing well the identity of those who had not paid a deposit, Fagin spoke to one, demanding he get off. He refused. Fagin threatened him that he would be *'off in a minute'*, to which he replied *'I doubt it.'* Furious, Fagin got off the coach, shouting at the occupants that he would drag them off in a minute. Within that time the accused and five mates left the coach, announcing that they were taking the train and anybody could join them.

Arguments began amongst the remaining passengers. Shane, realising reliable fighters had left the bus, now demanded to no one in particular that the six be allowed to travel, and looking about him said, *'There's loads of little "chabbies" here . . ... What they gonna do when t' feytin starts? . . . Them who go every week should be on, it dun't matter if they ain't booked.'* Oliver sprang to the younger Blades' defence, arguing that *'nobody goes every week, we all miss matches, and we were little dickheads once'*. Fagin listened, then politely told a group of six Blades in their teens to leave. They did so without complaint, and were given their money back. The other six, standing nearby, then got back on. The dispute never was mentioned again, and the pair never ran another vehicle. In South's words, it was *'too much aggro'*.

There were always others willing to take over when an opportunity arose, and Nick and Gordon ran four coaches to four games in 1987. With the team relegated to Division Three in 1988, there was no real need for a big away mob, and though coaches were run occasionally, the operator changed for each excursion. Over 1989–92 only three full coaches per season were run, by either Dene, Eddy or Yifter, and for a while mini-vans came back into vogue. Then from the 1990s, with the growth in car ownership, Blades would simply travel away in convoys of cars when 'trouble' was expected, for the police had no way of controlling this form of travel. The largest such convoy occurring in 1990, when 18 vehicles travelled to Leeds (see Armstrong 1994). As a response the police had then to record the registration plates of all cars they suspected of harbouring hooligans, and thus their database was now both personal and also inanimate, in the form of vehicles.

Away game travel changed continually as a result of police impositions, and the police tried to pre-empt this by warning coach operators of the consequences of ignoring police-imposed departure times and instructions to travel along predetermined routes. When police effectively controlled routes into the city centre meant it was thus no longer an option for the Blades, they would 'jump off' the coach near to the ground, with traffic lights or heavy traffic providing the opportunity. For this reason from 1987 police would board coaches on the outskirts of the town and sit by the front and emergency doors. Another tactic was for police vehicles to 'capture' vehicles and escort them at high speed to the ground. Unable to stop fans travelling, at times they would stop fans alighting at their destination and decide the occupants were 'drunk', and so prevent them seeing the game.

From the mid-1980s Blades, alighting from coaches at away matches, would be forced to walk from coach door to turnstile via a police human 'wall', with an officer training a camcorder on them. On one occasion in 1991, before a departure for a game in London, the Sheffield police videoed everyone boarding a coach outside a London Road pub. Another time everyone boarding had to give the Sheffield police their names and addresses. By the early 1990s only those football 'innocents' and those without resources to buy or to hire a car with their mates regularly travelled by coach.

Thirsty Work? Hooliganism and Pubs

As Wittgenstein (1958) averred, the only place where real philosophical problems can be tackled and resolved is the railway station. In the 1970s, train stations became one of several key termini at which the disembarkation of visiting rivals could be reasonably expected. In this sense, the established pubs of away fans are chosen from an array of 'stations' that are accidentally presented by the forces of social control. Ironically, the association of group with territory is therefore precipitated by those who would publicly seek to unhinge these deviants from such a permanent seat of residence. It became usual for a local 'welcoming committee' to attend these locales; but their success was reliant upon precedents, guesswork, the relative effrontery of opponents, and the predictability of police strategies. With the football ground ceasing to be the main arena of hooligan contestations from the early 1980s, a network of pubs became the focus for the meet-ups and challenges, and it became the norm for up to two hundred Blades to rendezvous in pubs hours before the kick-off. Sometimes the arrival of visitors was surreptitious, sometimes blatant; it all depended on *their* calculation of opponent reputation and subsequent *risk*. At times rivals could appear blatant, and could face accusations that their public display was only conducted behind the safety of police protection, for the fans loved the ultimate 'pose' of shadowing a traffic-stopping police escort of rivals who are unable to do anything much in the way of a response. For this reason the home lads despised such police escorts, being fully aware of what was going on.

Pubs chosen for these meetings were required to be spatially set within the mutually accessible zones, along public transport arteries, or within walking distance of the football ground. An accommodating (and profit-orientated) manager and staff were also required. The down-side to the realisation of profit, however, was the occasional inconvenience of broken windows, and there was also the secondary stigma that police and non-frequenting public tend to view such pubs as a spatially distinctive 'hooligan' home. For the visitors, established drinking places became confirmed over the years, and tended also to be located away from the city centre – in Blades' case London Road. The pub was the holding point for the 'turnout'. The numbers gathered varied, for the reputation of Their Boys and past history played their parts. Those with no status in Blades' eyes were dismissed with stock phrases, *'They're nowt'*, *'They're shit'*, *'They're not worth turning out for'*, *'Not worth getting nicked for'*, *'They don't know what it's all about'* or *'They haven't got any "Boys"'.* Lesser rivals could be appreciated for trying, *'They always turn out'*, *'You'll always get a feyt'*, *'They're game but they're crap'* or *'We run 'em every time.'* If the opposition was considered *'good'*, various warnings would have it: *'They're game as fuck'* or *'Top Lads'.* For totally insignificant rivals Blades did not wait in the city centre or even look out for rivals the whole day. In effect there was no one to fight, even if they did bring a couple of hundred or even thousands of followers.

The identification of group with setting resulted in the construction of mutually dependent concepts of violation and defence in hooligan exchanges. It was pubs that permitted the enactment of various hooligan strategies for those within them and those seeking to approach them as aggressors. The most common ritual was the 'walk round', in which one set of opponents did not enter the pub, but walked past it. For the walkers, honour is earned by perceivably intimidating their opponents, to the extent that no response is offered from the sanctuary. Claims of a moral victory are dismissed by those inside, on the grounds of unfulfilled promise, in that neither an attack nor an entry has been attempted. For those outside, such a defence may be anticipated and negated through a phone call to an known adversary inside the pub, and a declaration of group intent. In this circumstance, the element of surprise in arriving outside the pub is forfeited in the interest of provoking an *'off'*. This is not always acted upon nor believed by the respondent. Hoaxes and *'wind ups'* are a notorious corollary of football hooliganism, as techniques for ridiculing opponents. More commonly, prior warning will not be given of attacks, and these, when initiated from the outside, tend to be limited to the surrounding of pub doors (the boundaries between the opposing groups), the smashing of windows (breaking down false perimeters) and the exchange of missiles (bottles, bricks, glasses). On such occasions, entry to a pub is hardly ever attempted. Those inside participate in exchanges to the extent of throwing missiles, but typically remain inside unless their numerical superiority is unquestionably established. However, the often exaggerated term of 'pub wrecking' encapsulates the activities of those outside only; social etiquette decrees that where pub management and staff have welcomed those inside, no serious or concerted damage will be done to the premises.

There is, of course, another scenario, in which pub space as territorial power may be further contested and confused, when one group knowingly enters the public space previously established by their opponents as their own. There are three general instances in which this procedure may be applied and each is known, through colloquial expression, by idioms embodying the contextual application of idealised masculine norms:

1. *'Sounding out'/'sussing'*: by intrusion: the entrants are unknown or unrecognised by their rivals and effectively 'pass' as ordinary pub customers. The significance is only immediately meaningful for the entrants and in its retelling to fellows in other circumstances – although useful tit-bits may be learned of the nature and identity of opponents.
2. *'Acting wide'* or *'Giving it the big 'un'*: as transgression: a recognised individual or group of hooligans enter their rivals' pub, but in a fashion that is ambiguous to their hosts, owing to its timing (outside match-day hours) and (low) numbers.
3. *'Taking liberties'*: the hooligans consciously trespass into the rivals' pub as part of a transparently oppositional collective ('mob-handed' or 'firmed up'), with the intended impact of *'winding up'* the hosts to the extent of a violent response, procuring fight or flight.

One notion central to each of these spatial penetrations is the entrants' acknowledgement that the meaning of their activities is almost entirely dependent upon rival interpretations. The differences between *'sounding out'*, *'acting wide'* and *'taking a liberty'* within the others' social space are really determined, firstly by the degree of recognition of these rivals, and secondly by the time–space context in which the entry is made. Greatest status is inevitably reserved for those willing to make the most public and offensive arrivals upon their rivals' spaces, though these occasions tend to be relatively rare outside match-day contexts (when such sudden appearances are jeopardised as much by police impositions as by the larger numbers of opponents). Intrusions or transgressions are the more regular modes of entry, with the latter containing stronger social tensions (and anthropological interest).

Blades did not want to bite the hand that fed them; they did not want to bring trouble to or damage to pubs that made them welcome. However it was not always possible to protect 'their' pubs from idiot Blades, because no one had the right to dictate the 'correct' behaviour. Thus, in 1986 The Stamp, whose landlord was very welcoming to the Blades, was visited by half a dozen rivals at lunch-time. Twenty Blades later entered and a few threw missiles at the six, who replied likewise. In a one-minute mêlée, a woman glass collector was knocked over. Most of the twenty Blades took no part and left the scene embarrassed about the damage, ashamed and shocked that a woman could be hurt, and aware of the landlord's anger. This incident was not spoken about, and Blades later dismissed it as 'stupid'. Silence prevailed because of a collective shame over what was considered 'out of order' – an attack on numerically inferior opponents who were not really Their Boys, the frightening of an innocent and the abuse of hospitality of one of the landlords who had been most accommodating. That said, it happened; but there was no internal Blades' punishment of the miscreants.

For all the potential trouble match-days provided, the pubs on London Road were remarkably incident-free. A fight around a pub once a season in the period 1984–92 was the norm. One in January 1984 saw windows broken and furniture damaged. Only one fight, in January 1985, could be considered 'big', and resulted in damage consisting of a few broken glasses and one broken window when twenty rivals were attacked by a dozen Blades. Later years saw only one lunch-time of damage. In 1986 rival lads were found in two London Road pubs. In the former incident one premise received a smashed window and a broken stool and glasses as twenty Blades ran from The Lansdowne to the front door, broke a window, and then stopped. In an earlier incident half a dozen fought a similar number of visitors with missiles. The latter pub suffered around twenty broken glasses arising from a brief fight lasting about 30 seconds in which a dozen Blades confronted a dozen visitors around a pool table. Both pubs remained open, and were back to normal in half an hour. The proprietors 'went mad', yet no Blades were barred and the matter was forgotten by the following home game. The years 1987–90 saw no match-day trouble along London Road. What damage did arise was from Owl incursions into the area, and occurred only once a year. At other times they were either met on arrival on the street or, finding no Blades around, did not damage 'their' pubs. Unoccupied rival pubs were never damaged. The year 1991 saw a brief scuffle inside two pubs when Manchester United were the visitors, and 1992 saw artefacts thrown and minor-scale fights with Aston Villa supporters. Nearer to the ground, a pub adjacent to the visiting supporters enclosure saw two fights per season in 1990–3, but these were small-scale and involved half a dozen people in total. In a ten-year period, 1983–93, the total damage to pubs was four windows broken and a few dozen glasses thrown. Probably a couple of stools were damaged beyond repair too.

Unexpected Creativity

In the space of the ten years or so between 1970 and 1980, the football ground went from being the front stage for the expression of animosities to being the back stage, where analysis and post-mortems between rivals could be shared through epithets and humour concerning 'no man's lands'. The new venues of contested rivalry became the more contextual and inconsistent centres of the train-station, the public house, and the city centres. And the streets *en route* to these sites also became avenues of contestation in themselves. In this sense football hooliganism became increasingly dominated by temporal rather than spatial considerations. Ironically, the strategy of forcing hooligans on to the streets rather than having them ensconced in a known pub led to greater policing problems, particularly when groups of opposing hooligans were also in town. For theirs was a polluting presence that could only be purified by confrontation.

Where police control strategies inhibit the prospect of tackling opponents (or even of gathering effectively), temporary spaces may be identified for hooligan purposes. For either set of rivals in these circumstances, the affective or symbolic content of these spaces becomes essentially arbitrary. These territories offer instead purely pragmatic, action-facilitating properties, well away from the observing eyes of police cameras or plain-clothes officers. The time and location for such exchanges is agreed upon beforehand, through personal communications via the hooligan network. We are talking here of the potential 'privatisation' of football hooliganism, for many participants: a violent exchange in surroundings devoid of an affective input represents a concept alien to the match-day experience. But its post-1980 manifestation pointed towards the logical culmination of the consistent increase in police constrictions upon the use of public space by football hooligans.

Notes

1. Throughout a decade of such dramas the Shoreham End was 'taken' unequivocally once by Manchester United, twice by Leeds and twice by the Owls in testimonial matches. At other times other clubs' fans remained on it for the duration of the match, but at the side of the Blades mob – notable attempts were made by the hooligans of Chelsea and Newcastle. A few other fan groupings made the expected forays, only to be taken off under police escort around an hour later. Such incursions were commonplace when the visitors were from Stoke, Birmingham and West Ham.
2. In 1975 *The Star* (9 March) reported that hidden cameras operated by police were being used to watch fans at Hillsborough during Wednesday's home games. The procedure was stopped when the club and police identified legal problems in the 'action replays'. Hidden cameras were rejected without trial by the United Board of Directors, the Club Secretary being quoted as saying *'there can be 40,000 people in our ground, it would be very expensive to have cameras keeping an eye on them'*.
3. The first all-ticket game at Bramall Lane came in 1978 for the visit of the then notorious Manchester United fans. In a crowd of 29,000, 400 visitors stood on the Shoreham End and sporadically fought Blades throughout the game.
4. A match between United and Wednesday at Bramall Lane scheduled for a Saturday afternoon in November 1992 was moved on police demands to midday Sunday, so that fans would not create traffic problems with city-centre shoppers and would not be able to drink before the game. The same fixture the following year was played at 3.00 p.m. on Sunday, thus allowing all those who wanted to drink to do so. The police did not want this kick-off, but the club and, more importantly, TV did, as the match was broadcast live nationally.
5. Disturbances in opposition grounds involving Blades mostly occurred at the last away matches of seasons 1987/8, 1988/9, 1989/90 and 1990/1. The earliest, at Huddersfield, saw a United victory, resulting in a traditional end-of-season pitch invasion that prompted the home fans

to run on, but to retreat when outnumbered. The charge continued over the seats and out of the ground. Disorder a year later at Bristol City started with skirmishing between rivals on the terraces that spilled over on to the perimeter of the pitch and involved fifty combatants from each side. The match was delayed a couple of minutes whilst police cleared the area. The last away game of 1989/90 at Leicester was the day United were promoted to Division One, and pitch invasions occurred three times during the match when United scored three of their five goals. The final whistle resulted in a mass invasion by about two to three thousand. The home fans stayed on the terraces, but after 10 minutes also took the field to challenge Blades, who promptly chased them off the pitch and out of the ground. The same match had seen scuffles in two stands throughout the match, when rival mobs of lads found themselves in close proximity. The incident in 1991 was again at the last away match: this time Coventry fans were chased off the pitch. The following season's last match saw a pitch invasion at Wimbledon, and attempts to perform improvised trapeze, with a few fans swinging on the crossbar of the goals, breaking it in two. Whilst two of these events involved fights and chases, the other two were celebratory. (One was celebratory with a 'necessary' chasing off of the watching and baying equivalent lads.)

6. Around three hundred youths climbed *over the perimeter fences*, mainly from the kop, and ran on to the pitch. Two opposition players were attacked by two youths, but not hurt. As the teams quickly left the field, the fans spent ten minutes walking around taunting visiting fans, who had a fence plus police on foot and horseback in front of them. A few arrests were made. In September an FA Commission cleared United of any blame, and no charges were brought. Warning notices about bad behaviour were displayed around the ground and in the match programme for the first three games of the following season.

7. Three pitch invasions occurred, involving hundreds of youths in the last ten minutes. One assaulted a rival player who had earlier been involved in an exchange of punches with a United player. In total three arrests were made and nine fans ejected. No charge was brought or penalty imposed by the FA over the incident.

8. At the end of the game a group of visitors twenty-strong directed chants towards Blades on the John Street terrace. Neither faction attempted to escalate matters. The police, however, decided to arrest some of the visitors. Over the next ten minutes forty officers on foot supported by eight mounted police at the scene arrested seventeen Chelsea fans; it was a ridiculous exercise, bar providing action and arrests for police who had no disorder to deal with.

9. Cars were damaged and overturned and fans assaulted. During the 1984/5 season a total of three cars were overturned on the same day, one before the match, and two after. One of the latter vehicles contained four visiting lads: one sustained an injured leg, the severity of which was not known. The following season damage was caused to two vehicles as a result of Blades pursuing rival fans. Three youths, having quickly jumped into a vehicle, were surrounded by a dozen Blades. Frightened, the driver drove erratically and at high speed through the Blades, hitting two nearby cars before driving off. The following season one empty car was overturned and a mini-van had its windscreen broken by a brick.

10. Returning from a night match at nearby Doncaster in 1979 Blades threw light bulbs out of windows, repeatedly pulled the communication cord, and picked up and carried the ticket inspector. After the train had been stopped at a sub-station the three hundred or so on board were then made to walk under police escort 11 miles back to Sheffield!

11. A facial injury was caused to a 14-year-old girl in 1976 when a group of United fans travelling to a match threw a piece of furnishing out of the sky-light of the coach they were aboard. Media headlines about the incident saw police asking for witnesses and claiming they had a suspect. Whether anyone was charged over the incident was never published.

12. A weekend in Brighton in May 1985 saw seventy Blades stay two nights. The Friday night produced a small-scale fight with a dozen youths believed to be Everton fans enjoying a holiday and awaiting their side's game in Europe. The fight also produced a broken pub window. There were no apparent casualties in the events, albeit one youth did get struck over the head by a bottle. The resort of Blackpool was always a popular port of call for football fans following their team in the north-west. Blades spent the night there regularly throughout 1986–93. The only time that matters turned violent occurred on Easter Saturday 1986. A coach full of Blades (returning from Carlisle) fought a coach full of Newcastle supporters (their side had been playing in Liverpool): the net result of this street brawl was one unconscious rival fan. Unfortunately for him, the punch came from a fellow north-easterner. In the confusion of a hundred men fighting the combatants were unsure who was who. No police arrived in the duration of the fight of about five minutes, and the participants ended matters themselves. Later in the night brief scuffles ensued with youths from Leeds and Manchester. One Blade was kicked to the floor by some of the former, and required 20 stitches in a mouth wound. The more genteel resort of Bournemouth

hosted Blades for a weekend in May 1987 when United played at nearby Portsmouth. Around a hundred Blades enjoyed two days without incident bar two brief confrontations with local lads at the end of each night out. There were no apparent injuries to either side, albeit four Blades were arrested. Whilst the sight of a hundred drunken Blades singing in the town at midnight was unnerving for some, that was the extent of the fear.

The most popular long-distance away games were at Ipswich and Norwich, when hundreds of Sheffielders would combine the match with a weekend in the resort of Great Yarmouth. In 1986 Blades met in a pub after watching the team play at nearby Norwich. The group sang and drank until the pub closed, and caused no trouble even though locals told them the local lads were out to get them because of an incident when a group of twelve Blades on the previous night had fought a similar number of local lads outside a disco. Around sixty Blades continued Saturday night in the same disco. For one and a half hours Blades realised local lads were in there eyeing them up, and an uneasy peace lasted until 12.45, when two Blades got into a scuffle with locals that resulted in the sixty Blades joining together in seconds in face-to-face confrontation with a similar number of locals. In between the two, seven bouncers linked arms and kicked out at anyone who came near them. Plastic glasses and a few plates were thrown between the two groups; one Blade got knocked out by a punch and one local received a bloody nose. The police arrived, and all the Blades left the club. Outside, 'snide', i.e. discreet, punches were exchanged between the groups with police looking on, until most Blades walked to their lodgings escorted by police. The twenty or so that remained became involved in chasing and missile throwing along the sea front and in the back streets with the locals. None was injured or arrested. The locals continued a vigilante-type patrol until 3.00 a.m., and then went home. Aside from the 1986 incident the only other acts of violence in the resort occurred in 1991 when a peripheral Blade pulled a car aerial off a parked vehicle and struck one of two passing youths. The action resulted in a charge of actual bodily harm and the later arrest of a Blade who fitted the description of the assailant, but was not actually the one involved. He had to face two court appearances before being found not guilty. The assailant was considered an idiot by Blades who knew him.

Chapter 9

The Perpetual Antagonists: Blades–Owls Contests

They who lose may win tomorrow.

(M. de Cervantes (1605), *Don Quixote*)

The difference in the form of opposition shown towards Owls compared to that shown to Their Boys was based primarily on the fact that Blades shared the bright lights of Sheffield city centre with Owls; a *modus vivendi* of sorts *had* to operate. Intra-city animosities thus tended to be functionally suppressed within working and educational hours and certain leisure contexts, or limited at least to verbal exchanges and light-hearted teasing known as 'football banter'. However, leisure periods carry the possibility of willing participants' becoming engaged in more intensive and potentially violent exchanges with city rivals. As illustrated in the first three chapters, issues that could produce a prolonged vendetta could arise from the most trivial of origins. Outside these hours, further ambiguity pervades the identification of football and non-football spaces; and the sting is never allowed to be entirely neutralised, as the continuation of close-season disputes demonstrates. Additionally, the personalisation of animosities between individual rivals, usually founded in prior engagements, can threaten to break into a reanimation of collective rivalries. At any juncture, some form of balance in the distribution of access to leisure resources, i.e. city-centre pubs, will have been achieved, and routinely (and confidently) regarded as established territory for one side or another. The entry of opposing groups to these spaces is thus regarded as consciously transgressive and assumed to be intimidating, unless otherwise explicable.

History and Hardness: The Pursuit of Animosity

In recent decades both these once-proud clubs have been in the lower echelons of English football, with United in Division Four for one season in 1981/2. United were league champions in 1898 and 1900 and FA Cup winners in 1899, 1902, 1915 and 1925. United's last visit to Wembley came as beaten finalists in 1936. By 1997, the Club had spent 59 seasons in Division One, 28 in Division Two, 5 in Division Three and 1 in Division Four. Wednesday last won the FA Cup in 1935 and the League Championship in 1930. Wednesday have been 62 seasons in Division One, 26 in Division Two, and 5 in the Third Division. In recent decades Wednesday suffered a similar fate to United. Relegated from the First Division in 1970, they were in the Third by 1975 and nearly relegated to the Fourth, at a time when United were near the top of the First Division. As a result there have been few competitive matches between the two sides, and from 1980 to 1992 the only fixtures played were the annual South Yorkshire knockout competition known as the County Cup or testimonials for long-serving players.

The success of one club does not bring a unity in the City, and Blades always supported Wednesday's opponents, regardless of where they were from. Whatever was to hand could provoke some to disagree. When football arguments are based on the success of the club's football status, the result is something of a foregone conclusion when the presence of one in a higher division states the obvious. So then arguments were found in relative match attendance figures: basically the issue was who had the more loyal following. The comparative loyalty of supporters of the two teams was of great symbolic significance from the late 1970s onwards. No clubs in recent times have fallen from such heights to such depths in so short a time-span and yet kept such support home and away. In the golden days of 1972 United's ground was packed with crowds of sometimes over 40,000 and never below 24,000, with a seasonal average of 33,000. The season they were relegated to the Second Division the average crowd was 22,000. More startling was their 15,000 average in season 1981/2, whilst they were in the Fourth Division. Wednesday crowds were always on a par with United; their fans, as well as Blades, stood by them in the lower divisions. Such attendances made United and Wednesday two of the ten best supported teams in England and Wales in the early 1990s. Derisory comments and subtractions for estimated away followings were always made when Blades looked at the Wednesdays home attendances and, no doubt, the blue and white faction did a similar calculation.

For the hooligan combatants, the decades have seen them contest the concept of who were the 'harder' fans of the two clubs. Whilst Wednesday were 'harder' than Blades in the mid to late 1970s, Blades were reluctant to concede this status, and could only express their disgust at the publicity the Owls received for some of their hooligan exploits.[1] In September 1980 a match at Oldham between the homeside and Wednesday was delayed by 30 minutes after missiles were thrown from the visitors' terrace on to the pitch. As a result of these actions and the attendant massive publicity, the FA banned Wednesday fans from their next four away games, and forced the club to pay £3,000 compensation to each club visited for loss of earnings. For some reason the standing areas of Hillsborough were closed for four home games as part of the punishment. All those involved paid to sit in the stand, and the club thus gained financially! Blades were disgusted, not by the Owls' behaviour, but because they envied them their notoriety. In previous seasons Blades had twice run across the pitch at Oldham and had not received a single line in the press.

Somewhat contrarily Blades had the reverse complaint twenty years later. Blades were, in fact, perplexed by the local media's playing down of events surrounding the Owls and Wednesdayites; one incident in 1994 stood out. In February, Wednesday played at Old Trafford against Manchester United. During the game the Wednesday following began chanting the theme of a 1970s TV series, 'The Dambusters', accompanied by holding their arms aloft in a pretend 'Bomber Command' formation. The home fans reacted furiously, believing this to be an insult related to the 1958 Munich air crash that killed half their glorious young team. The net result was fights outside the ground afterwards, as the home fans attacked Sheffield vans and coaches. A total of 30 arrests were made. This made a front-page story in *The Sheffield Star*, but not headlines. A few weeks later Manchester United were at Hillsborough. Fights outside the ground resulted in 22 arrests and one hospital casualty, the product of being struck by a missile. The Police Superintendent in charge of match policing described the evening as one that *'went very well'*, with *'minor incidents'*. The four journalists assigned by *The Star* to compile a story could not or did not bother to elaborate on the statistics or police claims (3 March). Blades were stunned that such events did not bring massive political and journalistic condemnation, but attributed such silence to the Wednesday club being somehow accoladed as the more 'respectable' of the two clubs and the one adopted by the political powers of the city and the local media.

Football Constructs and Binary Opposition

There were various forms of hostile but non-violent opposition around the notion of football loyalties that centred on identification with respective colours, fan numbers and football chants. Thousands of United fans (and Wednesday fans) took part in some or all of these oppositions. The association of club colours has always been taken seriously. From their beginnings United have always worn a kit of red and white stripes, with

Wednesday in a similar one of blue and white. Match-days see colour-demarcated ground division; but colour rivalry also exists outside match-day. Some United fans could never wear blue sweaters or jackets or paint their homes blue, and this worked in reverse. Colour prejudice also affected smoking habits, with some Blades never purchasing the popular Embassy Regal cigarettes because of the blue and white packaging, preferring plain Embassy, with their red and white packaging. Others just said *'blue and white bastards'* when talking about all matters concerning Wednesday.

One aspect of the rivalry is found in the relative status of the two clubs. When the Football League doubled in size in 1882 the fourteen founder members permitted two more teams to join. In a ballot, Wednesday were admitted to Division One, United to Division Two. Because of this Wednesday have since been seen as the city's premier club, giving the United fans a chip on their shoulders and an inferiority complex in respect of their more famous neighbours. Such a status is certainly evident environmentally. At Wednesday's Hillsborough ground, a magnificent cantilever stand was built in the early 1960s to host the 1966 World Cup preliminary rounds. It was only a matter of time before United had a similar stand in an attempt to compete for similar international status. Completed in 1975, it crippled United financially for the next decade.

Status (and prejudice) is more than structural, however, and many Unitedites believe the local powers that be are against their club. As many a Unitedite will tell you, *'They'* are *'all Pigs'*. Thus, the elected members of Sheffield Council have been dismissed since the 1970s (bar a few honourable exceptions) as consisting of an unofficial branch of Wednesday's Supporters Club. However, the evidence was not overwhelming, although to Unitedites the Council's anti-United bias was typified by their refusal of the early 1980s development plans for Bramall Lane. The link between Council and Wednesday has a long history, and, as Fishwick (1989: 30) notes, Wednesday, as the older club, always had closer links with the local élite than United. Furthermore, Unitedites believed the local evening paper, *The Star*, had, and still has, a Wednesday bias. United fans have still not forgiven its 1973–4 *'Save Our Owls'* campaign, as Wednesday struggled at the bottom of Division Two. This campaign consisted of *The Star*'s producing and distributing thousands of stickers, posters and badges, and advertising discount admission prices. The 'Save Our Owls' logo adorned the top of the sports page for two weeks, though the campaign failed, for Wednesday failed to win any of their last seventeen games and were relegated. In 1980/1 United were able to fall all the way to Division Four without even the hint of a similar campaign, and, in their opinion, received fewer 'photo specials' in the paper after a big match and had fewer comparable slogans to the 'Good

Luck to the Owls' printed on the sports sheet before big games. Many United fans despise such publicity, but have to buy the newspaper because there is no other source of local football news.

Blades and Owls existed in a world of binary opposites (cf. Lévi-Strauss 1966). Blades' criticisms of their rival supporters formed an all-embracing definition of what Blades were *not*. Both the mainstream, 'ordinary' Wednesday fans, as well as hooligan Owls, were lambasted. The *'typical pig'*, a male Wednesday fan (in the 20–40 age range) was the epitome of everything Blades considered themselves not to be. Ecologically he was inferior, and spoken of as *'From that end of town'*, i.e. to the north of the city, from large Council estates built during the 1940s and 1950s. To Blades, these places produced something equivalent to a social moron, manifested in clothing and consumption styles. In the mid-1980s their industrial work-wear outer garment, known as a donkey jacket, was seen to illustrate stylistic ignorance, and was accompanied by what were seen as for them *de rigeur*, cheap, brand-label, ill-fitting jeans. At the match they stereo-typically wore football scarves as appendages (*passé* by the 1980s) and thereby earned themselves the derogatory label of *'Christmas trees'*. In later years, whilst retaining the jeans, such men were recognisable by the 'official', club-approved and marketed, Wednesday T-shirts and team shirts. These were worn at what Blades considered to be the most inappropriate times and places, such as visits out with the family, socialising in Working Men's Clubs, or at holiday on caravan sites at various Yorkshire and Lincolnshire resorts – which were derisorily seen as the perceived natural vacation habitats for such types. The Blades could profile the 'perfect pig' (males): *'eat crisps with their beer . . . talk like old men . . . are little and fat . . . have bad hair cuts . . . wear pig jumpers (V-neck sweaters with club insignia on) even in summer . . . sit next to silly old women in the stands when at the match . . . have match programmes sticking out of their ill-fitting jeans pocket . . .'*.

Assembled in the ground or on transport to a match armed with flasks of tea and 'potted meat' (beef spread) sandwiches, they constituted what the Blades derisively called in parody of hooligan constructs *'Wednesday's Picnic Crew'*. Such people were dismissed by Blades as *'thick bastards'*, and were easily imitated by adopting a vacant facial expression and slow chants of *'We love you, Wednesday'* (or whatever chant was their flavour of the moment). Every Blade claimed to know such caricatured Wednesday fans, and deep down all knew their equivalents amongst Unitedites, for some had family members who fitted these categories. However, Blades could chat and laugh about such 'types' with their knowing and sympathetic audience, whose mutuality was based on a presumed realisation that they were a cut above these fans in style, intelligence and resources.

Because of the large numbers of police and their readiness to jump on any outbreak of overt hostility at 'derby' matches, various covert performances against, what Blades considered, such social imbeciles were enacted. This produced a practise which needed a degree of discretion and the presence of 'offensive bodies'. There was no shortage of this category – basically Wednesday fans who, ever the simpletons in Blades' eyes, considered their duty to walk along John Street to the visitors' enclosure making as much noise as possible in proclamations for their team. Not deserving of any serious form of violence from Blades such people could not be ignored. Thus, on his way to the Bramall Lane End in the midst of the pre-match throng the visiting singer could find himself on the receiving end of various 'scutches' (blows to the head made with a flat palm) from Blades walking beside him. The first would shock the receiver who would remonstrate, but the Blade would continue walking without even turning to face the accuser whilst another Blade would repeat the action (to the unwitting Owl). Realising remonstrations were futile and that police were unaware of these actions amidst the crowds the 'offensive body' tried to make his way quickly to the turnstile, usually more determined than ever to voice his loyalties. Blades meanwhile laughed at these figures they considered so ridiculous.

There was, thus, a spectrum of hostility that many partook of. However, the violence occurring between 1965 and 1995 could not really be attributed to the history or structure of the clubs or to the city fathers' predilections. The reasons for violence appear to lie in constructs of power, breaches of appropriate masculinity, and personal vendettas, and it is to these that analysis now turns.

Kops and Bus-Stations: 1960–1970s

The beginning of inter-city fights in the mid-1960s saw the origins of Blade–Owl intra-city manifestations. Tactics were similar to those used against 'away' supporters, and Ross, a participant, recalled the early days. Significantly, he took pride both in the fight and the media coverage.

There weren't no segregation and the Ends would be mixed. When we played 'em at t' Lane, we'd get into t' ground early, stand at t' back o' t' kop and start throwing things at 'em as they came in through t' turnstile at t' bottom. The police usually had to escort 'em in on to t' terraces, then we'd feyt on and off throughout t' match. Then we'd go home and it wo' forgotten about. Our famous match was at Hillsborough in 1966. Weeks before at matches Blades were all singing 'Don't forget your eggs', and when we got on their kop, we pelted 'em with hundreds of eggs, they got covered in it! . . . next season, though, it got a bit dangerous. A Blade threw a small tube of acid at 'em, it splattered a few Pigs.[2]

History alone, however, is an insufficient explanation for the violence of recent decades, if only because relations between the two sets of supporters have not always been as bad as they were from the mid-1980s onwards. Older Blades told of days between 1940 and 1960 when rivals stood peacefully together at city 'derbies'. Even in the late 1960s and early 1970s some Owls and Blades, mates in other social contexts, would attend the home matches of rivals and stand with their Owls or Blades mates. During the early 1970s *some* (relatively few) rivals would occasionally (at maximum twice a year, and not for the same opponents each year) join up to confront fans from outside the city, but would keep their separate identity by wearing their own team colours. Such unity was rare, however, and throughout the 1970s, whenever United had played a home game and Wednesday had played a nearby away game (and hence would be arriving back in Sheffield between 5.00 and 6.00 p.m.) Blades would chant *'Pond Street'* (the name of the bus station across from the train station). After the game hundreds would then walk the mile to this location to wait for Owls disembarking from trains and buses, and then get involved in fights and chases. This was the extent of Blade–Owl competition at the time.

By the 1980s, the factions were not enacting any socio-economic or personal-geographical association of 'neighbourhood' or 'territory'. On the contrary, what Owls claimed as 'theirs' in the 1980s had in fact been Blades' in the 1970s. In 1978, a group of Blades began meeting on Friday nights, as part of a weekly reunion of those who had followed the team on a pre-season tour of Switzerland. Up to forty were gathering by 1979, and in a sort of response a similar number of Owls met nearby. Ironically, considering the 1980s fights, Blades would gather in pubs on West Street and Owls would be in pubs nearby. In the course of the night the factions would often find themselves in the same pub and fights would begin. The following week there would be revenge attacks, and soon procedures became ritualised around certain pubs and streets on a Friday evening. Amongst the Sheffield-residing Blades were others from Rotherham, two of whom had a personal 'thing' going with some of the top Sheffield Owls. They would sometimes even gather as a Rotherham Blade entity to fight their adversaries. That said, hostilities were not a weekly event, and were dropped over the summer of 1979. After eighteen months the hostilities ended for no good reason, bar the excuse one participant gave: *'they all got to know each other. Others grew out of it . . .'*. There was no wider sociological explanation offered by the participants, nor was one sought.[3]

Despite this genesis of the relationship of factions and pubs, and despite previous hostilities, there were to be long periods of relative tranquillity and even rapport between Sheffield-residing Blades and Owls. In the early 1980s, Blade–Owl relationships were only strained to the point where stares at each other were the norm in pubs the factions found themselves sharing; but matters were generally peaceful. This was due to the main actors of each faction *'getting along'*, whilst others shared an entrepreneurial interest to the point of trading goods. Evenings saw them sharing the same city-centre pubs, often with Blade or Owl mates, and a *majority* of each faction tolerated the other to the extent that this held the potentially hostile in check. Another factor was that the Owls had one particular black youth (an ex-boxer) that Blades were all wary of! And when fights did break out in these years, it was 'outsiders' who were blamed: Rotherham and Village Blades fighting 'Townie' Owls. That said, there is one annual event that needs neither match-day nor pub identification to define the customary occurrence of a somewhat un-festive occasion. Christmas Eve lunch-time drinking in the city-centre pubs has become one of the year's best 'sessions'. As a tradition, it was founded in the half-day closing for factories and businesses that accompanied the great years of employment, when everyone went from work to the pub. Since the 1970s, amidst drunken revellers and last-minute shoppers, the fun for Owls and Blades begins around 3.30 p.m., when the rivals pursue their own business. In the 1980s crowds would gather around a large Christmas tree at the top of Fargate Shopping Precinct, where carols were sung – rather irreverently – by the drunks. One carol, 'Mary's Boy Child', would see Blades and Owls chant their own words as to who really 'ran away' on 'Boxing Day'; fights would follow.

Whilst the Sheffield Blades had no control over their colleagues from elsewhere, these in turn were dismissive of city-based colleagues who would not join them in their fights, imitating derisively to each other the city Blades' claims that they *'could not because we know 'em'*. This denigration stated that good Blades should not have good relations with an enemy, though there was always a degree of piousness in such claims, for close scrutiny would show even the most vehement Blades would have friendships of sorts with some Owls or Wednesdayites. Coming from the same region, it was inevitable that some of each faction would know their adversaries personally. A few were related to the opposition; some had attended the same school; some worked in the same premises. And because some shared the same neighbourhood there was always confusion as to whether, as a 'good Blade', you should have Owl mates. And in confrontations, what did one do when the opponent was recognised and known? Was it all contextual, and was the only 'good pig' a bashed one? The answer was nobody knew for sure, and there were no hard and fast rules Blades had to abide by.

Negotiations and Dramas: Masculinity and Semantics

For the hooligan participants the Blades and Owls crucially exist in a world of situational ethics. That the Owls were appalling did not need to be debated in Blade circles. The question was how *'bad'* they were. This vision of their badness was primarily founded in relation to their perceived cowardice, yet was offset by the somewhat contradictory notion and accusation that charged them with unsupportable violence in relation to Blades. Exactly what to do with such an ambivalence caused confusion, and because no two situations were identical and because the participants were never exactly the same as on previous occasions, there was always a degree of negotiation both intra- and inter-group. There were various accusations made against Owls that appealed to the Blades' collective consciousness; and when statements were made, these had to be derogatory. Whether you, as an individual, believed them or whether they were patently untrue was immaterial to the laugh they provoked and the *communitas* that grew from the shared constructs. It was as if Blades enjoyed being disgusted by the supposed antics of their city rivals, and zeroed in on specificities to reinforce and replicate this perception in two definitive ways.

Specifically, it was said, Owls were bullies. Ready to fight when outnumbering Blades, they would not do battle when numbers were equal. And whilst Blades disagreed about how 'hard' individual Owls were, none ever admitted to collectively thinking Owls were 'harder' than Blades (although it was permissible to admit they *had* been in 1974–84). Yet their weakness was also a subject of disagreement. Many agreed with Ged's mid-1980s evaluation that *'They've got four or five who wanna' know . . . at most twenty.'* These five or six he called the *'"umbrella" . . . behind which the others hide'*. There was debate on an individual level as to who had the 'harder' lads. Not that it mattered; for when Blades had run Owls, their individual 'hardness' was academic and vice versa. Because of the nature of losing and winning, in the circumstances described on most occasions no one was ever certain what was a total victory, or had excuses to hand to explain or excuse the apparent defeat.

Generally, it was argued by Blades particularly in the late 1980s, that the Owls disgraced the name of Sheffield by their hooligan inactivity, by saving their occasional violence and biggest turnouts for Blades, instead of doing the 'correct' thing and opposing the 'lads' either from or in other cities: *'They go all t' way to Manchester, not to feyt Mancs but so they can get off their coach in Sheffield later and go lookin' for Blades.'* Owls' home and away games provided Blades with gossip to the effect that Owls were a disgrace to the 'good' name of the city in hooligan circles. Thereby inventing a sort of mythic appeal to the city fathers, Blades complained that Owls' inactivity in hooligan matters shamed the city on a national level! Stories about how few Owls travelled to away matches, resulting from observations (from a distance) or from details given in trust by Owl mates, supported these modes of thought. Other observations suggested Owls had not 'turned out' in Sheffield to repel rival fans from other cities, and this was proof to all that they did not really want to fight. Irritatingly, Owls could never be made to admit to having been 'done' or 'run', nor would they accept that Blades were 'top lads' in the city. And this collective vision gave Blades a reason to exist and something to talk about: *'It's more than rivalry; it's about who's top in Sheffield. It's about reputation, say when you're down in London and you're in a boozer and they* [i.e. fellow hooligans] *want to know that United can "do" Wednesday.'* Thus the desire for a good reputation nationally set the agenda for behaviour in Sheffield.

The influence of intra-city rivalry is also suggested by the uncertainty that Blades had in dealing with the match-day entry of some outside hooligan formation that was following its side in some game against Wednesday. The hooligan code of honour would normally require the Blades to intervene, and effectively 'police' the home spaces by confronting any hooligan visitors with maximum menace. In the circumstances four honour-seeking strategies were available to the Blades. They might:

1. Act with complete lack of interest, arguing neither opponent has sufficient status or capability to merit their attention or the danger of being arrested. This is a comparatively risky option, however, as hooligan status is rarely gained or reproduced by inaction. For inaction also undermines the principle of effective group re-assembly against the rival others, upon which the hooligan formation is essentially predicated.
2. *'Wind up'* local rivals by monitoring the visitors' activities more closely than their real match-day opponents. This might extend to treating some visitors as 'guests', and showing them around the town before appalled city rivals. The danger of this strategy relates to the lack of hooligan status derived from neutral or positive interaction with visiting fans;

for honour is only gained through intimidating their city rivals into non-intervention.

3. Take on *either* the visitors *or* the city rivals. If adopted, this strategy should be directed at the most potent formation present, as little honour is gained from challenging the formation with lowest numbers and/or hooligan status.

4. Take on *both* visitors and city rivals. This offered by far the greatest scope for attaining honour, and the possibility of reproducing rivalries over an extended period of time on match-day.

All these social dramas took place around and inside city-centre pubs. Such spaces were holding stations and theatres for collective ideals and consequent performances. The station that the various pubs provided in various locales facilitated Blade–Owl dramas as depicted in Blade-speak. In any pub along West Street, Owls were already cowering, fearing to leave this area of the city centre, because they knew they would 'get done' by Blades should they appear anywhere else. If Owls were in a neutral pub venue (i.e. without Blade or Owl claims) they had entered only because the pub 'bouncers' were their mates and would protect them by barring entry to Blades. If gathered in large numbers, the obvious question Blades asked each other was why did they not walk along London Road? The answer to Blades was obvious – they dare not! But the props could be moved to anywhere in the city, and the individual actors were forever changing. At times the audience to any confrontation was only consenting adult Blades and Owls; any external audience was always made up from unwilling spectators, in a drama in which they wanted no part.

One constant in all this was the desire of another group of muscular males, namely the police patrolling the city centre, to prevent all this, though usually they could only respond to events. Compared to the confusion existing in events with Their Boys, the local police were much more in control of local events when they took part in them; for they knew the city centre as well as any of the combatants, and consistently reinforced the association of football loyalties and certain pubs by tolerating Blades on London Road and often escorting them back there when they found them in the city centre. Their job, however, was made more difficult when Blades and Owls negotiated impending confrontations over the phone. And, of course, a major problem for the police was in anticipating the unexpected, for violence and the drama surrounding it were never totally predictable. At times Blades did not go *directly* to the Owls' location, but would meet hours before they knew Owls would be gathering. This is significant, for it illustrates the creation of tension that was an essential part of such occasions;

and I would venture that the use of pubs as 'stepping-stones' could help keep the situation non-violent. If, for example, Owls spotted Blades getting close they could decide on the basis of their relative numbers to fight or flee. Such a procedure also permitted those Blades who might not really wish to fight Owls either to disappear along the way, or to be a drink behind, and thus a pub behind, as the Blades got nearer to West Street or to the pubs where Owls were regularly to be found. Such staggered progress provided a face-saver, both at a group and on an individual level.

The Appalling Other

Various constructs of appropriate masculine conduct were available to the factions seeking justification or moral virtue for their actions. These were multifaceted, but founded in local ideas of honourable masculine norms. Stock phrases contrasted and contradicted these norms and made clear the Owls' immorality. They were accused variously of:

1. *'They Hammer Chabbies'* (i.e. assault youngsters). This accusatory statement of violence directed against young and aspiring, rather than established and well-reputed, Blades came complete with voice intonation and sneer. In Blades' eyes, it was what Owls did all the time. A couple of young Blades across the years did get bashed by Owls, but in circumstances of their own making. This was conveniently forgotten, however, because it clouded an issue that Blades wished to see as being stark and clear. Gossip about Owls on an individual and communal level pervaded Blade gatherings. Blades always spoke of Owls *'going around in a mob'* in city-centre pubs. Obviously this was because they dared not venture out in small numbers for fear of meeting Blades, not because Blades would attack them, but because they could not stomach the possibilities of a fight that had equal numbers. Information on who, where and how many Owls would receive the derisory stock responses: *'Stupid pig'*; *'He's a wanker'*; *'Their top knobhead'*; *'Did he have his running shoes on?'*; *''im who runs backwards shoutin' "Into 'em!"'*; *'Showin' 'is heels as usual?'*; *'I've seen t' back of his head on West Street a few times'*; *'Been on t' floor more times than Ginger Rogers'*; *'Had more slappin' than a creosote brush'*; *'Doin' his impression of a starfish?'* Such statements were not really meant to elicit laughter, and indeed were considered contemptuous statements of fact. Matters could, and did, get very personal. Uncertain of an Owl's identity, others would expound his details: *'That big kid with all t' hair who thinks he's really cool'*, or *'Him wi' t' blond hair who's always*

bouncin' about . . . thinks he's a reyt hard case.' Even those on good terms
with specific Owls under discussion would enjoy the *'slagging off'*,
although some might venture an opinion to the contrary by trying to
'put a word in' for the abused, saying he was *'alright'* or *'not a bad lad'*.

2. *'They "Start" On Kids Out On Their Own'* (become confrontational when
the numerical odds are in their favour): When Owls were sighted alone
or two-strong in pubs, Blades, if in a group, would point the individual(s)
out to one another almost as if looking for guidance on what was an
appropriate response. Rarely were such Owls attacked or even
approached in such circumstances, and if a Blade got aggressive, then
others pulled him off, telling him it was *'not reyt'*. That said, a couple of
Owls *did* suffer threats from Blades on a couple of such occasions that
were totally out of order and other Blades knew this. No doubt these
instances would be taken back to other Owls as examples of despicable
bullying by Blades; yet the most the Owl received was one blow and
verbal threats. If there were instances of some mob-handed attack on
an isolated Owl, Blades never boasted of this circumstance. And Blades
would always believe that even if an Owl was momentarily outwardly
friendly and non-hostile, later in the evening he would tell Owl mates
where Blades could be found. Blades, of course, would never conduct
themselves in such a manner.

3. *'They Bring in Them Who've Nowt To Do Wi' It'* (introduce individuals
who have a reputation for fighting but are not real Owls, and by taking
the issue to inappropriate times and places introduce non-combatants
to what is essentially a private matter). Protagonists on both sides
worked to an ideology that had it that not only were Blade–Owl events
time-specific, but their personnel was issue-specific. The social process
was *'football-related'* and others, female or male, who were not *'into'*
football should, decently, be kept out of it. Over the years various individuals who appeared amongst the Owls were, in the opinions of Blades,
'not real pigs'. Instead, they reasoned they had joined the Owl cohort
because of an Owl mate's requesting their presence against the Blades.
Such individuals were usually renowned fighters, which only made
Blades believe the Owls more appalling for having to bring in *'hired help'*
to oppose them. That said, such accusations were few and far between
and the individuals so accused were not usually out with Owls again.
That they were on some specific occasion might be more to do with
simply having a drink with a mate who was an Owl and who met with
other Owls. Blades did not wish to see matters in such complex ways.

Personal issues were forever interesting in this group dynamic. In the
years 1983–95 two visits were made to the workplace of a Blade by Owls:

once when three called to Gordon's depot; the other involving one Owl and Mick. In the first instance, Gordon saw via the firm's CCTV cameras three well-known Owls walk into his workplace. He rounded up two mates and three wooden bats, and the three ran towards the Owls. The latter were shocked, for they had come with a question, not offering violence; and wanted only to discuss who might have been phoning with threatening messages, claiming to represent the 'BBC'. They were wrong in identifying Gordon, and after a 20-minute chat departed amicably. The other visit was a product of a chance encounter. One of the Owls' Top Lads, out shopping with his wife, saw Mick involved in a similar pursuit. Recognition from city-centre confrontations led the Owl to insult Mick. The two squared up in the store until startled wives pulled them apart. Days later Mick and Kenny on their way to play football one Sunday morning saw the same Owl. Stopping the car, they alighted and chased him home, and, as he bolted the door, banged on his windows. The following day the owl, with two others, appeared at Mick's workplace armed with a wooden bat. Arming himself similarly Mick chased the Owl off the premise and, having cornered him, the pair agreed to a fight without weapons. The fist-fight was ended by passers-by and the personal issue was not resurrected ever again.

There were two other scenarios where hostility had no precedence, both involving the same Owl, who was accused of having 'said something' about Gordon's wife (he had attended the same school). The following Sunday lunch-time, and having done his homework, Gordon knew the Owl always visited a nearby pub with his father, and so he parked his car outside the Owl's house and waited two hours. The Owl did not leave the house; and, believing he had stayed at home out of fear, Gordon let the matter drop. In Blades' eyes the Owl had shamed himself enough. This same core Owl was a regular in city-centre fights, and, being fat, was an easy target to identify. Victim then turned predator a year later, when the Owl was guilty of 'offering out' a Blade, Ben, whilst he was out shopping with his wife. The Blade accepted and a fight ensued in the car-park, but soon stopped. The only reason for this conclusion the Blade could give later to his mates was that the pair felt rather stupid at this incongruous situation. Both departed unscathed. It was such scenarios that made the Blade–Owl conflicts so different from conflicts between Blades and Their Boys.

4. *'They Come Down Hidin' Behind t' Coppers'* (parading with a hooligan/hostile intent but using the police as protection against attack): This oft-repeated accusation occurred mainly, but not exclusively, when either

of the two sides were at home for a city derby. Obviously, when the game was at Bramall Lane, Blades presumed the Owls would know where they would be – along London Road – and therefore believed Owls should (as 'visitors') bring the issue to them. If Owls did, however, arrive near London Road, Blades always accused them of doing so in a calculated, cynical way, knowingly using the police as protection. Of course the police would intervene in any impending dispute, and *en route* to the match this would mean that police would have to separate the factions and give the Owls an escort to the Bramall Lane End. Either way, Owls considered the occasion good for a 'pose', and never missed an opportunity to shout to watching Blades that they were on their 'manor' and taunt them by asking what had they done about it, or what were they going to do about it? The answer was that they could do nothing with so many police around, and so they simply got angry and resentful. Owls did this in 1986, 1992 and 1993, and on the last occasion did not arrive until 2.55 for a 3.00 p.m. kick-off. The few Blades that remained outside at this time fought them before police escorted the seventy Owls to the match. To make matters worse, the Owls appeared along London Road at 11.30 p.m. that same night, when there were few Blades around, and so the Owls had done everything Blades detested them for within the space of eight hours.

5. *'They Smash Windows and Run Off'* (damaging the exterior of a pub containing Blades, but not waiting around for Blades to come out): Blades believed Owls only arrived in Blade territories when the majority of the latter had either gone home or entered nightclubs. Blades thus credited Owls with calculating a somewhat cowardly optimum time that they could walk there and find fewest Blades, i.e., after 11.30 p.m. Of course, the Owls would deny this, and appeared on London Road around twice a year between 1987 and 1992. Those Blades who remained would always fight them. But in discussing this 'tactic', Blades would calculate that had Owls arrived 20 minutes earlier they would have found double or triple the number of opponents. True 'victory' in football-related conflicts was more than breaking pub windows and running away. Its high point meant making it impossible for rivals to leave the pub, either because the weight of numbers outside or around the door prevented it, or because the others were too scared to come out. Thus Blades would claim moral victories when they went along West Street or wherever they found Owls, because in many situations they could claim that *'None of 'em 'd come out o' t' pub.'* Blades of course were a different calibre: *'We'd 've 'ad a go,'* they would state in hindsight.

6. *'They Could've Killed Us . . . But They Din't Wanna Know'* (not seizing the chance to do what Blades believed Owls ought to have done): Not every encounter between Blades and Owls was a hostile one. As has been illustrated, there were many circumstances in which there was agreement as to when the issue was 'on' and 'off', or other circumstances were in play. That said, there were also numerous situations which were ambiguous, and each faction, not knowing the 'correct' response, usually left the encounter without recourse to violence. To some Blades, in some circumstances, this was worthy of repeating to colleagues, because it illustrated the cowardly nature of the Owls. At times this occurred when Blades entered a pub to find themselves more numerous than the Owls; they would then savour the occasion of watching Owls watching them. The rivals could even co-exist in the same pub, albeit at opposite ends of the room and constantly watching the others with a general air of anticipation that it was *'gonna go'* any moment. All would be standing, all of them clutching their beer glasses (useful potential missiles). At times nothing happened; one group would depart, and Blades (and no doubt the Owls) would discuss who was out amongst their rivals and generally express their own disbelief and incredulity that they had not *'killed 'em'*. At times I stood with Blades, and although outnumbered they would deliberately stand close to or even amongst groups of Owls. No acknowledgement took place: Blades chatted, Owls did likewise. And when the latter left Blades would comment contemptuously that no one had *'said a word'* or even looked at them whilst they performed this obvious symbolic challenge.

7. *'They Left Their Beer and Fucked Off'* (in their haste to depart, fearful of the Blade presence, the individuals involved were prepared to waste a drink): Departing from licensed premises out of fear and without having finished the contents of the pint glass, was, in its critical retelling, considered to be perhaps the most appalling breach of male etiquette. It not only spoke of cowardice, but of a level of it so great that it led to undignified and hasty exits. Great store would be set by the fact that the opposition made no attempt to walk away slowly, heads held high. Because of their imagery, such accounts always provided a laugh for Blades in the retelling, and the actions of the departed would usually be enhanced: *'They were feytin' each other to get out o' t' door'*, and *'They were screamin' "Women and children last"'.* Such actions were all the better if the teller could add how the Blade presence was not deliberate or even in pursuit of Owls. Hence quotes such as *'We'd only gone in to look at t' birds in there'* or *'We weren't bothered about a feyt. They just bolted.'* To walk into a city-centre nightclub and find unsuspecting Owls also inside

was, on occasions, the excuse for various performances. Thus Blades would retell how, two-strong or twenty-strong, they had stood near the offending rivals or surrounded them, or stared at them. Amidst this mutual recognition it was not unusual for not a word to be exchanged. On such occasions, it must be said, Blades did not often have a violent intent, for the context was not right. However, rather like a child enjoying power over a puppy, Blades would watch and smirk as they discussed Owls' reactions, and would surmise, from various kinds of evidence, what they construed to be Owl attempts to conceal their fear: *'They're all looking into their beer'*; all *'pretending to laugh at summat which in't funny'*; *'keep watching t' door hopin' some mates will come in'*; *'keep going to t' toilet in a group'*; they would rather *'walk half a mile to t' other bar than buy a drink near us'*.

Violence: Words, Rituals and Death

The Blade–Owl conflict had its own semantic way of interpreting encounters that resulted in violence. These differed from the accounts relating to Their Boys, but were consistent with a Sheffield male working-class vocabulary that required the pursuit of another male in the honour-bound hope of teaching him a lesson for some misdemeanour. Four terms in particular were used: the most innocuous was to *'pull'*, which described the means of getting the attention of a rival. This was usually accomplished by one man squaring up to and verbally threatening another in front of an audience of mutual male friends. No actual assault would take place; any humiliation would be verbal, and was embodied in the absence of violence from the accused. The venue was invariably a Sheffield pub, and the scenario was always retold to Blades, for example, *'I pulled 'im about what he wo' shoutin' at t' Blades other neyt.'* The next stage was a *'clip'*, defined as a flat-handed blow or 'scutch' around the head. A punch could be similarly classified. The blows were meant not so much to cause injury, but more as a gesture of audacity and dominance, which, if not responded to, was the end of the scene: *'. . . clipped 'im, then let 'im go'*. Implicit in this was the poor showing by the *'clipped'*, for he had not responded and therefore was unworthy of more punches. Giving *'whacks'* or being *'whacked'* defined situations when assailant(s) tried to hurt an individual by repeated blows, or succeeded with one good blow. Those suffering a whack had to run to avoid more. The severest occasion of dominance was being *'hammered'*, where the victim fell over and received kicks as well as thumps. At least two rivals were required to deliver blows before a Blade would thus describe some situation he had been in as a *hammerin'*.

As the adage of 'hurting the one you love' would have it, so it would seem that the Blade–Owl contests reflected the fact that the nearest is not always the dearest. There were far more injuries in Blade–Owl disputes than in contests between Blades and Their Boys. This is not surprising, for these intra-city confrontations were more frequent and less controlled by police. The question then is, was the actual violence *greater* and, if so, why? The answer, to an extent, is that issues of a personal nature were often intertwined, and thus were absent when Blades opposed rival fans elsewhere. That said, the injuries were rarely a product of weapons' being carried in anticipation. And, in regard to weapons, the same 'norms' Blades used relating to Their Boys were always applied to the Owls. This might seem to be contradicted by tales of the use of petrol bombs; but these were one-off, freak events, which, considering the frequency of Blade–Owl disputes, should be considered as a statistical 'blip', and almost a hindrance to the analysis.

Yet, whilst there were endless possibilities for the exchange of punches, few participants were ever hurt, and considering the numbers involved not that many ever actually got punched. Listening to Blade accounts of such 'chances – missed' against various Owls, one could gain the impression that the history was one of a series of lost opportunities. And whilst the scenarios described above illustrate the preponderance of threats, there were situations that failed to manifest even the hint of a threat; while yet others saw core Blades intervene to prevent colleagues from showing or offering violence towards Owls they knew. At times, local knowledge could prevent violence; at others discretion was the better part of valour, simply because combatants knew individual reputations of fighting ability, i.e. 'hardness'. As a result some Blades were wary of some Owls and vice versa. At times the mere presence of known 'faces' was enough to decide the issue, and rivals fled. Alternatively, many literally talked their way out of trouble, for example, claiming to those they knew to be harder than themselves that they had no violent intent on this occasion.[4]

From the mid-1980s Blades and Owls said that someone would get killed in their vendetta. One United fan (not a Blade) was killed in 1993, after the Sheffield FA Cup Semi-Final at Wembley. His assailant was an Owl, a one-time participant in Blade–Owl conflicts, but by the 1990s no longer seen in the eyes of Blades or Owls as one of Their Boys, for he had 'retired'. In court, Judge Loughland described the death a *'tragic misadventure'*, which is what it was. The victim was not 'one of the lads' in the football hooligan context, but was simply 'one of the shirts', i.e., a fanatical supporter. His death was attributed to a punch received at the hands of the retired Owl, and he died from a skull fracture and brain haemorrhage after six days in hospital. The subsequent inquest and trial showed that at sixteen he had undergone heart-valve replacement, had never worked since, and needed constant medication. Of course, his assailant was not to know this. Boarding the coaches after the Wembley game the rivals had exchanged the ritual abuse, with the victim part of a group exchanging insults with Owls. A fight broke out and punches were thrown, and resulted in a mistaken death when the one punch he received made him fall and bang his head: a million-to-one chance. That said, a most significant aspect was the *lack* of response or any talk of revenge by Blades. Within a couple of days the network gossip provided a full account of the circumstances, and realising that, they too, could have ended up killing a rival with a one-in-a-million blow, they did not pursue the matter. Moreover, a few Blades knew the accused, and some even liked him. And though a week later twenty mates of the deceased arrived at the pub the assailant was known to frequent to 'do' him (he was not in at the time), that was the extent of the pursuit of vengeance. The Old Bailey trial took a week, and on a charge of manslaughter the Owl received a three-year jail sentence.[5] But there were no repercussions or vendettas over this incident, for it was not regarded as a Blade–Owl 'thing', and because of cross-cutting ties it did not become a Blade–Owl drama.

Loving the Enemy? Owl Mates

A dialogue of some sort always prevailed in Blade–Owl issues, for some of the Top Lads of each faction knew each other well enough to chat, while others were at a lesser level of intimacy that was known colloquially as 'on nodding terms'. This acquaintance saved both factions on a number of occasions from further violence. Some protagonists recognised that amongst their equivalents there were *'good lads'*. Some Blades and Owls had mates in the other 'side', and illustrated in this a recognition that, outside of football loyalties, they were no different. Such friendships originated mainly in school, sometimes through residence, and occasionally in the workplace. And in a few cases they were created by playing in the same Sunday football teams. A couple of 'mates' had actually met through the Blade–Owl hostilities, by simply talking on the streets after a fight and taking the role of the main negotiator in some potentially violent encounter. Such people could therefore not really fight each other in Blade–Owl situations. And recognition of the 'game' and the courageous 'other' produced an admiration that sometimes extended to a handshake when the two groups squared up to one another. There was, in a sense, a mirror image here, which some Blades recognised. Others, of course, could not and did not want to recognise this; for it simply it confused matters, and they were happy in their wilful 'hatred'.

For those that had mates across enemy lines confrontations proved a dilemma. Some would move away from those they knew, and if fights did occur try to make contact with someone they did not know. Yet others, when questioned about such a possibility, argued that combatants from either side should accept the likelihood of assault and see it as contextual and not to be taken too personally! Thus in Blade–Owl confrontations surnames and personal insults were shouted in proceedings, and post-mortems were occasions of personal diatribes. Thus at one time Gordon saved a top Owl from a *'kicking'* when other Owls ran off, leaving him alone and surrounded by twenty Blades. Two years later Gordon and Ray were being attacked by Owls when this same Owl pulled their assailants away and ensured safe passage. Even Alan, a top Blade who couldn't abide Owls, was once rescued by this same Owl as he was being kicked along West Street. There were always people who, either from a sense of 'fair play' or because their personal ties extended across the divide, would intervene to ensure that few ever got seriously injured. In altercations the participants of both sides worked to the notion that: *'he's had enough'* – a factor illustrated quite simply by an absence of resistance from the man suffering the blows.

As illustrated repeatedly in the ethnographies, Blades knew the names and/or identities of their assailants, but would never reveal their identities to inquisitive police. To do so would be dishonourable: a man was expected to be able to respond to an injury or insult with his own version of retribution or punishment. For this reason Blades and Owls had an unwritten rule that none of their numbers would give evidence in the witness box against the other. One Blade arrested for assaulting an Owl even phoned the home of a leading Owl asking him to explain to the Owl victim that, in the impending identity parade, he should, ideally, fail to recognise him. The Owls played their part – the Blade was not picked out and the Blade was not charged. To the exasperation of police, even the recently injured would not admit their injuries to be a product of Blade or Owl fights, and indeed an Owl could go up in the estimation of Blades when they realised how his silence in the face of police inquiries had saved some of them from arrest and fines or custodial sentences.[6]

At times, the Blade–Owl conflict was considered completely off-limits by both parties. On a couple of occasions Blades and Owls were placed in the same police cell, and in the circumstances (three occasions in five years) the detained chatted and each left with a better opinion of the other. Moreover, I noted the individual subsequently felt a certain obligation to speak well of his adversary, when denigrated by colleagues. At times, rivals found themselves sitting on the same bench, either as defendants or in the court's public gallery, and even sharing some defence solicitors. Other occasions saw rivals lining up in opposing football teams on Sunday mornings, when the game was played to the rules and handshakes accepted. A few Blades told stories of having attended weddings, to find an Owl and his fiancée as guests. Such recognition did not bring hostility, but a discreet chat and laugh about their respective factions. Other former combatants were to become neighbours through buying or renting properties. The most remarkable instance involved Pear, who, on one occasion, following a fight and chase, had stood over an Owl who had been caught and beaten to the floor, and dropped burning matches on him (none ignited his clothing). Surrounded by Blades, the Owl appealed to their better nature, and various Blades helped him up and walked him away from London Road, as Pear cursed a lost opportunity. A year later Pear discovered his new next-door neighbour was the very same Owl! The two had a chat and agreed that as both now had wives and children, they would drop hostilities and ensure their respective factions did not bring matters to 'the door'.

There were constant messages between the factions. Blades often knew when the Owls were turning out and when they were likely to be on London Road. That said, some messages were false, for opponents enjoyed 'winding up' rivals by making false claims and threats. When the clubs played matches, however, the issue lost any ambiguity – it was *expected* that the factions would meet, for they were honour bound to turn out. Thus, it was often a question of finding where the Other was, and then sending an invitation over the phone. This was not difficult. Owls, knowing roughly where Blades would be, would phone the pub and ask for Blades by name, and invite, threaten or abuse them. Most of the time nothing came of the calls, because the Owls were not where they said they were, or were just calling to be abusive. More importantly, the call offered the chance for each group to deride each other's mobs, whilst dozens shouted abuse in the background. Some Blades would phone the Owls both on Friday and Saturday nights and, on a few occasions on Sunday lunch-times. Knowing where an individual Owl drank, a couple would phone the pub, and, asking for him by name, would warn him that 'the BBC' would be shortly coming through the pub door after him. Message over, they would return to have a drink with fathers and relatives. For some, the wind-up was more fun than confronting the opposition.

At times, those considered appallingly violent by the wider society were the same people who acted as mediators to prevent conflict. Both 'Kivo' and other villagers responded to my hypothetical question as to whether locality could overcome football loyalty by arguing that it could cause a dilemma. This hypothetical situation never actually occurred, and, if it had, I believe there would have been sufficient 'umpires' in the form of football-inspired friendships to prevent a fight, for this sort of negotiation was a significant factor in disputes in both the city and the region at large. It would be wrong, therefore, to say that Blade identity would necessarily overrule any local identity. In some circumstances it did, but not in others; and each area had its own local issues. The villagers fought local Blade–Owl battles occasionally, and Rotherham had their own local 'war' with Leeds fans to pursue (see Armstrong 1994). Put simply, each district had its own dynamics and personalities. In some places and on some occasions Blade identity overcame all others; but it all depended on the incident. There *were* occasions, for example, where disputes based on perceived insults and subsequent threats were mediated peacefully, thanks to the intervention of Blades in both camps. Ironically, then, Blades could occasionally be said to be contributing to a more tranquil city or neighbourhood.

Segmented and Disorderly

According to the logic of 'Ordered Segmentation', group and locality are closely linked, and rival city fans should aggregate to tackle the arrival of a greater outsider with a prodigious hooligan reputation. I cannot find a single sustainable example of this in Sheffield.[7] Furthermore, whilst the Sheffield hooligan rivalries do have a small number of no-go areas at mutually recognised leisure times, there is no other recognisable association of group with place. At times, violations of balances of power in the city can take place, but these are suppressed by the activation of other codes of masculinity; in particular that of gender deference or situations which individuals enact and in which they temporarily shed their oppositional identity for a familiar and reciprocally passive social persona. It is also wrong to attack a rival out with non-recognisable mates as male company, for that is a state (at that moment) of a non-hooligan identity. A two-club city produces interaction with persistent socio-ethical problems that are regularly negotiated but never fully resolved. There are no 'rules of disorder' here (or elsewhere), but there are norms and guidelines, appropriate within ideals of local masculinity.

Blades and Owls compete, but for what prize is difficult to establish. If the 'Pigs' were the fools and bullies Blades made them out to be, then surely there would be little to be gained from repeatedly proving superiority. And even after the 'Pigs' had been chased, they still met and drank along West Street, for Blades did not want it as their 'patch'. Territorial gain was therefore not the motive, but displays of power were; and whenever there is power there will be resistance. In Blades' relations with the Owls there is recurring struggle, with victory perpetually having to be won. In the situation, both factions allow themselves the ritual context of conflict in order that one or the other can assert their dominance effectively. However the Blades did not know quite what to do with 'victory'. They inevitably sought an admission of their superiority, but the Owls' refusal to accept defeat gave Blades something more important, a permanent reason for expressing solidarity through socialising. The two groups are thus involved in a symbiotic relationship, and in a sense are Siamese twins or Binary Opposites, each essential to the other's existence.

Whilst Blades and Owls worked on such mutual allegations and assumptions, the ambiguity of so many situations meant that in most instances each side had an opportunity to claim a valid excuse for explaining either their inactivity or apparent defeat. Such explanations to absent Blades would usually be embellished with figures of the number of Owls involved, which would be said to have increased by 25–33 per cent – with the main protagonists' names being recalled. The listeners would express anger and the need for vengeance, which has therefore to be based on this full possession of the facts. Inevitably the act of vengeance would produce some accusation of bad masculinity, more often than not in some form of bullying. The bully must then be taught a lesson, and in pursuing this, each side created the seeds to sow further conflict. This, combined with elements Walker (1987: 51) saw as essential for Sicily, is applicable for men in many places and walks of life: *'The conventions of the vendetta are time-honoured, and followed not only by Sicilian peasants by also by football teams, colleges, politicians, book reviewers, and media personalities. Usually such justifications are permissive; but sometimes they are obligatory: retaliation and Omerta are not only allowable but the only correct behaviour.'* Blade–Owl encounters were not inevitable, and the outcome of meetings could differ depending on previous incidents.

Notes

1. In March 1976 Owls made headlines after trouble at their match at Rotherham. Sixty fans were arrested, nine fans needed hospital treat-

ment, and a train was damaged on the return journey (*The Star*, 22 March 1976).

2. If publicity were anything to go by there were more Councillors who watched Wednesday than United throughout the 1980s, though what this actually meant was difficult to argue. United fans, however, had their own litany of mistreatment. Thus, in 1984, with Wednesday winning promotion to Division One, a civic reception at the Town Hall was given for the team. Then, as United were surprisingly promoted to Division Two a few weeks later, they too were given one. Of course, for the United fans, this only occurred because the Council had been driven to this show of impartiality. Later, in 1990, with United promoted to Division One, Blades awaited similar treatment to that which the Council had afforded Wednesday in 1984 – an open-top bus ride around the city. Blades, however, are still waiting their triumphant parade.

3. Headlines in *The Star* in September 1968 stated the club would ban for life those responsible for throwing the substance (acetic acid) that burned five young men at the testimonial match. Two needed hospital treatment; the others were treated at the ground. A week later the culprit received the amazingly lenient sentence of a three-year probation order.

4. For the Boxing Day fixture in 1979 between United and Wednesday at Hillsborough, the kick-off was at 11.00 a.m. and there was not a single arrest. For the return fixture at Bramall Lane, played on Easter Monday 1980, around 300 Blades met in the Peace Gardens in Sheffield city centre, and, not finding any Owls in city-centre pubs, they entered the ground to find 150 Owls on the kop! One 22-year-old Owl received a two-inch wound to his back, the result of a stabbing, and one WPC sustained three cracked ribs after being kicked by a female supporter. A total of 42 arrests were made, nearly all being charged with threatening behaviour.

5. The media, as always, tried hard to represent the issue in the worst possible light. The *Daily Telegraph* reported the first day of the trial under the heading 'Invalid Soccer Fan Punched to Death', and then added opinion from the Prosecution Counsel that the issue was *'an unprovoked attack . . . only crime was that he was wearing the red and white striped shirt of Sheffield United . . . set upon for no apparent reason'*. The paper did not report the rest of the trial, where readers would have learned of very different circumstances.

6. The longest period for retribution was five years. One Blade was stabbed in the back in a fight with Owls outside a West Street pub in 1990. Requiring an overnight stay in hospital and eight stitches, the Blade knew his assailant, but would not inform questioning police of his identity. In

1995 a Blade–Owl city-centre fight resulted in the Owl receiving a beer glass across his neck and needing seven stitches in the wound.

7. Significant to any theory of Ordered Segmentation is the fact that United and Wednesday followers would never dream of travelling together to fight for the England national team. The latter had fewer fans following England than the Blades. Until 1990 none of the Owl lads went and, on the only occasion one did, he went with a Blade mate. The one Owl who did follow England post-1990 used the friendships made with London hooligans to confront Blades alongside the Londoners.

Part IV

Theory Reconsidered

Blades provided a resource network and, at times, an alternative, informal justice system. With the primary aim of reforming miscreants by punishment, those who offended issues Blades considered worthy of offending faced retribution. The official agents of the state were not expected to intervene in such matters, bar attempting to prevent the protagonists meeting in the first place. Following the accomplishment of retribution, Blades expected their adversaries, be they Their Boys, Owls, or pub bouncers, not to reveal the identity of their aggressors or assailants.

Encompassed in these dramas were issues that could run for years, or conversely, be quickly forgotten, dismissed as having been deserved, or accepted as fair in the nature of consenting participants. Every issue had its own negotiations and circumstances which meant responses had to calculate variables that included: severity of injury, perceived level of insult, degree of bullying, and the level of culpability of those involved. No one could predict how matters would be resolved because Blades did not consistently share the same degree of motivation. More importantly, no individual amongst Blades could demand conformity in behaviour from the others. No individual could claim to be the 'Top Lad' – unable to name such an individual in the 1960s, Blades could not put a name to such a status thirty years later. This facet, so incomprehensible to police, was easily explainable in Blade circles. Firstly, Blade gatherings were egalitarian – there was nothing to be gained from claiming such a status. Secondly, such a status could not be conferred without testing, which would provoke internal feuding. Thirdly, because of the fluid nature of Blade gatherings, new faces appeared and old ones disappeared which meant that 'membership' was always in a state of flux.

Chapter 10

Match-day Mores: Honour and Shame

*So soon as ever thou seest him, draw, and as thou draw'st, swear horrible; for it comes
to pass oft that a terrible oath, with a swaggering accent sharply twanged off, gives
manhood more approbation than ever proof itself would have earned him. Away!*

(William Shakespeare, *Twelfth Night*, 3,4,181–6)

To the outsider, violence is the *raison d'être* of a Blades gathering. This is
wrong. Blades' micro-ontology emerges through various shared constructs
of the Other. From this they create theatres of rivalry against idealised terms
of reference. In the event, various territories are constructed and defined
as appropriate and facilitating, and these enable various performances to
be conducted in a routinised and implicitly 'safe' manner. Such ritualised
procedures, like symbols, operate simultaneously on many levels, and have
a multiplicity of meanings for the participants (Turner 1974; A. Cohen 1974).
Most are mannered, stylised, and coherent, containing elements of role,
script, audience and stage (Goffman 1967; Chaney 1993: 17–23); tied in are
patterns of procedures: location, timing and language. Such confrontations
require a theatre, commodities, and an exchange of what Shields (1992: 7)
calls 'looks' and 'gazes'. Blades play to various audiences, and, like
thespians worldwide, they and their fellow performers need to adhere to
the boundaries of the plot and understand the script. That said, some fluff
their lines, whilst others ham; still others fail to respond on cue, and some
have to improvise constantly. The outcome is hooligan dramas that are
contextual, negotiated and improvised. Such performances provide for
major and minor roles; we have heroes and villains, with 'Top Lads' in the
hooligan 'crews', the onlookers, various fellow supporters as willing
participants by proxy, the disgusted public, and the theatre critics –
journalists and police, who report on what they see as the appalling
performance.

Competing Moralities: The Hooligan Game

Like all competitions, hooligan rivalry was contrived, and the 'prize', although culturally defined, satisfies various individual desires. Both sides accept some basic rules of conduct; both have a chance of winning, and conduct that would make the game impossible is prohibited. Obviously, any total elimination of the opponents is not an aim, for the game could not be played again. However, some used what rivals considered a breaching of the norms, or unfair or 'dirty' tactics (particularly the use of weapons). These social indiscretions are rarely, if ever, admitted by the perpetrators, for to do so would undermine the claims to a successful performance against appropriate opponents. Each hooligan encounter thus becomes a form of cultural collateral to be bartered over. There are no refunds until the next encounter. Losers may seek to negate their debts by claiming an unfair exchange; victors will ignore these face-saving appeals for compensation. Blades gamble reputation within a system that trades in futures. To receive credit, participants claim to be upholding a 'fair and equitable' system of exchange that cannot be found to be counterfeit.

A notable aspect of challenge and response in terms of honour, as Bourdieu (1977: 105) pointed out, is that a man ought only respond to the challenge of an *equal*. It was in accordance with such notions that Blades violence was not random, but was very discriminatory. Within this contest the aim of humiliating rivals played a larger part than injuring them, and the highest honour in this context was acquired by 'running opponents'. This created *the* most visible form of superiority, and was a victory greater than any involving actual physical violence.

Having seen the social drams of Chapters 2 and 3, it makes sense to refer to Blade encounters (even physical ones) as *'competitions'*. Immediately it has to be said these terms are being used and have the same meanings as those attributed to them by anthropologist F. Bailey (1969), who, using analogies drawn from games to analyse the behaviour of politicians, argued that much world-wide adversarial behaviour – although seeming to follow no rules at all – was based on a kind of minimal consensus of what extremes or boundaries of behaviour could be tolerated. If, as Bailey argues, there were no such groundwork of accepted rules, then it was correct to speak of 'fights' between opponents. Commonly, however, even when political behaviour might seem violent, there were rules tacitly, or explicitly, accepted, and such rules could be divided into two groups – first, into those that were proclaimed ('normative'). These set broad limits to possible action, and allowed the players a choice; moreover, they are general guides to conduct, allowing a 'right' or 'wrong' judgement that can justify behaviour.

Others were tacit ('pragmatic'). Dealing with the effectiveness of action, they are, as Bailey postulates, wide-ranging, from accepted ways of winning without actually cheating, to ways of cheating without being found out.

Regardless of the nature of the competition, Bailey argued that what is needed for victory is invention and new strategies. These can include a deliberate deviation from normative rules (what is considered 'fair play'), or may arise because the rules do not anticipate all possible strategems. Hence innovation need not offend existing norms, and the competing personnel may be wide and loose enough to permit individuals who make outlawed moves to partake, even though in a sense they do not understand the rules of competition. If victory is the outcome, because cheating is effective, then others may follow suit. Such 'pragmatic exceptions' (1969: 113) could build against the normative rules and result in either a new set of rules or end with a 'stocktaking' to restore the desired norms. Confrontation, as a product of competition as well as being a message of one's strength, Bailey argued, could also be a challenge *'which the receiver has an option to receive and act upon'* (1969: 100). We might therefore describe the hooligan encounters as a choreography, where a challenge is thrown down, which, if accepted, has as an end-product a victor and a vanquished. In the course of this decisions are made under *'conditions of uncertainty'* (1969: 70), and these arise when there is no apparent rule to guide action or where there are several possibilities. Such occasions are rare because *'most decisions have the agony taken out of them by being routine'* (ibid.: p. 69). Competing teams in these hooligan social dramas can function without leaders or normative rules for allocating authority, and this facilitates the adoption of pragmatic rules that enable some to *'coerce or influence others'* (p. 35). When a decision has to be made *'The art seems to be that of uttering highly acceptable generalisations (i.e. normative themes) in such a way that each member of the audience can give the particular meaning which most pleases him'* (p. 86).

A similar paradox in the means and ends of violence is found by Bailey. He describes how *'orderliness depends upon anticipation, upon expectations being fulfilled'* (p. 121). The paradox, as he points out, is that *'the prize goes to the team who can act in a way unforeseen by its opponents, and, perhaps, unanticipated in the rules of the game'* (p. 121). Hence the ingenuity the Blades and their rivals showed at times in both finding each other and avoiding the police (Bailey's 'Umpires'). Like umpires in a game, the police must not identify with either side. Their concern is with the arena in which the game takes place and the regulation of the rules, although as umpires they can modify or introduce new rules to cope with unanticipated disorders. Then again, they may also help the competitors communicate or suggest solutions to difficulties and diminish uncertainty, and at the same time, can announce a decision and enforce it without reference to the competitors. Through such 'umpires', Bailey argued *'the public at large seeks to protect itself from violence and disorders'* and in turn *'the holders of these roles represent the public and are the means of making articulate and forming public opinion'* (pp. 132–3). Without specifically relating to them, Bailey's whole theory could have been written to articulate the role of the police in football hooliganism.

Challenges: Discrimination and Response

The rival hooligan teams had clear ways of identifying their adversaries. From the mid-1960s to the late 1970s Blades, like all young football fans elsewhere, wanted onlookers (both football supporters and the general public) to know what they were and who they identified with. They thus wore clothing, scarves, hats and badges, which marked them out as football fans. This was their most standard symbol of 'otherness'. For *some* Blades in the late 1960s and early 1970s, however, a more transparent obviousness was provided by the 'skinhead' fashion of close-cropped hairstyle, 'Ben Sherman' label shirts, Levi 'sta-pressed trousers', or jeans deliberately shortened to reveal Doc Marten 'bovver' boots. There were also seasonal and optional extras, with braces worn but covered in winter months by designer label 'Harrington' jackets and three-quarter length 'Crombie' overcoats. Cloth badges of the football club could be sewn on to the breast pocket, accompanied by a woollen scarf knotted around the neck or wrist. A few emphasised their difference further with paint-sprayed gold or silver boots. Alongside them on the Shoreham End would stand those colloquially known as 'grebo's' – youths with long hair who wore a combination of leather or denim motorcycle jackets and denim trousers. Others wore Doc Marten boots with government surplus army 'bush' (camouflage) jackets, whose shoulder lapels and cuffs were useful for tying team scarves around. These also provided an ideal site to exhibit the current symbols of hooligan victory, and the scarves of opposing teams stolen from rival fans displayed as battle honours. That said, some bought such artefacts from sports shops and then wore them, only to tell and re-tell great tales of heroism about their capture.

Around the early 1970s a new style briefly appeared. Copied from the character of Alex in Kubrick's controversial 1971 film of Anthony Burgess's (1962) 'A Clockwork Orange', the Shoreham End now contained youths in boiler suits, some wearing bowler hats, some pit helmets. A few wore face make-up and others carried walking sticks. They were, of course, intentionally outrageous. The celluloid youths they copied were danger-ously violent nihilists and they knew no norms. This fad lasted only one season. However, each participant arrived attired as he wished, and the late 1970s saw a proliferation of artefacts and styles within the hooligan 'scene'. Different scarves, sold by the club souvenir shop and city sports shops, created not only good business, but a variety of appendages on the terraces. For the 1979–80 season, some Blades supplemented scarves with red, white and black Tam O'Shanter hats and, between 1980–2, others took on cloth caps and Donkey jackets with National Coat Board (NCB) initials on the back in celebration of a 'hard' mining image and self-parody of being Northern. The 1982–3 season saw sweatshirts borrowing the designer label of the 'Lonsdale–London' boxing club, which announced that the wearer was a supporter of 'United–Sheffield'. The link was significant, for Lonsdale meant 'hard', fit and fighting. Even without speaking or any obvious garment to indicate football loyalty, hooligans could always identify their equivalents. Metal pin badges became *de rigeur* in 1981–4 amongst Blades. This was the club's insignia worn on the left breast of either the summer T-shirt, autumn V-neck jumper or winter jacket. This suited the change when participants no longer sported the more obvious football favours, yet fans still needed to show one another whose side they were on (not least so that Blades did not attack Blades). The badge did this perfectly. Rivals knew what to look for, the tiny badge – worn 'correctly' – said symbolically who you were and that you were 'game'. By 1982 an even smaller tie-pin badge was worn with the same design. Apart from this badge, the 1980s Blades did not sport any other overt symbol to signify group identity.

Some Blades of the early 1970s preceded the 'Casual' style of the 1980s and were dressed at the match in the height of contemporary fashion – platform shoes, high-waist 'baggy' trousers (Oxford Bags), some with side pockets ('Birmingham Bags'), V-neck pullovers ('Northern Soul jumpers') and wide-collared shirts. Many also wore football scarves, but favoured the less obvious 'silk' variety, which was less bulky, smarter and easily concealed up the sleeve or inside the open-necked shirt. Such concealment produced a few scenarios. Should a rival hide a scarf under his other clothing he could be challenged to prove where he came from: questions would range from the direct *'Where yu from?'* to the more devious *'Got time on yu pal?'*, when the reply would reveal the accent. Should this be well-disguised or the Blades be in any doubt, further questions would be asked, such as *'What part of Sheffield yu from?'*, sometimes followed by the challenge *'Name a boozer there.'* If 'sussed', the victim could try to walk in a nonchalant manner and fool his observers into thinking he was a 'home' fan, or walk away anticipating a kick in the rear or a blow to the side of the head, or preferably, stand near a police officer. Alternatively, he could run like hell or, on seeing fellow supporters, appeal to their loyalties in seeking refuge. Another ploy, not always convincing, was to suddenly discover a limp, the reasoning being that fellow hooligans would surely not strike an invalid. Some even tried to pass themselves off as mentally disturbed, though 'actin' like a mong'' was difficult. These techniques, more spoken of than used, caused much mirth in recollections of the hooligan past.

The 1980s saw fundamental changes in the nature of Blade gatherings. What was at one time an uncohesive mob gathering in a confined area and along specified routes had changed to produce more cohesive gatherings, wherein those gathered knew that the day's events would sometimes be an *ad hoc*, improvised process liable to take place over a wide area. Hooligan competence and therefore honour was manifested in being able to recognise equivalents. The actors had to look for the appropriate information from the store of role plays which they and fellow hooligans recognised as signifying intention. Upon 'decoding' the representations, the response would vary between ridicule and violence. And whilst violence was never a random event, it is true that the 1960s and 1970s had seen instances of attacks on any rival of the same age. From the 1980s, however, confront-ations of the 'firms'/mobs/crews and the subsequent incidence of violence were far more discriminating. Blades explained their more discriminating style by referring to their greater sophistication: they did not *'need beer to feyt'* or wander around singing silly threatening songs to an uninterested public. Ironically, the new style required the football hooligan to define himself against the stereotype of the hooligan as a beer-guzzling, scarf-bedecked, noisy, objectionable oaf. And so, whilst the 1980s Blades also drank beer and took drugs, they were more instrumental about when and how much, for they had to avoid police, who would quickly quell and contain them if they suspected them of being drunk.

Dressing for the 1980s

Consumer style provided an identification upon which any two groups could negotiate. In Blades articulation, there was something called *'Football'*, which encompassed a male look and comportment and with which they claimed they could always identify even in a busy street. Such identity was a configuration of symbols – clothing worn, numbers in the group – and, most importantly, the context – the times, such that a location in the city-centre streets or in proximity to the football ground between midday and six meant 'Their Boys'. Blades worked with this knowledge, taking and realising the signs in a combination of demeanour, comportment, eye movements and clothing, with various subliminal categories which, on questioning, could be reduced to stock replies. Katz (1988) terms this the mutual identification of common essences.

This made life easier for non-combatants. Those not considered part of the game and not worthy of attention were dismissed in various terms: *'scarfies'*, *'hats and scarves'*, *'shirts'* (because they wore scarves or the club colours, a *passé* thing to do); or *'beer-bellies'* (older, scruffy supporters aged 30–40, whose physical attributes counted them out of the challenge, as their only intention was being to drink and watch the match). Other descriptions, such as *'anoraks'*, *'train-spotters'*, *'speedway fans'*, the *'radio brigade'* and *'football virgins'*, were also negative categories derived from appearance. Basically this was 'bad' clothing within a Blades' definition, for hats and scarves signified only a devotion to the team and suggested they had nothing else in life in the way of identity. A radio signified a desire to know what the rest of the football world was doing, and its listener represented to Blades a *'fanatic'* commitment. Older untouchable males would be classed as *'old blokes'* or *'normal supporters'*. Younger supporters of similar age to Blades who, because of appearance, were not worth challenging were termed *'jiffs'* and *'stiffs'*. These terms cannot easily be defined, but could include rival lads dressed in a displeasing manner to Blades' eyes. Their clothing and actions signified a total lack of understanding of hooliganism; so much so that to confront them would have been futile, for there was nothing to be gained. Again, if opposition was presented by *'game'* youngsters that Blades did not consider worthy of fighting (15–17-year-olds), they would dismiss them to each other as being *'just chabbies'* (a Sheffield term for baby or youngster), *'kids'*, or *'little knobheads/piecelets/divvies/ trendies'*. In spite of all their attempts to be more discriminating in their actions.

Deportment within Spaces

Silence and discretion were often required in hooligan scenarios. During the 1970s and 1980s home matches would often see Blades on John Street shortly before kick-off, either standing around the petrol station forecourt or in the road, hands in pockets and silent. This is where the visitors' turnstiles were located, and visiting fans would stand around watching for their hooligan equivalents. Sometimes rival fans would deliberately walk into each other, thus allowing each other the chance to get a quick (and discreet) exchange of punches before quickly separating. Others exchanged discreet verbal insults, and this suited everyone. Rivals gained the acknowledgement they were seeking, while Blades had made their point in having recognised their equivalents. The nearby police, who had made the whole interaction possible, remained unaware. To the innocent eye nothing had happened. By the 1980s the innocent eye could even be unaware of performances enacted on a 'mob' level. To an unknowing public this partisan existence remained unseen, even as a hundred Blades regularly walked around Sheffield city centre or other towns on a Saturday afternoon. And this was the situation until the Blades found their equivalents, when a shopping public would suddenly see an event unfold that would seem to occur without premonition, for questions about rival identities were now unnecessary.

The nature of the mob-to-mob challenge was dependent on two things: the presence of police and the relative strengths of the two groups. If police were nearby Blades would quietly look 'mean' and 'shadow' rivals by standing or walking closely. Even under police escort a couple of Blades could sometimes 'tag along' with rivals, inviting them to 'Drop back' and 'Turn off.' Such invitations were symbolic rather than practical, and were made to impress watching Blades and annoy rivals, for with police around little or nothing could actually be done. Significantly, Blades knew they could not be assaulted. To strike with so many police around would mean almost certain arrest.

Then again, recognition could take place with the police not obviously nearby. Should two mobs identify each other with police elsewhere, a shout of 'Who are these?' or 'They're here' would precede subsequent shouts of 'Come on, then', and lead to fight or flight. If the two groups were numerically similar they would generally run towards each other, slow to a standstill at about ten yards apart, and in the ensuing 'stand off' some would 'bounce about' on the balls of their feet, inviting rivals by gesturing with their arms and hands to 'Come on.' Others would stand relatively still, but the air was full of shouts: 'When you're ready', 'Get 'em' and 'Oo! . . . Oo!', a noise Blades made preceding all confrontations from 1981 onwards, similar to that made by the warriors in the film 'Zulu!', and later changed to a chorus of 'B-B-C'.[1] Eventually, participants would run across the inevitable space that developed between the opponents, and a flailing of arms and legs began. One side would invariably 'back off', sometimes to run away, at other times merely to drop back a few yards, reassess the situation, and then go forward again. The arrival of police meant the fight was over, as it invariably scattered participants. And this, for the most part, was actually what match-day football hooliganism was.

Extending Invitations

Police tactics were responsible for much of the post-1980s discrimination and decorum. The desire to avoid them meant that invitations of various types and in various names were extended. This can be illustrated by various incidents. One memorable one occurred in 1987, when, after a match, a mini-van of rivals from Portsmouth drove into Sheffield bus station and challenged twenty waiting Blades. A three-minute twelve-a-side fight ensued, with two rivals repeatedly kicked on the floor before police arrived, scattering the combatants. Ten minutes later the same van pulled up outside a pub where Blades were awaiting entry. Heads appeared from its various windows shouting *'Cheers lads . . . good one . . . we owe when you come to Pompey.'* Somewhat startled, the Blades considered them *'game'* for both their actions and their attitude, and though this was not typical and was never to recur, it does illustrate that participation was consensual and appreciated, and that the factions spoke the same language.

Two groups frequently recognised each other, but almost equally often knew that police were nearby. In such situations a messenger would cross the divide and suggest a place the factions could make their separate ways to sort out the issue. One Saturday morning in the late 1980s, Sheffield railway station witnessed fifty Sunderland lads in the buffet bar. For an hour they watched the approach roads. Eventually, a youth checked out the pub across the road. As there were no Blades in there, the rest made their way towards it. Before they entered, however, a Blade, Dom, appeared, saying *'We know who you are, let's tek a walk where there's no coppers'*; and he specified a place. He then took this information to thirty Blades in The Stamp, who walked to the suggested venue. However, the visitors lost confidence and returned to the station before a fight started.

When, like some doors, opportunities were bolted, creativity and dialogue could unlock them. In the middle and late 1980s, when rival lads entered a pub by the railway station, the landlord would sometimes lock them in, and Blades could find themselves in the frustrating position of knowing where Their Boys were, but unable to do anything about it. On one such occasion Blades' invitations through the windows for the forty rivals to 'come out' came to nothing. From another pub, a few hundred yards away, Jade phoned the pub, asking to speak to *'any o' them lads who've come in from Huddersfield'*, and told the visitor that if they were not out in ten minutes *'We're comin' down to smash it up.'* Minutes later the visitors left, and Blades pursued them into the railway station. After a brief scuffle everyone scattered as police arrived.

Four years later fifty Leicester lads were in the same pub, and once again the landlord barred the door. One Blade, Bernard, left others gathered in a nearby pub and was allowed to walk alone into the bar-room. With family in Leicester and knowing one of 'Their Boys', he asked of his whereabouts, but learned he had not made the journey. He told 'Their Boys' Blades were forty strong and would be down soon, and they replied they wanted to finish watching the boxing on the pub TV. Bernard took this information back, and when the boxing ended Blades walked out of their pub, and the Leicester fans also came out. In the ensuing confrontation the visitors were chased back to the station, a few receiving a 'kicking' on the way.

One of the strangest fights, certainly from the point of view of the preamble, occurred in November 1992, when Blades again fought Leicester fans in London's West End. The forty-strong Blades were a motley collection from two vans and five carloads, who agreed to rendezvous after the match in Covent Garden. The only pub to let them in was the one they settled in, and after half an hour they were joined by fifty Leicester fans who were also having a night in London, having travelled from Portsmouth. Whilst the mutual recognition of 'Football' was immediate, most fans of each faction enjoyed a chat about what the other had been up to and compared stories and opinions of other crews. About a quarter from each side did not mix, and remained in small groups watching suspiciously. After an hour one Blade (a total peripheral) without warning punched a Leicester fan. Things turned hostile. Many Blades rounded on their colleague, telling him his actions were stupid, and a minute later the Blade assailant, expressing regret, told his victim as recompense he could have one free punch at him. The victim accepted the offer and, as the factions stood around, thumped him across the cheek! Far from ending hostilities, however, this was the cue for one of the Leicester lads to launch a punch at another Blade. In the following minute bottles, glasses and stools were thrown, resulting in the Blades' running Leicester fans out of the pub and across Leicester Square, with one from each side being arrested whilst brawling.

At times Blades were enticed by false stories and pen and paper. In 1994 six core Blades standing outside the Reading FC ground waiting for tickets were approached by a local in his late twenties who had obviously sussed them. The story he told was that four young Sheffield fans entering a nearby pub that the local mob met in had been 'jumped' and beaten up. He considered this bad form, and suggested the group go to the pub and sort out such bullies. The Blades, wary of the possibility of his being an undercover policeman, thanked him for the information, but stressed they were not hooligans, and walked away. Ten minutes later he returned, and gave a street diagram as to how to get to the aforementioned pub. Blades thanked him, but once again refused to rise to the bait. Thus, despite good intentions on one part, it needed the others to accept the offer for a scenario to begin; sometimes, smelling a rat, they would not play the game.

Reputation and League Position

The primary purpose for gathering amongst Blades was to feel good. The best feeling was afforded by being considered part of some élite masculine entity. Thus, if the groups were accorded the status of being 'hard' and fearsome, nobody amidst Blades would argue with that. The trouble was that not all were agreed on how reputable the Blades were, and opinions on how hard Blades were changed over the years. In the late 1980s Blades all believed they were one of the top 10 'firms' in England, but who was better than them was the topic of much debate.

When discussing Their Boys Blades did not really have the benefit of knowing personalities like they did the Owls. Thus opinions were often reduced to various stereotypes. Supporters from Liverpool, 'Scousers', despite being the 1970s media inspired loveable 'scally' rogues were, in hooligan circles, renowned from the early 1970s for 'thieving and slashing', and were particularly renowned for stealing garments from rivals. Fans from Manchester, 'Mancs', in the mid-1980s, were believed to carry Stanley knives, but both City and United had a 'good' reputation for being 'game' with Blades. Newcastle supporters, 'Geordies', were stereotyped as overweight, badly dressed, and often drunk (akin to Scottish supporters). Considered not to have a "mob" of identifiable lads instead *'they all just get pissed and feyt'*. They were, all the same, renowned and respected in hooligan circles. Londoners, 'Cockneys', were mimicked by walking with a bounce, rolling shoulders, and moving the head from side to side saying; *'wanna know?'*, *'Owriyt'*, *'Wanna pop?'* in exaggerated London accents. Such fans held a certain mythology. In the 1980s they were rich in appearance with expensive, casual, pastel-coloured clothing, supplemented by gold jewellery and distinctive hairstyles. They were also considered 'well-organised', a vague recognition of their ability to 'suss' out rivals in the metropolis and arrive at destinations having avoided police. They were believed to be sometimes 'tooled up', i.e., knife carrying, albeit no Blade was ever slashed by a Londoner. Generally London crews contained a high proportion of 'old' lads i.e. from their late twenties onwards. Some considered London firms to be in a 'different league' from Blades, in that they played harder, had older players and had more training; a product of living in London, a place many Blades considered 'weird' and 'violent'.

For all their adversaries Blades did not have any long-standing enmity with *any* other hooligan group other than the Owls.

There existed various folklores of how Blades' 'rep' was gained that did not accord with the media constructs of notoriety. In fact, hooligan culture found some acts defined as 'football hooliganism' deplorable, even if they did bring mass publicity. On the contrary, the conferment of reputation was considered best when attained quietly and effectively. Events would be passed along the 'Hooligan League', which operated informally via gossip exchange, so that *'what really happened'* could be set against what the media reported or did not know. Such exchange came from seven contexts:

1. **'Nighters'** (later known as 'Raves'): i.e. all-night 'Northern Soul' music discos held in the Midlands and the North in the early and middle 1980s. These attracted hooligans from various cities to dance and chat about their escapades. This music and style were superseded from 1987 onwards by House or Acid Music 'Raves', which many football 'lads' frequented.
2. **Working Away**: Blades met other lads whilst on contract work in other cities, principally on building sites. Others travelled via long-distance driving jobs, and a few away at college met with local hooligans.
3. **Summer Holidays**: Mediterranean resorts from the late 1970s onward would find hundreds of hooligans on holiday, or working in bars and discos, or in other entrepreneurial activities where stories were shared and friendships made.
4. **England Matches**: Although only a few dozen Blades ever travelled abroad in the years 1982–94, those that did had the chance to meet equivalents. Fixtures between England and Scotland in the middle and late 1980s witnessed Blades amongst the English gatherings.
5. **Family:** Blades had relatives, invariably male cousins, with the occasional brother-in-law, in other towns. Family visits were the scene for the secret exchange of information.
6. **Custody and Court-rooms**: Blades arrested and placed in police cells could find themselves with rivals, with whom they would spend the hours chatting. When in court facing charges following arrest, rivals occasionally went for a drink together; some kept in contact.
7. **Hooligan Tourism:** Various Blades would, on occasion, travel to games not concerning 'Their' team to see what other hooligan groups were up to. At times they would make themselves known to the other lads; at other times they were 'sussed' and challenged as to who they were. As neutrals, they were usually afforded a welcome as guests or spectators

for the day. Contacts would be made, and one day their hosts would reciprocally be their guests. From 1987 individual Blades had friendships with the lads of Nottingham Forest and Everton. This however did not prevent fights when the teams played each other for the next couple of years. Thus, liaisons were always contextual, and contested and contrived.

The perception of how 'hard' Blades were varied with individual rival hooligans and even amongst the Blades themselves. The late 1960s and early 1970s Blades were considered then and in retrospect to be a 'hard' mob, and Bramall Lane was 'risky' for visiting fans. A few years later, in their own and, they presumed, other fans' opinion, Blades were a 'soft touch'. There was no good explanation why, but at this time many rival 'mobs' stood on the Shoreham End (even though only three – Leeds, Manchester United, and the Owls – ever 'took' it completely). Although at the time they were a First Division team, on occasions the away support was minimal, as Blades were afraid to attend certain notorious grounds. Then, owing to a combination of more effective policing and the safety afforded by this, the away following increased. On top of this Blades' self-confidence and 'reputation' rose as a result of winning various hooligan confrontations; and relegation to the Third Division in 1979, and the Fourth in 1981, meant that Blades' success in confrontations with smaller groups of opponents bred a certain confidence. In their own estimation, Blades could now pull a *'good'* (i.e. large) turnout, and in their own opinion were *'game as fuck'* (i.e. willing to confront opponents whoever and wherever they were). This change, Blades explained, was time-specific, and founded in the team's success a decade previously in the First Division: *'We're all a product of United's mid-seventies' success. All t' young lads in Sheffield wanted to go to Bramall Lane. Everybody went wi' their Dad and watched all t' feytin' on t' Kop. Eight, ten years later here we are, we watched it happening then, grew into it, and we're all of similar age'* [Ray]. And whilst age-grouping may explain the numbers who constituted the Blades, their *'gameness'* had to be proved; when it was, it had little to do with *actual* physical violence.

It is crucial to this phenomenon that in many instances events worth remembering contained little violence, or violence without apparent injury or innocent victims. Blades particularly prided themselves on being one of the first rival mobs from outside London to challenge the feared Millwall on their home ground, when in 1980 fifteen coach-loads travelled, including two coaches of Blades, and fought the Londoners in streets around the ground before and after the match. One incident, regarded by many as significant, came after a match at Lincoln in 1982. In the two preceding seasons Blades had struggled in confrontations against these unknown and, as it proved, underrated rivals. For this August match a hundred Blades travelled by service train, and successfully repelled a lunch-time attack on a pub they were in. After the match came the crucial confrontation, when Blades walked on to adjacent grassland, in normal expectation of an attack by the home lads. They duly arrived, without any police. The Blades 'stood' their ground in the face of a charge. Furious punching and kicking lasted for two minutes, and ended with the home lads losing momentum and running. This fight was spoken of by many Blades in 1983–5 as being a turning-point in their self-realisation.

The next test of nerve arose in September 1984, with the visit of Yorkshire rivals, Leeds, and their notorious hooligans. Across the 1970s Leeds had 'taken' the Shoreham End and chased Blades outside the ground, and the number of Blades travelling to Leeds was always very small because of their hooligans' notoriety. Because the two sides were in different divisions, they had not met since 1978; and by 1984, Blades, like hooligans everywhere, knew that the police had now largely managed to control the segregation of fans inside the ground and the transport routes to it. 'Trouble' now only came to those who went looking for it, and even then was usually contained by the swift arrival of police. Because of this, fans were more arrogant in their challenges to those perceived to be of a higher hooligan rank. Thus emboldened, on one early afternoon two hundred Blades arrived via three coaches in Leeds city centre and chased the locals. Blades considered that they had 'done' one of the country's 'top' crews on their home ground (see Armstrong 1994). That said, only about ten of the mob got a punch in, no rivals were hurt, nothing was damaged, and three Blades were arrested. Leeds fans claimed that Blades had met only their young lads, and by the time they had gathered their forces the police were protecting the Blades.

Some occasions provided the scope to build a reputation without so much as a punch being thrown. In 1987 the London team, West Ham, had a following regarded nationally as being the country's 'top' crew; and, at one away game in the capital, Blades decided to present them with a challenge. Three coaches disembarked their passengers well away from West Ham's ground, and Blades arrived a hundred strong via the Under-ground on the main road to the ground half an hour before kick-off. Within a minute over a hundred rivals poured out of two pubs, but a fight was prevented by police (as Blades had anticipated). No punches were exchanged, but Blades felt they had 'done themselves proud'. Surrounded by police, they were virtually paraded through the streets to the ground. Years later a hundred Blades paraded along Tottenham High Street before and after a match, shadowed by Their Boys, but saw a large-scale fight prevented by the swift arrival of police. In these two scenarios only two Blades managed to strike opponents, and two Blades were arrested. This minuscule level of disorder was considered a tremendous 'show' by Blades. For the home fans the Blades incursion was a mere five hundred-metre walk surrounded by police. This might seem over-playing the issue, but this was how hooligans operated; and it clearly illustrates that violence was not always necessary for *'good shows'* and *'gettin' a result'*, for an expressive performance was just as satisfying.

Semantics of Victory and Defeat

The aftermaths of these various performances were embodied in linguistic constructs. The post-mortem would, at times, hear Blades expressing appreciation and praising rivals for their courage: *'They were good lads'*, *'Wun't budge'*, *'The mesters'*, *'Top Lads'*, *'had come for it'* or *'wanted to know'*. The post-match 'chat' was also an analysis of technical play, *'We backed 'em off'* or *'had 'em on their toes'*, *'went steamin' in'*, *'straight into 'em'*, *'waded in'*, *'lot went'* or *'Blades went barmy.'* If the confrontation was limited to verbals because of police presence, a prominent rival could be accused of *'showing off'*, *'posing'*, *'giving it the big 'un'* or *'thinking he's a reyt hero'*. He could also be variously described as a: *'knobhead'*, *'divvy'*, *'daft cunt'* and *'silly bastard'*. An individual who had been beaten was *'ragged'* (well beaten and kicked), or it was said he was *'clocked, then let go'*, which described receiving a couple of punches thrown before being allowed to run away. If, during a fight, a rival or one of the Blades fell and received blows by foot or fist, this was termed getting: *'turned over'*, *'hammered'*, *'bashed'*, *'pasted'*, *'wasted'* or getting *'a tousing'*. When a proper defeat was inflicted, i.e. rivals had run in all directions, Blades used exaggerated and violent metaphors: *'Killed 'em'*, *'Scattered 'em'*, *'Blasted 'em'*, *'Spidered 'em'*, *'Skedaddled 'em'*, *'Done 'em'*, *'Wasted 'em'*, or *'Wrote 'em off.'* Other terms used of the other party in such transactions were *'swam'* (descriptive of the erratic actions rival fans used to get away), *'legged it'* (ran away), or *'done a Dexy's'* (taken from the name of the pop group 'Dexy's Midnight Runners') or *'doin' t' Offman's'*, a term peculiar to Sheffield (a play on words, since the phrase was used to describe running, as in *'I'm off, man!'*). Another humorous term for those who fled was *'chip butty throwers'*, a metaphorical depiction of times when opponents were reduced to throwing all they had to hand before running, including their food.

Blade narratives habitually exaggerated violence. So that at a very mild level a single thump or *'back-hander'* was described as having its victim *'whacked'*, *'smacked'*, *'clipped'*, *'scutched'* or *'slapped'*. If a thump had been effective a Blade could claim that such actions *'decked him'*; that *'he copped for one'*; that *'I thought . . . Bumpff . . . fuck off'*, and *'had him spinning/wobbling'*; his *'knees had gone'*. Then again, the punch could be perceived to have educational effects: *'I smartened 'im up.'* Blades laughed about giving, receiving, or watching one of their own or the other lads creep amongst rivals to deliver an unexpected punch known as *'the sidewinder'*. Accounts and descriptions of slight or minimal violence provided laughs; but *not* when someone got hurt. Significantly, real injuries were never laughed about.

Norms and Nutters: Controlling the Impulsive

There is no clear definition of the degree of involvement ideally required, for each Blade assessed the situation for himself, and the 'structure' was dependent on an agent's ability to take part with others in activities that in performance produce the individual self. In these non-institutionalised social settings the precise role of a Blade was a personal matter, to be continually negotiated within parameters and according to 'norms'. Norms however are ideas of what people *think* ought to be, and not actual behaviour itself, and are, for the most part, *situational* (Strodtbeck 1965: 206–7). Indeed, at times, it seems that, as Klein and Crawford (1967: 88) posit, norms only exist in myths, since in actuality the only 'norm' is *'the acceptance of a wide variety of illegal acts'*. And whilst Becker (1963: 128) argues that all groups have rules to define situations, the question in this context remains as to whether all the participants could state what these were. Even if they could, such rules do not specify a rigid role-reaction; rather they are a guide, an 'Ideal Type' for both behaviour and situation. But these can vary with the requirements of the moment, and more than one can be applicable, or may just as easily be ignored.

Because there was no set degree of commitment (or antagonism) specified, the seriousness with which an individual took the pursuit of rivals would vary with the day, the opponents and the inclination. Along with shifting this challenge-response came a variable level of commitment as to what was the 'correct' level of hostility to enact as a Blade:

On match day I drink a few pints, look tough and occasionally run around pretending I'm gonna hit someone. That's football hooliganism for you. [Tufty]

Football feyts? . . . they never last more than about 60 seconds, hardly anyone gets a thump in, nobody carries weapons and it's not every week. For most people it's about getting together, all going on a journey, having a few beers, a laugh, a quick battle. Then home. [Ged]

All you need to do is put them down, kick 'em a few times, then leave 'em. [Jim]

I hate this attitude some Blades have when they know there's five in the pub of 'Leave 'em, they're not doin' owt!' . . . if we were five strong in their pub we'd get a reyt hammering, so it's only right they should get t' same. [Nev]

Glasses and bottles are acceptable . . . anything you can get hold of, you know, a bar stool, ashtray, bottle, because they've got the same chance; but knives are out of order. I don't like distress flares though. [Greg]

Although violence was minimal, limiting the behaviour and potential violence of particular individuals proved difficult. This produces fundamental questions never before addressed or answered by previous research, and prompts one to ask: 'What was the "correct" way of acting as a hooligan'?, 'What was a legitimate accessory in the confrontations'?, and 'What were the grammars of motive?'

We can start by looking at methods of control, and though Blades were agreed the code was *'Their Lads and blokes who wanna know'*, others could (occasionally) vary in their assessment as to who were their equals, and who indeed were *'looking for it'* and showed they *'wanna' know'*. For some, this included any rivals of similar age with tattoos, for such bodily adornment was seen as a signifier of masculine pretension, with an implicitly violent potential. Such an overtly masculine message was seen as a statement that the wearer would have the competence the message implied. That said, it was only tattooed match-goers who were challenged, invariably near the ground. And from observations, the number of times a victim was chosen simply because he was tattooed occurred about once a season between 1984 and 1992. This never was at a 'mob' level, and the challenge was often restricted either to verbal abuse or one single punch, which usually elicited no response and was not continued. Another signifier was clothing. Should a perceived adversary be wearing garments that mirrored what Blades wore, then by his garments he was displaying a status that Blades would not worry in responding to, and his clothing implied a degree of cultural collateral that he should ideally be able to exchange. He was thus a legitimate target.

The core Blades, and amongst these those considered the 'hardest', were the most discriminatory in their violence. On occasions such Blades were even at the forefront in demanding that other Blades cease hostilities.

Once in 1989 against Manchester United a few visitors were challenged by a group of peripheral Blades. Considering the visitors not worthy opponents, two of the Top Blades (Mick and Kenny) demanded Blades leave them and look for Their Lads. Another time, in 1992, a handful of visiting fans were enjoying a drink in a pub near the ground when a Sheffield youth I had never seen before hit one without provocation. One of the top Blades (an ex-boxer) considered the assault cowardly, and thumped the aggressor. The latter had mates, one of whom was renowned for his part in fights in the 1970s. His threats met with one punch and unconsciousness. These were the only two incidents I witnessed in a decade. The core Blades were no angels, but they had no desire to hit out randomly, and were appalled at those who did. More important to my argument was the fact that whoever did the defining could never anticipate any particular punishment for a 'wrong' definition.

Acceptable behaviour was not just applicable to violence. Some aspired to a decorum in socialising that others could not maintain. Occasionally, *some* did abuse hospitality, but there was nothing others could do. In the 1990s, for example, two incidents occurred when drunken individuals damaged without rationale Sheffield pubs to which Blades had previously been welcomed. These excesses were considered by most Blades to be out of order. Blades used a variety of terms, such as *'oddballs', 'tapped', 'not all there', 'off his head', 'fuckin' idiot', 'just mad'*, for people who, invariably the worse for drink, acted with unnecessary aggression or manifested behaviour likely to attract the attention of police. The term 'nutter' was rarely heard.[2] When these pejorative names were used, no one was *consistently* labelled. However, the aggressive reputation of certain individuals was considered useful and even comforting, for it meant that if fights began there were those more capable of fighting. As one core Blade argued, *'If a young lad comes along and does summat stupid yu don't wanna' tell 'im to piss off because he'll tek over from you one day; like when we pack it in, and you want the best for t' Blades.'* All individuals wanted the best for Blades, and the best was not being 'run' by Owls or Their Boys.

Challenging the Umpires

It is evident that the outcome of certain interactions between rival football fans was influenced by a timely police arrival. Their very presence at some confrontation was extraordinarily influential, and it was remarkable how few police were needed to prevent large-scale disorder ever breaking out. Football crowds are full of fit and excitable young men, often fuelled on alcohol; yet fights or incursions on to the field of play have been so few in number across the years that any such event makes the headlines. And even how relatively few police officers are needed to prevent disorder outside the ground is a matter that is often overlooked. Then again, police were always able to enter a pub containing perhaps two hundred Blades and be almost assured they would not be assaulted or even subjected to verbal abuse. Between 1980 and 1994 assaults on police by Blades were so rare as to be worthy of chronicling, if for no other reason than to remind ourselves just how abnormal such events were:

1. The last 'Away' visit assault occurred in October 1981, when a Blade was arrested following a confrontation with the home fans. A single police officer making the arrest was surrounded by some fifty Blades shouting 'let him go', and was pushed to the ground and kicked by some half dozen, who then ran off. The officer picked himself up, with no apparent injuries.

2. In 1984 seventy Blades were outside a pub watching a drunken (peripheral) Blade place a beer glass on the road in the path of passing vehicles. The police arrived, and the group went quiet; some left, walking off to the football ground. One Villager, who rarely attended matches but was always drunk when he did so, walked away with a beer glass. In reply to a woman constable's question as to what he intended, he unwisely said he was going to throw it. Moments later she and a male colleague attempted to take the glass from him, and this led to some pushing and pulling between him and his mates. One Blade she seemed to have decided to arrest ran off. The WPC followed and grabbed him. He swung round and struck her, causing her to fall. And though he managed to escape and avoid arrest, he later spoke of the event across the years as a matter of some shame, explaining he was drunk and thought he was striking a man and not a woman.

3. Only on one occasion in the fifteen years of participant research (1980–95) was a PC assaulted at Bramall Lane when I was present. This happened in 1986, during an after-match protest against the Manager outside the South Stand. Some fifty Blades were running to join a wider gathering, when one PC ran at and grabbed one Blade. In one motion the Blade swung and struck the officer a single punch to the face, causing him to fall. As the assailant ran off, the PC got up and walked away.

4. The only obvious injury in the Bramall Lane ground occurred in March 1985, when a wooden seat thrown by a Blade struck an officer, who needed assistance from colleagues as he was led away (see Armstrong 1994).

In contrast to what the police may wish to present and some media commentators to represent as a terribly risky duty (cf. Graef 1989), in fact football hooligans are one of the easiest public disorder-prone groups for the police to deal with. The macho canteen culture of operational police officers not only easily anticipates football-related action, but some even welcome it, for a variety of reasons. Sociologist Holdaway (1983: 60), drawing on his years as an officer in the Sheffield force, could write: *'The local football ground is another place where arrests can be made readily, especially by the special squad of officers employed there. If juveniles are arrested they are ejected from the ground; adults are charged and taken to court, usually providing overtime for an officer.'* As it did for the Blades and Owls, the match provided the police with an opportunity to demonstrate their own masculine credentials.

Blades believed that *their* local police were the 'hardest' in Britain, and at times were inclined to boast about this – especially to men from other towns. Assaulting one of these officers of the law was thus regarded as being an unwise activity, regardless of the circumstances. In their defence of that undefinable activity of 'maintaining law and order', it was understood that any magistrate would sentence such an offender to imprisonment. Moreover – and there were many who could testify to it – the police would inevitably administer their own form of 'instant retribution' or 'instant justice' once an assailant was under arrest. Any subsequent 'not guilty' verdict, it was widely believed, would lead to a police vendetta against the miscreant. For the population, of all ages and persuasions, knew their force was not some 'whiter than white' organisation, and they were not so naive to have notions of their local bobby's being some televisual 'Dixon of Dock Green' philanthropist. Many of the older generation, for instance, recalled the national notoriety of the 1963 'Rhino Whip Affair', when a regime of police violence and fabrication of evidence was disclosed.[3]

The Absence of Blades $CODE\ OF\ CONDUCT$

It is of significance to the debate on the manifestations that hooliganism takes that the city that invented and mass-manufactures the Stanley knife and in fact probably more knives than any other city, certainly in Britain and probably in the Western world, should find that those considered by all in it as appallingly violent did not carry, in any capacity, knives. In this cultural milieu knife-carrying is ostracised to the extent that most men would consider anyone with one weak to the point of cowardice in feeling the need to carry such an implement. To put it another way, carrying a blade implied to the vast majority a preparedness to use a level of violence beyond ideas of reason and honour. Benny, explains the 1970s situation: '. . . .we never carried knives. It wo' rare for anybody to do that. Originally some carried poles from their banners and flags which they could use in a feyt. But at back o' t' kop there wo' always rubble . . . small bricks, stones, bottles: people used that. . . .. Before police began searchin' everyone at t' turnstiles you could tek owt in.' The extent of violence was different in some ways, yet the same as decades later in other respects.

Because of this only three woundings resulted from sharp edges carried by a Blade at football matches in Sheffield in the 1980–94 era. All were consenting adults involved in hooligan rituals. One victim in 1980 was an Owl standing deliberately on the Shoreham End as part of a mob of a hundred trying to 'take it'; 'jabbed' by a then regular Blade's penknife, he received minor buttock wounds requiring three stitches. Another more serious wounding occurred in 1982 a mile from Bramall Lane: the opponents were Barnsley. Dempsey, who was present, told me the story: 'About sixty of us waited in t' 'Howard' [a pub]. We watched t' Barnsley Special get a police escort, then, about a minute later thirty of Their Boys who had broken away came out. We got 'em in a sort of ambush which ended with them geddin' chased, and two got slashed on the back.' The two protagonists (using Stanley knives), who were aged fifteen, received three years' youth custody, and never returned to the Blades. It took ten years for the next wounding of two visiting Manchester United fans, found in a pub by sixty Blades in the early evening. In the ensuing fracas one visitor received a minor wound caused by a piece of glass, but would not accept hospital treatment nor describe his attackers to police. The perpetrator, a core Blade whom I knew well, had never before carried glass before and was never to do so again. It was a mystery why he did so on that occasion.

In the years 1980–1994 (over 500 away matches) woundings committed by Blades at or *en route* from away games numbered three. The first, in October 1982, occurred when a hundred Blades stopped in a Midlands town and a few dozen fought with local youths. An 18-year-old Blade stabbed a penknife into the back of a local youth, causing a wound that required three stitches. Weeks later the assailant received nine months' youth custody. The only other time occurred in 1989 before a game at Hull, when a mini-van containing peripheral Blades was confronted by local lads outside a pub; in the ensuing fight one local waving a bottle was slashed by a Blade carrying a Stanley knife. From a mining town north of the city, and only occasionally amongst Blades, he received a nine-month custodial sentence.

Whilst few ever carried a weapon, others, particularly in the mid-1980s, knew that actions indicative of possessing a knife could be a useful deceit. The required performance when facing rivals was to stand still, and, usually wearing a weird and false smile – which suggested one knew/had something they did not – with one hand inside the jacket pocket threaten onlookers by inviting them to come nearer. The 'knife' could alternatively be signified as hidden in the groin. A youth with his hand half-way down the front of his jeans was making a statement that was not sexual. This did not happen regularly. However, this pretence could not be sustained: if a weapon had not been revealed by the second such gesture rivals would then shout to each other something akin to *'He's got nowt'*; having drawn attention to himself, the pretender would be a prime target for attack.

Small but heavy wooden implements better known for facilitating the game of 'rounders' (a miniature form of baseball) were readily available from sports shops. On three occasions in the early 1990s eight Blades considered the impending circumstances needed them, and, as a result, two Owls were struck over the head. Another weapon available was far more indiscriminate. This was noxious gas, freely available in France and thus brought to England by individuals who travelled to Europe on holiday. Of two varieties – 'CS' or 'Mace' – these substances were contained in small metallic canisters, and when sprayed at an individual were immobilising, but when released in a general direction could also debilitate dozens in the vicinity. Such a device was never used at a match and never used against Their Boys, but was used in a fight between Blades and bouncers in 1991. Over the years 1980–94 I know of four individuals who had such substances, but only two who carried them with them in anticipation of a fracas. Whilst the above proceedings were personal, in that they involved combatants at close quarters, on a dozen occasions in ten years projectiles were fired that, had they struck an individual, would have caused injury. These were indiscriminate in their targets, and therefore not all participants agreed with their use. These nautical distress flares (bought or stolen from camping and boating outlets) were slightly larger than a fountain pen; they could be easily concealed, and were fired by being placed across the palm of one hand whilst the other hand pulled the ignition. A 'whoosh!' noise was followed seconds later by the illumination of the flare, which could travel around 80 yards. A dozen Blades carried and fired them in the 1984–5 season, usually outside the ground in set-to's with rivals, though a couple of times they were released in the ground; three were fired outside the ground and one inside the season after; and subsequently one was fired against the Owls in a confrontation on West Street in 1990 and two in fights with bouncers in 1993. Fortunately, apart from the fight with the Trio (see

Chapter 3) they never hit anyone; whether they were fired deliberately over the heads of their intended targets is impossible to ascertain. The majority of Blades did not consider such devices necessary, and the same majority did not want to carry them because they realised serious charges would be brought if the perpetrator of such a discharge were found. The one occasion the noxious substance was released illustrated how random the effects could be: in the enclosed area it wafted into, with the aim of hitting a specific group of ten bouncers, it also caused innocent nightclub-goers distress.

Pragmatic Responses

When fights began whatever was to hand was considered by Blades as legitimate to use, because rivals usually had similar opportunities. With police searches at turnstiles, carrying missiles of any kind was considered 'too risky'; possession of such items would inevitably lead to prosecution. By the 1980s, with most fights outside the ground and around pubs and in city centres, when 'the off' (as such situations were defined) began various items were requisitioned from wherever they were situated: milk bottles, milk crates, bakery trays, litter bins, traffic cones, advertising boards, vegetable displays, pub stools, beer glasses, drinks bottles, ashtrays, and pool-table cues and balls. It was from missiles that most injuries in football hooliganism occurred – in particular, thrown glasses. In 14 years (1980– 1994) I witnessed twelve rivals receiving wounds from such 'glassings'.

Rivals did occasionally receive repeated kickings from a variety of Blades, often when they were laid prostrate. In the narratives of hooligans there was in all memories the character of the *'poor bastard'* – this individual being the one who when his group had got 'run' was the one unfortunate enough to fall over when pursued. Having fallen, he was easy prey to those chasing, and for his prior activities he would be the one who would, almost invariably, receive repeated kicks from the pursuing forerunners. That said, this denouement was not inevitable, and, whilst this may sound perverse, the fact of the matter is that Blade mythology held that it was preferable to be kicked by half a dozen than by one. With numerous kicks being aimed, the aggressors usually missed their target or kicked parts of the body that could withstand blows. Also, Blades surmised that in a large pursuing group there were always people who would pull the aggressors off and permit the victim to get up and run away. This *did* happen. From so many of the situations wherein the position of a victim looked dire it was amazing to see him rise and depart not too worse for wear soon after. In such situations Blades knew that you *'curled up in a ball and covered your head'* –

and waited for the kicking to stop. Whilst Their Boys got up and walked in such situations, there were similar scenarios with Owls that left them semi-conscious or unconscious. The reason for this contrast? – the recognition that a few Blades had for their out-of-town opponents. In such situations the sympathy possibly available to the unlucky 'Their Boy' was not extended to an Owl, who might have been accused of doing to a Blade what was being done to him now.

Even so, such attacks on Owls tended to be about once or twice a year between 1985 and 1994. Thus not only did few Blades inflict a serious injury on opponents; very few in return received one. Over a 14-year period 1980–94 the most serious injuries Blades received happened miles from football grounds and hours before or after games. There was one broken jaw, and a fractured skull (see below). Stitches were required by ten individuals for small cuts, a result of missiles thrown in or outside pubs. No Blade died; none spent a night in hospital as a consequence of contacts with rival fans around a match. Only two received small wounds, the result of the use of knives in a fight with Bristol City fans in a park adjacent to the ground in 1989. Thus whilst *potentially* a lot of people could get hurt in such disorders, amazingly few ever did. Because few Blades ever suffered injuries, they did not perceive any group of rival fans (bar the Owls) as worthy of holding a vendetta with, even when a death had occurred.

Match-Day Death

For all the absence of horrific statistics of injured or maimed, one rival fan did die opposing Blades. In October 1986 a 17-year-old Bradford fan died having been struck by a car driven by a stranger after a match at Bradford. The incident had a prehistory. Months earlier, thirty Blades travelled over-night Friday to their Saturday match in London, stopping at a motorway service station (Leicester Forest). They found forty Bradford lads similarly travelling to their match on the South Coast. One Blade the worse for drink insulted them, and in the ensuing fight a Blade had his jaw broken by a blow from a rival wielding a bat, and another (the instigator) sustained a fractured skull when he fell and banged his head whilst running. Blades smashed a window of the Bradford coach before police arrived. Blades were allowed to resume their journey, but the Bradford fans were detained, and three arrested and charged with affray, and one was imprisoned for nine months.

Five months later United played at Bradford. Whilst the Blades' coach, carrying sixty, included the two who had sustained the injuries, there was no talk of revenge. The police were prepared for the day, and on the outskirts of Bradford the coach was 'captured' and all occupants made to give police their names, addresses, occupations and places of work, and then made to enter the ground at 2.00 p.m. accompanied by a police escort. Inside the ground, Blades found a dozen photocopies of the *Leicester Mercury* with headlines of the May incident left for their benefit. Across the pitch the Bradford lads periodically chanted 'Leicester Forest'; Blades did not respond. Afterwards a dozen Rotherham Blades (none of whom were at Leicester Forest) travelling in cars were 'sussed' by local equivalents. Realising the situation, one Blade squared up to a rival, and the Bradford lad ran away – directly into the path of a car, and was killed instantly. Five Blades were immediately arrested, but released hours later without charge. Considering the hysteria that the media could have generated out of this, it was unusual to note that news of the death did not appear in the papers.

The return fixture at Bramall Lane in March 1987 saw eighty Bradford lads arrive at midday in a fleet of cars and vans. Gordon, at the time shopping, saw them and, realising they were Bradford's 'lads', forgot his pursuit of consumption and approached the eighty, informing them that if they wanted a fight London Road was the place. Gordon meeting Jim and Liam similarly shopping, the three led the eighty on their way, shouting insults as they walked before them. Near to London Road another Blade saw the situation and ran to The Lansdowne, whereupon thirty Blades ran out and chased the visitors, kicking three who stood their ground, before police arrived. Blades expressed surprise that Bradford had brought so many lads and had had the courage for the first time ever to walk through the city centre, believing this was due solely to their wanting to 'put on a show' for their deceased colleague. But whilst they had come 'mob-handed', they had also 'got run': Blades were not impressed. The issues of both the motorway services events and the death of the youth were never mentioned again, and visits to Bradford were never considered special. Two months later *The Star* reported that the coroner had recorded a verdict of 'Accidental Death' on the Bradford fan; whilst accepting that the fatality was a *'spin-off from football hooliganism'*, he added that *'there was no evidence to suggest the youth had been involved in any fighting'*.

The Articulation of Boundaries

Empirical research suggests that when a subject or action is preceded by verbal justification that makes it possible, then such behaviour can be instigated (cf. Hartung 1965). Specifically, Blades used three of the five possible defences that Sykes and Matza (1957) termed 'Techniques of Neutralisation' in statements that sought to justify their actions. One was 'Denial of the Victim', whereby the opponent was regarded as having received his rightful punishment, articulated by the statements: *'shun't come lookin' for us wi' bats'*, and *'they know what risks are . . . they shouldn't give it big 'un if they can't tek an hammerin''*. Basically, this presented a *'serves 'em right'* philosophy. The second – 'Condemning the Condemners' – shifts the focus from the act to those making judgement and their various hypocrisies, spites, and secret deviations. Thus, Blades were aware that those who condemned their actions – journalists, police or the lawcourts or *'blokes at work'* who offered their opinions – were also not without sin. For many a wife-beater, they knew, thought hooligans were appalling, and many a police officer thumped innocent people. Journalists were despised for their occupational necessity of lying, whilst workmates always had some secret vice. Barristers, it was firmly believed, would lie for any cause for a price, whilst Magistrates and Judges would never understand what it was to have mates and loyalties. This Blade vision of an 'Appeal to Higher Loyalites' meant the requirements of the micro-group in certain contexts took precedence over any wider morality.

Ideas of honour set the boundary of the hooligan competition and provide the reason the rival groups exist. That said, the desire for honour does not account for motivation or action, although, as Friedrichs (1977: 284) noted, honour provides a code for both interpretation and actions on two levels. One is as a *'system of symbols, values, and definitions'* to think about and interpret a phenomenon. On a second level honour embodies the acts which organise *'categories, rules, and processes . . . which may be specific to the given culture'*. Honour is thus both an individual and a group attribute that has to be claimed and maintained, and is therefore a *power mechanism* used to initiate and resolve conflicts. Men individually or collectively lose honour if found incapable of replying to a challenge. As Bourdieu (1979: 106) might argue in this case: *'Evil lies in pusillanimity, in suffering the offence without demanding amends.'* But there were various contexts where ideals were not achieved. Such demands were sometimes absent; at times such offences had to be tolerated, as were negative verbal statements, which as Pitt-Rivers (1966: 77) argues, can sometimes alone challenge honour. Crucially, honour is culturally specific, and only exists in systems of stratification (cf. J. Campbell 1964; Pitt-Rivers 1965, 1966; Peristiany 1965; Davis 1977; Gilmore 1977; Brandes 1987). But, in the hooligan domain the horizontally arrayed gathering also contains honour, based in ideas of gossip and superiority via disgust, sometimes at action and sometimes at inaction.

Honour and shame were produced simultaneously in various audiences, and judged by different criteria via 'the court of reputation' (cf. Wikan 1984; Brandes 1987). Whilst fellow hooligans can be both honoured and shamed by their counterparts, the wider audience, (i.e. the public at large) tend to see the various groups' very pursuit of honour as shameful. As Bourdieu (1979: 115) states, honour is the ethic appropriate to an individual who always sees himself through the eyes of others; his self-image is inseparable from the image of himself he receives back from others (cf. J. Campbell 1964: 268). In the Blades' eyes honour is besmirched by letting 'Them' (Owls or Their Boys) get away with 'It', in situations defined by a number of clichés, such as *'bullying'* or *'tekin' liberties'* and *'Givin' it big 'un'* (all of which cover a variety of acts and events). Blades thought they should always respond to this, because they *'Can't be 'avin' that'*, justifying the response on the grounds that they *'Can't put up wi' that.'* This is done by showing courage *('Bottle')* in confrontations, and illustrating an ability not to run away, but to *'stand your ground'* in order to produce the masculine enhancing performance recognised and epitomised in the phrase *'good lads'*.

Notes

1. The same procedure was used by the police. The 1982 ACPO Public Order Manual recognised the battle cry as a 'morale booster' for public order policing, able to 'relieve stress' (see Northam 1989: 89).
2. Identifying a career structure and roles for the various participants, Marsh *et al.* (1978) defined the 'nutters' as *'individuals whose behaviour is considered by the fans to be so outrageous as to fall completely outside the range of action based on reason and causes'* (p. 70). The 'nutter's' function is described as a *'visible demonstration of the limits to legitimate action'*, and shows other fans what they should not do as well as providing them with living proof their own wider moral propriety. And so even though their behaviour is described by fellow hooligans as *'going mad'*, *'wild'*, *'crazy'*, Marsh saw a sense of order in what the nutters did, for *'even going crazy involved the following of certain conventions and restrictions'* (p. 71).
3. The incident arose in 1963 out of a Sheffield Crime Squad attempt to extract information from suspects. The squad was established to concentrate on burglaries and, in the course of one particular inquiry,

arrested three known criminals. At CID headquarters the three were beaten by two detectives with an old-type truncheon known as the Rhino Whip, because of a plaited hoop at one end. Other members of the squad witnessed the assault, which included between sixty and seventy blows on one of the accused. In court one took off his shirt to reveal his injuries and named the officer responsible. The court granted permission for them to be examined and photographed. The Chief Constable called for an inquiry, but in the meantime the squad fabricated evidence of a fight between the defendants, made false pocket book entries, and buried the Rhino Whip. The Chief Constable publicly claimed his men would never have treated prisoners that way and that the injuries were a result of sexual perversion. The defendants' solicitor took out a private prosecution against two members of the squad; they pleaded guilty in Magistrates Court to assault, were fined and lost their jobs. A month later one appealed against his dismissal and made allegations against senior officers. The second officer similarly appealed soon after. The Home Secretary appointed a two-man tribunal, and after a 12-day hearing in which squad members denied everything, he dismissed the appeal. The tribunal had strong words for the Chief Constable, saying that he *'lived somewhat in an ivory tower, barely able to accept the men under his command could be guilty of truly infamous conduct'*. Interestingly, Percy Sillitoe's renown as the gang-buster of the Mooney gang, infamous for his violent methods and those of the Flying Squad, was quite clearly still admired thirty years after he had left Sheffield. One of the detectives showed photographs of him to the defendants before proceeding to beat them.

Chapter 11

Cultural Capital and Blade Gatherings

Here is a picture of society in which there are scenes but no plot.

(Richard Sennet (1977) *The Fall of Public Man*, p. 36)

Blades constitute a 'quasi-group', *not* an organised collectivity. There is a form of organisation of sorts, but this is Goffmanesque and is 'attenuated, extremely variable in duration, and difficult to determine' (Burns 1991: 359). Mutual friends, for example, are sufficient an introduction to enable an individual on his own to join members of another group of Blades if he should happen to see them at a match or in a pub. In this informal way a Blade builds a wide circle of acquaintanceship, which varies in intensity from what may be a simple visual recognition on the periphery to a close companionship at the centre. Out of this gathering certain individuals take roles and responsibilities. Some organise transport to games, others gain recognition because of fighting ability, courage, or wit – but in no sense is there a regular or formal leadership. There is, however, an idea of mutual responsibility, and a commitment such that if, as a Blade, you see another Blade confronted or set on, then you have an obligation to help. At the very least, it is better for Blades to 'run' other fans than to see Blades get 'run'. Having said all this, however, it must be acknowledged there are some who are known to 'go looking for it' (i.e. seeking confrontations) with rivals; though many more participate only, as they see it, if they cannot decently avoid it.

In terms of participation, the most essential requirement for being a Blade was free time, with money coming a close second. An enthusiasm for United and an antipathy towards Wednesday were prerequisites, as was a willingness to hit or be hit in the pursuit of Blade confrontations. Gatherings consisted of various groups of 'The Boys/Lads', whose constituency depended upon neither locality nor similar background, but did require a reciprocity in attitude and peer-group social competence. Together this produced a loose-knit group with a range of shared presuppositions. All Blades were long-standing United supporters. A lad 'became' a Blade by travelling to away games, entering pubs where Blades meet, joining in the gossip, confronting Their Boys and Owls, and when necessary looking 'mean' towards match-day rivals. One did not necessarily have to practise violence, for, to borrow from the poet Milton's reflection on the frustration of blindness, *'they also served who only stood and waited'* – or at least did not run away. Reflecting upon their initial involvement, all spoke of 'when I started' as a Blade, but this was not consistent in definition; and thus they were deciding themselves when their hooligan days began. Feeling they had to do *something* to 'become', they would signify the crossing of the boundary from mere watching, i.e. changing from being enthusiasts, to being 'one of the Lads'. But so vague is this definition that one feature of this association network is that a Blade can be part of this process for years and yet never actually assault anyone.

Blades: Resources and Cliques

The most accurate analogical depiction of the football hooligan life comes from Wallman's (1984) theory of 'urban resource networks', for football hooligan formations work in accord with this author's three ontological characteristics: time, information and identity; and their mutual resources relate to emotional and material contents.

1. *Time* is a critical requirement, for in a straightforward sense without this resource there is no possibility of engaging with fellows and rivals. At an individual level, time may also be interpreted in a more biographical sense, for a 'football hooligan' identity carries with it more 'significant others' (peers) than later stages in a young man's life can allow for. At the collective level, time is also encultured by the resource network in designating periods when it is legitimate or otherwise to act aggressively towards rivals and others.
2. *Shared identities* are also vital, for identification with a particular team is a general precondition. However, within this commonality there must be generally shared cultural identifications regarding the formation and its cultural practices, particularly in connection with the reproduction of male leisure practices.
3. *Information* and its exchange provide the circulation of knowledge that links the structuring of the group by time to the preconditions of shared identification. Information here relates to the formation's cultural collateral, and specifically relates to issues and news conjoining time and identity, whilst its control and dissemination distinguishes participants and non-participants.

Trying to account theoretically for Blade gatherings presents problems. It may well be argued we should look to USA 'gang' studies for answers (cf. Thrasher 1927; A. K. Cohen 1955; Miller 1958; Yablonsky 1962; Bloch and Neidershoffer 1958; Cloward and Ohlin 1960; Wolfgang and Ferracuti 1967; Short 1968). However, no single empirical work or theoretical premise can neatly encapsulate the Blades' world (cf. Downes 1966; Patrick 1973), and what is explanatory for American urban lower-class culture is not applicable in Britain (see Mays 1963: 249; Patrick 1973: 156; Valentine 1968). Anthropology provides a wider set of applicable explanations; and the gatherings under the titles of both 'the Blades' and 'the BBC' seem to fit well with Boissevain's (1974: 174) description of a *Clique*: '*a coalition whose members associate regularly with each other on the basis of affection and common interest and possess a sense of common identity.*' Furthermore, the author argues the Clique consists of a: '*relatively constant collection of persons who see each other frequently for both emotional (or expressive) as well as pragmatic (or instrumental) reasons. It has an objective existence, in the sense that it forms a cluster of persons all of whom are linked to each other. It also has a subjective existence, for members as well as non-members are conscious of its common identity*' (ibid.). Such Cliques have (ibid.: 76), '*little or no internal specialisation*', with '*no clear-cut principle of recruitment*' bar one of shared characteristics and a latent mutual affection. And whilst there is a 'core' who, as 'primary members', participate constantly, there will also be 'secondary' members without 'clear-cut norms of behaviour'. Such gatherings do have a sense of common identity and, via this, a consciousness develops that inspires loyalty.

We could also apply Mayer's (1966) concept of 'category' and 'quasi-group', and see that Blades are a category in which on average each individual has a few core mates, but that this can, for some, include up to a couple of dozen, to constitute a quasi-group. This contains those present and those absent who are considered ideologically to be reliable and a resource to draw on. Finally we could also take Geertz's (1966) four categories of 'fellow men'. Thus, we would see that at any one time there were *Consociates*, who interacted continually and would know each other well. Alongside these would be dozens, at times hundreds, of *Contemporaries*, sharing the same temporal locations and of a similar mind. Also present at such times could be *Predecessors* and *Successors*, the former known to some (but not all) by what they had done for the Blades' cause in earlier years, and the latter category present, but either too young or not yet confirmed as part of the Blade scene.

Time: Leading the Young Astray?

Institutions that depend on hierarchies cannot believe that a group that acts in concert can do so without some form of recognised and organised hierarchy. As information about hooliganism comes from the notorious hierarchies of police, media and academe, not too much thought has ever gone into challenging established wisdom. What needs to be stated early on is this: Blade gatherings did not lend themselves to structure or organisation, and there was never an accepted or recognised hierarchy. What was true for the late 1960s was true twenty years later. Individuals chose their level of commitment and participation, and whilst the situation was not the random and chaotic *jouissance* of the 1970s, the post-1980 formation had little in the way of organisation beyond self-selection. In contrast to both police beliefs and popular wisdom there was absolutely no leadership of elders who organised and prepared younger aspirants, only to slink into the background when fights began. Indeed, there was no recognised senior leadership or direction whatsoever, for the opposite was the truth.

Two particular groups spanned the early to mid-1980s. One in the early part was synonymous with the clothing, criminality and charisma of one Blade, Dempsey. The other grew out of fights with the Owls, and was bigger than any individual. The early 1980s core hooligans were known sometimes as the 'Young Lads' and sometimes as 'Dempsey's Mob'. Numbering around twenty and with four West Indians, they were 'game' fighters, despite their stylistic and sartorial obsessions. Older Blades, both at the time and in later years, referred to this gathering as the 'Bad Lads', because they introduced a new element to away games: they would pass up the beer drinking in favour of stealing designer clothes in strange towns or as they travelled along the route. The two groups of 'shoppers' and 'drinkers' would meet up later in the day, or stand together if a fight was imminent. However, no one from either faction had the right of leadership. When the numbers grew, Dempsey, along with his brother, and twenty to thirty colleagues, travelled to away games on scheduled Service Trains. At departure time any young Blade could, and did, stand near them. Dempsey and Fagin, the two 'Top Lads' in this gathering, regarding them as 'hangers on' and 'little shitheads' who were liable to run away in fights, and would thus tell them to 'Fuck off'. Enforcing such a command was impossible. The youngsters would merely sit in another carriage then trail the group. Their persistence would pay off, helped by showing 'game' in any ensuing fights with rivals. Over time they would no longer be abused, but were free to travel and sit with this core. For a few, such devotion could be expensive. A few were 'taxed' of designer clothing in a simple process: older, harder Blades would occasionally praise a garment and ask the wearer if he could try it on. He would then walk away with it. There was little or nothing the aspirants could do. That they remained as Blades and wanted to be involved is still one of life's mysteries!

The gathering of the Bad Lads/Dempsey's Mob tended to grow out of a high rate of school-leaving unemployment, as lads from various districts migrated to the Fargate precinct in the city centre to 'hang around'. Friendships were struck up, and from this came sporadic shoplifting. One underrated assistance in all of this was the City Council's bus-fares policy, which throughout the 1970s and early 1980s provided Sheffield with the cheapest public transport in Europe. This helped deconstruct any strongly held *local* identity in favour of the city centre. These young men were also to benefit from the growth in mass travel, visiting places their parents had only dreamed of. Open and receptive to new ideas, they were the ones who returned to the city with European fashions and European con-sumption patterns – they brought knowledge of the drug 'Ecstasy' to Sheffield. In later years, a few who began promoting 'raves' were able to because they had the collateral in terms of money and, more importantly, had the *network* provided by Blades that facilitated their acquisition of premises, music, technology, drinks, publicity for the events and muscle to man the doors. In this sense, the reputation acquired via football fighting meant their reputations went before them as promoters and as security doormen.

Later, in 1985, the 'Young Lads' took over the mantle as the vanguard of the Blades. This gathering of some thirty youngsters (aged 18–20) had waited in the wings for two years, unsure of where they stood in relation to the elder Blades. However, one game so appalled them they decided to go it alone and let others follow on. For the much-anticipated fixture at Leeds in November 1984, the Young Lads – twenty strong – were aboard a coach consisting mostly of Old Lads and their mates from various pubs. This mixture, it was believed (wrongly), would contain the occupants guaranteed to be seeking a fight in the city centre before the game. Of five coaches that departed early that day, four travelled into the city centre of Leeds and one stopped in a pub in the suburbs. Disgusted, the Young Lads stood outside this pub and arrived at the ground under police escort. On hearing that the others had managed a slice of the action, they vowed to run their own coaches, because these older fans were disgracing Blades' name, as they would *'rather drink beer than feyt'* (see Armstrong 1994). This young gathering was to fight the Owls across the next five years, and constituted the core BBC.

Time: Commitments Curtailed

Blade identity was purely dependent on an individual's doing what Blades did, and when they no longer did this they were no longer Blades. All Blades had 'days off' (i.e. missed matches), and none went to every match, for they would often be short of money, working overtime, attending weddings, or playing football. Anyone with a suspended sentence (*'bender'*) or court appearance pending usually stayed away, lest he be led into temptation. A few stayed away because of *'trouble wit' coppers'* – a way of saying they were the targets of some police vendetta. Many missed the away games having failed to make the departure point. Friday night travels were unpredictable, for one never knew how much alcohol could be consumed or where one might wake up. And time – the most important factor in Blades' life – would one day catch up with them all.

For most, leaving was not a dramatic step, but a gradual process that began by missing 'big' away games, not being part of the regular turnout, and (for a core Blade) absenting himself from the Friday night drinking sessions. Anyone could leave at any time. An individual could tell others he was *'finished'*, or *'not bothered any more'*, or refer to his status as *'retired'*. Questions as to what had become of such individuals met with stock replies: *'packed in'*, *'calmed down'*, *'hardly ever comes out now'*. Although disapproving sentiments would occasionally be expressed about the influence of girlfriends, no one could really criticise, for it would happen to them; and they all knew it. Many who 'left' still attended matches; some even drank in the Blades' pubs, but in non-hooligan company; or, if with active hooligan mates, they no longer joined in the match-day 'walkabouts' or joined the call-out when Their Boys or Owls appeared.

A common belief in Blade narrative was that, as you got older, *'It* [i.e. trouble] *comes to you rather than you go looking for It.'* For this reason Blades of all ages (and even those officially 'retired') believed that even if you were not seeking it, you could still get into confrontations. The status of 'retired' was open to some ridicule, and some would laugh and use a sort of 'football-speak' to say how they were *'comin' out o' retirement'*, or *'makin' a comeback'*, or *'might 'ave a rush o' blood'*, or be *'puttin' in an appearance'* for a 'big' game. In reality they were wearing the hooligan mantle again for a few moments in their lives. Some saved it for a couple of games a year. Some saved it only for the Owls.

Being a Blade, then, was in its earliest manifestations and up until the late 1980s essentially a young man's pastime. And the majority enjoyed that world-wide prerogative of being 'young and foolish'. As Blades commented, however, some got *'dafter as they got older'*, and some seemed to live their life backwards by being hooligans later in life after non-eventful teenage years. By the 1980s the vast majority of Blades were aged between seventeen and twenty-eight, though a number were older. Up to this era a hooligan who over-stayed his time in this local culture was regarded by the younger ones as like some ageing hippy is considered in other contexts. Gossip would classify the reality: *'Thirty-two and still a hooligan? I hope I'm not doin' it wi' t' Blades when I'm his age'*, younger ones would comment. Others were more sympathetic, and realised the resource that older men could find when circumstances left them behind: *'All his mates are married; he'd rather come out wi' us than drink alone or stay in. There's nowt wrong wi' that.'*

In the 1980s a few core Blades were married, and some had children: as a consequence their 'hooligan' activities were less frequent. At one level this was because a Sheffield background militated against a man's prolonging his Blade days, with close family networks creating the very high possibility of being seen by people you knew when out with the lads. On another level, after 1986 there was a fear in some that age might be equated with leadership by the police and prosecution counsel. Most significant, though, was the tie of marriage, for this brought the problem of the demands for respectability, especially in a small city where the general belief was expressed in the adage: *'You get more relatives – you have to leave it out.'* There was also peer group pressure, and a man in his early thirties has few mates of that age to discuss hooliganism with. Should he attempt this, most would be contemptuous of what was considered the prerogative of the young single male. This quiet and unspoken form of social control means that most Blade days were numbered, for marriage and children brought more important 'significant others', along with financial commitment. Money and time were therefore better spent on them than on long-distance trips, on fines or on possible prison visits. Memories were all that remained after 'retirement'.

A desire for good memories and the ancillary tales was often cited as a reason for being part of the Blade cohort. In their memories Blades could laugh at being run, or even admit to being scared, though such admissions took time. It was not a done thing to confess too quickly after the event. Significantly, the memories of Owl encounters seemed not to include admission of defeat or fear. Thus, oral history was not always truthful. Few would ever care if, in years to come, the account was embellished, or that some of those present were guilty of glory by association or of wearing a disguise of hardness by a process of osmosis, i.e. by being in the company of those who *were* hard. Blade gatherings *did* elicit memories, and generally they were selective. Violence was often edited out or quickly glossed over in favour of an account that was funny or farcical to the point of self-denigration. Many men heed this, for when they reach the age of anecdotage, such activity can still make them interesting in the eyes of the young. In the 1990s, however, there were many Blades who were near to or in their thirties. There was no more sinister reason behind this than the fact that having grown up together over the previous decade many enjoyed the easy sociability Blades offered. These lads were not chasing rivals around the streets before and after matches, but were willing to confront Owls when the occasion arose. Ironically, a few of the times when such occasions arose grew out of a thirtieth-birthday or stag-night celebration in the city centre for a Blade that Owls mistook for a 'Blade mob' out for them. Two such occasions ended with large-scale pub fights and hospital casualties.

Time: Summertime Blades 1982–92

Bearing in mind the sociological belief in 'violent types' and impulsively violent young men, we could well ask a question not previously raised by research – namely, how de we account for the hooligan outside the football season? As the ethnography shows, the *raison d'être* of the Blades was a football match, and a *collective* identity more or less died outside the football season, to be resurrected at the early August pre-season friendly games. In the summer Blades often followed the popular all-male lunch-time Saturday drinking 'sessions' evident throughout the city, with their *individual* identities relegated to the easier (and more familiar) local neighbourhood friendship circle. A match, then, allowed disparate individual Blade elements to coalesce as a collective, and for this reason the first and last matches of the season were joyful occasions, usually played in warm weather, the day witnessing much shaking of hands, with participants celebrating the rebirth or temporary demise of the Blade entity. These days were usually the occasion for large gatherings to go on a pub-crawl, during which they would inevitably approach West Street.

Whether there was a summer gathering of any sort depended on the year, and from the early 1980s various gatherings occurred, albeit they were one-off celebrations and prone to a sort of carnival excess. Such early gatherings did not have the Owls rivalry as a *raison d'être*, but were 'piss-ups' pure and simple.[1] By the mid-1980s the symbiotic relationship Blades had with Owls could offset the propensity to gather outside the football season. In 1984 and 1985 Blades regularly gathered and fought Owls in the city centre. Following a defeat by the Owls in May 1986, Blades did not meet all summer, but, when they had avenged this defeat, they met in the following summer. The issue was not just the situational position of Blades–Owls, however, for it also depended on which Blades were around (not abroad), and what events were taking place. From 1988 one regular gathering was on the day of the FA Cup Final. This would usually see around a hundred Blades meet in a pub and drink all afternoon whilst watching the game. Likewise, across the summers of 1990 and 1994 Blades gathered in pubs for the World Cup matches, as these were always more enjoyable when watched in company, and would always provide a degree of extra amusement in the ridicule shouted at the pub TV screen. When no such ordered occasions offered themselves, Blades were left to their own devices as to when and where to meet. In the summer of 1988, both Friday night and Saturday lunch-time would see thirty-plus Blades gathered along London Road, simply because the era produced Blades of the same age who had time on their hands. By 1991 this had fallen off to a degree, because of pressing problems of finance, family and work commitments. Then the number rose again, for no apparent reason.

These same years saw Blades begin what was to become a seven-year annual summer day-trip to the Lincolnshire Seaside. For two years (1987–8), fights broke out at the end of the night, the first time with nightclub bouncers, and the second with another coach-party of young men. On each occasion a few Blades were arrested. That said, their next five journeys to the coast were peaceful and eventless, producing only hangovers. The other summer events Blades travelled to and that ended in fights occurred around various 'stag-nights'.[2] Any excuse for a gathering would suffice, for there was always someone with a birthday or impending marriage to celebrate. From 1992, if no day-trip was planned, a midsummer Sheffield rendezvous would do.

Celebratory 'piss-ups' occurred in 1993 and 1994 when one Blade was about to marry, and another to turn thirty. On the first occasion, one hundred and fifty began a pub crawl at midday Saturday, ending up in a pub at midnight. The police became aware of events around 7.00 p.m. when they visited a pub from which a Blade had stolen two guitars belonging to a band due to play a gig later in the night, and called up a car to take the goods away to be sold. A drunken 'peripheral' then broke a small window when two pubs barred him entry, and the police arrived in numbers and began chasing seventy Blades into a residential area that had a large black population. Youths from the estate took to the streets on seeing the commotion. Two dozen or so began talking to Blades they knew, and the police left the area to avoid inciting a further confrontation. Blades then drifted quietly into various pubs. On the second occasion around a hundred celebrated, but this number was doubled when wives, girlfriends and children met up for a disco and buffet. These occasions suggested a considerable move toward conformity by this 'class of 1985'. Blade identity *could* therefore be automatically sustained away from the club and the match in other contexts that did not need a game of football; and it was this that provoked accusations from some that they were something of a parasitic gathering on the body of football, who were organised for other unrelated serious crime.

Time: England Away

There were various other avenues that Blades could have used to manifest a violent nature. The most obvious would have been to have followed the England national side abroad at any time after the late 1970s. European games involving the national side were often the occasions for a disorder that was hugely publicised and condemned. Such excursions did not appeal to Blades sufficiently to provoke them to attend in large numbers. This is not to say that football followers from Sheffield had no interest in the national side; far from it. Indeed, Blades watched televised games involving England, though not many attended even when England played at home. A few Blades did go to games at Wembley and twice got into fights, once in Central London with Scottish fans before an England–Scotland fixture, and a few years later when fifteen Blades were part of an England following that fought Scottish fans in Glasgow. Yet this was the full extent of Blade hooligan involvement around England's *domestic* fixtures in the fifteen years between 1980 and 1995.

Participation with the England followers *abroad* was a different matter however, and significantly an *individual* affair. Observation would show that one Unitedite had travelled with the mainly Southern-based Chelsea fans since the early 1980s, but, living as he did in London, he was unknown to the Sheffield 'core'. The one local residing 'core' Blade who took an active part in foreign affairs would usually travel with mates from Nottingham, to become literally a flag-flying Blade. Along with a dozen other Blades, he later attended the European Championships in Germany in 1988, but none of them went as part of a 'mob', and the maximum was four in a car. Two years later, twenty Blades, mostly older villagers with non-hooligan mates, attended the 1990 World Cup in Italy. Only four went with the England 'Lads', and only one saw any hooligan action. During the European Championships in Sweden in 1992 only a dozen Blades attended, and none were involved in any fights. Generally, Blades were dismissive of the

England followers, many of whom they considered were *'into t' NF'* or later the BNP – i.e. sympathetic to the political aims of the National Front or the British National Party. Criticised by many stay-at-home Blades for being 'Nazis', southern-dominated and indiscriminately violent, their ideas and escapades appealed to very few.

Time: Absent Friends

Like all social groups, Blades had to deal with death and tragedy, and they grieved and sought to ease the pain for the victim's friends and relatives. During the research three Blades died, and their demise was marked by tributes. One who died in 1985 in an accident at work had been recently married. A bucket collection was held in the London Road pubs, an autographed football was obtained from the club, and a benefit 'do' was organised with a darts competition, a comedian, and a pop band made up of three Blades. One hundred Blades and a hundred friends and relatives gathered, though perhaps only 20 per cent of the Blades present actually knew the deceased. But that did not matter; the occasion was to show respect for a colleague, and the night ended with half an hour of Blades chants and another bucket collection. The benefit raised £600. Another Blade died in 1987, having overdosed with heroin. Peripheral for the previous four years, he was best known for once having 'coshed' an Owl. Little was known about his family circumstances; however, thirty-five Blades on a seaside excursion remembered his short life in a disco pub. Informed of the event, the DJ asked all patrons to honour a minute's silence, which was followed by a few Blades chants. Glasses were raised and pints drunk to the deceased.

A death in 1989 was the most emotional. A peripheral Blade, aged 29, was well-liked and was the elder brother of a very popular core Blade. His funeral was attended by forty Blades, who produced a £100 impromptu 'whip-round' for his mother.

The largest fund gathered from Blades' pockets financed the buying of a computer. In 1992 an accident in a hotel swimming-pool left the brother of a former core Blade of the mid-1980s a quadriplegic. The event, organised by his brother, saw over three hundred attend, including seventy core Blades, and even a few of the Owls' Top Lads who were the victim's mates. The evening saw entertainment by comedians and singers and fund-raising raffles. Others who suffered various misfortunes had Blades to thank for financial relief. In 1985 a Blade who broke a leg in a disturbance at an away match was given £50 from a whip-round in a pub after the next home match.

In later years two Blades who were imprisoned also received financial assistance. In one instance, the Blade (wrongly) imprisoned on a charge of assault for six months was given £200 via his fiancée. Another Blade jailed for six weeks for accumulated non-payment of fines received £80 when one Blade offered to have his hair shaved off if Blades would sponsor him. It was this ethos of mutuality that, in part, made Blade gatherings a significant part of the lives of many young men.

Information and Identifiers

The only factor distinguishing Blades from non-Blades was one of access to information, a resource gained from time spent amongst Blades, where activity was regulated by background expectations and talk. Essentially the appropriate information was largely structured by the phenomenon the Blades were involved in, and so the chat on match-days or when travelling would always touch on what Owls/Police/ Their Boys were up to and what Blades might/ought to/should do in response. Listening to this continual discourse allowed an individual to learn what was 'expected'. But most of this chat was *not* just about Their Boys or Owls or violent intent. Rather, it was a continuous narrative relating to experiences common to Sheffield male culture.

There was no real doctrine or body of fables that had to be learned and lived by. What 'oral transmission' there was consisted of older lads telling Blade audiences of past events; and there was no one with the role of 'Narrator'. These stories accorded with the form of Goffman's (1959) *'theatrical account'*, essentially consisting of the telling of that which might have happened. At times it could be entirely accurate and factual; while yet other stories lay somewhere between the two formats. It did not matter, particularly, for the essential was that a laugh was provided by the tale, and as Garfinkel (1956: 106) would say *'If the interpretation makes good sense, then that's what happened.'* The recipient listener, if intent on maintaining a Blade identity, had a duty to show interest and add to the subject, thus producing, in Goffman's (1971: 62–94) terms, a *'supportive interchange'* or what Malinowski (1922) would term 'phatic communication'. Overtly nothing was happening, yet in actuality Blades were playing the part of being Blades. Such encounters passed the time and made life enjoyable, and this pooling of 'knowledge' frequently made sense of events and was therefore as important as any actual confrontation.

Whilst there were terms such as 'Young Lads', 'Old Lads', and others based on either group or geographical identities, the concern with identity did not lead to the ascription of particular roles, but merely ensured individuals became familiar to many others. Some had value added to mere recognition, with comments along the lines of *'game as fuck'*, *'has a bounce now and then'*, *'handy'*, *'tasty'*, *'gets stuck in'*, *'He'll have a go'*, *'He loves It'* or *'He's into It.'* And though commitment to the cause and fighting ability was one possible defining attitude, others required a combination of characteristics – district (i.e. abode), mates, age, and frequency in match attendance. In the latter case, descriptions varied from *'goes everywhere'* to *'just comes now and then'*, and could be combined to produce a kind of 'technomony', i.e. being identified with a particular mode of transport, such as *'Travels wi' Max's lot'* or *'Goes in that white van to all t' away matches.'* An individual could thus walk around city-centre bars on Saturday night and identify dozens of Blades in other social contexts, and be able to describe him to others using such terms.

The gathering was loose, so one did not have to know others intimately. This fact had unexpected advantages, for when police wanted Blades they had arrested to identify others from photographs, in all honesty they often did not know them, or knew nicknames and little else. Some, for no good reason, however, were over-concerned with identity, constantly *'sussing out'* who was *'him by t' fruit machine?'* or *'tall kid wi' t' leather on?'*, and *'Who's he knock about wi'?'* Some Blades answered my research-inspired curiosity about various *'new faces'*, and revealed just how keenly they were observing events: *'He's just started comin'''*; *'He only turns out for big matches.'* Some however knew the identity of almost everyone in a pub of a hundred and fifty, particularly after the mid-1980s, when strangers had to be accounted for lest they were undercover police.

Information: Who Counted?

I could not find a single example of a Blade's being ostracised for being considered *'useless'* or having let Blades down in some way. There were two reasons for this: the first was because those in the know did not want to publicise the matter and risk causing argument and recrimination; the second was that Blade encounters were so ambiguous and ephemeral that most incidents were open to interpretation, and circumstances could always provide excuses. As no one had the authority to demand conformity of behaviour, there was no procedure for ostracising an individual who might have breached acceptable norms. Thus, should an individual wish to carry a weapon, he could do so, because no one had the authority to demand he did not. However, shared values about what was 'right' meant that excessive violence (actual or attempted) was extremely rare. And because of the ephemeral nature of fights with Their Boys, even in a crowd of two hundred, few would actually throw punches. For all the posturing and shouting in any confrontation, the vast majority were merely spectators. Thus, any Blade who claimed he had done or was going to do something, when others knew he had not or would not, could merit the titles of *'bullshitter'* and *'bottle merchant'*, and of someone who *'talks a good feyt'*. Blades realised that not everyone fought and not all were particularly good in combat. An awful lot were simply 'posing' at being tough guys, though everyone was welcome, because no one was consistently special or could guarantee to be there when trouble started.

The only thing occasionally used to provoke conformity was ridicule, manifested in the vague idea of shame; but this was not so strong as to force those shamed to depart, or to give up their ways. Thus when a Blade, having sighted the impending rival mob, ran into a pub full of Blades shouting *'They're here'* the vast majority of occupants would immediately depart to meet their opposition. Some, however, remained inside, particularly for home matches. There were various reasons for this – they might have just bought a pint; or considered from experience that the 'call-out' was a false one; or regarded the pursuit as futile for a variety of reasons – they might know police were outside, or that the rival mob was small and others could therefore do the job without them. Some might just not have the motivation required that day. When the other Blades returned they never berated those who had remained to their faces: some would exchange stares, and others mutter about unmotivated Blades. Such disgust, all knew, was best kept low-key and voiced in the company of Blades who had gone out. Thus one could hear complaints of:

> *'Some would rather drink beer than feyt.'*
> *'Shout of "They're here!" went up and half of 'em went and bought two pints each.'*
> *'They all hid behind the 'Green 'Un' when they heard a coachload of Millwall had just tipped out.'*

All knew colleagues varied both in motivation and courage, and that some in their ranks did not really want to fight because, quite simply, they lacked the *'bottle'*. And whilst in hindsight they could be dismissed as *'wankers'* and *'shitters'* for not doing the Blade cause any good, there was a realisation at the same time that they were not making it any worse! After all, such people made the numbers up, and when the hooligan issue was a visual one (which it often was) this made opponents think Blades had a (numerically large) *'good mob'*. By the early 1990s, when the Blades had a self-selecting core of 30, they believed that no one amongst them would ever let the others down, particularly against the Owls.

But, because of the 'permeable' conglomeration that was the Blades on match-day, nobody, including the participants, could say with authority how numerically strong they were. More importantly, no one knew what numbers could be 'relied' on in confrontations. Answers to this question produced varied responses:

> *'There's 30, sometimes 300.' [Barry]*
> *'There's 15, never been more than that really, all t' rest just make t' numbers up.' [Ray]*
> *'There's 50 who are good as gold and about 100 who are just "posing".' [Declan]*
> *'In a season there's about 70 to 100 who wanna' know.' [Jim]*
> *'There's six I know who won't leave me if I'm getting "done".' [Kenny]*

All accepted that whilst a 'core' would fight for the cause, the vast majority were making up the numbers. (I estimate at any one time a sixty-strong 'core' was supplemented on match-days with forty outer core and up to 200 peripherals classifiable as *'fringers'* or *'occasionals'*.) But this was not a stable gathering, and some could reappear after months of absence and return to the core. And who knows how many were *'reliable'* or *'good lads'*? If they were good one week, this did not mean they would be good the next. In truth, Blades often had to chose the company of colleagues they did not know well, and there was no guarantee that a performance one week would be the same the next. Partnership was thus a risky business.

Information: Directives or Clichés?

There was nothing in daily conversation that distinguished Blade from non-Blade. The only thing of note was that the former would occasionally use words or phrases that non-hooligan males might not relate to. So, whether voicing opinions or suggestions, sentences would be pre-phrased: *'We* ought to . . .', *'Blades should* do that' . . ., *'This is* crap', *'We're* all over as usual.' Suggestions would usually be open-ended, the initiator hoping for agreement. Alternatively, an individual structuring some conversation on a particular issue that was concerning him could enquire *'What d' yu reckon?'*

or *'Do you think they'll turn up?'* Blades organised themselves by sentences that were understood by those in the know, loaded with significance, and usually not explicit.

One could know every hooligan term and phrase, but nothing altered the fact that any facet of 'Leadership' was related to consensus. In Blades' existence, only a limited number of possibilities existed. Ideally they had to confront and 'do' Owls and rivals when these two groups presented themselves. But disagreements arose around two issues – how they were to do it and, on occasions, what level of violence was necessary? Then again there were issues of how to achieve these ends, where to meet or to travel, where to go in the ground; and occasionally, where to stop for a drink. Because there was no recognised leader, when things went 'wrong', and did not turn out as expected, exasperated individuals would exclaim to no one in particular: *'This is fuckin' daft'*; *'What we doin'?'*; *'We should be in their town centre'*; *'They'll be on West Street/waiting in their city centre . . . what we fuckin' about here for?'* The core Blades, especially, had an ironic, even world-weary, view of their colleagues' abilities to plan anything. Thus, throughout the 1980s, as Blades fruitlessly patrolled the streets or wandered aimlessly around foreign fields, comments such as: *'All over as usual . . . no one's got a clue what to do'*; *'What the fuck's happenin' here?'*; *"Fuck this, I'm goin' in t' next boozer we see'* were regular.

Internal dissension was more regular in away games, when Blades decided to stop off *en route*. There was no pleasing everyone, and whatever the destination chosen there were disgruntled voices. Few pubs would allow fifty or a hundred men in, so Blades often had to split up, and some would be bored with the venue after an hour or two and suggest moving, whilst others would wish to remain. Whoever won the debate, the coach would be guaranteed to contain sulking passengers. And though such occasions did not end in tears, there was usually an argument, a great deal of 'bitching', and a promise by some never to travel with such company again. When this *did not* happen Blades were often amazed, for it was almost expected that the day would end in acrimony of some sort.

What 'leadership' there was to be seen and heard was basically a matter of individuals voicing opinions and using accepted sentences, which, although usually terse, were understood by everyone 'in the know' – but would probably require unpacking by outsiders. This manifested itself via common understandings, wherein comments or gestures implied the obvious without being articulated. This avoidance of the explicit was in itself unconscious, and worked because most Blades could fill in the blanks via what Cicourel (1973: 53) would call the *'et cetra'* assumption. In essence we can see *'phatic communication'* (Malinowski 1922: 312) occurring through remarks that *'create and maintain a situation, an atmosphere of sociability'*. The truth of the matter is that one could be a leader or follower at various times in varying circumstances. Whoever 'led' was the one who could, in some way, satisfy the group's momentary requirements.

In some circumstances various Blades would put forward ideas. These were then acted on. Blades would laugh and ridicule the situation and point out how the 'yellow jersey' (i.e. the *Tour de France* cycle race leader's garment) was now being worn by whoever had had the idea that prevailed. Any attempt by an individual to propose a course of action was fraught with problems. If the idea was not acted on and Blades were unsuccessful, the initiator could piously spend the rest of the day saying 'told you so'. But if the plan was accepted (by consensus) and went wrong in that police 'captured' the group, or the home lads were nowhere to be found, then the instigator could face ridicule and even verbal hostility. For this reason, individual Blades were reluctant to set themselves up. More importantly, the element of surprise, so crucial in hooligan encounters, meant that many a fight began without formal proceedings.

During confrontations anyone could and did shout anything. Most such yells were threats and accusations across the factions, though there were individuals whom others expected – by virtue of their fighting ability or previous hooligan experience – to *'hold it together'*. In such situations 'instructions' were shouted by *anybody*, albeit those who had been around longer knew the score better and were more confident in shouting out a proposed course of action. The shouters served both to encourage and to comfort, signifying to other Blades that somehow there was somebody who knew what was happening. Quite simply the yells were stock phrases: *'Are we 'avin' these or what?'*; *'Into 'em'*; *'Stand Blades'*; *'Don't fuckin' run'*; *'Drop back a bit, then run into 'em'*; *'Let 'em come a bit nearer'*; *'Get the bastards'*; *'C'mon Blades'*; *'Everybody out' [if in a pub]*; *'Watch out for t' ambush.'* If the confrontation ended in victory various Blades might congratulate the group (and in effect themselves) with phrases such as, *'That wo' marvellous, Blades'*; *'That's more like it'*; *'That's the way'*; *'Fuckin' brilliant.'* If defeated, phrases such as *'That wo' crap'*; *'Shit'*; *'What we doin'?'*; *'Fuckin' rubbish, Blades'*; *'Disgrace, that'*; *'Made us look daft'* were heard. Anger required and produced only terse comments, whilst joy restricted the need for any deep analytical statements as well. There were no lengthy recriminations, because no one person or group could be blamed for being run, and as each situation was different there was no template that the participants could use as a yardstick of worth.

Information: Faces in Places

Part of the problem was that any gathering under the name of Blades was so loose, permissive and lacking in a boundary that there were always *'new faces'* present. Occasionals would always appear – what the core Blades in some derision called *'day-trippers'*; these lads were not normally part of the Blade gathering, but were mates of Blades who came along for matches, either because they were workmates, or family, or blokes from some local pub. Dozens of individuals would go to one or two away games a season, and some got drawn into incidents. Their presence was usually that of 'tourists', i.e. either wanting to be part of the day's events or simply wanting to have a 'Story to Tell'. And though a few did things that got them arrested or left regular Blades amazed, such day-trippers were usually disappointed, for action was not always easy to come by, as the free-for-alls that were frequent in the 1970s were over by the 1990s. The same lack of regularity applied to confrontation with Owls, and anyone could get drawn into hostilities in a pub or out on a pub crawl with Blades. Thus some fought Owls once in their lives, some fought them once a year – usually on the last match of the season's mass stop-out by Blades. Others got heavily involved, but then dropped their involvement for years before finding themselves back in old scenarios.

For some participants there was no ambiguity. Certain individuals were known to all Blades because of their previous Blade performances. Somewhere or somehow they had done things that earned them the accolade of peers, for they had either *'stood their ground'*, or punched a rival with such force as to knock him over, or contrarily had been defeated but had gone down fighting against greater odds. Such individuals (*they* knew who they were) now had the right to ask those of similar prestige about the moral worth of others in Blade company. So they could, and did, ask *'What's he ever done?'*, or remark that some individual *'wants to be one of t' lads but hasn't got it'*. The 'it' referred to was a combination of qualities. Either they lacked a certain street-wise collateral, or they were unwilling to stand and fight, or they were unable to fight and take the consequences of either a beating and/or arrest and court appearance. In contrast, these 'hard' men were prepared for consequences and confident they could handle themselves well enough in fights or in the courts to be able to continue to be regular participants. Then again, a few others were regular and willing fighters because they had *not* thought too much of the consequences; or if they had received a fine or even a custodial sentence, neither proved deterrent enough in circumstances of 'necessity'.

Yet for all this surface comradeship, the pursuit of a common enemy and the laughs to be had, there was never total trust amongst Blades. Suspicion manifested itself most frequently in rumours of an informer ('coppers' nark') in their ranks. In gossip with trusted close mates nine names were mentioned between 1988 and 1992 (my own, proposed by various Blades, made it ten). There were various suspicions as to why an individual might be 'grassing' (informing), and though some had reasonable foundation, others were quite ridiculous. Having been arrested, five became subject to suspicion when they were released without charge, for, although they had been frequently arrested, they did not face the court and possible custodial sentence. This was proof, some thought, that they had done a deal with police, and in return for the dropping or reducing of some charges had given names or told of some likely future events. Not everybody was convinced by the varied stories Blades inevitably told on leaving police custody, but never once did a Blade accuse another to his face of being an informer. On the whole, however, such fears were sporadic, and when periods of anxiety ended, the subject of the 'nark' was ridiculed. From 1988, whenever a 'core' Blade (beyond suspicion) was arrested the others would joke in his company that he was *'the grass'* or *'givin' names and addresses'* and how he would now *"ave to leave Sheffield'*. Blades joked about this subject precisely because airing it reduced anxiety.

Identity: Tolerance and Sensitivity

Blades knew that both in wider society and amongst Blades the issue of race was sensitive. The first and last instance on this issue that caused a momentary division occurred in February 1985, when United were playing at home to a side containing a (Sheffield-born) black winger. A few bananas had been thrown at him as he came close to the John Street terrace, and the chant of *'Nigger, Nigger lick my boots'* originated towards the rear of the John Street stand. The 'Young Lads' combined with the remains of the 'Bad Lads' were not impressed, for both were groups containing a high percentage of blacks. Two West Indians in the latter group were sitting at the front of the stand, and stared at the chanters (mostly Rotherham, Villagers and the more peripheral Blades). One walked to the row where the main instigator was sitting and threatened him, as dozens of watching Blades at the front of the stand and the terrace shouted threats towards those who had chanted, yelling: *'Fuckin' shut up'* and *'Pack in wi' that shit.'* As police walked to the scene the two returned to their seats and thanked Blades for their support. Over the last decade it would be fair to say that the perpetrators of racist remarks from amongst Sheffield United fans have been from the more mainstream and non-hooligan supporters. The Blades core always contained blacks, and no one would have voiced such opinions.

⌊One incident with racial overtones occurred in early 1990, when a mixed-race Blade was beaten up by four Blade sympathisers of right-wing politics.⌋ The victim was twenty-one years old and peripheral to Blades gatherings, partly because he had served a two-year prison sentence for burglary and had been charged with the rape of the occupant – an elderly woman. Although found not guilty, it was believed that he *had* raped the woman, and his identity and crime became a source of gossip amongst Blades. Two British National Party (BNP) activist Blades were unable to tolerate this, and when eighty Blades were gathered in a London Road pub after a match, one asked him to 'step outside'. The youth naively did so, and found two other Blades (their mates) waiting. The ensuing attack was ended on the intervention of one of the older Blades, and the victim was taken away by ambulance – never to return amongst Blades. Controversy smouldered on, as the black Blades considered the attack to be racially motivated and were said to be ready to fight his assailants. However the attackers stressed the issue was not a racial one, but was the result of the crime and his boasting. The matter was dropped and never spoken of again.

The ambiguity around race was such that incidents could be cited either to support or to refute various positions. The incident involving Prince (the black Blade beaten up by other blacks in Chapter 2) outside the chip shop is useful for exploring Blades' perceptions of violence and racism. The fact that white Blades had failed to defend him is perhaps indicative of a kind of 'racism'. However, the matter was unrelated to football and concerned an allegation of 'grassing' (informing police), and was therefore regarded by Blades as a private matter between five black youths, one of whom was Prince. Had the assailants been Derby fans, Blades would not have stood back. However, the fact that they were from Sheffield affected the response on one level, because it was a personal matter. On another, there was fear, for black youths are stereotypically regarded by white working-class lads in Sheffield as '*risky*', and renowned not only for being good fighters but for having the resources or the potential to gather other black youths in the city in subsequent revenge, '*You feyt one you feyt 'em all*' being a well known recognition of this capacity. Black youth had a collateral of fighting ability greater than their numbers, and for this reason they were welcome in hooligan cohorts, and during the period of this research constituted one in ten of the core Blades.

Identity: Inherited Intelligence and Police Constructs

From various sources Blades knew a fair bit of what police were thinking about them, for they exchanged information received first- or second-hand from various publicans and solicitors. The former revealed information given as part of the city-centre Pub-Watch Scheme (a late-1980s initiative that saw police produce intelligence sheets relating to actual or potential disorder around public houses and night-clubs), whilst information from solicitors was a product of listening to the prosecution and defence chatting informally in court foyers. Information even came from police officers themselves, for some Blades had relatives in the job, and a few installing windows or building extensions entered the homes and chatted amicably with unsuspecting policemen of various ranks. A couple played in football teams with policemen, and, over a pint, these might inadvertently reveal what their colleagues were thinking or reveal details of surveillance measures. At various times in the middle and late 1980s, there were parents who variously held positions as a magistrate, a prospective city councillor, and a probation officer, and who remained unaware of one aspect of their sons' social lives. In fact, from their wide network Blades knew when police borrowed the vans of nationalised utilities to use for observations and knew when and where cameras were erected to video them on Saturday before and after games.

Like the police, the Blades used the latest technology to discover what the 'others' were up to. Before a Sheffield 'derby' in the early 1990s at Bramall Lane one Blade carried a radio scanner borrowed from a radio enthusiast, and, sitting in a pub with thirty others, provided entertainment from the police radio frequency. Thus Blades were probably the first to hear that the surveillance cameras planned for a site across the road from a pub were to be moved because the landlord had absconded with the takings on the previous night and the pub was now closed. They were also to learn of a camera and detectives in a flat in the high-rise block behind London Road. The officer, in his words, *'could see all the way to Derbyshire'* and recognised a few *'well-known faces walking the street'*. However, he could not see the Blades laughing at him from inside the pub, though none of this knowledge was acted upon.

Other information came from police carelessness. In 1989, at an away game, a Sheffield plain-clothes police officer accidentally lost two pages of a 'mug shot' dossier. Found by passing Blades, it was passed around, and those in it learned of their status in police eyes. Two years later two similar sheets of intelligence were 'obtained' from West Bar police station, by a combination of police carelessness (leaving a door and the file open) and the opportunism of a visiting non-hooligan United fan who simply pulled two sheets out and gave them to Blades that he knew. These contained photographs, nicknames, and 'intelligence' as to whether the accused was a 'recent member' or 'leader' of the BBC, and who were 'suspected drug-dealers'. Police knew of the circulation of the sheets, for one Blade arrested in December 1991 after a home game had them on him. As he was searched before being placed in a cell the documents were found, taken from him and given to a CID Officer called to the Charge Office. The Blade was charged with being drunk and disorderly, and told others that the police did not question him as to where he got the mug shots.

Identity: Negotiations of Justice

In Sheffield there was never any overtly dramatic arrest or spectacular prosecution of those alleged to be core hooligans. There were, however, small-scale arrests that, on release, brought a documentary receipt that was known thus colloquially as *'gettin' a pink'*. The subsequent court case was a drama akin to the dialogue of the deaf. The court process needs the individual to acknowledge facets of behaviour and character using understood vocabularies of motive such as admitting to having drunk too much or having momentarily taken leave of one's senses or having been impelled into events through keeping bad company. The influence of liminality, communitas and carnival were beyond the court's terms of reference and understanding. In this social drama the possibility of explaining that one disliked Owls to the extent that one felt compelled to thump and chase them was impossible. Moreover, to say that Their Boys got what they deserved because they were knowingly *'takin' liberties'* and *'givin' it big 'un'* would not hold water. Thus the various courtroom factions played the game using an agreed 'third' language, and employing the 'necessary' clichés and explanations learned from fellow offenders, pro-bation officers, or defence counsel and solicitors. Blades thus acquired and used their own theories of delinquency causation to impress, facilitate and soothe the magistracy and judiciary.

Faced with a minor charge, a guilty plea made economic sense; for a fine would usually be less than the accumulated travel costs and lost wages due to adjournments and days off work. Guilt, of course, was not a necessary component in the decision; rather, it was simply a matter of what made life easier. For this reason amongst others, any study of hooligan activity based on criminal statistics must be treated with considerable scepticism, for the contrary route would become the criterion for action if a Blade faced a more serious charge. Then, the rule was always 'plead not guilty'. In such a situation, Blades were well aware that some plea-bargaining might well result, and an affray could be reduced to the lesser charge of threatening behaviour. Blades were also well aware that serious charges often required more than just a police witness to the allegation. In the event, trial at Crown Court before a jury meant they were more likely to 'get off' or 'walk out' than if their case was heard by a magistrate. This belief was based on the understanding that twelve good men and true were likely to take a more cynical view of police evidence than some magistrate, who, by virtue of his or her office had spent little or no time living 'on the edge'. Blades simply knew that judges and magistrates were from a different social background, certainly to theirs and often to that of many jurors.

Some charges preferred against Blades implied a more sinister causation of hostility. In September 1991 five peripheral Blades were arrested following a midnight disturbance with a group of predominantly black local youths outside a North London fast-food takeaway, this following a night in London after a match at Chelsea. The five faced a Crown Court case in February 1992 on charges of violent disorder under the Public Order Act 1986; for one, the charge included racial assault, and another two faced the further charge of criminal damage. After four days in Crown Court the judge directed the jury to find all the defendants not guilty on the grounds of insufficient evidence. The incident was never a racial matter, for two of the arrested Blades were actually black. However, I believe the overtones of football fan violence and racism had probably come to influence the prosecution of this specific charge.

In all, only four core Blades and one peripheral one were jailed in the fourteen years 1980–94. The greatest number of fans imprisoned occurred in March 1985, when three were jailed. Two had thrown stones, and a third fired a distress flare, and this young man – barely seventeen at the time – was the only Blade in the group. Somewhat peripheral, he was leading a less than exemplary life elsewhere, and soon after vanished from Blade gatherings. Another Blade who was to see a prison cell was most definitely a core member whom police were keen to classify as a 'leader', and he was imprisoned on a variety of charges following repeated arrests. At one time he was awaiting trial on three consecutive charges of threatening behaviour arising from match-day incidents and disturbances with Owls. His custodial sentence was no doubt helped by fabricated and nonsensical evidence to the effect that he had struck a pensioner during a fracas. The other custodial sentences were equally farcical. In 1989, whilst in a street near an away ground George had grabbed a fellow Blade, demanding he stop taking photographs of other Blades involved in a nearby fracas. After he had been arrested, the police construed this as an attack on a rival fan and he was given a three-month custodial sentence. The fact he was black probably did not help his case. In 1991 Callum was imprisoned on a charge of affray following a late-night disturbance between thirty Blades and a similar number of Somalis in London. Callum, the only Blade arrested, was not even involved in the disturbance, having arrived on the scene after the event. Moreover, he was incapable because of a combination of drink and drugs, but was charged with assault and affray. Evidence of failed identification from two Somalis was discounted, and his eventual conviction may have had as much to do with the influence on the jury of his six-foot frame, his thickset appearance and a balding head, as they perhaps included a stereotypic vision of a racist thug in their deliberations. Finally, a 28-year-old fanatical follower was gaoled after he had shown no more than a regular dissent with a referee's decision at the end of the game, as the latter walked to the players' tunnel. Wagging his fingers, he said *'Thanks for nowt tonight, ref.'* The court heard the referee had been frightened, and, without any supporting evidence, the magistrate said *'it seems fashionable to attack referees, but that must stop'*. The Blade's previous football-related convictions (although four years earlier) allowed the magistrate to assert that these had not deterred him, and that he regarded the incident as *'very serious'*. After a sentence of a month's imprisonment and a ban from entering football grounds for 12 months, a front-page article and photograph in *The Star* completed the emphasis on what was hardly a horrific crime. Thus across the ten years 1984–94 only two individuals were gaoled for offences occurring around the match – one for firing a distress flare, and the other for entering the pitch to abuse a referee; the latter received a one-month sentence, the former nine months. The rest were gaoled for acts that occurred miles from the ground, or hours before or after the match, and would not be defined as football hooliganism until the early 1990s, when the category was expanded by police bureaucratic categories.[3]

The basic principle in English law, in the matter of football hooliganism, appeared to Blades to be that the winner was the side that could create the 'better' evidence, so that at times they would deny doing what I am convinced they had done. Equally, it is my opinion the police claimed to the courts to have witnessed more than they saw. The subsequent outcome seems to depend on whose version of events (the 'facts') the magistrate or jury accepted. I feel the police version of events consisted of small-scale lies – 'verballing': basically, inventing statements and attributing them to the defendants and embroidering their actions. Thus in police and prosecution evidence the accused could be said: to have his fists clenched; to be kicking out with his feet; to be beckoning people to come towards him; to be shouting something abusive, offensive, or threatening (or all three). I also believe the police would claim that 'shoppers' were jostled and 'innocent bystanders' had to seek refuge in order to help a prosecution case. This infuriated defendants, as did the issue of 'football' when introduced by police witnesses without good reason. Arrested for fighting Owls hours from a game and miles from a football ground, police would stress the 'football' nature of the issue. Aware of the emotive response this could provoke in the minds of magistrates and juries, Blades thought it unnecessary and vindictive. No doubt police thought it justified.

The courtroom contestation would often depend on other, non-verbal, but changeable, criteria. In the 1970s many Blades, knowing some charge would be of a minor public order nature, had a somewhat cavalier attitude. Arrest would often be followed by the cliché *'gonna see Gerry on Monday'* – Gerry being the city solicitor (and later Labour MP for Huyton, Merseyside) Gerald Bermingham, whose solid court reputation had made him a Defence favourite. In later years the choice of solicitor was more individual, but could be based on recommendations from fellow Blades who had 'got off' with some particular practitioner's assistance. The 1970s were days of a defence strategy based on attire and appeasement of the bench: 'wear a suit and go guilty', i.e. look respectable in the eyes of the middle-class magistrate and one might be rewarded with a 'not guilty' verdict or a small fine for not contesting the issue. Such ploys were enhanced by the mid-1980s and later by a rational and calculated policy that considered the charge to be faced and made a more comprehensive attempt to manage the impression created and to use 'credible' witnesses. This was sensible for two reasons. One was that years of stories of Football Hooliganism had made punitive sentences highly probable. The second was that police from the mid-1980s began to press more serious public order charges.

Identity and Reputation

To gain convictions the court has to rely on a guilty plea and/or the evidence of prosecution witnesses. Blades knew any outcome often depended on the availability of such witnesses, and that all cases relied to some degree on police evidence. In the eyes of the court, the police officer is a 'professional witness', who has been trained and rehearsed in court procedures. Blades knew such expertise was their main danger, because they were sure no Blade (or Owl) would dare 'nark', i.e. turn informer, and provide prosecution evidence. Because the police were understood to fabricate evidence with verbals and the like, some Blades were prepared to be creative with the truth. And whilst there was no organised perversion of justice, in four cases in five years (1985–90) I know that some Blades were willing witnesses for mates, even when they had not been at the incidents that resulted in the arrest. These lads were nothing remarkable in Blade circles, but they did have a smart appearance, and in their own words had an ability to '*talk posh*'. I witnessed their ability to 'suss out' magistrates and jurors, for they knew from watching various trials what 'sold' to the courts. Claiming expenses when a case was outside Sheffield, they invented loss of earnings from mythical jobs, made cash from train travel though they had been given lifts by the defendants, and sought reparation for expenses and recompense for hotel bills that were also fabrications. As entrepreneurs, they could make £100 from a witness appearance, and then gained another pay-off from the laugh they later enjoyed with other Blades about these tactics.

Without such witnesses an accused needed to illustrate to the bench or jury a degree of social conformity. Thus, at times, they would play the legal system by using some occupational or romantic status. When facing a serious charge, Blades knew it was a good idea to be employed or have a written promise of a job, and so non-existent job references were made available from mates, whilst genuine ones sometimes came from a fellow employee or employer friends of the family. The reasoning was that magistrates would not readily impose a custodial sentence on someone with a 'stake in conformity'. However, if a fine was the expected outcome, it was advantageous to be 'unemployed', for this might reduce the amount to be repaid and set repayment at a minimal weekly amount. If, however, during the proceedings, things were not turning out as expected or envisaged, a Defence Counsel could be told to mention a forthcoming engagement or marriage, thereby illustrating an involvement with more serious significant others.

Throughout a case, the proceedings were always pervaded by the importance of presentation. Those aspects of demeanour, which are an essential part of hooligan encounters, were therefore extended into the courtroom. A dress code that was smart and clean was a prerequisite, as were verbal exchanges that were both polite and avoided slang. From their solicitors and other Blades a novice-accused soon learned that magistrates were particularly hostile to swearing and demonstrations of lost temper under questioning. Furthermore, any belief that the police either had fabricated evidence or were pursuing a vendetta was unmentionable. It was always thought by Blades that magistrates were fully aware of police fabrication, but simply did not want the accused to articulate the issue. For if anyone was going to shout 'the Emperor has no clothes', then it was certainly not the 'hooligan' who was expected to do it.

The influence of legal impositions varies with the individual. Of those imprisoned, few seemed to have 'learned their lesson', and most returned to Blade days and ways. Blades subjected to fines generally kept away from trouble until they had been paid off. Those on a suspended sentence were very wary about the possible repercussions of their actions, and city-centre curfews were mainly adhered to, but did not change a person's nature. Those Blades sentenced to Community Service Orders that prevented match attendance, or who were to report to police stations on Saturday afternoons, fulfilled them and did so, but could be usually discovered amongst Blades in after-match activity. And those Blades who were subjected to some personal vendetta by an individual officer had to put up with it.

Identity: Common Criminals?

There was no stereotypical Blade, and there was no stereotypical background. Contrary to New-Right prejudice, the majority of Blades were not from single-parent families – in fact only a handful were. Whilst a good percentage were from families with a second marriage, the majority of participants were from nuclear families. Contrary to popular prejudice, the majority of Blades were not expelled from their schooling career: very few received expulsion notices albeit few could claim to represent a success story for the British educational system. A very large percentage had come to the attention of the criminal justice system. That few had been deterred from activities that were likely to result in arrest is significant, as is the fact that only a handful had ever seen the inside of a prison cell. Finally, very few Blades were 'unemployed'. Whilst this status was widespread amongst their peer group in the region, the activities and consumption that being a Blade required were out of reach of those without a decent financial income.

At Blade gatherings were men with various convictions unrelated to Blade activities, such as drunken driving, shoplifting, burglary, theft of vehicles, criminal damage and assault. None of this was a product of 'organised' crime; rather, it was individualistic and opportunistic. No Blade had a criminal record for rape or sexual assault, and if there were any spouse-beaters they kept very quiet. Yet in the late 1980s, of two hundred Blades travelling to one away game, two out of three had convictions not directly connected to football (see Appendix). These were mainly drink and public order related, for many of these young men had a life away from Blades that brought them into contact with police and the courts. From the eye of a lens an interested observer would have noticed amongst Blades and Owls some individuals who either went on to and were actively involved in professional crime. Their football loyalties combined with the permissive atmosphere of hooligan gatherings meant that they could relax in fellow company and, should they be so minded, check out the resources that they could draw upon. Basically, anything could be sold in this network and non-material collateral could be exchanged in that individuals could enjoy talking to those involved in crime and a life (which included prison) that was unknown to them. Myths could be traded and laughs had and, if the day offered the chance of confrontation, life was more interesting. In no way, though, were professional criminals organising the others.

There were thieves amongst Blades, but not always honour amongst thieves. And the theft that Blades did indulge in on match-days was small-scale and sporadic. From the 1970s, along the 'away' journeys, various goods were stolen, in a practice referred to as *'robbin''*. This varied from the widespread practice of thieving food from over-priced Motorway Services, to the more individual and experienced theft of designer clothing, jewellery and electrical goods. Such artefacts would then be sold amongst fellow travellers, and so long as this activity did not subsequently result in some vehicle's being detained by police, no disapproval was shown of the perpetrators. Occasionally some theft could be personal and opportunistic. In the mid-1980s a few unattended handbags were stolen from West End London pubs (a practice known as *'dippin''*), and leather jackets were 'relieved' from unattended backs of pub chairs. Such incidents of theft occurred perhaps six times in the ten years between 1984 and 1994. I witnessed the more serious offence of 'robbery from the person' on some three occasions in ten years, and this was only ever perpetrated on 'Their Boys'. The circumstances were always the same, the theft occurring after the victim had been beaten to the floor. One was relieved of his designer training shoes, and two had leather jackets taken. These victims were unlikely to run to police and make a complaint.

Some practices were financially favourable to Blades, the most memorable from a footballing perspective being the fraudulent production of season tickets for Bramall Lane (and Hillsborough). A couple of dozen Blades managed to see a quarter of the season with such counterfeits, obtained at just under half the club-approved price, before the police found out. That said, the perpetrators were never discovered.[4] Other fraud involved obtaining goods 'cheaply' at the expense of both banking corporations and travel insurance companies, ironically using false names, but ones taken from the United and Wednesday team players of the 1970s. The claims made by the Football Intelligence Unit (see H.A.C. 1994) that football hooligans were involved in passing counterfeit currency had a degree of truth, but only to the extent that many thousands of men in many towns and cities throughout Britain in the early 1990s had access to false currency at around one-third cost price. Sheffield was not exceptional in that such currency circulated in leisure areas and across the football ground turnstiles.

Like millions of others of their age group, many Blades took drugs, and others could supply them. As a result a few amongst Blades had drug-related convictions, and a couple served custodial sentences for supplying. That said, in the period 1986–93 there was no 'addict' amongst Blades and not all Blades took drugs. Those who did, used them sporadically for 'recreational purposes', i.e. weekend use of marijuana, or 'speed' (amphetamine sulphate), or (post-1986) 'trips' of an hallucinogenic with an LSD derivative. From the early 1980s Blades had smoked or swallowed drugs *en route* to away games, often sitting with others who would not touch such substances. On a coach or van the smokers usually sat by the windows, and should police vehicles be seen would throw the offending articles away. Contrary to police beliefs based on rumours following fights in the city, there was no drug market contestation against Owls or amongst Blades. In fact in 1991 Blades who heard that police believed their vendetta with the Owls was related to control of drug markets decided to parody the construct. One group from a south-east district of the city subverted the image, producing T-shirts with the graphic of a Blade 'stoned' on a cannabis cigarette under the motif of a cannabis leaf with the initials BDS (see Figures 3–6). This doubly subverted the hooligan construct of the BBC, and the 'new' (and very short-lived) Blades Drug Squad ran coaches to three away games, where the cost included a ready-made 'joint' to smoke *en route*.

Identity: The Urban Élite

Blade socialising provided a network of sociability that was both a material and an emotional resource. Blades formed Sunday football teams, helped others find work, lent money, and gave discounts on goods and materials when work permitted. Pub and nightclub 'bouncers' permitted wait-free and admission-free entry. Gym workers ensured favourable rates and bookings. Civil servants told interested parties about licences for shops, while others warned of DHSS raids. Two moved into financial consultancy and managed other Blades' pensions. At another level Blade company was an emotional resource. Thus, Blades married sisters of Blades, and, when some love-affair broke down, London Road and the Blade gathering were a haven that accepted all comers, even after years of absence. When moving to a new district, local Blades could make the newcomer welcome, inviting him to watch or play in the Sunday morning football team. For the few serious shoplifters and designer-label counterfeiters Blades' gatherings were a useful market.

At other times the aid and back-up was to right wrongs by violence; for which other group in Sheffield could gather 150–200 young men when deemed necessary? In many respects Blades (and Owls) knew they were a city resource without equal. They were an urban élite, believing they had a network and a cultural collateral that no peer group had; and, as a result, could look down on those culturally unwise 'mugs' who did not have the personal abilities for 'handlin' themselves', or to articulate the 'verbals' necessary to overcome tricky moments with rivals or authority figures.

Blades had no basis for any clear-cut leadership, indeed no real basis for the exercise of any kind of authority. On occasions, some individuals exerted an *ad hoc* influence: some might have more attractive ideas, and these might be pursued, but not necessarily with any clear recognition as to who originated the scheme. Whoever took the lead did so not by force, or the threat of it, but by others' willingness to comply and *not* disagree; the rest had, for the moment, allowed him to exercise leadership. Blade gatherings did not lend themselves to duty-bound obedience, and no decision was enforceable. No possible advantage could be served by creating the role of 'Leader'; for should this individual be 'whacked' by rivals or arrested, then the symbolic loss could make the rest back down. The 1987 imaginary leader and joke figure 'Fletch' was the antithesis of the Blades. In his 'late twenties', he was older than the majority, and he came from London – significant because of the Blades' conceptual association of the capital with a fan of violence of a greater severity than theirs.

The Blades had media-inspired images of themselves that were not simply reducible to 'class', for the Ideal Hooligan also came out of the airwaves. Blades, however, were not 'cultural dopes', and although they tended to feel they should be doing whatever others were up to, they adopted some elements and transmogrified what they saw and read into the local context. Football hooliganism was never a homespun thing; but when media images were combined with cultural constructs about what was 'acceptable' and 'out of order', this produced the Blade–Owl, Blades – Their Boys conflicts. The 'BBC', in their pseudo-formal existence, had the trappings of corporate identity – calling cards, badge, song, and in London Road a fixed meeting-place – yet the lack of any formal organisation was their essence. The BBC was *never* dependent on personalities, as the tasks it represented were greater than any individual. Those who invented the name and produced BBC artefacts eventually left the scene, yet the BBC 'Ideal' lived on for another ten years. A quasi-make-believe unity developed in the face of Owls or Their Boys, and to outsiders the *de facto* gathering was given a basic identity by the circulation of artefacts that depicted Blades as dangerous and organised. But this was a creative process that was largely ignored in journalism and by police intelligence, and has been insufficiently stressed by previous academic research.

The match was the Blades' *raison d'être*, even if they met hours before it was played and stayed together hours afterwards. It served the purpose of facilitating contact between the different groups and individuals, and an away match allowed for more extensive exchanges of view, wider experiences, and the swapping of ideas and rumour. If on occasions the Blades did appear to act as a unit, this was because a kind of fortuitous structure was given to the channels of gossip by the institutionalised nature of the Sheffield pub crawl. Sometimes visits to pubs would be made with the explicit hope of encountering particular Blades, but whether or not this was the case the effect of the pub crawl was not only to enhance the levels of general gossip but to talk of and consider ideas of future intentions. It was an institution only in that it enabled an organisation as acephalous as the Blades to appear sometimes as if it had a head. The only resource needed for those wanting to be part of it was time and enthusiasm for United.

Notes

1. The changing nature of Blade gatherings was manifest by meetings outside of match day. Whilst these had begun on Friday nights from 1978, the close season summer gatherings began in 1980 when Benny and others went into nearby towns which resulted in brawls with locals. The following summer Benny and twenty others restricted their pub crawls to Sheffield, beginning, ostensibly, by celebrating Benny's dog's birthday. The dog, however, was refused entry to a nightclub, possibly because it was attempting to walk sideways having swallowed amphetamines. The following year saw a pub crawl in honour of a rubber tyre, which one youth wore around his middle all evening. This was followed, weeks later, by a large cut-out cardboard crocodile taped on to a T-shirt, imitating a 'trendy' football fashion of wearing Lacoste

design T-shirts with the emblem of a crocodile stitched on to the left breast.

2. In 1987 a ten-strong Blades' stag-night group fought bouncers in the nearby towns of Rotherham and Chesterfield. The Rotherham incident, arising over an argument between Blades and bouncers over entry to a pub, ended with one Blade getting knocked out and Blades being 'backed off'. The second argument, at the end of the night, ended with eight Blades being arrested and five found guilty of affray. No bouncers were arrested and none was reported hurt. In court four Blades were find £1,800 each, which two paid. On appeal, two had their fines reduced to £400. These draconian fines were no doubt helped by the introduction of 'football hooligans' and the cabalism of the 'BBC' into the prosecution evidence.

3. In October 1988 four fans aged between nineteen and twenty-one were arrested and charged with assault. Two of the four were also charged with wounding. Two were found guilty and sentenced to three and a half years, and two were cleared at Derby Crown Court in October 1989. The facts were that the four had watched United lose at Chesterfield, and later, after drinking in Sheffield, they had stated an intention of finding rival fans to fight with. Their search led them to a group of local lads who were accompanied by a 66-year-old man walking his dog. The aspect that fascinated Blades was that one of the two convicted came from Essex, and the other was from a very upper-middle-class area of Sheffield. The Essex man was reported to have urged on the others, saying *'Let's chin that old bloke'*, a matter which appalled the Blades. Neither was part of any Blade gathering on London Road, nor had they ever travelled with 'the lads'; yet a reading of the media reporting of the events would suggest these two epitomised Blade thinking and behaviour.

4. In 1992 a season ticket scam at Bramall Lane was discovered by police. Three people faced minor charges of attempting to gain entry without a valid ticket. Tickets for United's games had been forged the previous season and sold along the Blade network. When United played Wednesday at Hillsborough in 1992 a few dozen 'tickets' were made for those unable to get them and those unwilling to pay cash they knew would go to Wednesday's coffers. Realising there was money to be made, two entrepreneurs amongst Blades saw their market opportunity. A 'friendly' printer copied the season ticket design, and they made 80 for United and 80 for Wednesday, and sold the lot at under half the proper price. The 1991/2 season scam worked; then police got wind of it at a home game. Police stationed various officers – plain-clothed and

uniformed – at *every* turnstile that accepted season ticket vouchers. When they found a bogus ticket the owner was arrested and his home was searched for evidence. This latter action was needed, for those arrested with a single voucher sensibly stated that they had just bought the solitary voucher 'off a bloke in the pub'. Police were not fooled; but the fact that they arrested only 7 out of 160 suggests that their operation was not that extensive.

Chapter 12

Peace in Our Time? The Future

The yob is never the boy you know – only the one you don't. As in all bigoted mythologies, the yob is that alien and bad creature by which the familiar and the good is culturally defined: the 'them' by which 'us' is created.

(Rosalind Coward (1994) 'Whipping Boy', *The Guardian*, 3 September)

For an anthropologist, the 'hooligan problem' is one of trying to account for behaviour that many individuals exhibit in different ways and to encompass within this the response of various audiences. Analysis primarily embodies a need to explain why some young men enjoy the *performance* aspects of *threat* and would endure various police impositions to enact these. The hooligan issue, as we have seen, is not so much a problem of physical violence as one of male aggressive performances in a highly controlled decontrolling of emotions and expressions (see Elias 1982). 'Violence' is often a pejorative term that more objectively could be said to state that physical confrontation is occurring in the wrong place between the wrong people (see Riches 1986). And, as we have seen, Blade activity includes aggressive performances considered matter 'out of place' or 'polluting' by most onlookers because they are considered as not appropriate or not in the proper context (see Douglas 1970), and that challenge the common-sense assumption that sport is a vehicle for tolerance and understanding.

Pursuing the Indefinable: Theory Reconsidered

For the young men participating in acts defined as football hooliganism, a variety of wants and meanings are attained. Academic theory *cannot* provide any one single and simple explanation for their motivation. Many pre-existing academic theories on the causation of football hooliganism are inadequate (some are totally ridiculous); thus answers as to why some are attracted to join the Blades' rituals have to be sought from a wider theoretical perspective. The answer, I believe, is to be found in the reasons A. Cohen (1974: 137) lists as to why people take part in any ritual or ceremony: to *derive comfort, perform a social obligation, achieve recreation, discover their identity, pass the time, be with others, and for an endless variety of other private personal purposes.* These reasons, he adds, are always affected by relations of power between both individuals and groups. And in contrast to what he (1974: 55) calls the *'contractual role'* of occupation, where the self is least involved, there exist *'non-contractual, non-utilitarian roles and activities in symbolic action'.* Quoting Victor Turner, Cohen notes how some individuals take 'periodic leave' from work relationships or contractual activities to seek 'Communitas' in recreational pursuits with people with whom they are not usually involved contractually. The question remains, however, as to why some people seek such pursuits.

One answer is the state of modern living. Since the 1960s we have seen modern life increasingly conducted with the help of technology and back-up from a range of social services. For most people in Britain there is now no epic of poverty and war, for life is relatively safe. Put another way, the modern world has produced what Durkheim defines as 'social anomie'. The resulting realisation of futility has generated what Mary Douglas (1970) terms 'ritual poverty', and created an absence of occasions for persons to exhibit their desired selves. Significantly, she points out that some things are impossible to experience without ritual. Similarly Klapp (1969) described how this sense of futility leads to 'symbolic poverty', and argues that modern society lacks vital gossips, meaningful relationships, fulfilling rituals, and a sense of place (1969: 318). And, in an urban milieu, as Klapp (1969: 319–20) contends, the absence of strong identification and reputation can lead some to seek an alternative or compensatory activity that may see them define themselves by some *'action or ordeal'.* Enslaved by ideas of rationality, technology and economic systems, man loses creativity and experiences disenchantment (see Weber 1930: 181; 1948: 139). Modern-day consumer lifestyle increasingly lacks any sense of danger or ordeal, and the problem then becomes one of transcending monotony (see Huxley 1954). From this the challenge which many accept is to create excitement via scenarios where the regulating boundaries are forever being re-defined and approved, and the fun of the event is overcoming them.

Discovering the Other

Tied in with this, I would argue, there is the consequent political crisis, which to borrow from Habermas (1976) is a crisis of *legitimation.* The problem is in making legitimate that which is no longer relevant. What, Habermas asks, are the principles and criteria with which to value and judge others? Another aspect of society not explored in this debate is the response to state oppression. British society, as Marcuse (1970) argues, suffers from 'surplus repression', in that it is governed by a range of regulations far beyond those necessary for an orderly existence. Such over-regulation combines with other symptoms of modernity, such as rage and disenchantment, and the repression of emotion. However, repression inevitably seeks release in alternative outlets, and that which is denied becomes the most hotly pursued. In this way, Blade gatherings became liberated from convention and cliché, and became carnivalesque in structure, in that they parody the established forms (1970: 7–10). And, as in 'Carnival', Blade activities – although liberating and progressive – could go beyond 'meaning', and drift into excess, and be explainable simply in the delight of being deviant. For living in a rapidly changing and fashion-obsessed world, a stable moral order is difficult to establish. This theoretical vision of events is supported by Cohen and Taylor (1992: 225), who argue:

> *Never before has life offered so many opportunities for us to articulate our freshly-won individuality; but paradoxically, the acceptance of any or all of these opportunities may merely serve to re-introduce the sense of meaningless routine and repetition against which we initially established our sense of individuality. In these circumstances, some may decide that only extreme escape attempts now work. Only the most outrageous, violent, surreal endeavours will resist co-option.*

Furthermore, as Lasch (1978: 53) argues, in an age of diminishing expect-ations, the Protestant virtues no longer excite enthusiasm. Outside the workplace is where people seek authentic and realistic experience, and this encourages the presentation of self as a commodity, where many seek alternative excitements to fill the gap and leisure time permits challenges and creativity.[1]

In this milieu, to find out who you *really* are some people pursue danger, in what I will call Trial by Ordeal (see Bellah *et al.* 1985). Thus has developed in many people a culture of 'risk-taking' with no settled world tradition or accepted world authority (see Giddens 1991; Beck 1992). How this risk-taking and ordeal construction is chosen is often dependent on economic resources, or what is locally or socially available. Some climb mountains, some take white-water canoe holidays, some go off-piste skiing, or holiday in war-zones; others walk along London Road or West Street in Sheffield. Taken to extremes, the risk in hooliganism has elements of the sublime, in that it is occasionally terror-producing. It is human to be frightened, and such situations are all about extending human possibilities. Being a Blade therefore allowed an individual to explore personal, social, cultural and physical limits, and just as importantly allowed for innovation, because as Foucault (1977) recognised, in transgression the issue in question was the limit rather than the identity of the culture. For in the pursuit of such movement, various selves can be gathered, gain credit or, in turn, be discredited.

Many theorists, however, have ignored the construct of fun, which, as Klapp (1969) noted, does not have to be confined to relaxation or amusement, but is evident in any search for identity – and can vary from banal amusement to offbeat experiences, cults, poses, and bizarre drama. Another way of gaining enjoyment lies in provoking misfortune for 'others', and this again was a Blade's delight. Such an activity was akin to ideas of 'Play', which, as Huizinga (1955: 13) suggests, should: contain elements to absorb the player's interests, have no material gains, contain its own boundaries according to fixed rules, provide for group formation, and include *'order, tension, movement, change, solemnity, rhythm, and rapture'* (1955: 17); the players need a high level of physical intimacy, a shared sentiment and emotional familiarity, and partake to achieve a consequence of social prestige (1955: 38–42). This describes the Blades. The activities that encompass 'football hooliganism' are socially constructed dramas and games that cannot be channelled into any notion of a constructive or benign pastime. As Lasch (1978: 100) asserts: *the search for fun*

> *Games simultaneously satisfy the need for free fantasy and the search for gratuitous difficulty, they combine childlike exuberance with deliberately created complications . . . Yet the 'futility' of play, and nothing else, explains its appeal – its artificiality, the arbitrary obstacles it sets up for no other purpose than to challenge the players to surmount them, the absence of any utilitarian or uplifting object. Games quickly lose their charm when forced into the service of education, character development, or social improvement.*

What Blades do, then, is a product of choice in the pursuit of the indefinable 'crack', 'laugh', 'buzz': basically, enjoyment based in uncertainty, as the individual confronts the drama.

The inverse of structured play is the unleashing of elements of rebellion, and there is little doubt that football support generally *and* football hooliganism both contain elements of rebellious carnival (see Thomas 1964; Burke 1978; Gluckman 1963; Eco 1984; Ivanov 1984; Giulianotti 1993). Carnival can consist of the pleasures achieved by subordinates who oppose the established. As Bakhtin (1984) postulates, it combines elements of excess, laughter, degradation and offensiveness, to produce an 'egalitarian second world' lying outside and beyond that preferred by officialdom. As Stam (1982: 55) describes it, carnival produces disrespect, and with this a *'radical opposition to the illegitimately powerful, to the morose and the monological'*. Thus, with their chants directed at players and powerful officialdoms, football fans ridicule the self-important and self-regarding guardians of propriety. Other Blade performances reproduce Barthes' (1975) notion of 'Plaisir and Jouissance', where 'Plaisir' is the cultural enjoyment that empowers the ego, whilst 'Jouissance' is explained (see Moore 1988: 191) as a violent pleasure that dissipates cultural identity to the point of discomfort, and unsettles the subject's relationship to language and representation. To borrow from cultural analyst De Certeau (1984: 18–26), Blades, I contend, are involved in the 'guerrilla activity' of resistance. Exhibiting *'tenacity, trickery and guileful ruse'*, Blades consistently resist the authoritarian forces of the media, the judiciary, and the police by small incursions that continuously deploy ways of cheating the social constraint, and always invoke the construct of Power – an aspect that is missing from many previous theoretical analyses of this phenomenon.

Blades enjoy having to construct the possibility of power, and, as Foucault (1979) argued, where there is Power there is resistance, for this necessarily sustains the concept. Baudrillard's (1988: 179) argument that 'power' arises out of the activity of making situations real and grave enough to make insults matter is significant here, and fits those opportunities when Blades had their 'successes' by denying a rival *'a core of uncertainty'* (1988: 32–4). Thus the hooligan group who, in the face of adversaries, could say 'we shall not budge' and gain the reputation of being predictable, would thus become the winners. However, there were many ways of expressing dominance, and although Blades' actions were unscripted, most hooligan activity was played within confines, with the police permitted the role of umpire and the State feared for its role in providing the courts of retribution. As Lukes (1972) would say, true power lies with those institutions whose existence is not challenged or barely acknowledged. And so Blades gained pleasure from raiding impositions and constructing reactions. But, crucially, the only power Blades have in regard to the State is, to borrow from Hebdige (1988: 18), *'the power to discomfit'*. And this, for what it's worth, is what Blades can achieve.

Explaining the Other

As the research found, the facts are that around twenty to twenty-five Blades and Owls required hospital treatment in the 15 years (1980–95). The hospital beds occupied by Blades and Owls encompassed twelve nights in total, and in issues with 'Their Boys' (the hooligan element of other clubs) Blades perhaps put five in hospital in fifteen years, and had the same number of their own ranks treated. When Blades fought about matters unrelated to football, or with opponents without a fan identity, then their obviously injured victims numbered some five persons. Some might cite the 'hooligan' relationship to the two deaths mentioned earlier, and my reply would be that the one occurring after the 1993 FA Cup semi-final was a million-to-one chance, whilst the other, in 1986, was the result of running into a car. I do not feel a Blade would ever have set out wilfully to see an opponent killed, for this was simply not on the agenda. The number of police officers needing medical treatment after meeting Blades was three in fourteen years. Though these statistics may be unacceptable, the purpose in specifying them is to give the matter some kind of perspective.

For all the numbers participating and the emotions engendered, Blades violence was on a world-wide or even a city-wide perspective relatively negligible, and I would argue, consistently devoid of hatred or vicious sadism. And though Simmel (1950) noted how in real conflict *'it is useful to hate the opponents'*, this was not really the case here. Blades and Their Boys had a contextured contest within agreed parameters, and even across their frequent confrontations many Blades knew Owls as 'normal' acquaintances. The fact remains that, despite the outpourings of the police, the Blades were simply not organised for extreme or even well co-ordinated acts of violence. Consistently the stereotypes and the reality have been at odds, and between 1980 and 1994 Blades did *not* wreck any trains, or any other form of public transport. They never attacked a lone person when they were twenty strong, and they were not prepared to be sheep-like and follow-my-leader. No child or elderly person was ever attacked, and the use of weapons was so rare as to be noteworthy. So, we can ask: why the three decades of demonology towards groups of young working-class males probably unprecedented in British history?

One possible explanation lies in perceptions and prejudices, and the role provided by Blades and their like in permitting observers to talk of barbarism as a product of both birth and behaviour. Opinions and ideas on the Blades and their equivalents are preached by what Becker (1967) would call the hierarchy of the credible, in this instance invariably repre-sentative of the middle class: journalists, senior policemen, politicians and some sociologists. For them the young male working-class football fan is an icon of revulsion. This is an academic issue, because as Sorel (1961: 80) has stated: *'It is very difficult to understand proletarian violence as long as we think in terms of the ideas disseminated by middle-class philosophies; according to their philosophy, violence is a relic of barbarism which is bound to disappear under the influence of the progress of enlightenment.'* Described by the above authorities, we read how 'hooligans' (often synonymous with all young male working-class fans) do not walk, they 'swagger', whilst some appal their social betters by various vulgarities: shouting in public, drinking alcohol from cans. Sometimes, in warmer climes, they will look neither chic nor elegant as they expose pale skin and that symbol that stigmatises the lower orders – the tattoo. Revulsion here is as much aesthetic as it is political. Furthermore, these fans, often in unison and in public, express opinions on cultural style, on race and gender, that millions agree with but rarely or never dare articulate. This is a crucial point – they say the unsayable; the onlooker has then to express outrage.

What exactly the football hooligan exemplifies depends entirely on the diagnosis offered for the hooligan 'disease'. As a receptacle for all political prejudices, he is as functional to our society as dragons, sorcerers, and Communists were to other times and cultures. For some, the football hooligan instils fear as the icon of a white working class. This occurs, as Mary Douglas (1970) would argue, because their behaviour and presence demonstrates the frailty of social control: 'they' manifest the weakness of valued restraints. Yet, I would argue the unreasoned fear of the activity of the 'Mob', as a dangerous and atavistic collective, is a result of the increasing isolation and atomisation of British society. This concern is part of a complex socio/political experience that has grown considerably in recent decades, and coincides with the events collated here as 'hooligan activity'. Increasing insecurity caused through cultural uncertainty, rising unemployment, loss of faith in Church and State, the privatisation of welfare services that were to protect from cradle to grave, and other political processes that have generated a 'feel-bad' factor have all generated fears of crime and unfounded concerns about victimisation that have little objective reality. In this situation, the fearful and unknowing have been unable or unwilling to challenge icons and symbols, or to question the alleged 'truths' about both football fans and hooligans. Thus, they have allowed governments, the police, the media and the sociologist to pontificate and proselytise, for only these people, it seems, can save us from each other.

Inappropriate Masculinity?

Concern with fan-violence has, even for many academic authors, almost exclusively concerned itself with limited gender-centred analysis around issues of 'aggressive/troubled/ hegemonic/empowering masculinity' and its consequences (see Brittan 1989). We need to consider whether 'masculinity' is a concept or a something that can be neatly defined or decoded.

Furthermore, when seeking to analyse group behaviour via some notion of 'masculinity' we should be aware that this is, surely, an extended collection of instances and not some essence that can be captured and bottled. There is no agreement, however, as to the antidote to this process; and memories are short, for British society was never free of both the revelries and the incivilities of young men (see Humphries and Gordon 1994; Brewer and Styles 1980; Pearson 1983). It was not always thus, however. Between 1945 and the late 1950s things were apparently different, in what some refer to as a 'tradition-bound society', normalised by local residence and marriage patterns, occupational inheritance, and family networks that were constraining of individualism. Since the 1960s, however, social patterns have changed because of increased social and geographical mobility, new employment patterns, increasing unemployment, new technologies, and trans-national media influences. The result is that Blades, like their peers and contemporaries, are not as deferential or class-bound as their predecessors.

In the past male identity was largely derived from the work situation, but this has lost its gender specificity, as many of the former 'macho' industries and occupations have declined or died. Male socialisation norms via occupational life patterns have consequently declined, and unemployment has meant an absence of the disciplines of Labour. Today, the ethos of work status is less important, and has given way to the individualistic criterion of status related simply to the amount of money earned. To tens of millions, then, Tradition has been replaced by survival. And for those who have it, work is now seen mainly in instrumental terms, so that what an individual can purchase and consume is, in many instances, more important than occupational status. If we accept that 'tradition' is ending, the individual thus becomes the bearer of many possibilities, and Tradition-bound rationality is replaced by deindustrialised role-playing with others in emphatic performances that may have no apparent meaning or purpose.

In all this, masculine identity has become problematic, with the 'yob' and the football fan perhaps standing as a root metaphor and symbol of many of the ills of society. The diagnosis for these ills varies depending on the practitioner, yet extremes of male behaviour are still at work in the City, in the police, in the media and in most other professions. The newly discredited male might therefore be seen as the fall-guy at the end of an era of what is somewhat myopically identified as a period of progress and reason; for, as the dissenting feminist voice of Rosalind Coward (1994) points out, the icon of the 'yob' *'is carrying the weight of masculinity which, for a variety of reasons, middle-class society finds increasingly unacceptable, and rhetorically dumps onto the men of the lower class. He is a classic scapegoat; lugging around the sins of our culture while the rest of us look sanctimoniously on.'*

Whereas the position of women used to be the corollary of the civil liberties enjoyed by men, and summed up in the phrase 'a man does, a woman is', the tendency in a stagnant society is to oppress and deny an open-ended possibility in masculinity, so that the scope of men to become something else by what they do is now the object of fear and loathing. Thus, in a society that has never before been so uncertain, many male characteristics have become an unwelcome reminder of past glories that, following the social changes that swept the Western world from the 1960s, now hold little kudos. In this situation, Coward's 'men of the lower class' can be narrowed down to the 'football hooligan', who is perhaps the most significant symbol that epitomises the disorganised society, a symbol that is reaffirmed, almost ritualistically, by condemnation and legislation.

The appearance of hooliganism coincided with the end of national service, and was thus part of an era of change, when horizons for young men altered dramatically. From 1963, young men were no longer conscripted into the military, and the State no longer planned their lives for three years, or controlled their bodies to the extent that it had the right to send them off to die. With the ending of empire and the 'civilising process' of imperialism, there was now no way to legitimise and applaud state-controlled violence. In the circumstances, it becomes almost ironic to reflect that compared to the way their forefathers conquered by pursuing mayhem, the acts of the hooligan pale into insignificance. Society might well refuse to condemn out of hand those young men who like to fight, and who prefer action as a substitute for thought. For the ability to be introspective is a luxury not available to many, and leaves us with a group who, in the past, have often been prepared to fight at great risk for what others define as 'evil'. And hooligans in one context can easily become 'our brave lads' (see The Falklands and the Gulf War expeditions), or cannon fodder (Kipling's 'Tommy Atkins'). Then again, with the growth in private security, those same sections of society who use the terms 'thug' and 'yob' so liberally might do well to realise that it is often those same young men with those same personal and physical proclivities that allow them to sleep so well at nights.

Football Hooligans: the Uncivilised?

Because the Leicester Centre make it central to their argument, we need to ask: has the structure of people's thinking and feeling changed over the last century, as the concept of the Civilising Process teaches us? As anthropology shows us, each culture by education 'civilises' into its own patterns of restraint, and each generation has its own 'barbarians'. But are there fewer people today involved in personal violence? And are we really 'choirboys' compared to our ancestors, as Elias (1978a) posited? Such a question even confuses the acolytes: so that Dunning *et al.* (1988: 212) writes *'the Civilising Process does not attempt to take account of social changes or nuances of "lived experience".'* We might ask then, where does this sit in relation to Elias's argument (1978b: 155) that human nature is changeable? For a fundamental question that springs from this assertion is to ask, what does being 'civilised' mean? Elias (1983: 111) offers us the following definition: *'Affective outbursts . . . are signs of weakness; the restraint of emotions, the curbing of affect, leads to a calculated and finely studied behaviour in dealing with others.'*

A wealth of ethnographic data, however, suggests that many illiterate peasants show just such qualities, even though they are not versed in the use of the handkerchief (Hobbs and Robins 1991). Are football hooligans the antithesis, then? Of course they are not: for they have to exhibit restraint and demonstrate competence in their interactions in order to conduct their performances. Inevitably, the impulsive would not last long in such an arena; for a degree of social competence is essential, and the 'loose cannon' would never survive for long in such company. Elias's mistake, then, is to associate cultural competence with personal hygiene, for the civilised person must be a bourgeois performer with various deceits and hypocrisies, as if *'wearing a mask is the essence of civility'* (Sennett 1977: 264). The virtues of civilisation are presumably corruption, duplicity and vice. Blades wear many such masks at different times of their lives. It would seem that the suppression of emotion is the acme of male civilisation, or that, as Freud (1963) would argue, civilisation is built on the renunciation of instinct. Yet across history, from the days of the Stoics onwards, we know that civilised restraint was often in vogue, and did not suddenly flower in the nineteenth century.

We might also ask, what has happened to this process now that the urban milieu is regarded today as the epitome of danger and all that is fearful; and why is it that these locales are seen to contain growing intolerance (not the least to those defined as hooligans)? This in turn raises further questions as to the true nature of citizenship and its opposition in the construct of being an 'incorporated' subject. It also queries the ideological growth of the free market and tolerance; and asks how to account for those who become disenfranchised in the process. Do we dismiss them as being uncivilised, because the very nature of poverty bars them from participating in those aspects of civility that bourgeois society has promised and continues to promise, though it continues to see massive discrepancies in wealth and social opportunity? If the test of a civilised society truly lies in the way it treats its weaker members, I contend that Britain is uncivilised, and moreover has become increasingly so since 1979, with the onset and development of the Tory-inspired 'free market' philosophies.

In the event, the process Elias proposes is interesting, but is a generalisation that anthropology cannot accept.[2] We therefore need to consider what degree of 'incorporation' differentiates the hooligan, because we are not told by the pundits. Putting it another way, we might ask who are the 'established', and who in reality are 'the outsiders' (see Van Stork and Wouters 1987). If, in the past fifteen years, we have truly seen a brutalisation of manners, be it in advertising, in screen depictions, and on both football and rugby pitches, then where stands the Civilising Process in the political ethos that promotes Individualism at all costs? What can we make of such a theory of class isolation? As Bourdieu (1984) noted, the lower-class culture argument implies an ethos so exclusive that it must presuppose no contact with middle-class agencies such as the school; this is an obvious absurdity.

The Eliasian construct ultimately proposes that those who commit violence at football matches are an uncivilised throwback in social evolution.[3] Yet the latter half of the twentieth century has seen 130 wars with 27 million dead, whilst the first eight decades of the century saw 99 million die in warfare – a figure twelve times greater than that for the previous century and twenty-two times that of the eighteenth century (Sivard 1989; Hobsbawm 1994). In the last decade further millions have died in wars waged against non-combatants by powerful regimes that have used everything from the euphemistic 'ethnic cleansing' to indiscriminate bombing and shelling of food markets and civilian housing. In the same years of the hooligan headlines we have read accounts and watched TV newsreels showing children starved to death, shot dead by soldiers and hacked to pieces in internecine disputes. We have felt impotent in the face of state torture, which remains commonplace in many areas whose heads of government are fêted and welcomed by our politicians and monarchy. Meanwhile, we are one of the largest exporters of weapons and tools of torture to many brutal regimes and silently accept the imprisonment of political dissidents and mass rape as a natural by-product of these conflicts. Yet our politicians, police and many commentators rage against the comparatively innocuous activities of football hooligans.

However, it is simply not the case that if men manifest violent behaviour in some contexts this will then permeate all they do. Groups are not so neatly monomorphic, and many men across many cultures value and respect physical violence, admire verbal aggression, and condone displays of a tough masculinity. Like the Blades, the majority express these values only in limited social contexts, so that not all receive the same level of opprobrium.[4]

Tribal Gatherings?

I would postulate that Blades are, to use Bauman's (1992: 198–9) term, a 'post-modern tribe'. In a similar vein, Maffesoli (1988, 1991) reasons that we live in a *neo-tribal world*, different from the original tribal idea because the neo-tribal is the product of individuals promoting self-identity and self-definition, and results in gatherings with little cohesion, structure, obligations, or rites of passage. Such tribes gather and are forever colliding with others, for their boundaries are vague and self-definition never ceases. Thus any attempt to define the tribe is somewhat futile, for it is not about satisfaction, but about display, style, experiences of emotion, and creating community. Such neo-tribes (e.g. Blades) are fluid, unstable and transient, and the numbers present depend on the attractiveness of the issue around which people gather. When the attraction wanes, members leave and such tribes can die. Open to all, the post-modern tribe allows individuals to construct their own meanings and to participate under their own conditions. Maffesoli's essential argument is that there is no agreed universal idea of 'Civil Society', and, thus, any attempt to define a homogeneous moral standard is impossible.

As Wirth (1938: 22) noted, urban dwellers seek to escape drudgery by *'creative self-expression'* in *'spontaneous group association'* or partisan spectating. Put more simply, Blades were 'Something Happening' and provided someone to enjoy time with, and from the late 1970s they expanded the event across the whole of Saturday, so that their socio-spatial possibilities became increasingly enriched. Blades – tolerant of incongruity and contradiction – were typical of urban group formations. As novelist Martin Amis (1989: 41), writing on the characteristics of urban life, stated, *'In a modern city, if you have nothing to do (and if you're not broke, and on the street), it's tough to find people to do nothing with.'* The city person has many selves, the urban landscape is forever 'throwing up new cultural personas' (see Mort 1988: 218; Sartre 1965).

We might seek parallels in the realms of anthropological ethnography. Geertz's (1972) account of the Balinese cock-fight seems to be appropriate here, for it seeks to interpret culture and derive meanings from events. Adopting Bentham's idea of 'deep play' (in which the stakes are so high it was irrational to engage in them), Geertz (1972: 450) argues the Balinese attend cock-fights to: *'find out what a man, usually composed, aloof, almost obsessively self-absorbed, a kind of moral autocosm, feels like when attacked, tormented, challenged, insulted . . .'*. These cock-fighters, I suggest, are comparable with Blades in the way symbols are used to derive meaning. In the Balinese case, the cockerel acts as a symbol of allegiance to the group (albeit, unlike the Blades, this is based in kinship), and so Geertz (1972: 443) is able to explain this incomprehensible pastime: *'[when] men go on allegorically humiliating one another and being allegorically humiliated . . . but no one's status really changes . . . All you can do is enjoy and savour, or suffer and withstand, the concocted sensation of drastic and momentary involvement along an aesthetic semblance of that ladder.'* A vast array of similar sensations is available to the hooligan participants. Moreover, the 'stakes' in football – unlike the cock-fight – include the potential danger of arrest, which may well bring a fine and/or physical restraint. As Geertz says, masculinity is one of the themes caught up here, and Blades particularly indulge in such 'deep play' to win masculine esteem and honour. They seek achievement in actions and pursuits that, even later the same day, or later in life, may come to be regarded as fruitless, ridiculous or even shameful. For the social self is not always consistent, and we should not forget that consciousness and subsequent interpretation of events can vary with the situation and the age of the actor.

Such 'play' is totemic, in that the group celebrates itself around the identity of Blades and Sheffield United. Whilst self-interest may have been included in the rhetoric of 'doing right' for the club's name, ultimately the gathering was a celebration of themselves. Significantly, as Harris (1989: 98) remarked, totemic groups exist because *'the greatest significance of being a "Crow" is being different from Eaglehawks'* (read: Blades and Owls). More-over, there were perhaps *two* Totems here, in the form of 'Sheffield United' and the 'Blades' – the latter an idealised, heroic pursuit of masculinity: an ideal type of what men should do or ought to do. The club, then, is them, and they are the club; the club, however, would always deny they want them.

The 'Meaning' of Being a Blade

Because there is no precise social or legal definition of 'hooligan', we need to examine the meaning for the participants. What it *means* to be a Blade is inherited, narrated, interpreted and enacted differently at the everyday level by constantly changing participants. And the social dramas they enact renew the desired values and norms the participants hold or aspire to. Such dramas achieve a 'communion' between disparate individuals as they pursue achievement and selfhood. The company of Blades therefore provides: emotional ties of shared ordeals, the pursuit of reputation, and a common theme of discussion. Blades create a comradeship of fellow fans, but are Janus-headed; for in-group friendship is linked to hostility to others. But who gets drawn into this association or the circumstances under which they meet – like the precise role of the 'enemy' – can vary considerably. Football hooligans exist largely through the arrangement of mirrors (see Simmel 1950) and the construction of what Cooley (1956) called the 'Looking-Glass Self', wherein they see themselves in the shape of their rivals.

With all this cultural background presented, and yet with research unable to find a neat equation as to what 'makes' the hooligan, analysis had to address more contemporary cultural theory, which concentrated on ideas of selection, experiment and 'lifestyle' in what Kellner (1992: 158) calls the freely-chosen game. What we can title the postmodernist's persona produces the person who is not a neat unified category (Shields 1992: 16). The individual then selects various groups and locations to spend time with, in effect playing with identity, selecting commodities and expressing opinions that may be contradictory and may exist independently of a person's socio-economic background.

The crucial concept in becoming a Blade is affiliation, and in particular the way the subject is converted to a style of behaviour that is novel to him but is established in others. Even here, however, there are problems: for how can the process of learning be combined with personality, which is a product of learning? Affiliation simply does not explain why some rob banks or fight at football matches and others do not. And whilst emphasising the social process of transmission, it also minimises the individual process of reception (see Sutherland and Cressey 1960). We therefore have to be sceptical of deterministic arguments that reduce the subject's capacity for choice, for creating meaning, or for taking self-control (see Matza 1969). Maybe we can accept the principle that, in the case of football hooligans, such delinquency is learned, in that men imitate others and always have done (see Tardé 1890). But the manifestations can change: basically, new criminal activity is grafted on to old patterns via what Tardé (ibid.) called 'Fashion', and is particularly prevalent in cities and amongst large crowds.

Thus the 'Differential Identification' theory of Daniel Glaser (1956) is applicable. This shifts emphasis away from membership groups towards *reference* groups, the essence of which is that the subject pursues behaviour to the extent of identifying with groups *real or imaginary*. This theory focuses attention on the individual's ability to rationalise his conduct in an arena of voluntary behaviour. It allows for purpose, meaning and choice, and stresses the importance of the vocabulary of motive. Crucially, it draws attention to the mass media, as Glaser (1956) states: *'Criminal identification may occur, for example, during direct experience in delinquent membership groups, through positive reference to criminal roles portrayed in the mass media, or as a negative reaction to forces opposed to crime.'* Being a Blade can thus be said to be an imaginary act of identification with symbolic others and ideals (see Glaser 1958; Strauss 1969: 64–9; Lacan 1977), allowing a young man to play with a self-image through the company he kept and the events they participated in. In such fantasies people can pursue *collective* activities they would probably consider repugnant if practised alone (Simmel 1957: 313), and in its performance the participants enjoyed the journey or voyage from superficiality into fantasy (see Campbell 1989; Bauman 1992). Blades were therefore everything they imagined they were, for in being a Blade the individual – to borrow from Barthes (1985: 255) – can be *'everything at once, without having to choose'*.

Football hooliganism was therefore the thing to do for many young men who sought risk and excitement. For the participants it was a fashion that some pursued longer than others. As Baudelaire (1964: 32) noted, fashion is the essence of Modernity, for the fashionable live in the *now*, and more importantly cannot offer explanations for their pursuits. Fashion is tied to dissatisfaction, which manifests itself in various ways. One is through imagination (Heller 1985: 304), so that consequently we see narcissistic and competitive displays (see Simmel 1950: 343) that have the aim of giving strength, providing reasons to be proud, and, at the same time, provoke envy, admiration and anger. Using items of consumption and engaging in certain activities allows participants to seek for an unknown, and to try to close the gap between imagined and experienced pleasures. The events surrounding hooliganism were essentially narcissistic, and in these pastimes Blades always had an eye on the 'other' – real or imagined. We can therefore consider Blades' role in an age obsessed by appearances and dominated by corporate image-management (see Langman 1992: 47), and see how the events they indulged in generated the cultivation of a range of 'looks' that in turn encouraged the 'show-off' (see Ehrenrech 1983; Bourdieu 1984). Such displays may well attract the chronically bored and those seeking instantaneous intimacy, which includes tens of thousands of young men the world over. These displays contained another element of fashion in the totemic garment, where participant consumption patterns purchased a cultural capital (see Bourdieu 1984) of style and knowledge (manifest in that ephemeral but understood concept known as 'attitude'). Blades could at some times of their performances feel grandiose, yet later on, or in other circumstances, might well realise true emptiness and inauthenticity.

Dupes, Dopes and Viruses

Football hooliganism has always provoked the media to a feeding frenzy, and its very presence has induced the ecstatic media to anticipate their next carefree headline. Blades always courted publicity and were never in favour of privacy. They played with the media, wanting publicity that stressed their notoriety, but despising the same media for their ability to get facts wrong or to moralise about them. Blades also understood how privacy allows for the unquestioning acceptance of state force, and they thus contested that idea. Consistently they raided the enforcers' rights and boundaries, thus provoking them to restore their visions of privacy. Consequently they were inadvertently influential in generating the use of greater force and the extension of state surveillance, as the controllers set out to illustrate just who held the reins of power. In a sense, then, the process mirrors Baudrillard's (1993) argument that, via the media, we anticipate an event, watch the images, become appalled, and so encourage the men in uniforms to dish out the punitive response as they set out to civilise the barbarians.

All of this media outpouring is not some state-supporting measure, for I contend that the different arms of the complex entity that is constituted by the broadcasting systems cannot truly be considered to be under the control of any right-wing state apparatus. Rather it is an entity that serves itself, and will do all it can to fit the hooligan within its orthodox views, and for its own ends. It is hypocritical when the circumstance demands: as when it hands over 'hooligan' footage to the police, but fights their requests for film of much more serious disorder because this has been defined as being 'political'. Then again, the media will occasionally even interview themselves or do their damnedest to set the scene for some easy and sensational copy, as when they go out and 'find the hooligan'. Nor is the media world troubled by inconsistency, for its singular self-interest will see it change sides to suit the headline or the moment. Finally, in what can be seen as clear evidence of its lack of involvement in capitalist state collusion, it can face accusations from political pundits when it under-reports what they feel are matters that might have been better presented in their favour.

Maybe the fundamental question raised here is 'what the press are about'? Primarily they are story-tellers, purveyors of myths and legends in a competitive business where success is judged in terms of sales and controversies. Police stories help set the media agenda, because they suit each group; and there exists a long history of media-induced belief that public disorder is manipulated by sinister forces. We also have to accept that the media have their own agenda, and by their targeting of issues can 'make' a problem. The media thus provide the news that fulfils the expectations they create, whether or not they actually elicit fulfilling behaviour. Their agenda-making role will continue to present a public with commentators whom we can term the 'opinionate', pontificating upon an issue they often know little or nothing about, but presenting it within established parameters, where clichés will serve as a substitute for analysis (see Hall 1978; Whannel 1979).

Then again, it might be argued that those measures that have been introduced against the football hooligan are a Machiavellian thrust that has been state-orchestrated, involving all the various parties. In this version of events, the encompassing measures would include expansions in police technology, growth in police establishments, and extension of legal powers by a government that knew it had public support to demonise the fans. This scenario would suggest that any police representation of the hooligan was part of a state-inspired expansion of coercion, and not just a matter of some local force or intelligence unit justifying its own activities. I would not give the police such a degree of political sophistication. At the level of the local state, Labour Councillors and MPs want hooliganism 'smashed', and allocate police resources to achieve this end. This, I would argue, contrary to Hall *et al.* (1978), was not done out of a desire to produce a new Authoritarianism or strengthen 'Capitalism', or to panic voters into right-wing attitudes. It was done out of a desire, as City Fathers, both to help their own political careers by showing concern about Sheffield's image and to reassure the more law-abiding citizens that someone was looking after their interests. As Phil Cohen (1979) has stated: '... *Labourism is the working-class politics of public propriety and conscience, and it is no coincidence that its spokesmen have always been in the vanguard of those advocating the strictest legal repression of "hooliganism", "juvenile crimes", and working-class youth cultures in general.*' (125)

We can see the elected members as reacting to public opinion stirred up by the media in the interest (in so far as they are 'manufacturing' news) of profits from circulation. Policies may change with personalities, but local or national Government (Capitalists or Socialists) are opportunist and often incompetent. I am not convinced there is any overall plan, however, and thus I part company from Hall *et al.'s* (1978) idea of a conspiracy between police, media, government and capitalism. The parallels between the two sets of responses to 'muggers' and 'football hooligans' suggest that 'the interests of capitalism' explain neither. What we have seen, I believe, is a highly complex situation full of misconceptions, producing unintended consequences for almost everyone.

Legislators and Interpreters

Confusingly, the police and the media have continued to promulgate an image of the parochial and bovine nature of the hooligan fans, while simultaneously consistently stressing the dynamic, sinister and universal threat that people like the Blades offer to society. So if the academic left has failed to understand hooligan culture, and the politics of the situation mean they are without a support group to give their side of events, we might ask – as Hall *et al.* (1978) did – who will stand between the hooligan and the law? The answer, which he clearly did not expect, seems to have been that, at times, the courts have done so – in the shape of the judiciary, the jury and the magistracy. For they have at times been the only locus for airing any contradictory version of events, and have been able to 'blow the whistle' and show some scepticism of police evidence and media representations (see Armstrong and Hobbs 1988).

Though one cannot deny that disorder in and around the grounds has caused death and injury, the police response has been disproportionate to the problem. Football hooliganism has legitimised promoting and extending the tactics and ideology of a pervasive and intrusive surveillance culture. Coercion by observation has historically been a means of controlling those identified as the dangerous classes, and though such procedures were previously restricted to prisons or madhouses, the football ground has become the late-twentieth-century 'place of need'. As a result the match has been subjected to Bentham's Panopticism (total surveillance of behaviour), to the extent that it has become zoned, numbered and partitioned. The major justification for these innovations relates not only to the public disgust that the spectacular displays of 'hooligan' aggression generate among the observers, but also to the everyday possibility that 'law-abiding citizens' might be caught up in the crossfire. Yet such instances are rare, and usually prompt equally vociferous expressions of moral outrage amongst the hooligan element as in media or police circles. As Gary Marx (1988: 57) has noted, the new surveillance culture is highly supportive of *'stage management and scripted scenarios'*. Aided by electronic evidence, computerised predictive profiles (often based on non-criminal data) financed by private business through the provision of electronic equipment, and the funding of police officers for overseas trips, and supported by various public relations and press releases, a picture is purveyed to the public of virtue fighting evil and combating the beast to save the family (ibid.: 134–5). The mute response allows police *carte blanche* to persist in their tactics. For the police officer, it is no longer a case of interpreting the actions of individuals as 'criminal' or otherwise, and thus promoting on-the-spot decision-making on the basis of experience or 'feel' for the occasion. CCTV invites the officer simply to respond to orders given from the cameras' console room, or if employed there to simply log images of public events for future interpretation by a more 'qualified' (superior) officer.

The law will define itself by claiming to defend a collective sentiment. But Blades themselves claim to identify with a wider idea of consensus, and to act within the boundaries of 'normal' behaviour; for they have their own ideas of normal and pathological hooliganism. In functionalist terms we might even say that their activities serve one useful purpose, for they allow young men to test the boundaries of the permissible. The State, in the shape of the police and judiciary, has for many years tried to narrow those opportunities, and consequently the Blades have learned the way the boundaries of tolerated behaviour can vary, sometimes formally, via court appearances, but often via police-dispensed informal justice. Whether these responses produced a better citizen in the long run is open to debate. However, few of the participants who feature in the data to follow went on to a life of violence and crime.

The various pieces of legislation and technological innovations and the way they were implemented were not effective in 'curing' hooliganism. Police might deny this and claim that they were, but Bauman's (1987) thesis suggests that the police are no longer using legislation to neutralise phenomena but are now *interpreters,* and use the most recent technology and surveillance techniques to watch the hooligans.

Consequently, the police consistently and publicly claim success for their intelligence systems, using what Manning (1988: 42) has called 'the backward glance', in which meanings are filtered through layers of perceptions and assumptions. Recordings of hooligans in action are produced by police as commodities to be sold and consumed. From the edited footage and skilful presentation that make up the police public relations exercise, we receive only a two-dimensional vision of what, inevitably, are always multi-dimensional scenarios; and these have an automatic bias in their imagery simply because the police have the power to control and choose the location and what to record and present. Seeking certainty, the organisation studies its environment, records what it requires, and presents this as a set of what Young (1993) describes as 'institutional truths'. And, as he points out (ibid.: 161): *'even knowing the thing is a constructed reality with overtones of fiction never makes the presentation less persuasive; for the audience is left with no alternative to put in its place. Indeed it is the drama, the theatrical modes, the metaphors and the extreme ritualism which . . . control how the public reads [these] mythological truths.'* As Douglas (1987: 92) notes, authoritarian institutions, like the police, can only think in terms that justify their own behaviour and actions, and will always ask for more control. Furthermore, police do not like people whose thinking goes against theirs. Thus, causation in this world is reducible to dupes, manipulated by leaders whom neither the police nor the media can capture. And no one is willing to entertain simple consideration of participant hedonism, vicarious pleasure, or the enjoyment of risk. And here lies an on-going ontological problem, in attempting somehow to represent to the non-participant those complexities of feeling and sensation that hooligan practitioners seek and sometimes enjoy. What is being prosecuted, then, is not violence *per se*, but the semiotics of 'reputation' and 'hardness' and a form of behaviour that is seen to pollute such sanctified market-driven ideals as 'the family', in which the spectacle of spectating must be stage-managed and vacuous, but 'fun'. In these new circumstances the police re-define hooliganism to encompass swearing and over-elaborate move-ments, and rely on the Blades and their like to provide material for arrests and hence for their consequent proclamations of 'success' in their 'war' against hooliganism.

Enemies Within: The Coming Contest

Since the 1980s successive political administrations have pursued the idea of an individualised, privatised, bourgeois mentality, and seem to find any collective gut display of cultural solidarity to be both incomprehensible and threatening. It seems not coincidental that police have pursued all-seater stadiums and encouraged family-unit participation, so that the traditional male football supporter with his heartfelt passions is confined to individual seating that destroys the old terrace locations, with their somewhat chaotic and heaving human discourse. Of course this mirrors the political denial of any collective activity with the potential to represent an alternative vision of how things might be. As intimated previously, such fans are disdainful of the legal process, never seeking the protection of the law in their jousts, which are governed by more subtle codes than those the law can operate. However, law is a universalistic and imperialistic code that does not allow partisan opposition to its demands.

What we have is a historical and hegemonic struggle about what sort of social dramas are to be allowed to occur in public spaces, and whose code of conduct will prevail. As New Age Travellers, Ravers, Pagans and other collective, non-commercial assemblies that remain relatively unpenetrated by state regulatory and bureaucratic controls have found, such social action is anathema to those holding the reins of authority. And like the participants in these demonised groups, those involved in the inherent social drama that accompanies partisan fanship are simply not willing to have their games bowdlerised and licensed for acceptable commercial consumption. We should all be wary of the consequences of the law and order society that has developed since 1979. The result, to borrow from Kohn (1994), is a police force that dresses like NATO and talks like Tesco. We can see how the overt growth in police public order tactics from the 1980s on is an example of 'Empire coming home', so that the colonial tradition of policing is now part of the domestic tactic. Thus the tactics normally associated with despised totalitarian regimes have become commonplace – mass surveillance, random searches, random photography, restriction of movement, undercover plain-clothes officers listening to conversations they define as conspiratorial, and show trials presented and accepted (tautology) by an unquestioning media.

Nirvana Postponed

The war against 'hooligans' has a long way to go, whatever their definition. Transgressing is more than ever an attraction in a post-industrial urban milieu where a devastated economy propels some to seek meaning in individualistic deviance that can border on nihilism. It could be argued that police resources over the past decade could have been put to better use than patrolling football matches. Between 1988 and 1992 the South Yorkshire Metropolitan Borough suffered some of the highest rises in crime statistics in Britain, according to Home Office-compiled figures. Readers of *The Star* learned (16 February 1992) that crime had risen 11 per cent over the previous year, with specific high rises in robbery (30 per cent), arson (20 per cent), and burglary (18 per cent). Perhaps as an indication of the state of the socio-economic situation in the region in the 1990s, crime rose by three times the national average in South Yorkshire in 1992/3. Home

Office statistics announced crime in the region was up by 13 per cent, with specific crimes accounted for as follows: robbery (up 39 per cent), theft (up 4 per cent), burglary (up 28 per cent), violence (up 4 per cent), car crime (up 13 per cent), criminal damage (up 9 per cent), and fraud and forgery (up 4 per cent). The only crimes that went down were those under the category of sexual offences (*The Star*, 5 November 1993). The only causal factor offered later in the year by the Head of South Yorkshire CID was that 70 per cent of crime was drug-related (*The Star*, 10 December 1993). Within a post-industrial culture, with the casualisation of labour and the end of careers, there has arisen a drug-induced nihilistic youth culture involved in random robbery and petty burglary in a drug-related entre-prenurial culture permeated by the practice of debt-settling by extreme violence. In this milieu police and politicians will have scenarios to deal with far more serious than any enacted by Blades and Owls.

There will still be disturbances at and around football matches. Com-mentators will continue to moralise and pontificate and drone on about what lessons can be learned from various events, and sociologists amongst others will attempt to give a rationale to what are frequently irrational events. In all this the rhetoric that speaks of preventing the hooligan victory will continue, as a self-appointed caucus of 'decent and polite society' sets out to run things its own way. However, in seeking to stop hooliganism, the forces of submission and control are engaged in a futile task, for two aspects of their quest seem to be impossible. First, their intention success-fully to counteract the ability of young men to gather together, to construct a category of an opponent in 'the other', and then to fight with this group is something of a pipe dream. And the second chimera – dependent on their success in achieving the first objective – is the utopian idea of creating a violence- and prejudice-free society. In the circumstances, the pursuit of civility (Sennett 1977: 265) and the search for a pacified utopia will find little comfort in the messages of history or the accumulated anthropological ethnographic record (see Cameron 1976; Thompson 1978; Baxter and Almagor 1978; Corfield 1982; McKnight 1986). And, it should be noted, those willing to fight the Owls in 1996 were just as numerous as ten years earlier. Those willing to fight 'Their Boys' still numbered in the hundreds when the necessity was required, albeit such gatherings were not weekly any more.

The fact of the matter is that human society does display aggressive instincts, and there is considerable evidence to support a belief that there is a capability of hostility in everyone, for across most of history life has been nasty, brutish and short for the majority. The 'wild man' (or 'stranger') of Hayden White (1978: 150–2) does not only exist 'out there', but inside each and every one of us. Moreover, as Holub (1992) argues, this prejudice needs defending. For no matter which epistemological viewpoint you take – whether this be based in some symbolic or hermeneutic framework – there always exists 'prejudgement'. Taken at a wider level then, this means you cannot overcome social difference by some smoothing technique, for there will always be the figure of 'the stranger' to be suspicious of, to be feared or contended with, and to hate. Men, I would suggest, will always seek out some classifiable 'higher purpose' to fight and die for; and there will always be young men who, when honour has been felt to be transgressed, take a punch and give two in return.

Notes

1. We can note from Werthman (1970: 141) and Gill (1977) how adolescents can choose to be in such company and create risks that assist in the definition of Self. This accords well with one of criminology's most underrated theories, Lofland's (1969) two routes to deviance. Thus, he argues, paralleling his Threat–Encapsulation–Closure theory sequence of the *defensive* act, there is a sequence of Adventure–Enchantment–Closure for the *adventurous* deviant. In their 'Adventure route to deviance', Lofland noted how psychologists argue that *'uncertainty, unpredictability, threat, fear, frustration, anxiety and the like, when felt to be manageable appear to be labelled by human beings as excitement, challenge, fun or adventure'*. The argument, expanded, is that once in a state of seeking excitement, the possible consequences of being hurt are either not considered or are defined in such a way as to add to the excitement.
2. Academics from a variety of disciplines have similarly criticised and ridiculed both the Civilising Process and its application to explaining football hooliganism. For some the Elisian theory is a fusion of untestable and descriptive generalisations (Rojek 1985; Horne and Jary 1987; Lash 1985) that never explains the discovery made by Dunning *et al.* of the 'rough' middle and upper-class hooligans. It is a theory that avoids the complexities and implications of evolutionism, and has an implicit ethnocentric bias. It is a theory that has, at its root, a dangerous dismissal of other societies as somehow barbaric or untutored (Robinson 1987; Mennell 1989: 230). Applied to football it does not seem, in any way, relevant to literature from Europe and South America (see Dal Largo

and DeBiasi 1994; Archetti and Romero 1994). Finally, the most recent critic of the Figurationists, Lewis (1996: 235), states that the theory is both historically inept, lurching from one absurd generalisation to the next when discussing pre-1914 England, and in an attempt to sustain the viability of the Civilising Process, evidence has been conveniently suited to fit Elias's theory.

3. By 1991 their 'Fieldwork Co-ordinator', John Williams, on whose 'participant-observation and reporting skills' (Dunning 1994) the Centre supposedly founded its theories, publicly 'rethought' his position (Williams 1991: 177–9). As he has accumulated the ethnographic data for the Leicester Centre, we can ask what happens when he changes his mind, and what becomes of the model and theory that his 'evidence' is supposed to have supported?

4. As Matza (1969) pointed out, those defined as 'delinquent' share the values of bourgeois culture, not only its individualism, but also its machismo cult of violence, its taste for conspicuous consumption, and its thirst for daring and adventure. Promoting ideas of individual choice over determinism, Matza argues that people 'drift into' or 'flirt with' deviant behaviour sporadically and then return to conventionality. Such a theory sees in male 'delinquent' gatherings a mutual misunderstanding, with an individual plagued by notions of 'masculinity', to the extent that with others like him he infers the 'correct' attitudes and behaviour from his peers. They, in turn however, infer motives and attitudes from his attempts to keep up with them, producing what Matza calls a 'comedy of errors'. From friends and the mass media the actor in these social processes learns both the techniques for committing crime and the 'techniques of neutralisation'.

Epilogue: May 1994 –May 1997

A win was vital in the fight against relegation. The opponents, Newcastle, equally needed a victory to ensure a place in European competition. They would bring 8,000 followers, and this was to be the last game for the John Street Stand and terracing, which were to be demolished in favour of a £5m state-of-the-art 7,000-seater stand complete with 31 'executive' boxes costing between £9,000 and £16,000 per season to hire.

Amongst the expectant fans were Blades who knew the renowned and respected rival mob would appear sooner or later. It was 2.20 p.m. when they did – on London Road – as a hundred Blades stood outside a pub drinking in the sun. Six rivals took the initiative and approached the Blades, and the two sides chatted under the watchful eye of both uniformed police and football intelligence officers, one of whom videoed the occasion whilst his Sheffield counterpart stood across the road from the Blades reciting the names of those present into a dictaphone.

Police presence meant hostilities were limited to mutual accusations of non-appearance and an agreement to sort the issue out after the match. A 2–0 victory in front of 30,000 produced a jubilant home following and later an equally jubilant visiting one, as defeats elsewhere ensured that they would be in Europe. As agreed, the visitors arrived on London Road ten minutes after the final whistle; but police on horseback, in vans and on foot with truncheons flailing prevented a hundred-a-side battle. Thwarted, the factions went their separate ways.

The next three years were turbulent at various levels. Despite the above-mentioned victory, United were relegated the following Saturday and remain in Division One. The manager was to leave, as was the Chairman, Reg Brealey, after a year-long campaign by fans to get him out. The John Street Stand was not built for two years, crowds plummeted, and the club was unable to pay wages at one point. Under a new Chairman, Sheffield United became a listing on the Stock Exchange in January 1997, and the share-index rating appeared on the score-board at home matches. With the all-seater stadiums came muted crowds, and, in response, exhortations over the tannoy from the clubs DJ to sing in support of the team and adverts in the club programme for fans with musical instruments to bring them to games in the aim of creating something resembling an 'atmosphere'.

Matters with the Owls came and went. A pre-season friendly between the two sides in August 1995 saw a peaceful afternoon, but a violent night. At 9.00 p.m. fifty Owls in a pub outside the city centre phoned a pub in the centre knowing that thirty Blades were in, inviting them to meet. A fleet of eight taxis took Blades to their appointment, and in the ensuing fracas one of the Owls received a slab of concrete on his head. Detained for 48 hours in hospital, he became a *cause célèbre* for the local media. *The Star*, reporting the incident, interviewed his parents; local TV did likewise. A year later *The Star* ran a story about him and the incident, again interviewing his parents. The Owl himself never spoke, nor did the journalists ever reveal that the same individual was the only person charged and fined over the fracas, after being captured on an off-licence video camera throwing bottles at Blades.

The enquiries police made following the fight included a dawn raid in which eight individuals were arrested. None were charged. The perpetrator was never found by police, but one Blade, annoyed at both being arrested and the nature of the assault on the Owl, hit the culprit in a pub weeks later.

Five months later another dawn raid got four Owls out of bed following a Blade–Owl fight in a city-centre pub on a Saturday night. Knowing the whereabouts of forty Blades, fifty Owls attacked the pub, but in the missile crossfire a party of young women suffered injuries. Three required stitches to wounds caused by flying glass, and others suffered shock. Two Owls also suffered flesh wounds caused by glasses held in Blade fists. Another victim of the Blades was allowed his say in the local press when a Blade received a six-month custodial sentence. He had been part of a Rugby League team from West Yorkshire on a stag-night in Sheffield; the twenty-strong group fought twenty Blades outside a pub, the end-product being one of the visitors requiring stitches to a nose wound caused by a beer glass and one semi-conscious Blade, the victim of a punch from the visitors. The Blade, slumped at the scene when police arrived, was arrested and charged with unlawful wounding. The injury was not his doing, but he considered a guilty plea would be looked on favourably by the court and result in a fine. His plea brought him a custodial sentence and, to add to his woes, his 'victim' was allowed to express his disgust in *The Star* at what he considered judicial leniency.

The Sheffield police were to receive more technology in their fight against the hooligan, though they found it convenient to lose technology when it suited them. A £200,000 city-centre Closed Circuit TV surveillance scheme was used for the first time by police to watch football supporters in Sheffield for the 1996 European Championships. For the same event police received new 'flame-proof' boiler suits and a new extendable baton. A new £900,000 helicopter saw the tournament as its unveiling and first task, and police publicised the 'photophone', which would allow pictures of hooligans to be transmitted around football grounds in seconds. The £½ m policing costs of the tournament were paid for by Sheffield taxpayers. In the same year the police banned United players from their traditional last-game-of-season celebration, wherein they would throw their team shirts to applauding fans, arguing that such an action could incite crowd problems.

Surveillance cameras became more pervasive, but, in what may be indicative of the future of the police-hooligan contest, Blades began to accommodate them into their scenarios. In one ludicrous incident in September 1996, forty police in five vehicles, armed with three surveillance cameras, arrived at a local league football match to prevent disorder between Blades and Owls. The three Blades on one of the teams knew nothing about the 'impending' fracas. Their team and all their vehicles were videoed, their car registration numbers taken, and all were escorted into the city centre by a police vehicle motorcade. This 'intelligence'-led exercise never made the local press; neither did a Blade fight with fans from a town that saw, for the first time ever, a young Blade visit on reconnaisance to ascertain where the town centre CCTV cameras were located, and suggest to Blades that they gather in a pub out of range of the cameras. Soon after the Blade–Owl vendetta resulted in six Blades visiting a pub on the outskirts of the city to settle an issue. The resulting fracas, whilst captured on the pub's CCTV, was conveniently 'lost' when the proprietor sold it to Blades.

In 1997 a TV drama-documentary told the story of the 1989 Hillsborough Disaster, which did not flatter the South Yorkshire police. Whilst officers in the force shared a £1.2m compensation payout for post-traumatic stress syndrome in May 1996 (each receiving an average of £90,000), the relatives of the dead had the funeral expenses covered. The documentary implied that CCTV tapes of the incident had conveniently been lost when police realised how incriminating they were. The inquest in 1990 heard police state the cameras were not working; but an electronics expert in charge of their maintenance stated they were. The tapes were found in April 1997, and were not 'faulty' as police claimed, but gave good images; the Hillsborough inquiry was re-opened in July 1997.

Football became an issue in party politics when Labour published its 'Football Charter' in 1996. Wanting to see a European-wide register established of known and suspected hooligans, it demonstrated an ignorance of *de facto* cross-border police practices. Its other main call was to have fan representatives on the board of each club. Months later the then Shadow Sports Minister confirmed that Labour would be prepared to look at plans to bring back standing areas to football grounds.

The pursuit of nirvana showed signs of faltering in the city and the region. Between 1993 and 1995 recorded juvenile crime rose by 77 per cent ,and detected crime fell from 45,000 cases in 1990 to 36,000 in 1994 (*The Star*, 19 March 1996). An overall rise in crime of 15 per cent occurred in 1993, which meant that over the fourteen years 1980–94 crime had risen 150 per cent, and between 1993 and 1994 violent attacks on police doubled. The following year ten people died in drug-related deaths as incidents of drug-dealing and robbery increased.

Blades still gathered in numbers and still fought when necessary, but not at the match. Many no longer attended, as admission prices increased and forms of carnivalesque behaviour were surveyed even more. At times a hundred and fifty would gather in pubs, minutes from Bramall Lane, only to watch their team on Satellite TV. Departing at the end to pursue Their Boys, they continued their ways in what must be considered a post-fan format. Not for them the media-induced hyperbole and hysteria around the game; they became detached; they loved the game, but knew a rip-off when they saw one. The future was interesting . . .

Appendix: The Team Line-Up – Blades

This network of 190 individuals was compiled on the way to an away match in April 1987. Personal details were obtained by speaking with individual Blades. Some Blades may in hindsight disagree as to whom they are linked with; for some new companions appeared shortly after, and disputes distanced former mates. But such issues are pedantic compared to the bigger issue that this Appendix aims to represent – namely that there was no cohesive or stable 'membership' of the Blades. Those researchers who hope to list and label a hooligan group have misunderstood the fluidity and anti-structure that such groups exist by. Had research sought a network a week or month later the table presented would not have been the same.

For clarity the various sub-groups (Column 1) have been divided alphabetically. All individuals have been given pseudonyms. Next to the 'names' is an 'M' signifying marriage or cohabitation. An asterisk (*) indicates whether the individual had been expelled or suspended from school (for whatever reason – insubordination, truancy, being a 'disruptive influence', or violent conduct). Column 3 indicates age on the day of the survey (April 1987). Column 4 is employment status, and abbreviations are used to indicate variables:

Community Programme (Comm. Prog.)   Unemployed (U/E)
Self-Employed (S/E)   Youth Training Scheme
                                       (Y.T.S.)

Where applicable, Column 5 represents criminal records, both football-related (F) and for crimes outside (O) the football context. The number of such charges is given in brackets. The various offences are abbreviated as follows:

Charges:
Actual Bodily Harm (ABH)   Malicious Wounding (MW)
Affray (A)   Possession of an Offensive
Assault on Police (AoP)   Weapon (POW)

Breach of The Peace (BofP)
Burglary (B)
Criminal Damage (CD)
Drink Driving (DKD)
Drunk and Disorderly (DD)
Fraud (F)
Grievous Bodily Harm (GBH)

Possession of Drugs (PofD)
Robbery (R)
Shoplifting(S)
Theft (T)
Threatening Behaviour (TB)
Unlawful Assembly (UA)

Custodial Sentences are similarly abbreviated:

Youth Custody (Y.C.)
Prison (P)
Detention Centre (D.C.)

No details adjacent to a name indicates no criminal record.

Sheffield Blades: BBC Blades

Group	Name	Age	Employment Status	Charges/Number/Sentence
A	Box	23	Storekeeper	(F) TB
	Vaughan	21	Y.T.S.	(O) ABH
	Nick	22	Comm. Prog.	
	Ross	22	Electrician	
	Eddy (M)	23	Bouncer	(O) 2 TB
	Shane (M)	22	Comm. Prog.	
	Oliver	22	Labourer	(O) DD
	Greg	21	Labourer	(F) POW
	Des	22	Shop Assistant	
	Bobby	22	Store Manager	
B	Boggy	19	Draughtsman	
	Dene (*)	22	Machinist	(O) ABH (Y.C.)
	Steve	19	Sales Assistant	
	Prince (*)	19	U/E	(F) 3 TB (O) TB
	Trier	18	Removals	
	Kav	19	Y.T.S.	
	Blue	19	Sales Assistant	(O) B
C	Gamble	20	Student	
	Ronnie	20	Accounts Clerk	
	Boston	19	Computer Operator	

Sheffield Blades: BBC Blades (*continued*)

Group	Name	Age	Employment Status	Charges/Number/Sentence
D	Bright (*)	26	'Roadie' (Pop band)	(F) TB
				(O) ABH (D.C.)
	Paul	24	Shop Assistant	
E	Gordon	22	Sales Rep.	(O) DD
	Declan	23	S/E Electrician	
	Titch (*)	18	Tanner	(F) TB
F	Jim	21	Machinist	(F) 2 TB
				(O) CD
	Mel	21	Machinist	(O) TB
	Jerry	20	Student	
	Jocky	21	Gardener	(O) T
	Martin	21	Estate Agent	(F) TB
	Adam	20	Office Clerk	(F) TB
G	Fats	26	Shopkeeper	(F) 4 TB
	Matt	25	S/E Carpenter	(F) TB
	Colin (M)	23	Shop Assistant	
H	Sid	21	Shop Manager	
	Beefy (*)	22	Labourer	(O) GBH (Y.C.)
	Timmy (*)	21	U/E	(F) 2TB
				(O) TB (D.C.)
	Boyle	21	Machinist	(O) DD
	Hank	20	Plant Operator	
I	Parker	20	Labourer	(F) 2 TB
				(O) T ABH
	Tuna	22	U/E	(F) 3 TB
				(O) B (Y.C.)
	Martin	25	Demolition Labourer	(O) DD
	Alan	27	Driver	(F) 2 TB
				(O) DD
	Tash	29	Scrap Dealer	
	Binzo (M)	31	Civil Servant	
J	Luke (*)	19	Labourer	(O) ABH (D.C.)
				(O) TB (O) A
	Pear (M) (*)	20	Farm Labourer	(F) TB
				(O) A

Sheffield Blades: BBC Blades (*continued*)

Group	Name	Age	Employment Status	Charges/Number/Sentence
	Darren (M)	26	S/E Labourer	(F) 2 TB
				(F) DD
				(O) DD
				(O) TB
K	Fagin (M) (*)	23	U/E	(O) MW (D.C.)
				(O) T (D.C.) (P)
	Dom	23	Labourer	(F) 3TB
				(O) TB (P)
				(O) B (P)
	Bobby (*)	23	Painter	(F) MW (Y.C.)
				(O) T
	Les	22	U/E	(O) 2 MW (P)
L	Len	28	Bricklayer	
	Ralph	22	Electrician	(O) ABH
				(O) T
				(O) AoP
M	Will	24	Carpenter	(O) ABH
	Jolly	23	Butcher	
N	Limit	22	U/E	(O) 2TB
				(O) T
				(O) B (P)
	Pinkie	22	U/E	
	Bernard	24	Labourer	(O) MW (D.C.)
				(O) B (Y.C.)
				(O) T
O	Jake (M)	24	Foreman Labourer	(F) 2 TB (D.C.)
				(O) DD
				(O) TB
				(O) ABH (Y.C.)
	Lez	24	Builder	(F) 3TB
P	Ray	23	Carpenter	(F) 2 TB
	Jeff	23	Sales Rep.	(F) TB
				(O) T
	Ade	23	Office Clerk	
	Sam	22	Shop Assistant	(O) DD

Sheffield Blades: BBC Blades (*continued*)

Group	Name	Age	Employment Status	Charges/Number/Sentence
Q	Tim (M)	23	Sales Rep	
	South	32	Coach Driver	(O) F (P)
	Dougie	24	Miner	(O) TB (P)
R	Barry (M)	28	S/E Electrician	(F) A
				(F) TB (P)
				(O) A (P)
	Marvin (M)	28	S/E Builder	
S	Wasp	28	Draughtsman	(F) TB
				(O) DD
	Lionel	26	Gardener	(F) TB
				(O) T
				(O) UA (P)
	Fish	26	Gardener	
U	Jack	21	Gym Instructor	
	Sam	21	Solicitor's Clerk	
	Bud	22	House Warden	(F) 3 TB
				(O) MW

Individuals

Name	Age	Employment Status	Charges/Number/Sentence
Taff	24	Youth Worker	(O) 2 DD
			(O) 2 TB
			(O) A (D.C.)
Rod	22	Labourer	(F) 2 TB
Dors (M)	22	Labourer	
Jade	25	Driver	(F) 3 TB
			(O) B
			(O) MW (Y.C.)
Mick	17	Shop Assistant	(F) TB
Billie	21	Y.T.S.	(F) 2 TB
			(O) F
Eyes (M)	25	Machinist	(F) DD
			(F) 2TB
			(O)

Old Lads

Name	Age	Employment Status	Charges/Number/Sentence
Tufty	31	Manager (S/E)	(F) TB
Daniel	27	Account Clerk	
Josh	27	Lift Engineer	
Adam	27	Office Clerk	
Lewis	27	Skilled Engineer	(F) B
Porky	27	Youth Worker/Student	(F) TB (P)
Red	26	S/E Heating Engineer	(F) TB
			(F) DD
Colly	27	S/E Bricklayer	(F) TB
			(O) TB
Reece	24	Student	(F) TB
Chuck	24	S/E Electrician	(F) TB
Callum	19	Mechanic	

'Suicide Squad'*

Name	Age	Employment Status	Charges/Number/Sentence
Brian	20	U/E	
Steve	21	Labourer	(F) 3 TB
			(O) DD
Shaun	22	U/E	(F) 3 DD
			(O) GBH (P)
Mick	20	U/E	(F) 2 DD
			(O) 3 DD
			(O) T
Lenny	20	Labourer	(F) TB
Jimmy (*)	20	Labourer	(F) TB
Ben	19	U/E	(O) 2 DD
Clive	22	U/E	(O) DD
Eric	19	U/E	(O) DD
Tim	20	U/E	(O) TB
Des	21	U/E	(F) DD
			(O) TB
Alex	21	U/E	(F) TB
Ray (*)	19	U/E	(F) DD

* This self-parodying description was taken by this group of Blades from the same neighbourhood in 1986 following an altercation they had been involved in with rival fans in Hull. Heavily outnumbered, they had stood their ground and, in admiration, a watching Blade laughingly referred to them in later discussions at the Suicide Squad. These Blades would occasionally chant 'Su-su-su-Suicide' when in pubs for the amusement of other Blades.

'Drug Squad'**

Name	Age	Employment Status	Charges/Number/Sentence
Kieran	28	U/E	(F) B
			(F) 2 PofD
			(F) T
Wally	26	Painter-Decorator	(F) TB
			(F) DD
			(F) T
Percy	24	Steelworker	(O) TB
Ally	26	Labourer	
Jocky	27	U/E	PofD

** The term 'Drug Squad' was a similar self-parody to 'Suicide Squad'. Renown for their penchant for smoking 'dope', this group of Blades (all from the same neighbourhood) even had T-shirts made celebrating their favourite vice.

Max's Coach Blades

Group	Name	Age	Employment Status	Charges/Number/Sentence
A	Clem	21	Sales Rep.	(O) B
	Roger	21	Glazier	
	Gregory	21	Tool Repairer	
	Finny	21	U/E	(O) S
B	Mick	22	Scrap Merchant	(O) B
				(O) A
	Shaun	22	Security Guard	(F) 2 TB
	Tom	23	U/E	(F) TB
	Tony	21	Steelworker	
C	Del	20	U/E	(O) DD
				(O) TB
	Andy	21	Joiner	(O) DD
				(O) TB
	Gary	21	Y.T.S.	(O) DD
				(O) TB
	Mike	21	Labourer	(O) DD
				(O) TB
	Simon	24	U/E	(O) ABH (P)
	Alan	22	Printer	
D	Binzo	19	U/E	
	Colin	21	Labourer	(O) ABH (D.C.)

Max's Coach Blades (*continued*)

Group	Name	Age	Employment Status	Charges/Number/Sentence
E	Melvin	26	Scaffolder	
	Chris	24	Labourer	
	Max	23	Steelworker	
	Den	26	Carpenter	(F) 2 TB
	Ade	23	Complaints Officer	
	Vernon	23	Hotel Waiter	
	Joe	22	Cook	
	Dave	21	Nursery Assistant	
	Fingers	23	Factory Labourer	
	Malcolm	21	Fitter	
F	Steve	20	Plasterer	(O) TB
				(O) T
	Les	19	Machinist	(O) TB
	Pete	21	Fitter	(O) TB
	Mac	21	Groundsman	(O) TB
				(O) CD
	Frannie	21	Miner	(O) TB
	Jay	18	Electrician	(O) T
	Willy	21	Miner	(O) B (P)
	Dominic	20	Painter	(F) TB
	Mike	21	Bricklayer	(O) T
	Foxy	18	Confectioner	(O) T
G	Nev (M)	26	Chef	(F) 3 TB
				(O) 8 DD
	Howie	24	Steelworker	(F) 2 TB
				(O) DD
	Pete	26	Sales Clerk	
	Graham	24	S/E Carpenter	
	Mick	22	Steelworker	(F) TB
				(O) TB

Villagers

Group	Name	Age	Employment Status	Charges/Number/Sentence
A	Tom	29	Labourer	(F) 2 TB
				(O) TB
				(O) DD
	Mark (M)	24	Miner	(F) TB
				(O) DD

Villagers (*continued*)

Group	Name	Age	Employment Status	Charges/Number/Sentence
	Herbie	24	Miner	(F) TB
	Bone	22	Scaffolder	
	Austin	24	Miner	(F) TB
	Ern	24	Miner	
	Des	22	S/E Mechanic	(F) TB
				(F) DD
				(O) TB
	Dennis	23	YTS	TB
	Pops	22	Mechanic	
	Smiler	24	Miner	TB
	Ginger	24	Steel Fixer	TB
				DD
B	Jemmy	24	Miner	(O) B
	Frazer	23	Miner	(O) DD
	Richard	24	Factory Hand	
	Danny	25	Miner	DKD (P)
				TB (P)
C	Mocky	23	Machinist	(O) TB
	Zak	24	Driver	DD
	Del	22	Gardener	(F) TB
	Arthur	19	YTS	

Rotherham Blades

Name	Age	Employment Status	Charges/Number/Sentence
Brett	28	S/E Driver	(F) 2 TB
			DD (P)
Willy	27	Gas Installation Engineer	(F) 2 TB
			(O) MW
Brian	28	S/E Labourer	Manslaughter (P)
Howard	24	Skilled Machinist	
Louis	28	S/E Builder/Decorator	(F) TB
			(F) DD
			PofD
Graham	24	Factory Assembly-Line Steward	
Roger	28	Coach Driver	
Marcus	28	Publican	(F) DD
Joey	22	University Student	

Rotherham Blades (*continued*)

Name	Age	Employment Status	Charges/Number/Sentence
Anton	24	Labourer	(F) TB
Lenny	27	S/E Hod-Carrier	(F) TB
Matty	28	S/E Excavating Driver	(O) DD
Tex	28	Manager of Building Firm	
Curly	24	Draughtsman	
Kevin	24	Technician	AoP (Assault on Police) (O)
			(F) TB
Boggy	25	Metal Dealer	(F) 2TB
Leonard	23	Carpenter	

Bibliography

Abrams, M. (1982) *Historical Sociology*. Open Books, Somerset.

Agar, M. (1980) *Professional Stranger*. Academic Press, New York.

Allan, J. (1989) *Bloody Casuals: Diary of a Football Hooligan*. Famedram, Glasgow.

Amis, M. (1989) *London Fields*. Penguin, Harmondsworth.

Appleby, A. (1991) Talk given to conference 'New Times for Football'. Birkbeck College, 10 March 1991.

Apter, M. (1982) *The Experience of Motivation: The Theory of Psychological Reversals*. Academic Press, London.

Archetti, E. P. (1992) 'Argentinian Football: A Ritual of Violence?' *The International Journal of the History of Sports*, 9 (2), pp. 209–35.

Archetti, E. P. and Romero, A. (1994) 'Death and Violence in Argentinian Football' in N. Bonney, R. Guilianotti and M. Hepworth (eds), *Football, Violence and Social Identity*. Routledge, London.

Armstrong, G. (1994) 'False Leeds: The Construction of Hooligan Confrontations', in R. Giulianotti and J. Williams (eds), *Game Without Frontiers*. Aldershot, Avebury.

Armstrong, G. and Harris, R. (1991) 'Football Hooliganism: Theory and Evidence'. *Sociological Review*, 39 (3) (August).

Armstrong, G. and Young, M. (1997) 'Legislators and Interpreters: The Law and Football Hooligans', in G. Armstrong and R. Giulianotti (eds), *Entering the Field: New Perspectives on World Football*. Berg, Oxford.

Atkinson, P. (1990) *The Ethnographic Imagination: Textual Constructions of Reality*. Routledge, London.

Bacon, F. (1985[1625]) *The Essayes or Counsels, Civill and Morall, of Francis Lo. Verulam, Viscount St. Alban*, in John Pitcher (ed.), 1. *Of Truth*. Penguin, Harmondsworth.

Bailey, F. (1969) *Strategems and Spoils: A Social Anthropology of Politics*. Blackwell, Oxford.

Bailly, A. S. (1986) 'Subjective Distances and Spatial Representations'. *Geoforum* 17: 1, IV pp. 81–8.

Bakhtin, M. (1984) *Rabelais and His World*. Midland, London.

Baldwin, J. and Bottoms, A. E. (1976) *The Urban Criminal: A Study in Sheffield*. Tavistock, London.

Bale, J. (1982) *Sport and Place: A Geography of Sport in England, Scotland and Wales*. Hurst, London.

Baritz, P. (1965) *The Servants of Power*. Wiley, New York.

Barthes, R. (1975) *The Pleasure of the Text*. Hill and Wang, New York.

Barthes, R. (1985) *The Fashion System*. Cape, London.

Baudelaire, C. (1964) *The Painter of Modern Life and Other Essays*. Phaidon Press, London.

Baudrillard, J. (1988) 'Selected Writings', ed. M. Poster. Polity, Cambridge.

Baudrillard, J. (1993) *The Transparency of Evil. Essays in Extreme Phenomena*. Verso, London.

Bauman, Z. (1987) *Legislators and Interpretors: On Modernity, Post-Modernity and Intellectuals*. Polity, Oxford.

Bauman, Z. (1992) *Intimations of Postmodernity*. Routledge, London.

Baxter, P. T. W. and Almagor, U. (eds) (1978) *Age, Generation and Time: Some Features of East African Age Organisations*. Hurst, London.

Bean, J. D. (1983) *The Sheffield Gang Wars*. City Libraries Publications, Sheffield.

Bean, J. P. (1987) *Crime in Sheffield: From Deer Poachers to Gangsters, 1300 to 1990s*. Sheffield City Libraries Publications, Sheffield.

Beck, U. (1992) *Risk Society. Towards a New Modernity*. Sage, London.

Becker, H. (1963) *Outsiders – Studies in the Sociology of Deviance*. Free Press, New York.

Becker, H. (1967) 'Whose Side Are We On?' *Social Problems*, 14 pp. 239–47.

Bellah, R., Madsen, R., Sullivan, W., Swidler, A. and Tipton, S. M. (1985) *Habits of the Heart*. Hutchinson, London.

Bloch, H. A. and Neidershoffer, A. (1958) *The Gang: A Study in Adolescent Behaviour*. Philosophical Library, New York.

Boissevain, J. (1974) *Friends of Friends: Networks, Manipulators and Coalitions*. Blackwell, Oxford.

Bourdieu, P. (1977) *Outline of a Theory of Practice*. Cambridge University Press, Cambridge.

Bourdieu, P. (1979) *Algeria 1960*. Cambridge University Press, Cambridge.

Bourdieu, P. (1984) *Distinction: A Social Critique of the Judgement of Taste*. Routledge, London.

Bourdieu, P. and Passeron J. C. (1977) *Reproduction in Education, Society and Culture*. Sage, London.

Braithwaite, J. (1989) *Crime, Shame and Reintegration*. Cambridge University Press, Cambridge.

Brandes, S. (1987) 'Reflections on Honour and Shame in the Mediterranean', in Gilmore (ed.), *Honour and Shame and the Unity of the Mediterranean*. American Anthropological Association, Washington, DC.

Brewer, J. and Styles, J. (1980) *An Ungovernable People: The English and Their Law in the Seventeenth and Eighteenth Centuries*. Hutchinson, London.

Brimson, D. and Brimson, E. (1996a) *Everywhere We Go. Behind the Matchday Madness*. Headline, London.

Brimson, D. and Brimson, E. (1996b) *England, My England. The Trouble with the National Football Team*. Headline, London.

Brittan, A. (1989) *Masculinity and Power*. Blackwell, Oxford.

Brogden, M. (1982) *The Police: Autonomy and Consent*. Academic Press, London.

Bromberger, C. (1994) 'Football Passion and the World Cup: Why So Much Sound and Fury?', in J. Sugden and A. Tomlinson (eds), *Hosts and Champions: Soccer Cultures, National Identities and the USA World Cup Arena*. Avebury, Aldershot.

Bromberger, C., Hayot, A. and Mariottini, J. M. (1993a) 'Fireworks and the Ass', in S. Redhead (ed.), *The Passion and the Fashion*. Avebury, Aldershot.

Bromberger, C., Hayot, A. and Mariottini, J. M. (1993b) '"Allez L'o.m., Forza Juve": The Passion for Football in Marseille and Turin', in S. Redhead (ed.), *The Passion and The Fashion*. Avebury, Aldershot.

Brownlow, J. (1980) 'The South Yorkshire Steel Strike'. *Police Federation Magazine* June 1.

Bruyn, S. (1966) *The Human Perspective: The Methodology of Participant-Observation*. Prentice Hall, Englewood Cliffs, New Jersey.

Buckatzsh, E. J. (1950) 'Origins of Immigrants into Sheffield 1624–1799'. *Economic History Review*, 2nd Series, 2 (3) , pp. 303–6.

Buford, B. (1991) *Among the Thugs*. Secker and Warburg, London.

Burke, P. (1978) *Popular Culture in Early Modern Europe*. University Press, New York.

Burns, R. (1991) 'The City As Not London', in M. Fisher and U. Owen (eds), *Whose Cities?*. Penguin, Harmondsworth.

Cameron, A. (1976) *Circus Factions: Blues and Greens at Rome and Byzantium*. Clarendon Press, Oxford.

Campbell, C. (1989) *The Romantic Ethic and the Spirit of Modern Consumerism*. Basil Blackwell, Oxford.

Campbell, J. (1964) *Honour, Family, and Patronage*. Oxford University Press, Oxford.

Canter D., Comber, M. and Uzzell, D. L. (1989) *Football In Its Place*. Routledge, London.

Chambers, I. (1986) *Popular Culture: The Metropolitan Experience*. Routledge, London.

Chaney, D. (1993) *Fictions of Collective Life: Public Drama in Late Modern Culture*. Routledge, London.

Clareborough, D. (1989) *Sheffield United: The First 100 Years*. Sheffield United Publications, Sheffield.

Clarke, A. (1992) 'Figuring a Brighter Future', in E. Dunning and C. Rojek (eds), *Sport and Leisure in the Civilising Process*. Macmillan, London.

Clarke, J. (1976) 'The Skinheads and the Magical Recovery of Community', in S. Hall and T. Jefferson (eds), *Resistance Through Rituals*. Hutchinson, London.

Clarke, J. (1978) 'Football and Working-Class Fans: Tradition and Change', in R. Ingham (ed.), *Football Hooligans The Wider Context*. Inter-Action Imprint, London.

Clifford, J. and Marcus, G. E. (1986) *Writing Culture – The Poetics and Politics of Ethnography*. University of California Press, Berkeley, CA.

Cloward, R. and Ohlin, L. (1960) *Delinquency and Opportunity: A Theory of Delinquent Gangs*. The Free Press, New York.

Cockerill, A. W. (1957) *Sir Percy Sillitoe: The Biography of the Former Head of M.I.5*. W. H. Allen, London.

Coffield, F., Borrill, C. and Marshall, S. (1986) *Growing Up at the Margins: Young Adults in the North East*. Open University Press, Milton Keynes.

Cohen, A. (1974) *Two Dimensional Man*. Routledge and Kegan Paul, London.

Cohen, A. K. (1955) *Delinquent Boys – The Subculture of the Gang*. Collier-Macmillan, London.

Cohen, A. P. (1994) *Self Consciousness: An Alternative Anthropology of Identity*. Routledge, London.

Cohen, P. (1972) 'Working-Class Youth Cultures in East London'. Working Papers in Cultural Studies, 2. Birmingham University, Birmingham.

Cohen, P. (1979) 'Policing the Working Class City', in B. Fine, B. Kinsey, J. Lea, S. Picciotta and J Young (eds), *Capitalism and the Rule of Law. From Deviancy Theory to Marxism*. Hutchinson, London.

Cohen, P. and Robins, D. (1978) *Knuckle Sandwich: Growing Up in the Working-Class City*. Penguin, Harmondsworth.

Cohen S. and Taylor L. (1992) *Escape Attempts. The Theory and Practise of Resistance to Everyday Life*. Routledge, London.

Cooley, C. H. (1956) *Human Nature and the Social Order*. The Free Press, Glencoe, IL.

Corfield, P. J. (1982) *The Impact of English Towns*. Oxford University Press, Oxford.

Cornwall, A. and Lindisfarne, N. (eds) (1994) *Dislocating Masculinity: Comparative Ethnographies*. Routledge, London.

Coward, R. (1994) 'Whipping Boys'. *The Guardian* (September 3).

Cressey, D. (1962) 'Role Theory, Differential Association Theory and Compulsive Crime', in A. Rose (ed.), *Human Behaviour and Social Processes*. New York.

Critcher, C. (1979) 'Football Since the War', in J. Clarke *et al.*, *Working Class Culture: Studies in History and Theory*. Hutchinson, London.

Cunningham, H. (1980) *Leisure in the Industrial Revolution*. Croom Helm, London.

DalLargo, A. and Debiasi, R. (1994) 'The Social Identity of Football Fans in Italy', in R. Guilianotti, N. Bonney and M. Hepworth (eds), *Football, Violence and Social Identity*. Routledge, London.

Damer, S. (1974) 'Wine Alley: The Sociology of a Dreadful Enclosure'. *Sociological Review*, 22 (4).

Damer, S. (1992) *Last Exit to Blackhill: The Stigmatisation of a Glasgow Housing Scheme*, Discussion Paper No. 37. Centre for Housing Research, University of Glasgow.

Davey, R. (1983) *Pubs and People Around Sheffield*. Neil Richardson, Swinton, Manchester.

Davis, J. (1977) *The People of the Mediterranean: An Essay in Comparative Social Anthropology*. Routledge and Kegan Paul, London.

De Certeau, M. (1984) *The Practise of Everyday Life*. University of California Press, Berkeley, CA.

Donnelly, F. K. and Baxter, J. L. (1976) 'Sheffield and the English Revolutionary Tradition, 1791–1820', in S. Pollard and C. Holmes (eds), *Essays in the Economic and Social History of South Yorkshire*. South Yorkshire County Council, Barnsley.

Douglas, M. (1966) *Purity and Danger: An Analysis of Concepts of Pollution and Taboo*. Penguin, Harmondsworth.

Douglas, M. (1987) *How Institutions Think*. Routledge and Kegan Paul, London.

Downes, D. (1966) *The Delinquent Solution*. Routledge and Kegan Paul, London.

Dunning, E. (1994) 'The Social Roots of Football Hooliganism: A Reply to the Critics of "The Leicester School"', in N. Bonney, R. Giulanotti, M. Hepworth (eds), *Football, Violence and Social Identity*. Routledge, London.

Dunning, E., Williams, J. and Murphy, P. (1984) *Hooligans Abroad: The Behaviour and Control of English Fans in Continental Europe*. Routledge, London.

Dunning, E., Williams, J. and Murphy, P. J. (1987) *The Social Roots of Football Hooliganism*. Routledge, London.

Dunning, E., Murphy, P. and Williams, J. (1988) 'Soccer Crowd Disorder and the Press: Processes of Amplification and Deamplification in Historical Perspective'. *Theory Culture and Society*, 5, pp. 645–73.

Dunning, E., Murphy, P. and Waddington, I. (1991) 'Anthropological versus Sociological Approaches to the Study of Soccer Hooliganism: Some Critical Notes'. *Sociological Review*, 39 (3).

Eco, U. (1984) 'The Frames of Comic "Freedom"', in U. Eco, V. Ivanavov and M. Rector (eds), *Carnival!* Morton, New York.

Eco, U. (1986) *Travels in Hyper-Reality*. Picador, London.

Ehrenrech, B. (1983) *The Hearts of Men*. Pluto, London.

Elias, N. (1978a) *What is Sociology?* Hutchinson, London.

Elias, N. (1978b) *The Civilising Process: The History of Manners*. Basil Blackwell, Oxford.

Elias, N. (1982) *The Civilising Process: Power And Civility*, Vol. 2. Pantheon Books, New York.

Elias, N. (1983) *The Court Society*. Blackwell, Oxford.

Elias, N. and Dunning, E. (1986*) Quest for Excitement: Sport and Leisure in the Civilising Process*. Basil Blackwell, Oxford.

Elias, N. and Scotson, J. L. (1965) *The Established and the Outsiders*. Frank Cass, London.

Elms, R. (1989) *In Search of the Crack*. Penguin, Harmondsworth.

Engels, F. (1892) *The Condition of the English Working Class in England in 1844*. Allen and Unwin, London.

Erikson, K. (1962) 'Notes on the Sociology of Deviance'. *Social Problems*, 9 (4), pp. 307–14.

Evans-Pritchard, E. (1951) *Social Anthropology*. Routledge and Kegan Paul, London.

Farnworth (1982) *Wednesday!* Sheffield City Libraries, Sheffield.

Featherstone, M. (1991) *Consumer Culture and Postmodernism*. Sage, London.

Feldman, A. (1993) *Formations of Violence: The Narrative of the Body and Political Terror in Northern Ireland*. University of Chicago Press, Chicago, IL.

Fine, R. and Millar, R. (1985) *Policing the Miners' Strike*. Lawrence and Wishart, London.

Finn, G. (1994) 'Football Violence: A Societal Psychological Perspective', in N. Bonney, R. Giulianotti and M. Hepworth (eds), *Football Violence and Social Identity*. Routledge, London.

Fishwick, N. (1986) *From Clegg to Clegg House: The Official Centenary of The Sheffield and Hallamshire County Football Association 1886–1986*. The Sheffield and Hallamshire County Football Association, Sheffield.

Fishwick, N. (1989) *English Football and Society 1910–50*. Manchester University Press, Manchester.

Fiske, J. (1993) *Power Plays Power Works*. Verso, London.

Foucault, M. (1970) *The Order of Things: An Archaeology of the Human Sciences*. Pantheon Books, New York.

Foucault, M. (1977) *Discipline and Punish: The Birth of the Prison*. Pantheon, New York.

Foucault, M. (1979) 'On Governmentality'. *Ideology and Consciousness*, 6, pp. 5–21.

Freud, S. (1963) *Civilisation and Its Discontents*. Hogarth Press, London.

Friedrichs, P. (1977) *Agrarian Revolts in a Mexican Village*. University of Chicago Press, Chicago, IL.

Garfinkel, H. (1956) 'Conditions of Successful Degradation Ceremonies'. *American Journal of Sociology*, 61, pp. 420–4.

Garvin, J. L. (1932) *The Life of Joseph Chamberlain*, Vol. 1. Macmillan, London.

Gaskell, G. and Benwick, R. (1987) *The Crowd in Contemporary Britain*. Sage, London.

Gaskell, M. S. (1976) 'Sheffield City Council and the Development of Suburban Areas Prior to World War I', in S. Pollard and C. Holmes (eds), *Essays in the Economic and Social History of South Yorkshire*. South Yorkshire County Council, Barnsley.

Geary, R. (1985) *Policing Industrial Disputes: 1893–1985*. Cambridge University Press, Cambridge.

Geertz, C. (1966) 'Person, Time and Conduct in Bali'. *Cultural Report, Series No. 14. South-East Asian Studies*. Yale University, New Haven.

Geertz, C. (1972) 'Deep Play: Notes on the Balinese Cockfight'. *Daedalus*, 101, pp. 1–28.

Geertz, C. (1975) 'Thick Descriptions: Towards an Interpretive Theory of Culture' in *The Interpretation of Cultures*. Hutchinson, London.

Giddens, A. (1984) *The Constitution of Society: Outline of the Theory of Structuration*. Polity Press, Oxford.

Giddens, A. (1991) *Modernity and Self-Identity: Self and Society in the Late Modern Age*. Polity, Oxford.

Gill, O. (1977) *Luke Street: Housing Policy: Conflict and the Creation of a Delinquent Area*. Macmillan, London.

Gilmore, D. (1977) (ed.) 'Honour and Shame and the Unity of the Mediterranean'. *American Anthropological Association*, No. 22. Washington, DC.

Giulianotti, R. (1991a) 'Scotland's Tartan Army in Italy: The Case for the Carnivalesque'. *Sociological Review*, 39, pp. 503–27.

Giulianotti, R. (1991b) 'Keep it in the Family: An Outline of Hibs Casuals' Social Ontology', in R. Giulianotti and J. Williams (eds), *Game Without Frontiers*. Avebury, Aldershot.

Giulianotti, R. (1993) 'Soccer Casuals as Cultural Intermediaries: The Politics of Scottish Style', in S. Redhead (ed.), *The Passion and the Fashion*. Gower, London.

Glaser, D. (1956) 'Criminal Theories and Behaviour Images'. *American Journal of Sociology*, 61, pp. 433–44.

Glaser, D. (1958) 'The Sociological Approach to Crime and Correction'. *Law and Contemporary Problems*, 23 (4), pp. 685–93.

Gluckman, M. (1963) *Order and Rebellion in Tribal Africa*. Cohen and West, London.

Goffman, E. (1959) *The Presentation of Self in Everyday Life*. Penguin, Harmondsworth.

Goffman, E. (1967) *Interaction Ritual: Essays on Face-to-Face Behaviour*. Doubleday Anchor, New York.

Goffman, E. (1971) *Relations in Public: Microstudies of the Public Order*. Allen Lane, London.

Goffman, E. (1975) *Frame Analysis: An Essay on the Organisation of Experience*. Penguin, Harmondsworth.

Golby, J. M. and Purdue, A. W. (1984) *The Civilisation of the Crowd: Popular Culture in England 1750–1900*. Batsford Academic and Educational, London.

Graef, R. (1989) *Talking Blues: The Police in Their Own Words*. Fontana, London.

Guttmann, A. (1986) *Sports Spectators*. Columbia University Press, New York.

Habermas, J. (1976) *Legitimation Crisis*. Heinemann, London.

Hall, S. (1978) 'The Treatment of Football Hooliganism in the Press', in R. Ingham et al., *Football Hooliganism: The Wider Context*. Inter-Action Imprint, London.

Hall, S., Clarke, S., Critcher, C., Jefferson, T. and Roberts, B. (eds) (1978) *Policing the Crisis: Mugging, the State, and Law and Order*. Macmillan, London.

Hampton, W. A. (1970) *Democracy and Community: A Study of Politics in Sheffield*. Oxford University Press, London.

Harrington Report (1968) *A Preliminary Report on Soccer Hooliganism*, Chairman R. Harrington. Wright and Sons, Bristol.

Harris, R. (1989) 'Anthropological Views on Violence in Northern Ireland', in Y. Alexander and A. O'Day (eds), *Ireland's Terrrorist Trauma: Interdisciplinary Perceptions*. Harvester-Wheatsheaf, London.

Hartung, F. (1965) *Crime, Law and Society*. Wayne State University Press, Detroit, MI.

Hebdige, D. (1979) *Sub-Culture, the Meaning of Style*. Methuen, London.

Hebdige, D. (1988) *Hiding in the Light: On Images and Things*. Routledge, London.

Heller, A. (1985) *The Power of Shame*. Routledge, London.

Hey, D. G. (1976) 'The Changing Pattern of Non-Conformity, 1660–1851', in S. Pollard and C. Holmes (eds), *Essays in the Economic and Social History of South Yorkshire*. South Yorkshire County Council, Barnsley.

Hill, C. (1988) *A Turbulent, Seditious, and Factious People: John Bunyan and His Church*. Clarendon Press, Oxford.

Hills, G. (1991) 'Whatever Happened to the Likely Lads'. *The Face*, 2 (39), pp. 71–6.

Hobbs, D. (1989) *Doing the Business. Entrepreneurship: The Working Class and Detectives in the East End of London*. Oxford University Press, Oxford.

Hobbs, D. and Robins, D. (1991) '"The Boy Done Food": Football Violence, Change and Continuities'. *Sociological Review*, 39 (3), pp. 489–502.

Hobsbawm, E. 1994) *The Age of Extremes: The Short Twentieth Century 1914–91*. Michael Joseph, London.

Holdaway, S. (1983) *Inside the British Police*. Edward Arnold, London.

Holt, R. (1986) 'Working-Class Football and the City: The Problem of Continuity'. *British Journal of Sports History*, 3.

Holt, R. (1989) *Sport and the British*. Oxford University Press, Oxford.

Holub, R. (1992) *Antonio Gramsci: Beyond Marxism and Postmodernism*. Routledge, London.

Home Affairs Committee (1990) *Policing Football Hooliganism: Memoranda of Evidence*. HMSO, London.

Home Affairs Committee (1991) *Policing Football Hooliganism: Final Report*. HMSO, London.

Hopcraft, A. (1968) *The Football Man*. Penguin, Harmondsworth.

Horne, J. and Jary, D. (1987) 'The Figurational Sociology of Sport and Leisure of Elias and Dunning: An Exposition and a Critique', in J. Horne, D. Jary and A. Tomlinson (eds), *Sport Leisure and Social Relations. Sociological Review Monograph 33*. Routledge, London.

Howard, N. P. (1976) 'Cooling the Heat. A History of the Rise of Trade Unionism in the South Yorkshire Iron and Steel Industry, from the Origins to the First World War', in S. Pollard and C. Holmes (eds), *Essays in the Economic and Social History of South Yorkshire*. South Yorkshire County Council, Barnsley.

Huizinga, J. (1955) *Homo Ludens: A Study of the Play Element in Culture*. Beacon Press, Boston.

Humphrey, L. (1970) *Tea-Room Trade: Impersonal Sex in Public Places*. Aldine, Chicago, IL.

Humphries, S. and Gordon, P. (1994) *Forbidden Britain*. Testimony, Bristol.

Hunt, A. (1956) 'The Morphology and Growth of Sheffield', in D. L. Linton (ed.), *Sheffield and Its Region: A Scientific and Historical Survey*, British Association for the Advancement of Science. Sunley, Sheffield.

Hutchinson, J. (1975) 'Some Aspects of Football Crowds Before 1914', in *Conference Papers. The Working Class and Leisure*. University of Sussex, Brighton.

Huxley, A. (1954) *The Doors of Perception*. Chatto and Windus, London.

Inkster, I. (1976) 'Culture, Institutions and Urbanity: The Itinerant Science Lecturer in Sheffield 1790–1850', in S. Pollard and C. Holmes (eds), *Essays in the Economic and Social History of South Yorkshire*. South Yorkshire County Council, Barnsley.

Ivanov, V. V. (1984) 'The Semiotic Theory of Carnival as the Inversion of Bipolar Opposites', in T. A. Seabrook (ed.), *Carnival*. Morton, New York.

Jackson, B. and Wardle, T. (1986) *The Battle for Orgreave*. Vanson, Brighton.

Jones, S. (1988) *Sport, Politics and the Working Class: Organised Labour and Sport in Inter-War Britain*. Manchester University Press, Manchester.

Katz, J. (1988) *Seductions of Crime*. Basic Books, New York.

Kellner, D. (1992) 'Popular Culture and the Construction of Postmodern Identities', in S. Lash and J. Friedman (eds), *Modernity and Identity*. Blackwell, Oxford.

Kerr, J. H. (1994) *Understanding Soccer Hooliganism*. Open University Press, Buckingham.

King, J. (1996) *The Football Factory*. Cape, London.

Kitsuse, J. (1962) 'Societal Reaction to Deviant Behaviour'. *Social Problems*, 9 (3), pp. 247–56.

Klapp, O. E. (1969) *The Collective Search for Identity*. Holt, Rinehart and Winston, New York.

Klein, M. W. and Crawford, L. Y. (1967) 'Groups, Gangs and Cohesiveness'. *Journal of Juvenile Crime and Delinquency*, 4, pp. 63–75.

Knightley, P. (1975) *The First Casualty*. Deutsch, London.

Kohn, M. (1994) 'Trouble with Funny Hats' – Interview in *Sunday Review* of *Making the Peace. Public Order and Public Securities in Modern Britain* by C. Townshend. Open University Press, Milton Keynes.

Lacan, J. (1977) *The Four Fundamental Concepts of Psychoanalysis*. Penguin, Harmondsworth.

Langman, L. (1992) 'Neon Cages. Shopping for Subjectivity', in R. Shields (ed.), *Lifestyle Shopping: The Subject of Consumption*. Routledge and Kegan Paul, London.

Lash, C. (1978) *The Culture of Narcissism: American Life in an Age of Diminishing Expectations*. Norton, New York.

Lash, S. (1985) 'Historical Sociology and the Myth of Maturity: Norbert Elias's "Very Simple Formula"'. *Theory and Society*, 14 (5), pp. 705–20.

Lasch, S. (1990) *Sociology of Postmodernism*. Routledge, London.

Leach, E. (1954) *Political Systems of Highland Burma*. Bell, London.

Lefebre, H. (1991) *The Production of Space*. Blackwell, Cambridge, MA.

Levi-Strauss, C. (1966) *The Savage Mind*. Weidenfeld and Nicolson, Condor.

Lewis, R. W. (1996) 'Football Hooligans in England before 1914: A Critique of the Dunning Thesis'. *International Journal of the History of Sport*, 13 (3), pp. 310–39.

Lofland, J. (1969) *Deviance and Identity*. Prentice-Hall, Englewood Cliffs, NJ.

Lukes, S. (1972) *Power: A Radical View*. Methuen, London.

Lutz, C. (1988) *Unnatural Emotion*. University of Chicago Press, Chicago, IL.

Mackillop, J. (1980) *Ethnic Minorities in Sheffield*. Sheffield Metropolitan District Education Committee, Sheffield.

Maffesoli, M. (1988) *Le Temps du Tribus*. Meridiens Klincksieck, Paris.

Maffesoli, M. (1991) 'The Ethic of Aesthetics'. *Theory, Culture and Society*, 8 (1), pp. 7–20.

Malinowski, B. (1922) *Argonauts of the Western Pacific*. Routledge and Kegan Paul, London.

Manning, P. (1988) *The Narcs Game*. MIT Press, Cambridge, MA.

Marcuse, H. (1970) *Eros and Civilisation*. Allen Lane, London.

Marsh, P. (1978a) 'Life and Careers on the Soccer Terraces', in R. Ingham (ed.), *Football Hooliganism: The Wider Context*. Inter-Action Imprint, London.

Marsh, P. (1978b) *Aggro – The Illusion of Violence*. Dent, London.

Marsh, P., Rosser, E., Harré, R. (1978) *The Rules of Disorder*. Routledge and Kegan Paul, London.

Marx, G. (1972) 'Issueless Riots', in J. F. Short and M. E. Wolfgang (eds), *Collective Violence*. Aldine-Atherton, Chicago, IL.

Marx, G. (1988) *Under Cover: Police Surveillance in America*. University of California Press, Berkeley.

Mason, T. (1980) *Association Football and English Society: 1863–1915*. The Harvester Press, Brighton.

Mather, F. C. (1959) *Public Order in the Age of the Chartists*. Manchester University Press, Manchester.

Matza, D. (1969) *Becoming Deviant*. Prentice-Hall, New Jersey.

Mawby, R. (1979) *Policing the City*. Saxon House, Farnborough.

Mayer, A. (1966) 'The Significance of Quasi-Groups in the Study of Complex Societies', in M. Barton (ed.), *The Social Anthropology of Complex Societies*. Tavistock, London.

Mays, J. B. (1963) *Crime and the Social System*. Faber, London.

McClelland, J. S. (1989) *The Crowd and the Mob: From Plato to Canetti*. Unwin Hyman, London.

McClennan, D., Gibb, K. and More, A. (1990) *Paying for Britain's Housing*. Joseph Rowntree Foundation, York.

McKnight, D. (1986) 'Fighting in an Australian Aboriginal Supercamp', in D. Riches (ed.), *The Anthropology of Violence*. Basil Blackwell, Oxford.

Mennell. S. (1989) *Norbert Elias. An Introduction*. Blackwell, Oxford.

Miller, W. B. (1958) 'Lower Class Culture as a Generating Milieu of Gang Delinquency'. *Journal of Social Issues*, 14, pp. 5–19.

Moore, S. (1988) 'Getting a Bit of the Other: The Pimps of Post-Modernism', in R. Chapman and J. Rutherford (eds), *Male Order: Unwrapping Masculinity*. Lawrence and Wishart, London.

Mort, F. (1988) 'Boys Own? Masculinity, Style and Popular Culture', in R. Chapman and J. Rutherford (eds), *Male Order, Unwrapping Masculinity*. Lawrence and Wishart, London.

Mungham, G. and Pearson, G. (eds) (1976) *Working Class Youth Cultures*. Routledge and Kegan Paul, London.

Murphy, P., Williams, J. and Dunning, E. (1990) *Football on Trial. Spectator Violence and Development in the Football World*. Routledge, London.

Northam, G. (1989) *Shooting in the Dark*. Faber, London.

Orwell, G. (1937) *The Road to Wigan Pier*. Secker and Warburg, London.

Parker, H. J. (1974) *View From the Boys: A Sociology of Downtown Adolescents*. David and Charles, Newton Abbot.

Parkin, D. (1971) *Mental Illness in a Northern City*. Psychiatric Rehabilitation Association, London.

Patrick, J. (1973) *A Glasgow Gang Observed*. Methuen, London.

Pearson, G. (1983) *Hooliganism: A History of Respectable Fears*. Macmillan, London.

Pearson, H. (1994) *The Far Corner: A Mazy Dribble Through North East Football*. Little, Brown and Co., London.

Pearton, G. (1986) 'Violence in Sports and the Special Case of Soccer Hooligans in the United Kingdom', in C. R. Rees and A. W. Miracle (eds), *Sport and Social Theory*. Human Kinetics, Champagne, IL.

Pelling, H. (1963) *A History of British Trade Unionism*. Penguin, Harmondsworth.

Peristiany, J. G. (1965) (ed.) *Honour and Shame: The Values of Mediterranean Society*. Weidenfield and Nicolson, London.

Phillips, D. (1987) 'Football Fans and The Police', in T. O'Brien (ed.), *Proceedings of the European Conference on Football Violence*. School of Community Studies, Faculty of Social Studies, Lancashire Polytechnic.

Pitt-Rivers, J. A. (1965) (ed.) *Mediterranean Countrymen: Essays in the Sociology of the Mediterranean*. Mouton, Paris.

Pitt-Rivers, J. A. (1966) 'Honour and Social Status', in J. Peristiany (ed.), *Honour and Shame: The Values of Mediterranean Society*. University of Chicago, Chicago.

Pollard, S. (1959) *A History of Labour in Sheffield*. University of Liverpool Press, Liverpool.

Polsky, N. (1969) *Hustlers, Beats and Others*. Penguin, Harmondsworth.

Popplewell, O. (1986) *Committee of Inquiry into Crowd Safety and Control at Sports Grounds: Final Report*. HMSO, London.

Portelli, A. (1993) 'The Rich and Poor in the Culture of Football', in S. Redhead (ed.), *The Passion and the Fashion: Football Fandom in the New Europe*. Avebury, Aldershot.

Powerdermaker, H. (1967) *Stranger and Friend: The Way of an Anthropologist*. Norton, New York.

Pybus, S. (1994) *Damned Bad Place, Sheffield: An Anthology of Writing About Sheffield Through the Ages*. Academic Press, Sheffield.

Redhead, S. (1986) *Sing When You're Winning*. Pluto, London.

Redhead, S. (1990) *The-End-of-the-Century Party: Youth and Pop Towards 2000*. Manchester University Press, Manchester.

Redhead, S. (1991) *Football With Attitude*. Wordswith, Manchester.

Reid, C. (1976) 'Middle Class Values and Working Class Culture in Nineteenth Century Sheffield – The Pursuit of Respectability', in S. Pollard and C. Holmes (eds), *Essays in the Economic and Social History of South Yorkshire*. South Yorkshire County Council, Barnsley.

Riches, D. (ed.) (1986) *The Anthropology of Violence*. Basil Blackwell, Oxford.

Ricoeur, P. (1967) *The Symbolism of Evil*. Beacon, Boston, MA.

Ritzer, G. (1994) *The McDonaldisation of Society*. Sage, London.

Robins, D. (1984) *We Hate Humans*. Penguin, Harmondsworth.

Robins, D. (1995) 'Review of "Football, Violence and Social Identity"'. *Sociological Review*, 43 (1) (February), pp. 213–16.

Robins, D. and Cohen, P. (1978) *Knuckle Sandwich: Growing up in the Working Class City*. Penguin, Harmondsworth.

Robinson, R.J. (1987) 'The Civilising Process: Some Remarks on Elias's Social History'. *Sociology* 21, (1), pp. 1–17.

Rojek, C. (1985) *Capitalism and Leisure Theory*. Tavistock, London.

Rowbotham, S. (1976) 'Anarchism in Sheffield in the 1890s', in S. Pollard and C. Holmes (eds), *Essays in the Economic and Social History of South Yorkshire*. South Yorkshire County Council, Barnsley.

Sack, T. (1986) *Human Territoriality: Its Theory and History.* Cambridge University Press, Cambridge.

Sartre, J. P. (1965) *Being and Nothingness.* Penguin, Harmondsworth.

Schlesinger, D. (1991) *Media, State and Nation: Political Violence and Collective Identities.* Sage, London.

Scraton, P. (1985) 'From Saltley Gates to Orgreave: A History of the Policing of Recent Industrial Disputes', in B. Fine and R. Millar (eds), *Policing the Miners' Strike.* Lawrence and Wishart, London.

Sennett, R. (1970) *Families Against the City.* Harvard University Press, Cambridge, MA.

Sennett, R. (1977) *The Fall of Public Man.* Faber and Faber, London.

Shields, R. (1991) *Places on the Margin: Alternative Geographies of Modernity.* Routledge, London.

Shields, R. (ed.) (1992) *Lifestyle Shopping: The Subject of Consumption.* Routledge, London.

Short, J. F. (1968) 'Introduction: On Gang Delinquency and the Nature of Subcultures', in J. F. Short (ed.), *Gang Delinquency and Delinquent Subcultures.* Harper and Row, New York.

Sillitoe, P. (1955) *Cloak Without Dagger.* Cassell, London.

Simmel, G. (1950) *The Sociology of George Simmel.* Free Press, New York.

Simmel, G. (1957) 'Fashion'. *American Journal of Sociology*, 62 (May), pp. 541–58.

Simmel, G. (1971) 'The Problems of Sociology', in D. Levine (ed.), *George Simmel on Individuality and Social Forms.* University of Chicago Press, Chicago, IL.

Sivard, R. (1989) *World Military and Social Expenditures.* World Priorities, Washington DC.

Smith, J. (1993) 'The Lie that Blinds in Destabilising the Text of Landscape', in J. Duncan and D. Ley (eds), *Place, Culture, Representation.* Routledge, London.

Smith, M. (1976) 'Precipitants of Crowd Violence'. *Sociological Inquiry,* 48 (2), pp. 121–31.

Sorel, G. (1961) *Reflections on Violence.* The Free Press, Glencoe, IL.

Stam, R. (1982) 'On the Carnivalesque'. *Wedge,* 7, pp. 47–55.

Storch, R. D. (1976) 'The Plague of Blue Locusts: Police Reform and Popular Resistance in Northern England, 1840–57'. *International Review of Social History,* 20, pp. 61–90.

Strauss, A. L. (1969) *Mirrors and Masks: The Search for Identity.* Martin Robertson, San Francisco, CA.

Strodtbeck, F. L. (1965) *Group Process and Gang Delinquency.* University of Chicago Press, Chicago, IL.

Sutherland, E. and Cressey, D. (1960) *Principles of Criminology.* Lippincott, Chicago.

Suttles, G. (1968) *The Social Order of the Slum.* Chicago University Press, Chicago, IL.

Suttles, G. (1972) *The Construction of Communities.* Chicago University Press, Chicago, IL.

Sykes, G. and Matza, D. (1957) 'Techniques of Neutralisation'. *American Sociological Review,* 22.

Tagg, J. (1988) *The Burden of Representation. Essays on Photographics and Histories.* Macmillan, London.

Tardé, G. (1890) *La Philosophie Pênalé.* A. Storck, Paris.

Taylor, I. (1969) 'Hooligans: Soccer's Resistance Movement'. *New Society,* 7 August, pp. 204–6.

Taylor, I. (1971a) 'Soccer Consciousness and Soccer Hooliganism', in S. Cohen (ed.), *Images of Deviance.* Penguin, Harmondsworth.

Taylor, I. (1971b) 'Football Mad', in E. Dunning (ed.), *A Sociology of Sport.* Frank Cass, London.

Taylor, I. (1976) 'Spectator Violence around Football – the Rise and Fall of the Working-Class Weekend'. *Research Paper in Physical Education* 62, pp. 4–9. Carnegie College of Further Education, Leeds.

Taylor, I. (1982) 'Soccer Hooliganism Revisited', in J. Hargreaves (ed.), *Sport Culture and Ideology.* Routledge and Kegan Paul, London.

Taylor, I. (1987) 'Putting the Boot into a Working-Class Sport: British Soccer after Bradford and Brussels'. *Sociology of Sports Journal,* 4, pp. 171–91.

Taylor, I. (1989) 'Hillsborough 15 April 1989: Some Personal Contemplations'. *New Left Review,* 177 (September/October), pp. 89–110.

The Taylor Report (1989) *The Hillsborough Stadium Disaster.* Inquiry by Lord Justice Taylor, HMSO.

Thomas, K. (1964) 'Work and Leisure in Pre-Industrial Society'. *Past and Present,* 29, pp. 50–66.

Thompson, E. P. (1978) *The Poverty of Theory and Other Essays.* Merlin Press, London.

Thrasher, F. (1927) *The Gang.* University of Chicago Press, Chicago.

Trivizas, E. (1980) 'Offences and Offenders in Football Crowd Disorders'. *British Journal of Criminology,* 20, pp. 276–88.

Turner, V. (1957) *Schism and Continuity in an African Society.* Manchester University Press, Manchester.

Turner, V. (1974) *Dramas, Fields and Metaphors: Symbolic Action in Human Society.* Cornell University Press, Ithaca, NY.

Turner, V. (1979) *Process, Performance and Pilgrimage.* Concept, New Delhi.

Valentine, E. (1968) *Culture and Poverty: Critique and Counter Proposals.* University of Chicago Press, Chicago, IL.

Van Maanen, J. (1988) *Tales of the Field: On Writing Ethnography.* University of Chicago Press, Chicago, IL.

Van Stork, A. and Wouters, C. (1987) 'Civilisation and Self-Respect: A Comparison of Two Cases of Established Outsider Relations'. *Theory, Culture and Society,* 4 (203), pp. 677–88.

Virilio, D. (1994) *The Vision Machine.* BFI Publishing, Indiana University Press.

Waddington, D. (1992) *Contemporary Issues in Public Disorder.* Routledge, London.

Waddington, D., Jones, K. and Critcher, C. (1989) *Flashpoints: Studies in Public Disorder.* Routledge, London.

Walker, N. (1987) *Crime and Criminology. A Critical Introduction.* Oxford University Press, Oxford.

Walker, N. (1991) *Why Punish?* Oxford University Press, Oxford.

Wallman, S. (1984) *Eight London Households.* Tavistock, London.

Weber, M. (1930) *The Protestant Ethic and the Spirit of Capitalism.* Allen and Unwin, London.

Weber, M. (1968) *Economy and Society.* Bedminster Press, New York.

Werthman, C. (1970) 'The Function of Social Definitions in the Development of Delinquent Careers', in D. Glaser (ed.), *Crime in the City.* Harper and Row, New York.

Westergaard, J., Noble, I. and Walker, A. (1989) *After Redundancy.* Polity Press, Cambridge.

Whannel, G. (1979) 'Football, Crowd Behaviour and the Press'. *Media, Culture and Society*, 1 (2), pp. 327–40.

White, H. (1978) *Tropics of Discourse.* Johns Hopkins University Press, Baltimore, MD.

Wickham, E. R. (1957) *Church and People in an Industrial City.* Lutterworth Press, London.

Wikan, U. (1984) 'Shame and Honour: A Contestable Pair'. *Man*, 19, pp. 635–52.

Wiles, P. (1985) 'The Policing of Industrial Disputes', in P. Fosh and C. R. Littler (eds), *Industrial Relations and the Law in the 1980s.* Gower, Farnborough.

Williams, J. (1991) 'Having an Away Day: English Football Spectators and the Hooligan Debate', in J. Williams and S. Wagg (eds), *British Football and Social Change: Getting into Europe.* Leicester University Press, Leicester.

Willis, P. (1977) *Leaning to Labour: How Working Class Kids Get Working Class Jobs.* Saxon House, Farnborough.

Wirth, L. (1938) 'Urbanism as a Way of Life'. *American Journal of Sociology*, 44 (1) (July 1938), pp. 1–24.

Wittgenstein, L. (1958) *Philosophical Investigations.* Blackwell, Oxford.

Wolfgang, M. E. and Ferracuti, F. G. (1967) *The Subculture of Violence: Towards an Integrated Theory of Criminology.* Tavistock, London.

Yablonsky, L. (1962) *The Violent Gang.* Macmillan, New York.

Young, M. (1991) *An Inside Job: Policing and Police Culture in Britain.* Clarendon Press, Oxford.

Young, M. (1993) *In the Sticks: Cultural Identity in a Rural Police Force.* Clarendon, Oxford.

Young, P. M. (1964) *Football in Sheffield.* The Sportsman's Book Club, London.

Zukin, S. (1992) 'Postmodern Urban Landscapes', in S. Lasch and M. Friedman (eds), *Modernity and Identity.* Blackwell, London.

Index

footballers: player on crutches
   bullied by bouncer 73
Foucault, Michel 119; the docile
   body 127; institutions overcome
   individuals 136; power 299;
   transgression of limits rather
   than identity 298
Freilich xiii
Freud, Sigmund 304
Friedrichs, P. 258
friendship *see* social context

Garfinkel, H. 272
Garvin, J. L. 144
Ged the Blade: correct level of
   hostility 248–9; on Owls 211
Geertz, Clifford: deep play 13,
   306–7; fellow men 263;
   intentionality xiii
George the Blade: bait 61; on Derby
   match day 43; imprisoned for
   attack 283–4; White Rose–
   Lansdowne disorders 28
Giddens, Anthony 3
Gill, O. 317
Ginger the Village Boy 48
Giulianotti, R. 174
Glaser, Daniel: differential
   identification 308–9
Goffman, Erving: character and
   performance 3; supportive
   interchange 272; theatrical
   account 272
Gordon the Blade: calls truce
   because of police 38; against
   Chelsea and Owls 72; coach
   service 193; on Derby match day
   43; Easter in Hull 40; encounters
   Bradford fans 257; furious with
   Eddy's passivity 51; Owl
   encounter 69; rescues and Owl

222; threatens Owls in Golden
   Egg 46–7; and the Village Boys
   48; visiting Owls 216; White
   Rose–Lansdowne disorders
   28–9, 31–2
The Green 'Un (newspaper) 85
Greg the Blade: carries petrol bomb
   61; correct level of hostility 249;
   and the Village Boys 48; White
   Rose–Lansdowne disorders
   29–30
greyhound racing 23
Grimsby fans 53–4

Habermas, Jürgen: crisis of
   legitimation 296–7
Hadfield, Sir Robert 7
Hall, Stuart 16, 110, 311, 312
Hank the Blade: coach trip to
   Cleethorpes 35
Harris, R. 307
Harry the Blade: Easter in Hull 40
Hebdige, D. 299
Henley Forecasting Centre:
   Blueprint for Football 1991 129–30
Hill, C. 170–1
Hillsborough Stadium: cameras at
   the disaster 321; changes
   wrought by disaster 179, 180;
   crush disaster 105–6, 115; history
   of hooligans 86–8, 89–90; media
   coverage of disaster 103
Holdaway, Simon 105, 252
Holt, R.: contests not confined to
   the pitch 13
homosexuality: football as an
   outlet 18; not declared 157
honour: acceptable behaviour
   within the group 248–50;
   ambiguous encounters open to
   interpretation 273–5; amongst